Y0-BSF-647

Pacific Initiatives in Global Trade

Pacific Initiatives in Global Trade

edited by

H. Edward English

Papers and proceedings of the
Pacific Trade Policy Forum of the PECC,
Vancouver, June 26-28, 1989,
and related documents

Published for PECC by
The Institute for Research on Public Policy/
L'Institut de recherches politiques

Copyright © The Institute for Research on Public Policy 1990
All rights reserved

Printed in Canada

Legal Deposit First Quarter
Bibliothèque nationale du Québec

Canadian Cataloguing in Publication Data

Pacific Trade Policy Forum (3rd : 1989 : Vancouver, B.C.)

Pacific initiatives in global trade

"Papers and proceedings of the Pacific Trade
Policy Forum of the PECC, Vancouver, June 26-28,
1989, and related documents."
Prefatory material in English and French.
ISBN 0-88645-105-1

1. Pacific Area—Commercial policy—Congresses.
2. International trade—Congresses.   3. General
Agreement on Tariffs and Trade (1947)—Congresses.
I. English, H. Edward (Harry Edward), 1924-
II. Pacific Economic Cooperation Conference.
III. Institute for Research on Public Policy.
IV. Title.

HF1642.55.P32 1989   382'.3'091823   C90-097577-6

65512

Camera-ready copy and publication management by
PDS Research Publishing Services Ltd.
P.O. Box 3296
Halifax, Nova Scotia B3J 3H7

Published by
The Institute for Research on Public Policy
L'Institut de recherches politiques
P.O. Box 3670 South
Halifax, Nova Scotia B3J 3K6

Contents

CAMROSE LUTHERAN COLLEGE
LIBRARY

Services Trade Issues

Part III. Membership in GATT and 245

Foreword

*Chen-Fu Koo and
William Saywell*

As chairmen of the PECC member committees for Canada and Chinese Taipei, the committees which hosted the Third Pacific Trade Policy Forum in Vancouver on June 26-28, 1989, we are pleased to introduce the published proceedings of the Forum.

It is released at a crucial time in the Uruguay Round of GATT negotiations. These negotiations address three groups of issues.

1. traditional obstacles to agricultural and textile products trade.

2. new issues related to goods and services embodying intellectual property, and to trade in services generally.

3. urgently needed strengthening of world trade institutions based on the General Agreement on Tariffs and Trade.

As the end of the Uruguay Round is scheduled for 1990, the Forum addressed both those issues on which there must be progress in the current negotiations and others for which continued efforts will be needed in the future. PECC members believe that there is substantial capacity for Pacific leadership in consensus-building on trade matters. Initiatives such as those identified by the Forum should be fully explored.

The papers in this volume were prepared by various specialists from academia, business and government. Their views reflect their personal experience and expertise in trade policy, and are not intended to reflect positions of PECC Member Committees.

We wish to express our appreciation for the work of all those who have contributed to the success of the Forum.

Foreword

Rod Dobell
President
The Institute for Research on Public Policy

On a number of occasions the Institute for Research on Public Policy has collaborated with other policy research organizations, based in Canada or other countries, in conducting conferences and workshops and in the publication of background papers and proceedings.

This publication in several respects represents a new venture in collaboration. The Pacific Economic Cooperation Conference (PECC) is an international tripartite organization involving business, academic and government participants. Fourteen economies of the Pacific region are represented by the member committees of the PECC. Furthermore the "academic" participants are in most cases associated with major policy-related research institutions of their countries. As the IRPP has initiated several bilateral relationships with Pacific institutions, it is pleased to extend such networking activity through its role in the Trade Policy Forum of PECC.

On its own initiative, the IRPP sponsored a conference on Canada and the Pacific at the time of the Forum, June 28-29, in order to take advantage of the presence of Forum participants and to afford Canadians another opportunity to add to their knowledge of, and commitment to, Pacific cooperation. The proceedings of the related Institute conference are published in a companion volume, *Canada, the Pacific and Global Trade*, edited by Murray G. Smith.

The Coordinator of the Trade Forum, Ted English, organized its Vancouver meeting with the support of the sponsoring member committees, and the advice and collaboration of the academics active in PECC.

The Pacific Trade Policy Forum has identified and explored the key issues in the current multilateral trade negotiations—old issues such as trade-restrictive policies affecting agriculture and the textile sector, newer issues such as the impact on trade of patents, trade marks and copyrights and of national regulations affecting internationally tradeable services, and strengthening of trade rules to police subsidy and dumping practices. The search for consensus among Pacific countries on this range of issues can make a strong positive contribution to the success of the Uruguay Round. The breadth and calibre of these contributions indicate the roles that the PECC, and especially the Trade Forum, is seeking to play during the current crucial stage in the Uruguay Round of GATT negotiations and in strengthening economic cooperation among Pacific nations.

Concerns about unilateral trade actions of the United States and the European Community and shared objectives in strengthening the multilateral trading system emerged as key areas of consensus among the Pacific countries. Consensus-building in the Pacific can continue to play a constructive role in the search for global cooperation in an era of new issues and new alignments, both North-South and East-West.

Recent institutional developments in the Pacific indicate the intention of governments as well as the private sectors to expand their efforts. The PECC has recently established a small permanent secretariat in Singapore. The economic ministers of 12 Pacific countries held an inaugural meeting on Asia Pacific Economic Cooperation in Canberra in November 1989 and announced plans for four follow-up meetings. Two of these will be gatherings of trade Ministers in 1990, seeking to develop, during the last months of the Uruguay Round, common positions on some or all of the same issues addressed by the PECC Trade Forum. Thus this volume, and the companion Institute publication *Canada, the Pacific and Global Trade*, should make a timely contribution to strengthening economic cooperation among Pacific nations.

January 1990

Avant-propos

Rod Dobell
Président
L'Institut de recherches politiques

L'Institut de recherches politiques a eu l'occasion de travailler à plusieurs reprises avec d'autres organismes similaires, canadiens ou étrangers, au cours de la tenue de congrès et d'ateliers et pour la publication d'études sur des questions particulières et de travaux se rapportant à ces rencontres.

L'ouvrage que nous présentons ici est, à bien des égards, une nouvelle tentative en ce sens. La Conférence sur la coopération économique des pays du Pacifique (Pacific Economic Cooperation Conference – PECC) est une institution tripartite qui rassemble des hommes et femmes d'affaires, des professeurs et des représentants des gouvernements des pays affiliés. Les comités membres de la PECC représentent quatorze économies de la région du Pacifique. En outre, les participants venant du secteur "universitaire" ont des relations, dans la majorité des cas, avec les principales institutions de recherches politiques de leurs pays respectifs. Comme l'IRP se trouve à l'origine de plusieurs programmes d'échanges bilatéraux avec des institutions de cette région, il ne peut qu'être heureux de pouvoir développer ce type d'activité dans le cadre du Forum sur la politique commerciale de la PECC.

L'IRP a pris l'initiative de patronner une rencontre sur le Canada et les pays du Pacifique, qui a eu lieu les 28 et 29 juin lors de la tenue du Forum. Il mettait ainsi à profit la présence des participants au Forum pour fournir aux Canadiens une occasion supplémentaire de s'informer sur la coopération avec les pays du Pacifique et de renforcer notre engagement en ce domaine. Le compte rendu de cette rencontre organisée par l'Institut fait l'objet d'un autre volume intitulé *Canada, the Pacific and Global Trade*, préparé par Murray G. Smith. Le coordonnateur du Forum sur la politique commerciale, Ted English, a bénéficié de l'appui des comités membres qui patronnaient cette réunion ainsi que des conseils et de la collaboration des membres du secteur universitaire de la PECC pour organiser sa rencontre de Vancouver.

Au cours du forum, on a identifié et examiné les questions clés qui font l'objet des négociations multilatérales en cours : questions traditionnelles portant sur les politiques de restriction des échanges en matière d'agriculture et de textiles; questions plus récentes telles que l'impact sur les échanges commerciaux des législations relatives aux patentes, aux marques de fabrique et aux copyrights, ainsi qu'aux réglementations nationales affectant le commerce international des services, ou le renforcement des réglementations visant à contrôler les subventions et le dumping. La recherche d'un consensus sur ces questions variées, parmi les pays du Pacifique, peut contribuer d'une manière importante au succès de l'Uruguay Round. L'ampleur et la qualité des points de vue exprimés lors de ces rencontres sont révélateurs du rôle que la PECC, et plus particulièrement le Forum sur le commerce, entend jouer au cours de la phase cruciale dans laquelle est entré l'Uruguay Round dans le cadre des négociations du GATT, et de celui qu'elle veut tenir dans le renforcement de la coopération économique entre les pays du Pacifique.

Parmi les points majeurs sur lesquels les pays du Pacifique se sont mis d'accord pour en reconnaître l'importance, il faut relever les préoccupations vis-à-vis des décisions unilatérales prises par les États-Unis et la Communauté européenne en matière de commerce et la nécessité d'établir des objectifs communs pour le renforcement du système commercial multilatéral. La réalisation d'un consensus entre les pays du Pacifique peut continuer à jouer un rôle positif dans la recherche d'une coopération globale, à l'heure où de nouvelles questions se posent et où de nouvelles ententes se créent, aussi bien du Nord au Sud que de l'Est à l'Ouest.

Les créations récentes d'institutions spécialisées, dans la région du Pacifique, sont l'indice que les gouvernements aussi bien que les représentants du secteur privé entendent accroître leurs efforts. La PECC vient d'établir un petit secrétariat permanent à Singapour. Les ministres de l'économie de 12 pays du Pacifique se sont réunis en séance inaugurale à Canberra, en novembre 1989, dans le cadre de la coopération économique des pays de l'Asie du Pacifique, et ont annoncé un programme de quatre rencontres complémentaires. Deux d'entre elles se tiendront en 1990; elles rassembleront les ministres du commerce des pays intéressés qui tenteront de préciser, durant les derniers mois de l'Uruguay Round, les positions communes relativement à certaines ou à toutes les questions étudiées par le Forum sur le commerce de la PECC. Aussi cet ouvrage, de même que le volume complémentaire qui l'accompagne (*Canada, the Pacific and Global Trade*), devraient-il paraître juste à temps pour contribuer au renforcement de la coopération économique entre pays de la région du Pacifique.

Janvier 1990

Acknowledgements

An international meeting makes special demands on its sponsors and organizers, even in the era of facsimile machines. The 1989 PECC Trade Policy Forum was no exception.

From the time of the decision to hold the June 1989 Forum, however, a wide range of support was forthcoming: from those in national committees who recommended authors for background papers; from the authors themselves; from those in the sponsoring committees and those who administered the Central Fund, who together ensured financial support; from those who made and carried through local arrangements in Vancouver; from all who participated actively in the meetings; and finally from those who have served in editorial, design and secretarial capacity during the preparation of this volume.

Particular mention should be made of our luncheon and dinner speakers on Monday, June 26, Makoto Kuroda, former Vice Minister of MITI, and more recently Advisor to the Long Term Credit Bank of Japan and Salomon Bros (Asia), and David Tappan, Chief Executive Officer of Fluor Corporation.

Special mention is reserved for those whose names do not otherwise appear in this volume. First, Heather Gibb, of the Canadian Chamber of Commerce in Ottawa, who has been responsible for the secretariat of the Canadian National Committee until she went on leave in the summer of 1989, and Dee Pannu, who subsequently took over the same responsibility. Second, a very special thanks for services beyond the call of duty to Lorne Brownsey of the Victoria office of the IRPP, members of the staff of that office, and Connie Niblock and Lorraine Duke who were responsible for most of the communications both with authors and with all participants for whom local arrangements were required. Also Heather Brownsey who assisted during the last weeks prior to the meeting. A special mention should be made of the support during the Forum meetings of members of the staff of the Asia Pacific Foundation, especially Micheline Darroch. Graduate students Alan Dudley and Diana Tyndall were also most helpful at the site of the meetings. The third group to which thanks are due is the staff of the International Economics Program of the IRPP at its Ottawa office, which played a major role in preparing the manuscript of the book. The Director of the Program, Murray Smith, Lynda Lennon, Melanie McDonald and Maria Grandinetti, all deserve special mention for their highly professional support. Also thanks to Sheila Protti, and Lorne Brownsey who edited the papers.

Many others contributed to what we believe was a successful international event. To the best of my knowledge, thanks to all my colleagues, there were no international incidents.

H.E. English
Editor and
Coordinator of the Trade Policy Forum

PART I

OVERVIEWS

Introduction and Guide to the Book

H.E. English
Editor and Coordinator
of the Trade Policy Forum

The aim of the Trade Policy Forum of the Pacific Economic Cooperation Conference* is essentially to provide an international constituency for those leaders in the public bureaucracies of PECC members who are responsible for keeping the channels of trade open and effective in sustaining the record of trade as an engine of efficient development. So long as rounds of negotiations under GATT auspices continue as the most respected of multilateral mechanisms for limiting trade barriers, countries whose record of economic advance has clearly been based on market-driven export

---

* The Pacific Economic Cooperation Conference, is a tri-partite organization made of businessmen, academics, and government officials. It has held seven plenary meetings since inception in 1980. The member committees represent the following economies: Australia, Brunei, Canada, China, Indonesia, Japan, Korea, Malaysia, New Zealand, the Philippines, Singapore, Chinese-Taipai, Thailand, and the United States. The Pacific Island States are also represented by a collective delegation.

Inter-plenary activities include, in addition to the Trade Policy Forum, an annual Pacific Economic Outlook report, task forces or fora on agricultural trade and development, fisheries, minerals and energy, the triple-T (transportation, telecommunications and tourism), science and technology, and tropical forest cooperation.

3

orientation have a leading role to play, motivated by proven self-interest.

This book, and the Trade Forum meeting on which it is based, focus on the current "Uruguay Round" of GATT negotiations. In particular the Forum discussed those issues of highest priority to Pacific countries. Priorities among trade negotiations issues differ among Pacific economies, but there can be little doubt that collectively the issues addressed here cover most, if not all, the principal concerns of the public and private decision makers of the region. A consensus on these issues by the negotiators representing PECC members of GATT, and by those who aspire to full participation in multilateral negotiations, would go a long way to assuring the success of the Uruguay Round. This is because the issues serve the interests of countries at all stages of development. Substantial progress on these issues should also serve as a foundation for future multilateral and regional efforts to build an even stronger consensus on trade policy, as well as more effective procedures for resisting protectionism.

At a November 5-7, 1989, meeting in Canberra, twelve Pacific Economic Ministers, now called APEC (Asia Pacific Economic Cooperation), decided to hold two meetings of the region's trade ministers during 1990, the second of these in Brussels just prior to the final session of the Uruguay Round. At the PECC VII plenary meeting, November 12-15, in Auckland, the Standing Committee of the PECC offered its cooperation in the preparations for those ministerial sessions, and in particular called attention to the work of its Trade Policy Forum. The report of the June Forum, June 26- 28, 1989, in Vancouver was forwarded to the officials preparing for the next ministerial sessions, and those preparing for the next Trade Forum to be held in Kuala Lumpur in the summer of 1990. The report made a commitment to work closely with officials on the specific questions that are revealed to be essential areas for agreement as the Uruguay Round moves through its concluding phase.

Readers of this volume will find it useful to review first the Statement of the Standing Committee at Auckland and the report of the June 1989 Trade Policy Forum to the Standing Committee of the PECC, as these constitute a brief summary of the main areas of consensus achieved this year, and the starting point for the "big push" in 1990.

What follows are the major addresses, panel discussions, background papers on specific issues, and panel presentations of a group of professional economists reflecting their identification of the elements of consensus that emerged during the Forum discussions.

At the end of this volume are included statements of the GATT Deputy Secretary General and Canada's Minister for

International Trade, made during the final day of the Trade Policy Forum. Also included in appendices are the speech by the Prime Minister of Australia in Seoul, January 1989, which generated the APEC initiative, and one by the U.S. Secretary of State in New York in June, which endorsed the Hawke initiative. The volume concludes with the Statement issued at the end of the APEC meeting in Canberra, which features the proposals for Pacific Trade Ministers meetings.

Statement on Trade Policy by PECC Standing Committee

At the conclusion of the Seventh General Meeting of the Pacific Economic Cooperation Conference in Auckland, New Zealand, 12-15 November, the Standing Committee of the PECC expressed its strong support of the multilateral trade negotiations and for their successful completion by the end of 1990. The Standing Committee also welcomed the intention of the Asia-Pacific Trade Ministers, announced in Canberra on 7 November 1989, to meet in mid 1990 and again in December of 1990 to help achieve a comprehensive and very substantive result from the Uruguay Round of multilateral trade negotiations, and expressed on behalf of PECC its willingness to cooperate in the preparations for this activity.

Commitments made by Ministers representing GATT members during the Uruguay Round and in particular during the Mid-Term Review, covered further general cuts in tariffs, substantial liberalization of non-tariff barriers, extension of GATT commitments to cover agriculture and the services sector, elimination of trade distortion associated with inadequate protection and enforcement of intellectual property rights and with trade-related investment restrictions, avoiding unilateral and bilateral means of dealing with short term import surges and balance of payments problems, and the strengthening of GATT monitoring and dispute settlement procedures.

The Standing Committee calls attention, in particular, to the work of the PECC Trade Policy Forum at its June 26-28 meeting in Vancouver, Canada. The papers and discussions at the Forum concentrated on multilateral issues and proposals of greatest relevance to the economies of PECC members, including:

1. *phasing out of export and other subsidies affecting trade* in agricultural products, substantial improvement in access to markets by reduction or elimination of tariff and non-tariff barriers and identifying means of assuring security of supply that are "transparent" and less trade-distorting;

2. *reduction or elimination of tariff and non-tariff barriers that discriminate against trade in processed forms of natural products;*

3. adoption in 1990 of a plan for *phasing out of the quantitative restriction on trade in textile products associated with the multifibre arrangement* and elimination of related bilateral voluntary export restraints and other practices that are discriminatory and constitute evasion of GATT commitments;

4. generally, recourse to safeguards should be *temporary, non-discriminatory,* based on GATT-determined procedures; this to be accompanied by clearer definition of constraints on the use of subsidy-countervail and anti-dumping practices;

5. adoption of *adequate standards for the protection of intellectual property* so that they become a more efficient and equitable means of transferring technology, especially between developed and developing countries;

6. *liberalization of trade in services by adopting a framework agreement and by efforts to harmonize national policies* in such sectors as finance and air transport, in which Pacific leadership is regarded as desirable and feasible;

7. strong support for the improvement of the GATT system, especially through *monitoring of national policies affecting trade, encouragement of independent research and dissemination of results of such surveillance and study;* and a hope that new progress will be made in negotiations to solve the issue of China's status as a contracting party to GATT.

A notable feature of the Trade Forum was the active and *effective participation of those from newly industrialized and developing economies in the Pacific region.* They especially stressed the need for trade policies that would assure them access to markets, including the importance of liberalizing their own trade policies to reduce distortion in economic development and to increase their leverage in trade negotiations.

Ministers responsible for international trade in the Pacific region should confirm their commitment to prosperity and future growth on an unrestricted global trading system. The maintenance and strengthening of the system is in the common interest of the countries of the region. In this context, Pacific Ministers should also reconfirm their determination to improve market access for all PECC member economies and like-minded countries outside the region.

It was generally recognized that cooperation in the Pacific should not be directed to the formation of a Pacific trading bloc, but to the formation of regional initiatives that promote multilateral liberalization of trade and investment. These initiatives should be open to other countries and be consistent with GATT principles.

Participants in the forum were anxious to make sure that all regional economic arrangements in the Pacific and Europe should be outward-looking. In particular, a successful Uruguay Round is vital to generate confidence that the European Community's internal market will develop in a context of diminishing barriers in the Community's dealings with others. It should also provide assurances against threats posed to world trade by protectionism and resort to unilateral retaliation, in a situation of large trade imbalances, arising mainly from factors other than trade restrictions.

Report on 1989 Pacific Trade Policy Forum of the Pacific Economic Cooperation Conference (PECC)

The following report is based on the background papers and discussions of the third Pacific Trade Policy Forum, held in Vancouver, Canada, June 26-28, 1989. It makes considerable use of specific contributions of a representative group of Forum participants, who also comprised the membership of the concluding panel.[1]

The PECC Trade Policy Forum has had two previous meetings, in San Francisco in March 1986 and Singapore in January 1988. The San Francisco meeting and those of the trade task force which preceded it concentrated on identifying trade negotiation priorities of the Pacific economies in the period leading up to the start of the Uruguay Round. At the Singapore meeting, areas of Pacific consensus were explored. The Third Forum has involved efforts to make specific proposals concerning selected issues currently under active negotiation as the Uruguay Round enters its final phase, looking to a successful conclusion by the end of 1990.

The specific proposals that attracted widest interest at the Vancouver meeting have two time dimensions: one group that is offered in the expectation that they might be incorporated in the current Uruguay Round, another that is less likely to achieve acceptance among all GATT signatories until some time beyond 1990. For both groups it is proposed that the members of PECC should consider regional initiatives designed to achieve a degree of market openness and trade policy liberalization that might only later be acceptable to the whole membership of GATT. It is assumed that such initiatives would be open to the adherence of others, at least on a conditional MFN basis for non-tariff measures. This could contribute to preparations for a new GATT Round, at least on a selected group of non-tariff barriers.

If the Round is to be successful, it must produce a "package" which accommodates the national priorities of the negotiating governments in seeking better access to markets for primary, manufacturing and service exporters, in improving existing GATT rules and revising new ones e.g. for transactions in intellectual property, and in strengthening GATT. This was recognized by the Trade Policy Forum. Although the "package" of recommendations summarized below may not be completely acceptable to negotiators, we emphasize that both global and Pacific consensus will only be achieved if each participant is prepared to give as well as to claim better access, and to accept negotiated rules which involve "concessions" from their starting positions. Such concessions benefit users of imports in each country.

Finally, we emphasize that the Forum was devoted to trade policy, but that if conditions conducive to freer trade and investment are to be created and sustained, action is required on other fronts, notably correction of payments imbalances through improved domestic economic policies.

High Priority Sector-Oriented Issues[2]

Five of the highest profile issues in the Uruguay Round are:

(i) agricultural protection and subsidization;

(ii) tropical and other primary and related processed products, especially the escalation of protection affecting the latter;

(iii) textile and clothing protection through the operation of the multifibre arrangement, and related bilateral restrictions;

(iv) the role of the intellectual property and its abuse in distorting trade in high-tech goods and services; and

(v) the necessity of a framework for liberalizing and removing distortions in trade in services.

Following a summary of Forum proposals relating to the above sectors, suggestions affecting cross-sectoral measures and the rules and operations of the GATT system will be addressed.

Agricultural Protection and Subsidization

On this topic, the work of the Trade Policy Forum was related to that of other PECC activities, especially in the Task Force on Agricultural Policy, Trade and Development. Forum participants re-emphasized the "critical importance that agricultural reforms must play if the MTN is to be successful". Three "central objectives for these reforms" were cited as "reduction of import barriers," "greater discipline on direct and indirect subsidies," and reduction in the adverse trade effects of "sanitary and phyto-sanitary regulations."

The forum noted the role of the Cairns Group, with several Pacific countries as members. It has become a "fourth force" or "alliance for progress" in the agricultural negotiations and helped to bridge the gulf between the positions of major participants which existed at Montreal in 1988. The April meeting in Geneva produced commitments by ministers which the forum participants saw as a good basis for progress, both in the short and longer term. There is an accepted obligation not to increase existing levels of domestic and export support and protection and to reduce levels in 1990. Ministers also set longer term objectives to establish a fair and market-oriented agricultural trading system; operationally effective GATT disciplines; and substantial and progressive reductions in agricultural support and protection sustained over an agreed period of time, resulting in both correcting and pre-venting restrictions and distortions in world agricultural markets.

Any exceptions from the above framework should be treated as temporary or transitional, subject to a fixed period, phase-out schedule and regular review.

If the Round is to be completed in 1990, the Forum recognized that both the Cairns Group and the GATT negotiating committee needed to make rapid progress on laying better foundations for detailed negotiations to achieve the ministers' aims and to allow governments to implement the first stage of long term reform in 1991 as agreed.

Issues on which the Cairns group or the PECC through its relevant Forum and Task Force might work to seek more specific regional and multilateral consensus positions include:

1. The quantitative devices by which protection levels of non-tariff practices should be measured.

2. The feasibility of "tariffication" of non-tariff barriers and subsidies, and of setting bound ceilings where "tariffication" results in much higher levels than in other sectors.

3. The scope for "decoupling" to remove trade-distortion effects of domestic agricultural support programs.

4. Means of ensuring food security that would minimize trade distortion.

Restrictions on Trade in Resource-Based Products

The Forum addressed, in addition to agricultural products, minerals and energy, fish and forest products. In almost all these categories the region was reported as a net exporter, the notable exception being petroleum. Its dominant role in some of these sectors is reflected in a figure of 50 per cent of the world exports of fish (in value terms) and over 60 per cent of hardwood logs and lumber (in volume terms). The economies of Australia, Canada, Indonesia, Malaysia, New Zealand, Philippines, and Thailand are directly supported in a major way by these sectors, and the United States and China have a large stake in many of the same sectors. Other countries of the region led by Japan are among the largest importers of such products.

Papers prepared for the Forum indicated two major groups of problems affecting trade, in addition to the aspects of agricultural protection already summarized:

(i) the "escalation" of trade barriers on processed forms of natural products,

(ii) policies affecting market conditions, notably accuracy of market and investment forecasting in minerals and energy sectors, and supply conditions and policies.

Under the former heading, high tariffs and especially high effective rates of protection have been reported on some processed fruit products, sugar, livestock and fish products, paper, plywood and furniture, and some mineral and chemical-products. Non-tariff barriers such as out-of-date or unnecessary health and phyto-sanitary and construction regulations have also been identified as restricting trade in some of these product groups.

It is suggested that PECC members initiate collective regional support for reduction or elimination of escalation on such processed products during the Uruguay Round. Failing this, they should examine the feasibility of regional action on an MFN basis on those processed products traded predominantly within the region. As for the non-tariff barriers on the same products, a conditional MFN arrangement within the region could be practicable, and open to other trading partners on the same terms.

Market, investment and supply conditions and policies fall largely outside trade policy jurisdiction. Clearly, as the report on a recent Minerals and Energy Forum indicates, the lack of transparency of investment intentions and public policy can destabilize markets and may result in unilateral actions to protect market shares. Much remains to be done on regional co-operation in improving information flows for those sectors, as already suggested in past reports of the M. and E. Forum.

In the fisheries and forestry sectors increasing concern focuses on the ability to maintain supplies, and related natural resource management policies. In this respect transfer of technology was cited as an important complement to trade policies. In the case of fisheries, both improvement of transport facilities and more uniform observance of offshore legal and regulatory systems were cited, especially on behalf of the South Pacific Island states, in a report from the co-ordinator of the PECC Task Force on Fisheries.

Textiles and Clothing and the MFA

As the discussions of the Trade Forum indicated this sector has epitomized both the nature of industrial adjustment in the Pacific, and the strength of resistance to adjustment that can be built into both national policies and international agreements. As Professor Yamazawa's paper noted, textile products have led the way as manufactured exports for many countries and the more dynamic NIEs of the Pacific have readily moved up market in response to their own higher wage levels and the resistance of developed country markets to the acceptance of more standard clothing items, a resistance reflected both in failure to meet MFA commitments and extension of its restrictive application to a wider range of products and the use of bilateral quotas and VERs.

For many developing countries, especially of Asia, success in the phasing out of the MFA is as essential to the success of the Uruguay Round as are the positive results of agriculture and intellectual property. All that the April 1989 meeting in Geneva could agree is that "substantial negotiation will begin in order to reach agreement within the timeframe of the Uruguay Round on modalities for the integration of the sector into GATT". Those "modalities" should include "the phasing out of restrictions under the MFA" and "other restrictions on textiles and clothing not consistent with GATT rules and regulations", "the time span for such a process" of integration, and specifying the progressive character of this process "which should commence following the conclusions of the negotiations in 1990."

The basic elements of the "Yamazawa" plan for phasing out the MFA are as follows:

1. MFA restrictions should be phased out within five to ten years with no further extension possible, so that the transition would lead to firm adjustment commitments.

2. After considering tariffication and tariff quotas,[3] Yamazawa recommended as most practical a steady expansion of existing export quotas starting in 1991 e.g., individual quotas to be expanded 20 per cent each year for five years to become non-binding by 1996.

Added measures for simplified administration might include:

3. Abolition of quotas for minor suppliers, measured either by per cent of consumption, or per cent of unused quota.

4. Safeguard measures to be continued for the five year period but replaced by Article 19 of GATT thereafter.

5. Liberalization of tariffs and quota reductions on developing country textile imports should be proposed on a limited-reciprocity basis, the latter as an encouragement to adjustment and trade by some firms in the capital-intensive primary textile sector of developed countries.

PECC members should consider recommending to their governments approval of a strategy along these lines. In particular, the five developed countries might discuss some form of joint declaration of intent respecting significant expansion of quotas on January 1, 1991 (or sooner) on a range of products of particular interest to the Pacific NIEs and developing countries. For their part, the latter might consider parallel but more modest action to demonstrate their commitment to the liberalization of trade in this sector, so clearly of substantial importance to them.

Intellectual Property and Trade in High-Tech Goods and Services

The papers and discussion revealed a variety of perspectives and priorities:

(i) the need for *adequate* protection of patent, trademark and copyright holders, which implies the right to expectation of sufficient monopoly return to induce a socially desirable rate of invention and innovation (taking into account efficient use of other incentives and support arrangements);

(ii) the need for appropriate means to ensure that competition can also play a timely and effective role in promoting innovation, and limiting any tendency to excessive monopoly rents, e.g. in pharmaceuticals, where fundamental social needs must be met and elasticity of demand is low;

(iii) the need to accommodate the interests, especially of developing countries, in transfer and diffusion of technology as part of the development process e.g. in the use of software in education. Patents and the skills and the capital that often go with them can assure access to technology, but at a price that should be appropriate.

It was recognized that the WIPO and other specialized agencies have a comparative advantage in technical competence to identify common standards of a legally and administratively efficient system of protection of such property rights. The involvement of the multilateral trading system is most appropriate in ensuring that differences in economic and especially trading practices are recognized, and where necessary policed. A primary aim of the trading nations in the Uruguay Round has been control through GATT of "counterfeit" trade. Border controls are part of the answer but basic protection of property rights is also clearly important, so that originators or their licensees will be compensated for their investment. The latter requires a minimum acceptable standard regarding duration and size of compensation, but above this minimum, standards can be expected to vary among countries, depending upon level of development and social priorities. Multilateral rather than unilateral means are much preferred in the establishment of acceptable and enforceable standards.

It was also recognized that enforcement of standards will vary among countries. Sometimes this is a general problem, related to level of development of administrative services. Harmonization of administrative practice should also be an objective which can limit trade distortions.

It was suggested that the PECC promote consideration of a regional consensus in the Uruguay Round on minimum acceptable strategy for the control of counterfeit trade as well as agreement on measures to limit the incentive to evade reward of property rights, including acceptable compulsory licensing provisions and shorter terms for patents and copyright on certain clauses of products and related services. Application of the "exhaustion" principle in trade mark legislation might also be explored.

Recognizing that the Uruguay Round may not deal fully with all these matters, the Pacific countries might give consideration to the preparation of a regional code for minimum adequate standards to harmonize national practices on trade-related intellectual property, including a dispute settlement procedure.

Services Trade Policy Issues

The Mid-term Review in December 1988 reported more progress on this "new" issue than on any of those already reviewed. As the countries represented by PECC membership had all supported the negotiations on services the Forum welcomed this achievement. Among the principles adopted by the April meeting in Geneva, the Forum noted with approval the following:

(i) a broad definition of services trade was adopted including both the actual transborder delivery of services and the international movement of producers and customers;

(ii) acknowledgement that services might be delivered by various models including movement of goods, persons, direct investment, and electronic transmission;

(iii) such principles as "national treatment" are to be applied so as to achieve substantial market access reflecting liberalization both of relevant laws and of administrative guidelines so as to achieve substantial and balanced benefits;

(iv) the present negotiations will endeavour to go beyond an agreed framework, to "initial commitments" to enlarged market access in some sectors; and

(v) explicit recognition was given to the interests of developing countries, particularly to ensure that export opportunities will be opened up in areas where they have a competitive advantage, and that an important feature of trade in services will be the kind of transfer of technology that can make significant contributions to development, especially of human resources.

It was noted that important issues still to be clarified include:

(a) principles governing conditions for establishment and temporary movement of workers; and

(b) the prospects for success in testing the agreed principles in services trade sectors before the conclusion of the Uruguay Round. Among those first to be addressed in the negotiations are telecommunications, construction, transportation, tourism, finance and professional services.

The two sectors addressed in specific papers prepared for the Forum were financial services and commercial aviation. The latter involves an active export interest of developing country and NIE members of the PECC, as well as more developed economies.

Major points arising out of the sectoral papers prepared for the Forum were the following:

(i) For financial services, it would be economically most realistic to define the category so as to encompass the growing competition across some traditional categories such as trustee, working capital, and investment services. The variety of practice and regulation even among developed countries suggests the need for harmonization of regulatory practices, in order to serve both national treatment and reciprocity objectives.

(ii) For civil aviation services, practice is governed mainly by bilateral bargains, usually involving designated and often state-owned national carriers. In the light of trends toward larger international consortia, involving air transport and tourism services, it was suggested that there may be scope for harmonizing practice by an international or regional agreement on guidelines, though it was also noted that national interests in "infrastructure" services make it more difficult to reach broad agreement governing such sectors.

The following PECC activities related to the sector were suggested:

(i) The PECC should commend negotiators for the progress to date on agreement in principles governing the service sectors and should support particularly application of those principles so as to encourage service sectors of developing countries.

(ii) The PECC should examine the provisions of two bilateral free trade agreements recently negotiated in the Pacific (the Canada-U.S. FTA and the Australia-N.Z. CER) with a view to assessing whether and how their provisions for standstill and liberalization of barriers to transactions in services might be more widely applied in GATT and in the Pacific. A notable characteristic of CER which would be worth emulating is the principle that all services other than those specifically excepted should be eligible for national treatment and the exceptions be subject to negotiation within a defined period of time. The FTA's provisions for a standstill on existing regulations and for easing temporary residence regulations affecting foreign business representatives could also be worthy of wider application.

(iii) Examination of selected sectors of particular interest to the Pacific countries, with a view to identifying possibilities for harmonizing regulatory policies (e.g. the financial sector) or at the very least promoting transparency of practice among the PECC economies. Those sectors designated as highest priority for "testing of principles" achieved in the Uruguay Round might warrant further examination especially after the end of 1990, e.g., construction services and professional services (engineering and management). The Forum sees scope for co-operation between it and the proposed task force on transport, telecommunications and tourism, particularly on the best means of facilitating the movement of goods, people and information in the Pacific. There is a need to reduce or remove unnecessarily restrictive and distorting effects of existing regulations, to effect useful harmonization of policies in these sectors, and generally to develop efficient and economical networks of transport and communication in the region.

Trade Policy Rules and Strengthening of the Multilateral System

This second group of issues cuts across many sectors. Among the trade policy issues receiving highest priority attention in the public domain in recent years have been those associated with the notions of "fair trade", "the level playing field", etc. Specifically the sources of perceived "unfairness" have arisen out of subsidy differences between countries, at least for individual industrial sectors, and also allegations of dumping. To these "older issues" have been added perceived unfairness resulting from administrative guidance favouring domestic suppliers, and low or non-existent standards in some countries for the reward of intellectual property.

The last, mainly related to information-intensive sectors, has appropriately been considered earlier in this report. All the others are of more general relevance as they are likely to be raised in any sector across the spectrum of trading activity. At the Trade Forum, a concern was repeatedly raised about two aspects of this issue or group of issues, that were perceived as affecting the outcome of the Uruguay Round.

(i) the recourse to strong unilateral pressure by the United States government, compelled in part by recent trade legislation, using or threatening to use countervailing or anti-dumping duties, withdrawal of concessions under the GSP etc. as means of bringing about changes in the national policies of other countries.

(ii) the introduction of the so-called "super 301" which promises even tougher action against trading parties alleged to be responsible for the most serious distortions of bilateral trade with the United States.

It was recognized by Forum participants that such moves, at least "super 301", is a mechanism for bringing about a stronger result for the Uruguay Round, just as the agricultural subsidy programme initiated in 1985 was designed to bring about a breakthrough in the attack on agricultural protectionism. However, the problem with such strategies is that they must be plausible, i.e. they must be based on a sufficiently substantive case to command respect from trading partners. Otherwise there could be a serious loss in confidence that trade negotiations will lead to a balance of benefits. If unilateralism or bilateralism appears to work better than multilateralism for the U.S., there may be a breakdown in the confidence of U.S. legislators in the internationally preferred method. To quote Brian Hindley of the Trade Policy Research Centre.[4]

> "Unfair trade" legislation is being manipulated to achieve protectionist ends. Moreover, one effect of this manipulation is to "supercharge" the voluntary export restraint (VER) system. The apparently inexorable spread of VERs is widely regarded as the major threat to the survival of the GATT as an effective control on governments in matters of trade. The *combination* of unfair trade action and VERs makes for a much greater threat than is posed by either one separately.

The example chosen for examination at the Pacific Trade Policy Forum was subsidy-countervail, partly because of the recent experience with this issue in Canada-U.S. FTA negotiations.

Lessons from this experience and from independent studies include the following:

(i) Most subsidies have such a small effect on competitiveness that trade distortion is minor, and significant injury improbable.

(ii) Sector specific subsidies (or subsidy equivalents) that are "actionable" may lead to prolonged analysis and adjudication, and the anticipation of this procedure leads to *ad hoc* bilateral arrangements based on bargaining power rather than assessments of economic effects. (This problem appears to be increasing relevant to natural resource sectors involving the role of rents and the social costs of sustained development, which are particularly difficult to measure.)

(iii) an independent mechanism for surveillance and dispute settlement can be of great importance in reducing recourse to trade distorting subsidies and indiscriminate countervail or anti-dumping actions.

The PECC should consider the following actions:

(i) general support for the three-fold classification of subsidies prepared in the Uruguay Round, in particular by the Swiss;

(ii) strongest possible support for the strengthening of GATT surveillance of national trade practices in this area and for an improved dispute settlement procedure;

(iii) exemplary regional case studies, sponsored by the PECC but carried out by international non-governmental research consortia; and

(iv) a call for recognition of the linkage between trade rules and practices identified in this section and the GATT safeguards system and full exploration of means of strengthening that system in order to reduce the trend to proliferation of unilateral "unfair trade" actions, voluntary export restraints and other bilateral evasions of GATT.

The Safeguards System

At previous meetings on the Pacific, it has been clear that PECC countries generally support a non-discriminatory multilateral safeguard mechanism, that can be employed as a temporary means of dealing with import surges, but which is prevented from leading to protracted protection by provisions for automatic short term degression periods during which adjustment must be undertaken. This was viewed as the best means of discouraging unilateral and bilateral actions outside the spirit and letter of GATT including VERs and other gray area measures. With reference to the trade rules discussed above, it was suggested that parallel agreements in the multilateral negotiations should revise rules on anti-dumping, countervail and trade measures for balance of payments purposes to ensure that they do not afford alternative channels for safeguard-type relief. Furthermore structural adjustment in both developed and developing countries should be encouraged. If all these elements are in place, the use of the safeguards approach should become a much more attractive as well as a more economically valid alternative to other protectionist-oriented responses to surges in imports.

At the Forum Ambassador Smith of the U.S. pointed out that progress in GATT on a new safeguards code had been stalled for more than a decade and that the credibility of the GATT was at stake on this crucial issue of importance to all contracting parties. At the last major debate prior to the Punta del Este meeting, the dividing point was over *selective* application of safeguards, the EC being in favour of selectivity and everyone else opposed.

Smith suggested that the PECC could possibly contribute to breaking this "log-jam", by proposing a compromise solution of its own, i.e. retention of the MFN principle for taking action while providing for a vastly speeded up period in which to take action should injury be incurred or legitimately threatened by surging imports. Further, any restraint action would be degressive in application and sharply time-limited in duration. In short, the "trade-off" would compensate for quick action when there is injury.

Smith felt that PECC's putting forward something along these lines could provide some political impetus to resolving the safeguards standoff, and suggested the PECC explore the concept further.

Strengthening the GATT System

In large part, the strengthening of the GATT System will be accomplished by the success of the Uruguay Round in dealing with the issues already reviewed. Structurally, it can be greatly strengthened if the national application of trade rules and measures is better disciplined and the "safeguard and adjustment" system becomes the preferred alternative.

A strong surveillance programme and an improved dispute settlement system also makes the multilateral system more effective and better respected.

Several speakers at the Forum emphasized the particular importance of getting recognition by GATT members that measures which restrict or distort trade are often also costly and damaging to consumers and taxpayers of the country imposing the measures. In the past, there has been inadequate public analysis and discussion of the costs and benefits involved. More recently, there have been a number of useful studies which have more clearly and quantitatively assessed the domestic and international damage done, particularly in agriculture, but also through high protection of manufacturing and regulation of services. The Forum discussants saw merit in fostering such studies by independent research institutions as an element of the responsibilities of GATT members.

The PECC countries should take a lead in initiating exemplary national studies as a basis for the work of the independent review body which it is proposed that GATT establish to report on trade-distorting policies of members. It is intended that this will also promote public discussion in each member country of costs and benefits of its policies and of more efficient means of achieving their objectives.

GATT will be further empowered if the secretariat is able to play a more active role in the coordination of international policies parallel to and in cooperation with institutions as the IMF, the OECD and the World Bank which already conduct dialogues with governments on macro-economic and development policies. The Trade Forum did not devote much attention to these latter questions, because it was clear from earlier Forum meetings that

PECC members were unanimous in their support of proposals relating to the strengthening and developing of the role of GATT.

There was one topic relating to broadening of GATT that did receive the Forum's attention—the process and conditions appropriate to the active membership of planned economies in GATT. In particular, Forum organizers recognizing the membership of China in the PECC, and the Uruguay Round negotiations relating to China's membership in GATT, had requested papers from Australian and Chinese specialists on the subject. Papers were available but unfortunately the Chinese participant was not able to be present. Forum participants nevertheless found that session highly informative and constructive.

The discussions were further enriched by a paper from the Chinese Taipei delegation dealing with Taiwan's role and interests in the multilateral trading system. The presence of guest participants from Hong Kong and the Soviet Union helped further to define the nature of commitments and expectations in these areas.

There was general support for the proposition that PECC can play an important role in identifying the conditions and practical steps that would lead to full GATT membership for both of the PECC members economies not now in GATT. It was recognized that this would also have relevance to other countries of the Western Pacific not now members of either GATT or PECC. As a non-governmental organization, PECC was seen as playing a research and mediating role in this process.

The PECC should establish one or two small working groups (perhaps three to five persons in each) to prepare reports on "China and GATT" and "Taiwan and GATT".

Concluding Observations

The Third PECC Trade Forum was designed to produce more selective and concentrated discussion on a number of issues of high relevance to the economies to the region as well of central importance to the Uruguay Round. The background papers and discussions paid significant direct attention to three of the four issues now identified as essential to the success of the Uruguay Round—agricultural protection, textile trade and the MFA, and intellectual property. The fourth issue, safeguards, was addressed indirectly in the papers, especially in those on subsidy countervail, and directly in proposals emerging from the discussion.

Proposals included at the end of each section of this report have been revised and modified by the representative panel of seven who were responsible for the final afternoon session of the Forum. They are two kinds:

(i) Recommendations to PECC members, and through them to working parties of the Uruguay Round; and

(ii) Recommendations to PECC Standing Committee for further work, relevant to the period beyond the end of the current GATT negotiations, and including some suggestions for regional study and action.

It should be noted in particular that some of the recommendations involve issues of great relevance to Pacific trade that also overlap the interests of other PECC fora, task forces and working groups. Examples of such overlap include:

(i) the need for more and better information flows on market conditions especially in the natural resource based sectors; e.g. demand and investment projections in the mineral and energy sectors, and supply and resource management implications in fisheries and forestry sectors;

(ii) the need for clearer analysis of *changes* in national current account balances and the relative importance of trade and macro policies as explanatory factors; and

(iii) a variety of trade issues relating to service and high-tech sectors that concern both the Trade Forum and new task forces such as those on Science and Technology and Telecommunications, Transportation and Tourism.

The Co-ordinating Group and Standing Committee will be asked to consider assigning to one or more task force those topics that warrant continued study and/or further PECC action.

H.E. English
Co-ordinator of the Trade Policy Forum

Notes

1. Sir Frank Holmes (New Zealand)), Jeffrey Schott (U.S.) Soogil Young (Korea), Wilhelm Ortaliz (Philippines), Ippei Yamazawa (Japan), Djisman Simandjuntak (Indonesia), and H. Edward English (Canada). These persons have in many cases both academic and government or private, sector research experience. Among the papers prepared for the conference, three were offered by corporation executives or economists, as were two of the four lunch and dinner addresses during the meeting. Many of the other papers were prepared by persons with experience in private or government research institutions as well as universities.

2. Each of these issues is addressed by papers in this volume which formed the basis of discussions on the agriculture trade issue. See also the paper by William M. Miner in *Canada, the Pacific, and Global Trade*, edited by Murray G. Smith, Institute for Research on Public Policy, 1989.

3. Tariffication involves conversion of existing export quotas (and other NTBs) to equivalent tariffs, followed by their phased reduction, to allow systematic return to market forces. Problems with this approach include difficulties in estimation, a shift of rent from exporting to importing countries and differential tariffs against different exporters if strictly applied. Tariff quotas would be equally discriminatory if based on existing quota distribution.

4. See Hindley's article on anti-dumping in *Canada, the Pacific, and Global Trade*, cited in note 2 above.

Challenges of Diversity and Growth in the Pacific

G.A. Denis
Assistant Deputy Minister
Office for Multilateral Trade Negotiations

I am pleased to be welcoming all of you to Canada and to Vancouver. This city has developed as Canada's gateway to the Pacific. It looks increasingly outward to this rapidly growing, dynamic region. It is closer to the great ports and cities of Asia such as Yokohama and Seoul than is Los Angeles on this side of the Pacific or Sydney on the other.

My own interest in the Pacific Economic Cooperation Conference (PECC) process goes back to the first meeting of the Trade Policy Forum early in 1986 in San Francisco. I was impressed at the time with the high quality of the participants and the good papers and discussions. Ironically, soon after this PECC meeting, I moved on to the Canadian team for our free trade negotiations with the United States.

The free trade initiative provided an early opportunity to make substantive progress towards the removal of trade barriers and the reshaping of trade rules. I remember that on one of my many trips to Washington during these negotiations, I happened to meet Mr. Kuroda, who was still the senior officer in the Japanese Ministry of International Trade and Industry, in the lobby of my hotel. From our brief conversation, I had the impression that if the Free Trade Agreement (FTA) were going to remove barriers within North America without raising barriers *vis-à-vis* third countries, then the FTA would be a good deal for Japan as well as Canada.

Canada has been a strong supporter of the PECC from its inception; its tripartite nature has been very helpful in developing a cross-Pacific dialogue and in advancing our common interests. PECC's strong support for a successful Uruguay Round has been useful in formulating our common objectives in maintaining an outward looking Pacific region as a major and dynamic participant in the multilateral trading system.

Since all the proposals for enhancing economic cooperation in the Asia Pacific region emphasize the importance of successfully completing the General Agreement on Tariffs and Trade (GATT) negotiations, I would like to focus my remarks on these global negotiations. We in Canada look to the Uruguay Round as a key link or bridge between the Pacific, North America and Europe. If successful, the negotiations will provide the basic framework and rules within which Pacific trade and investment will continue to grow in the coming decade and into the next century.

Perhaps no other region depends more heavily on a successful outcome of the Uruguay Round than does the Asia Pacific Region. Before the negotiations began late in 1986, many of the challenges came from the Pacific because of the need for the multilateral trading system to adjust to the growth and diversity of the region. Countries in the Pacific therefore share a major responsibility in taking initiatives and bringing forward proposals which will help find solutions with respect to the complex Multilateral Trade Negotiations (MTN) agenda.

In making our own proposals in Geneva, we are increasingly mindful that Canada is very much a Pacific country, a Pacific trader. Our trans-Pacific trade now surpasses our trans-Atlantic trade. Four of our 10 largest trading partners are in the Pacific, and the rates of growth in exports and imports into and out of these markets have been extraordinary in recent years. Canada's exports to the Asia Pacific region grew more than 30 per cent last year. No wonder that the Cairns Group, which includes Canada, is seen by some European observers of the GATT as a Pacific-based group of agricultural exporters.

The MTN: A Response to Global Interdependence

The overall international context of Canada's participation in the Uruguay Round is the growing global interdependence that we share with economies across the Pacific.

It is based on our belief that maintaining an open world trading environment is a crucial element in sustaining the expansion of trade and investment. As the experience of several Asian economies has borne out in recent years, it is only in that kind of environment that satisfactory solutions to the current problems of international indebtedness of developing countries can also be found.

We view the reform and the expansion of the GATT system to new areas such as trade in services, trade-related intellectual property and investment issues as an important condition for giving the GATT the capacity to respond to the challenges which have accompanied the dynamic and export-led growth of most Asian-Pacific economies. We believe that the kind of strong and viable GATT, which has contributed so much to growth and prosperity around the Pacific Region, can only be maintained if international rules work for the benefit of all and if the level of mutual obligations go hand-in-hand with the evolving status of national economies in world markets.

Canada sees the timely and successful conclusion of the Uruguay Round as the best defence against the threats to the world trading system posed by protectionism and unilateralism ever-present in a continuing situation of large trade imbalances. The size and persistence of these imbalances have put political strains on the management of trade relations and undermined support for the open trading system, particularly in the U.S. A timely and comprehensive MTN outcome is necessary to defuse the U.S. Super 301 time-bomb. Such trade weapons are unlikely to go away if the issues underlying these threats are not resolved satisfactorily and in a trade expanding manner.

We also believe that a substantive comprehensive outcome of the Uruguay Round is necessary to maintain a reasonable balance between the forces of regional market integration and those of the global village where technology, capital and know-how flow increasingly easily across national borders. We see the expansion of trade and investment opportunities through non-discriminatory trade liberalization and the development of better and fairer trade rules as common links to both regional and global trading arrangements.

A successful Uruguay Round is a condition for ensuring that developments in Europe, North America and the Pacific will continue to be outward looking and that these regions will not turn into protectionist trading blocs in opposition to each other. Indeed, Canada's trade policy seeks to build on the Canada-U.S. Free Trade Agreement of January 1st, 1989 in order to reach out to the Asia-Pacific region, to Europe and to other parts of the world market.

We see the Free Trade Agreement as a stepping stone for enhancing Canada's trade and investment relationship globally. A large part of the competitive challenges facing Canadian secondary and manufacturing industries on the domestic and North American markets has been coming from Japan and from the newly-industrialized economies in the Pacific. As the FTA creates the foundation for Canadian industries to become fully competitive on a North American basis, these industries will be structurally in a better position to compete both domestically and in global markets.

The Uruguay Round: The Main Tasks

We are presently just past mid-way through the Uruguay Round negotiations and are now entering a more intensive phase. A great deal of activity in Geneva and in other capitals is underway to ensure that the directions and positions for the negotiations will be developed with a view to their completion at the end of 1990. In this regard, anyone who needs convincing about the enormous tasks ahead should simply bear in mind that the Uruguay Round is the most ambitious and wide-ranging set of trade talks ever undertaken in the GATT.

With the full contribution of all participants concerned, we believe that the Uruguay Round can advance the interests of its Asia Pacific participants in four important ways:

- By negotiating seriously to seek solutions to the difficult issues on the MTN agenda, we stand a better chance to keep trade and investment channels open. The MTNs are the best defence against any unravelling of the achievements of previous rounds. Maintaining pressures on those countries which have some catching up to do in opening up their markets for goods and services will be necessary to preserve even existing access conditions.

- By opening up further new market opportunities for agriculture, resource-based products and manufactured goods and services, the MTN can provide the right market signals to sustain economic growth and share it throughout the region. That market signal is that trade liberalization is the engine for new investment and employment opportunities.

- By putting in place better and fairer rules to govern trade in goods, the MTN can not only improve the multilateral trading system it can also demonstrate that the GATT can be overhauled and modernized through trade negotiations rather than through unilaterally imposed solutions. This would bring greater predictability and acceptance to the trading environment. The key issues that I see on this part of the MTN agenda concern safeguards, subsidies and countervail, intellectual property, and the GATT dispute settlement process.

- By enhancing a fuller involvement of the more industrially advanced developing countries in managing the GATT system and by their greater contribution to the overall level of trade liberalization obligations, developing countries will secure for themselves more influence on the shape of the future trading environment. They will also strengthen support for an open multilateral trading system by the major industrialized economies. This, I submit, is the best incentive for the major importers to continue on the road of structural adjustments to face new competitive forces from the Pacific.

This is what the 15 different negotiating groups in the MTN are all about. As this PECC Trade Policy Forum covers nearly all the issues on the MTN agenda, I shall not take the time to explore each or even several of them here. However, I should mention, in the light of extensive consultation with our private sector and of all the bilateral trade and industry engaged in promoting Canada's trade and investment relationship across the Asia and Pacific, that Canada's business community sees the key areas as agriculture, market access, trade rules, services, and dispute settlement.

Our private sector hopes that the MTN will assist in securing non-discriminatory and improved access to the growth and dynamic markets of the region through substantial reduction of Non-Tariff Barriers (NTBs) and tariffs, especially for value-added agricultural and processed resource products.

Our private sector attaches a high priority to ensuring that new and strengthened GATT rules and obligations will be accepted and applied more fully by all countries in the Pacific in a manner commensurate with the benefits that they get from the open multilateral trading system.

Our private sector hopes to diversify its exports of manufactured goods to the Pacific but believes that informal barriers, whether through national distribution regimes or through administrative guidance in various countries of the region, are as important as formal border barriers. They tend to be sceptical as to what the MTN can contribute in this respect.

Our private sector understands the need to continue the adjustment of Canadian production facilities to meet global competitive pressures from Pacific Rim exporters. However, they feel strongly about the need to obtain full and real reciprocal market access opportunities. In this regard, they see their competitiveness and, therefore, their global position enhanced by the Canada-U.S. Free Trade Agreement.

Our private sector is apprehensive about the future of the multi-fibre textiles arrangement; how the reintegration of this sector into the GATT will proceed; what period of time is envisaged for this process; what the new safeguards and rules will be; and what textile exporters themselves will be prepared to do to open up their own markets to greater competition from developing as well as from developed country competitors so as to permit a greater sharing of the adjustment process.

Our private sector perceives that mutually beneficial investment and technology through new rules on trade-related investment and intellectual property can help enhance the flow of investment and technology with countries in the Asia Pacific region. It wants to ensure, however, that improved standards of intellectual property will be supported by a system of non-discriminatory enforcement of intellectual property rights in cases of alleged infringements and by a truly multilateral system of dispute settlement.

Our private sector perceives successful international agricultural trade reform, with rules equally applicable to all GATT members and with substantial reduction of trade distorting subsidies and barriers, to be of very great importance to its future prosperity. The Asia Pacific region has major stakes in this agricultural reform because some of the major world markets and some of the most efficient producers and exporters are located in this region. Indeed, Canada, Australia, New Zealand, Thailand, Malaysia and Indonesia have been actively working together in the Cairns Group, cutting across developed and developing country lines, to provide leadership in seeking solutions to current day, pressing agricultural trade problems.

Conclusion

Tough choices are ahead of us on many MTN negotiating issues. These hard choices will have to be made in the next 15 months. Ministers reconfirmed at the December 1988 mid-term review meeting in Montreal that this round of negotiations should be completed by the end of 1990. The current international trading environment adds to the needs of this calendar because a successful MTN next year will help to contain the threat that the U.S. Super 301 exercise could lead to a series of actions damaging to the GATT trading system. It will help to ensure that the completion of the European Community (EC) internal market by 1992 will be achieved in an outward looking manner within the framework of the new GATT rules. It will also help to manage the continuing pressures for structural adjustment to the dynamic growth and the diversity of competitive challenges in the Asia Pacific region.

We must, therefore, maintain the momentum for a successful conclusion of the MTN. This forum can contribute to ensuring that governments will be prepared to face up to the hard choices because trade and investment flows will be significantly influenced by this outcome. We need to keep our horizons on the year 2000. I hope that the PECC discussions over the next three days will contribute to defining and to pointing the way toward substantial MTN results, both in terms of its scope and its depth.

Editor's Summary of the
Panel Discussion of Senior Officials*

A panel composed of senior trade officials of Japan, the United States, New Zealand, Korea, Thailand and Canada addressed the first session of the Forum. The title attached to this session was "From the Mid-term Review to 1992". This was intended to encourage comment not only on the final stages of the Uruguay Round but on the years immediately following, at least to the date of the consolidation of the European Economic Community. The panellists responded to this challenge, stressing particularly the following general positions to this challenge:

    i)   The role of market-orientation in the development of the Pacific economies, especially in the last 20 years, leads logically to their joint interest in ensuring the preservation and strengthening of the institutions of the multilateral system.

---

*   These included Ambassador Hideyuki Ukawa, Michael Smith (former Deputy USTR), David Gamble, Byong Kyun Kim, Karun Kittistaporn, and Germain Denis.

ii) It is necessary to monitor national policies that constitute resort to unilateral pressures on trading partners and to monitor also the evolution of regional groups to discourage inward-looking policies; this applying both to Europe and North America.

iii) Among the substantive trade liberalization issues on the agenda for the current negotiations on Geneva 1990, four seem to be primary to the Pacific countries represented; two, agriculture and textile trade restrictions, are traditional; two are new—intellectual property and services. If substantial progress can be made by the conclusion of the Uruguay Round on each of these issues, leading interests of all Pacific region countries will be served.

iv) There was strong support for all the major moves to strengthen the functioning of the GATT system but special emphasis was placed on the necessity of reinforcing the safeguards system so as to make access to it prompt, temporary and conducive to adjustment rather than mere protection. The general view of Pacific countries that safeguards should not be selectively applied was re-affirmed. In general this was viewed as a means of discouraging alternative bilateral or unilateral measures likely to be contrary to the spirit and probably also the letter of GATT.

v) The strategy appropriate to members of PECC and their governments that was supported by several panellists included use of specific issue alliances, such as that of the Cairns group attempting to identify the most affective means of dismantling agricultural protectionism. Application of this idea to consensus-building on issues such as textiles and intellectual property was supported by several participants. Services policy harmonization and stronger and more uniform handling of subsidy and countervail practice were also cited by some as areas for Pacific initiatives toward multilateral solutions.

vi) Concern was expressed that standstill on new protective measures, especially those incompatible with GATT commitments, had not been taken as seriously as earlier meetings of the Forum had hoped. New efforts to achieve greater transparency in national practice will make an important contribution to standstill and roll-back.

vii) Special concern was expressed concerning the prospects for solving problems affecting GATT membership for

PECC countries not now fully represented in the multilateral institutions. Recent events in China were seen as causing some delay in resolving China's membership status and a more gradual approach was seen by some as both necessary and desirable under the circumstances. Political instability in some other countries of the region was also viewed as a source of uncertainty that might affect trade liberalization for some time.

viii) Finally, it was acknowledged that strengthening of the trade system was affected by other policies, notably macroeconomic policies, mainly related to fiscal deficits and their impact on monetary and especially exchange-rate policies.

It was noted that the role of the PECC could be affected by the outcome of the Hawke initiatives. Participants stressed the importance of ensuring that the work of PECC, including that of the Forum in particular, should become a part of the foundation for any meeting of Ministers and other future consensus-building efforts of governments.

PART II

SECTORAL TRADE ISSUES

Review of Uruguay Round Agricultural Negotiations

Carol Brookins
President, World Perspectives, Incorporated

PECC Consensus on Agricultural Issues

In September 1988 the Task Force on Agriculture Policy, Trade and Development of the Pacific Economic Cooperation Conference met in San Francisco to discuss the agricultural issues facing member nations ahead of the December 1988 ministerial Mid-Term Review of the GATT's Uruguay Round of Multilateral Trade Negotiations (MTN).

Following that PECC meeting, a statement was issued covering the areas of consensus reached by the 15 nations represented (Australia, Canada, China, Indonesia, Japan, Malaysia, Mexico, New Zealand, Philippines, Singapore, Chinese Taipei, Thailand, and the United States) regarding mutual agricultural considerations and objectives for reform in the Uruguay Round.

In brief, there was general consensus that:

1.   . . . the pace and effectiveness with which agriculture can be brought fully into the GATT will be a key factor in determining whether the global trading regime evolves in the healthier direction of more inclusive and global market-oriented principles or whether it will move in the direction of bilateralism and protectionism.

2.   . . . (the) critical importance that agricultural
     reforms must play if the MTN is to be successful.
     Through the combined achievement of all the
     negotiations' objectives, countries can expect to
     realize major economic gains through a more
     efficient and effective use of national and global
     resources.
3.   Three central objectives for these reforms . . .
     remain essential.
     – Improved market access through the reduction
       of import barriers
     – Greater discipline on direct and indirect sub-
       sidies, including their phased reduction, and
       dealing with their causes
     – Reducing the adverse effects of sanitary and
       phytosanitary regulations
The above reforms must be achieved in the context of an
overall institutional strengthening of the GATT as
agreed at Punta Del Este, and they must be undertaken
in a coordinated manner.

The Chairman's statement from the September meeting
summarized the additional consensus on:

- the need to establish a fixed date by which the reform process
  is to be completed
- the desirability of an appropriate device to measure the level
  of agricultural protection and trade distorting support
- the legitimate concern for developing countries for "special
  and differential treatment" during the reform process
- the responsibility of both exporters and importers in
  providing food security
- the necessity for the Mid-Term Review to provide impetus to
  intensive negotiations over the two years remaining in the
  Uruguay Round.

Agriculture in the Uruguay Round at the Mid-Term Review

The December meeting of trade ministers failed to produce
agreement on the agricultural agenda, and special efforts were
undertaken by negotiating parties to reach accord by April 1989.
At the Geneva meeting of the Trade Negotiating Committee in
April, a mandate for negotiations on all key areas of the Uruguay
Round was forged with a target date for concluding an agreement
by the end of 1990. At that April meeting key provisions of the

PECC consensus on objectives and issues were included in the Framework Agreement reached on agriculture, and in the continued commitment to complete the MTN on schedule.

Major disagreement between the U.S. and the European Community (EC) over the context and objective of agricultural negotiations was resolved to the point that there could be agreement on language covering the areas to be negotiated. Although major issues were not resolved, I believe that the language agreed to gives a broad mandate to complete a comprehensive and substantial negotiation of agricultural trade and policy reform over the next 20 months.

EC demands for specific language or rebalancing (i.e., permitting tariff structure changes to include raising or imposing some tariffs if others are lowered, which would include adjusting the zero duty binding on oilseeds and non-grain feed ingredients) were rejected by the other negotiating parties. However, EC officials claim that there is nothing in the language of the agreement that precludes the introduction of this concept during the upcoming negotiation process.

Agreement on short-term reform commitments was very loose. The market situation improved to the point that there was no pressure on negotiators to make a major short-term adjustment in policy. Additionally, negotiators did not want to have to use political capital over the next year in trying to implement short-term commitments on politically sensitive import access issues—like dairy and sugar for the U.S.—when the real focus is on a major long-term reform package before the end of 1990.

It is true that the U.S. dropped its insistence on language calling for elimination of barriers to trade and subsidies by a certain date; however, that was not unexpected and in fact was part of the U.S. strategy from the time of its initial proposal. Compromise language calls for the objective of:

> ... substantial progress reduction in agricultural support and protection sustained over an agreed period of time, resulting in correcting and preventing restrictions and distortions in world agricultural markets. This goal will be realized through negotiations on specific policies and measures, through the negotiation of commitments on an aggregate measurement of support, the terms of which will be negotiated, or through a combination of those approaches.

Nothing was taken off the table from the original framework commitments of the Punta del Este Communique mandate in 1986. Additionally, and perhaps most importantly, the import access objective was strengthened and further clarified. Measures included under the import access section of the April Framework Agreement are:

> quantitative and other non-tariff access restrictions, whether maintained under waivers, protocols of accession or other derogations and exceptions, and all measures not explicitly provided for in the General Agreement, and the matter of conversion of the measures listed above into tariffs; (and) tariffs, including bindings . . .

This language is significant in two aspects. First, the concept of tariffication is specifically referred to for the negotiation. Second, there is direct reference to the EC's variable levy in the wording that is used as a matter of course in the GATT context when referring to the levy system ("all measures not explicitly provided for in the General Agreement"). What the concept of tariffication does is open up the negotiations to tariffication and to converting the variable levy to a fixed tariff, and then negotiating a time frame for rolling back tariffs.

The EC is not yet publicly prepared to "cross the bridge" and begin negotiations on tariffication; however, the ED delegates did not block reference to this concept in the document and some observers believe that they have privately taken a major step by accepting the above language. This is not to say that the negotiations will be easy, or that this is what the ultimate outcome will be. Much will depend on the market situation, other aspects of the negotiation (both in agriculture and in other sectors), the skill of U.S. negotiators in managing the EC and keeping U.S. commodity interests on board, pressures from other negotiating parties and relative trade-offs.

However, some observers believe that the EC is now isolated in opposing tariffication since the Japanese have already agreed to the concept and process in their 1988 beef and citrus agreements with the U.S. If tariffication is a part of the final agreement, the Japanese accord may well have been an important precedent in moving multilateral reforms under the GATT to that point, which is, in fact, an important step toward moving agriculture under the GATT system.

Tariffication is the key to real reform of the agricultural trading system. Not only would it put agricultural trade under the general liberalization process applied to other goods trade in the GATT system, but it would open domestic markets gradually to competition from imports. If combined with restrictions on export aids, this would force changes in domestic production policies, particularly if subsidies are leading to surpluses that cannot be marketed competitively in world markets.

An additional important point of the April agreement is contained in the health and sanitary language, which calls for the objective of

(1)   developing harmonization of sanitary and phytosanitary regulations and measures, on the basis of appropriate standards established by relevant international organizations . . . .

(2)   strengthening Article XX so that measures taken to protect human, animal or plant life or health are consistent with sound scientific evidence and use suitable principles of equivalence . . .

"Sound scientific evidence" is a crucial point in the current U.S.-EC dispute over the EC's hormone ban; the U.S. wanted that language in the agreement and the EC insisted on the addition of "suitable principles of equivalence" to balance the concept. The U.S. had no problem with that addition, given the emphasis on international standards.

A key area of the negotiation will focus on the role of the aggregate measure of support politics (i.e., tariff equivalent), given the EC's support for the concept, not only as a way of measuring compliance, but also as the actual item for negotiation. EC officials favour this because they see considerable policy flexibility in raising some barriers while reducing others and still being able to meet rollback commitments. It would include their concept of rebalancing. In fact, some EC officials are trying to put enough factors into a "tariffication" concept to turn a tariff into an aggregate measure. The EC's proposed aggregate measurement— the SMU, as contrasted to the OECD's PSE (producer subsidy equivalent)—currently excludes border measures (both access and export competition) and focuses only on internal support mechanisms. It could ultimately be possible to look at some version of the SMU as a vehicle for making commitments on negotiating down internal supports, while making a different agreement on reducing export subsidies and using tariffication for expanding import access.

The aggregate measurement concept is also looked upon favourably by the Japanese, the Nordics and the Koreans, who see this as giving them maximum flexibility in protecting as long as possible their most sensitive agricultural sectors. U.S. negotiators in principle introduced the aggregate measurement concept early on as a way of shifting the negotiating focus away from the traditional request/offer process on specific negotiations. While not objecting to incorporating the concept of the aggregate measure in a final agreement, U.S. officials will be seeking an agreement that provides the maximum amount of equity in order to keep all the sensitive commodity interests on board.

Additionally, negotiators will have to direct attention to writing rules and disciplines that lock in the policy changes agreed upon. Without an overhaul of the current rules, negotiating parties could ultimately drift back into policies that bring new distortions back into the agricultural trade system.

A very ambitious work program has been outlined by negotiators, with the agreement calling for participants to advance detailed proposals by December 1989 on the following items included in long-term reform:

- the terms and use of an aggregate measurement of support
- strengthened and more operationally effective GATT rules and disciplines
- the modalities of special and differential treatment for developing countries
- sanitary and phytosanitary regulations
- tariffication, decoupled income support, and other ways to adapt support and protection
- ways to take account of the possible negative effects of the reform process on net food-importing developing countries

Setting a loose December 1989 deadline creates a momentum for moving forward the difficult work ahead. The hope is that if the major papers outlining all the negotiating items and content are all on the table by December of 1989, negotiators will have all the elements to consider in preparing the text of a working document; this would then be the document used in negotiating the structure and content of the final package during that last year of the Round.

From June 1989 several months of the Uruguay Round are ahead when big public focus will be lacking and the hard work will be taking place in structuring complicated proposals. However, observers believe that the agreement structured in Geneva— despite all the omissions and loose interpretation in some areas— reflects considerable progress. Negotiators point out that they and their counterparts left the table in Geneva after a number of very hard fought battles; nevertheless, the general "unspoken" attitude that appeared to emerge from the session was a sense that something actually might come out of the GATT on agriculture in this Round.

What seems to be occurring is a transition in attitude from initial bravado, fear, and gamesmanship to a serious belief that agricultural reforms can and will be negotiated over the next 20 months, and more importantly, that the outcome can lead to growth in trade and world agriculture. If these perceptions are accurate, the early seeds of a belief in progress are crucially important to creating the attitudes—or conventional wisdom—in negotiations which accept the reform objective.

Prospects for Agricultural Reform

Although major issues remain disputed—and will be difficult to resolve—in the agricultural negotiations, there is reason to believe that we have the potential for moving global agriculture into a multilateral, progressive reform process.

All this aside, no outcome is certain, and there are substantial obstacles. First, the fundamental situation in world commodity markets may slow the momentum if stocks continue to fall due to weather and crop problems in the cereal sector. We have seen in the past that when pressures on budgets, stocks and trade are reduced, the potential for systemic reform is reduced.

Second, the EC will continue very reluctantly to undertake reduction of border protection, because many members view the variable levy structure as the major mechanism for preserving the principle of "community preference." And yet, reducing barriers to import access is one of the four key aspects of the GATT proposals.

Third, political pressures against major change in current systems and policies will increase from agricultural and farm lobbies throughout the GATT membership—including even strong advocates for reform like the United States.

Given the above and other potential obstacles, the PECC has a vital role to play in continuing its strong collective advocacy of the GATT agricultural agenda, and ensuring that it reaches a meaningful conclusion. That will require coordinated progressive reductions in all three key areas of subsidization and protection—domestic production supports, export subsidies and import barriers—because GATT members all protect their domestic agricultural sectors through a combination of these measures.

Additionally, harmonization of health and sanitary regulations is vital in providing international standards that can be used in effective dispute settlement procedures. This area is particularly crucial today in the era when environmental pressures are growing on national levels concerning the way food is produced, processed and marketed.

If the Uruguay Round does not produce satisfactory results, we can all be assured that bilateral pressures will continue on the agricultural trading system. We have already a number of cases currently under the GATT dispute settlement process—from an Australian case against the U.S. sugar import quota to a U.S. case against EC soybean support policy. Trade conflicts will escalate in the absence of meaningful commitments to multilateral reform, because protectionist policies will be challenged as no longer acceptable in the context of today's world trading system.

PECC member countries—both those in various stages of development and industrial nations—stand to benefit greatly from improvement in the agricultural trade regime, reduction of agricultural subsidies, and the higher rate of economic growth that will ensue. It is well understood that PECC members include a large number of the leading agricultural importers and exporters of a variety of products, and are among the most dynamic economies in the world today.

Given the diversity of PECC members' agricultural sectors, efforts at reaching a coordinated consensus on specific proposals for implementing the stated objectives will greatly assist the negotiating process. This can certainly be aided in part through the Cairns Group, but engagement by all PECC members would be particularly useful. New concepts could be developed for providing support to rural sectors not tied to commodity production, or trade distortion.

The PECC can play a leadership role in demonstrating to the full GATT membership that it is possible to harmonize systems that are very different through a common process. Through unified efforts in the Uruguay Round, member countries can cooperate to improve living standards in their rural sectors and bring new opportunities for agricultural and economic growth.

Trade Development in Processed Minerals in the Pacific Region*

Christopher Findlay
Coordinator
Minerals and Energy Forum (MEF)

Introduction

The Minerals and Energy Forum (MEF) convened a Specialist Group meeting in June 1989 to discuss issues involved in the development of trade in processed minerals in the Pacific region. The importance of this topic was noted at the last MEF in Seoul and was endorsed by the Working Group which manages the MEF work program. The meeting was organized under the headings of:
1. Supply Security and the Demand for Metal
2. Investment in Minerals Exploitation and Processing
3. Trade Development in Processed Minerals
4. Strategies for Achieving Efficient Locations of Processing in the Pacific Region.

This paper summarizes some of the points of the discussion at the meeting which were especially relevant to the Trade Policy Forum.

---

* A report of the Minerals and Energy Specialist Group Meeting held in Canberra on June 8-9, 1989. This report is a personal view of the author. Although the outline of this paper was presented to the meeting other participants may not agree with the detail of the paper and the weights given to particular issues. The papers presented at the meeting are available from the MEF Secretariat, see the list attached to this paper.

The concept of transparency emerged as a major theme of the meeting. However, a number of policy issues were discussed which were relevant to the concept of transparency. Two of these are familiar in terms of the trade policy debates, but another appeared to be a special feature of the minerals and metals sector.

Concepts of Transparency

Policies at the Border Towards Imports

Policies directed towards the import of processed minerals in consuming countries will affect the location of minerals processing. Usually the expectation is that countries losing competitiveness in an industry are more likely to adopt a protectionist response, depending on the relative degree of political influence of the losing groups.

In the East Asian context, however, the consuming industries have a strong continuing interest in policies affecting the metals industries, especially because growth of metal demand is expected to remain high. Even though under pressures to cut back the growth in capacity in those countries because of the influence of factors like rising wages, labour relations problems and environmental issues, the strategy being adopted by the processing industries is to relocate offshore and then import back the processed product. Under these circumstances, the protectionist response would only come from declining domestic industries in which firms did not relocate.

While this appears to be the general picture of pressures for relocation of processing in Northeast Asia, there are exceptions. In addition, there was concern expressed at the meeting that, where pressures for protection continued, the policy adopted would not be transparent but would take the form of voluntary restraint agreements, discriminatory trading agreements and special commodity agreements. Developments along these lines in North America were of special concern.

Policy towards Processing Activities

Countries well endowed with mineral resources have a natural interest in promoting local processing, but in some cases they adopt policies that actually reduce incentives for this. For example, there may be an expectation in the community that a resource deposit is highly valuable and that the developers can bear a relatively high tax burden. At the same time, those countries might expect that the developers of a deposit will also undertake substantial local processing, in the belief that the presence of the deposit is itself a major competitive advantage.

Analysis of the economics of processing suggests however, that location decisions are highly sensitive to a host of factors, only one of which is the endowment of the raw material. A number of other policies in resource rich countries are of critical importance, particularly those affecting the efficient supply of inputs in the processing industry like transport and construction services.

As an example of the sensitivity of the location decision to policy, it was noted how the use of subsidies, including direct payments, tax holidays, government provided infrastructure, low-cost loans, etc., for processing industries invoke a substantial effect on trade flows. A related issue of the impact of subsidies on the pattern of the world's coal trade was highlighted in this context.

Supply and Demand Outlook and Supply Security

Response to the loss of competitiveness may take a protectionist form but, as noted above, this did not appear to be a major motivation for policy towards the processing sector in the region. A variety of national objectives often grouped under the heading of "supply security" may be a more significant rationale for these restrictive trade and domestic policies.

The issue of supply security appears to be especially relevant for the minerals and metals industries. This may be because the processing of minerals is highly capital intensive, involves long lead times and because the products traded are not necessarily homogeneous. This means that trading partners will face relatively high price fluctuations in response to any supply and demand shocks if they traded on the basis of spot market prices. As a result they may unilaterally use a variety of methods to avoid being exposed to this degree of uncertainty. The pursuit of supply security may involve a cost, essentially an insurance premium, but the important issue is whether there are cooperative alternatives to unilateral policies for achieving those objectives.

There was some discussion at the meeting of the meaning of supply security. It was agreed that the term had many dimensions and its interpretation varied between countries. An important form of transparency is therefore to make the meaning of the term more explicit by discussing the requirements for metal supply, country by country, so that expectations could be fully understood. Just as importantly, exporting countries would also want to discuss their interests in market access to achieve greater stability.

These discussions among trading partners could include a review of the outlook for metals demand. They could also review the characteristics of the trade which would be regarded as desirable from the point of view of exporters and importers. This could include rules on how to deal with supply and demand shocks and their impacts on prices in the region and in the rest of the world.

The development of this sort of transparency would avoid countries taking decisions on metal procurement in isolation. The previous experience has shown that these decisions have been taken at some cost, in terms of the loss of gains from specialization and trade, and to some extent have been based on outlooks for regional trade which have then become self-fulfilling.

For example, an expectation that the trade in semi-finished products is likely to be relatively small and hence the market will be more unstable, is likely to come true if importing countries promote domestic processing and import raw materials instead. This discussion might be based on the judgment that the supply elasticity of raw materials is greater than that of semi-finished products. The adoption of such strategies has contributed to the familiar pattern of escalating effective rates of assistance further down the processing chain.

Strategies for Achieving Transparency

Use of Multilateral Negotiations

The use of Multilateral Trade Negotiations (MTN) strategies has obvious benefits in terms of constraining the use of trade distorting policies. This is especially relevant for countries losing comparative advantage, and without the countervailing power of a strong consuming sector.

A number of groups involved in the current MTN round have some interests in minerals and metals issues. These include the generic groups (tariffs, NTBs, and subsidies), the Natural Resource Based Products Group (NRBP) and the Trade Related Investment Measures Group. It was noted at the meeting that product coverage was still an issue in the NRBP Group, in particular whether to proceed beyond non-ferrous metals to include energy and ferrous metals in its discussions. There are also issues about the location of the substantive negotiations on these sorts of the products, that is, in a generic group or in the NRBP Group.

While the meeting did not come to a view on these questions, two points were clear. First, in the current round, progress was being constrained by a lack of direction in the negotiations. In that context, an important contribution would be a statement by Pacific countries on what were the priorities. That statement might be an appropriate agenda item for a regional ministerial meeting. Second, the lack of transparency of the policy mechanisms involved severely constrained the priorities which could be offered. At this stage, an exception to this problem appeared to be steel, as well as the related trade in coal, and these might be nominated as top priority issues.

Regional Strategies

A regional approach to some of these issues is sensible because of the present high degree of regional concentration in minerals and metals trade. There was some concern expressed that discriminatory trading arrangements would, as a side effect, divert some trade away from the Pacific.

Various regional activities might include the following:

Regular meetings of producing and consuming countries
Regular meetings of producing and consuming countries could be held to review their expectations of minerals and metals supply and demand in the region and to discuss their notions of security of supply and of market access.

It was argued that such meetings would have an extra benefit for domestic policy-making in supplier countries. This was to maintain the pressure in those countries to remove unilaterally policies which were raising the costs of local processing. It was important that policy-makers in those countries be exposed to the competitive pressures in the region to build processing industries, in order to focus their attention on domestic policy as well as that of their trading partners'.

Build a bank of data and information
A second purpose of regional initiatives would be to build the bank of data and information on these issues. These would include policy inventories, price comparisons and the analysis of the impact of the policies now in place, and, the effects of reforms. Research effort in these areas would contribute to the effectiveness of subsequent MTN rounds.

It was argued that the PECC and its Minerals and Energy Forum could serve an important function in being the coordinator of some of this activity. It was noted that most of these activities are in fact already part of the work of the MEF.

Minerals and Energy Forum
Specialist Group Meeting

List of papers tabled, available from Minerals and Energy Forum, % Australia–Japan Research Centre, Australian National University, GPO Box 4, Canberra, ACT 2001, Australia:

Department of Primary Industries and Energy, Australia
Towards the Efficient Location of Minerals Processing in the Pacific Region

Professor Peter Drysdale, Australia
Energy and Resource Trade Security
Chapter 5, International Economic Pluralism: Economic Policy in East Asia and the Pacific, Allen and Unwin, in association with the Australia-Japan Research Centre, Australian National University, 1988

Mr. Errol Muir, CRA Limited, Australia
Minerals Development in Resource Rich Countries

Dr. I-Lin Cheng, China Steel Corp., Chinese Taipei
Taiwanese Investment Strategies for Developing Overseas Minerals Resources: a case study of China Steel Corporation

Mr. Cui Yin-Yu, China National Non-Ferrous Metal Corp., China
Situation and Forecast of China's Non-Ferrous Metals Industry

Professor Chen Chia-yon, National Cheng Kung University, Taiwan
The Supply and Demand for Metals in the Taiwan Area and Its Prospectives

Mr. Kang Jong-soon, Korea
Aspects in the Development of the Korean Steel Industry

Mr. Andrei Baranovsky, Institute of Energy Resources, USSR
Development of Minerals and Energy Resources in the USSR and Cooperation with the Asia-Pacific Region

Dr. Allen Clark, East-West Center, United States
Tariff and Non-Tariff Barriers to Minerals Development and Trade

Mr. Kingsley Barker, Department of Foreign Affairs and Trade, Australia

Resource-Based Issues in the GATT Uruguay Round of Multilateral Trade Negotiations

Dr. Barry Lipsett, Department of Energy, Mines and Resources, Canada

The Canada-US Free Trade Agreement and Minerals Processing in the Pacific Region

Barriers to Pacific Trade in Fisheries Products

Gordon R. Munro
Coordinator, PECC Task Force on
Fisheries Development and Cooperation

It is particularly appropriate that the issue of barriers to trade in fisheries products be discussed in the context of a Pacific forum such as the PECC. The Pacific region is at once the single most important region in terms of world harvests of fish and the single most important region in terms of trade in fisheries products. The region accounts for more than 40 per cent of the world's harvest of fish. It also accounts as well for approximately 50 per cent (in value terms) of world exports of fishery products and 60 per cent of world imports of such products (Crowley, 1989).

Japan and the United States are of almost overwhelming importance in the region as importers of fishery products. Together they account for over 45 per cent of world imports of fishery products. Of the fish exporting nations of the world, eight of the leading 12 exporters are Pacific Rim countries. Canada is the most important followed by the United States, Republic of Korea, Thailand, Japan, China, Mexico and Indonesia. These countries collectively account for about 35 per cent of world exports (Crowley, 1989).

Upon taking an overview of trade in fisheries products in the Pacific, no one would suggest that the trade is bedeviled with barriers to the same extent as trade in agricultural products. Nonetheless, trade barriers continue to be significant, and much remains to be done before trade in fisheries products can be described as truly liberalized.

Tariffs range in excess of 100 per cent in some instances (Major, 1989) and, as in other areas, vary according to the degree of processing. There are many non-tariff barriers in existence. Some, such as sanitary regulations, are similar to those found in agriculture. One non-tariff barrier found in certain Pacific countries is particularly restrictive. This takes the form of global import quotas on fisheries products of particular species and types. Often import licences are issued to domestic processors who have little incentive to import. The foreign exporters become residual suppliers, with all of the risks that that implies (Crowley, 1989; Pereyra, 1989).

The second point is that, while barriers to trade in fisheries products are in some instances highly restrictive, the use of such barriers varies widely throughout the Pacific, as the appended tables indicate (Major, 1989). Australia, Canada and New Zealand, for example, have very low barriers to imports of fish products from GATT countries and from developing countries (Campbell, 1989). At the other end of the spectrum, both the Republic of Korea and Taiwan impose high tariffs, and Japan makes extensive use of quotas, in spite of the fact that all three are significant exporters of fish products.

It is interesting to observe in passing that in the Republic of Korea, a country notable for its restrictions on agricultural imports, the import liberalization ratio for fisheries products is even lower than it is for agricultural products—54.2 per cent vs. 70.5 per cent (Park, 1989).

The arguments for protection in developed countries and Newly Industrialized Countries (NICs) are similar to those found in agriculture. Once again, the Republic of Korea provides an example. There are in Korea small scale, chronically depressed, inshore fisheries which account for five-sixths of Korea's fishermen. Since all other attempts to alleviate the situation have been unsuccessful, these small scale fisheries can be maintained only through the use of stringent protectionist measures, or so the argument goes (see also Shinohara, 1989).

Having said all of this, however, there is some evidence that the heretofore highly protectionist countries have made some progress towards liberalization (Major, 1989). What is required is to find a means of ensuring that this progress continues.

The question of ease of access to markets for fishery products is of particular concern to the developing coastal states of the Pacific. As a consequence of the UN Third Conference on the Law of the Sea, all coastal states have gained the right to lay claim to fishery resources out to 200 miles from shore. Extended Fisheries Jurisdiction (EFJ), to use the legal terminology, is, of course, important to all coastal states. Developing coastal states, however, see the acquired fishery resources as having the potential to make a significant contribution to their rates of economic development. The Pacific Island nations are a case in point.

The extent to which these newly acquired fishery resources will make a contribution to the economic growth of these developing countries will depend upon the effectiveness with which the fishery resources are managed and the ease of access which these countries have to markets for fishery products. It should be noted in passing, that developing coastal states face not only artificial barriers to trade such as tariffs, but also natural barriers such as inadequate transportation facilities and inadequate facilities for quality control.

The PECC Task Force on Fisheries Development and Cooperation is giving increased attention to the issue of barriers to trade. The issue was discussed at some length at the Task Force workshop held in May 1989. The Task force will, not surprisingly, recommend to the Seventh PECC that the PECC encourage all of its member countries to continue their programs of trade liberalization with respect to fishery products. The Fisheries Task Forces does, however, desire to go beyond that.

It wishes to impress upon the PECC the necessity of ensuring that its developing coastal state members realize the full economic benefit promised to them by Extended Fisheries Jurisdiction. It shall, therefore, recommend to the PECC that it encourage its developed and newly industrialized country members to continue their trade liberalization programs by removing first their barriers to imports of fishery products from Pacific developing coastal states. Specifically, the recommendation will read as follows:

> The PECC should urge its developed and newly industrialized country members, when continuing their fisheries trade liberalization programs, to recognize the particularly great need of Pacific developing coastal states to gain access to markets by giving, within GATT rules, specific and special consideration to imports of fisheries products from Pacific developing coastal states.

In making this recommendation, the Fisheries Task Force hopes that it will enjoy the full support of the Trade Policy Forum.

CAMROSE LUTHERAN COLLEGE
LIBRARY

Table 1
General Tariffs and Quotas for Fish Products

	Aust. %	Canada %	Japan %	Korea %	NZ %	Taiwan %	USA %	Malaysia %
	GENERAL							
Fish – Fresh, Chilled or Frozen	Free	Free	0-10	25-30	Free	35.5	$0-$2.05/lb	Free
Fish – Dried, Salted or Smoked	Free	Free	15	25	Free	35-50	0-25	0-20
Crustaceans and Molluscs – Fresh, Frozen and Dried	Free	25-40	10-15	25	Free	50	0-110	Free
Squid	Free	Free	10-15	25	Free	50	5¢/lb	Free
Tunas – Frozen, Chilled	15	Free*	10	30	Free	50	Free	Free
Tunas – Canned	15	30	20	60	14	50	25	20

* Frozen tuna, if to be canned in Canada – 30% for frozen loins.

Source: Major, 1989.

Table 2
Tariffs and Quotas for Fish Products

	China % GENERAL	Singapore %	PNG %	Fiji %	Thailand %	Indonesia %	Solomons %	Philippines %
Fish – Fresh, Chilled or Frozen	120-150	Free	0-50	Free	Free	40+10#	30	50
Fish – Dried, Salted or Smoked	150	Free	0-50	Free	60	40+10#	30	50
Crustaceans and Molluscs – Fresh, Frozen and Dried	120-150	Free	Free	Free	30-60	40+10#	30	50
Squid	150	Free	Free	Free	30-60	40+10#	30	20
Tunas – Frozen, Chilled	150	Free	Free	Free	Free	40+10#	30	50
Tunas – Canned	180	Free	Free	Free	80	Rp 1750 per kg	30	50

Import Duty

Source: Major, 1989.

Table 3
Developing Countries Preferential and
Most Favoured Nations' Tariffs

	Aust. %	Canada %	Japan %	Korea %	NZ %	Taiwan %	USA %	Malaysia %
Fish – Fresh, Chilled or Frozen	Free	Free	0-10	25-30	Free	35.5	$0-$5/lb	0.20
Fish – Dried, Salted or Smoked	Free	Free	15	25	Free	35-50	0-4.8	Free
Crustaceans and Molluscs – Fresh, Frozen and Dried	Free	0-10	10-15	25	Free	50	0-18.0	Free
Squid	Free	Free	10-15	25	Free	50	5¢/lb	Free
Tunas – Frozen, Chilled	Free	Free	10	30	Free	50	Free	Free
Tunas – Canned	Free	9.8	8	60	0-10	50	6	20

Source: Major, 1989.

Table 4
Developing Countries Preferential and Most Favoured Nations' Tariffs

	China %	Singapore %	PNG %	Fiji %	Thailand %	Indonesia %	Solomons %	Philippines %
Fish – Fresh, Chilled or Frozen	80	Free	0-50	Free	Free	40+10#	30	50
Fish – Dried, Salted or Smoked	100	Free	0-50	Free	60	40+10#	30	50
Crustaceans and Molluscs – Fresh, Frozen and Dried	80-100	Free	Free	Free	30-60	40+10#	30	50
Squid	100	Free	Free	Free	30-60	40+10#	30	20
Tunas – Frozen, Chilled	80	Free	Free	Free	Free	40+10#	30	50
Tunas – Canned	180	Free	Free	Free	80	Rp 1750 per kg	30	50

Import Duty

Source: Major, 1989.

Table 5
Quotas

	Aust. %	Canada %	Japan %	Korea %	NZ %	Taiwan %	USA %	Malaysia %
Fish – Fresh, Chilled or Frozen	No	No	Yes	No	No	No	No	No
Fish – Dried, Salted or Smoked	No	No	Yes	No	No	No	No	No
Crustaceans and Molluscs – Fresh, Frozen and Dried	No	No	Yes	No	No	No	No	No
Squid	No	No	Yes	No	No	No	No	No
Tunas – Frozen, Chilled	No	No	Yes	No	No	No	No	No
Tunas – Canned	No	No	No	No	No	No	Yes	No

Source: Major, 1989.

Table 6
Quotas

	China %	Singapore %	PNG %	Fiji %	Thailand %	Indonesia %	Solomons %	Philippines %
Fish – Fresh, Chilled or Frozen	No	No	No	No	No	No	No	No
Fish – Dried, Salted or Smoked	No	No	No	No	No	No	No	No
Crustaceans and Molluscs – Fresh, Frozen and Dried	No	No	No	No	No	No	No	No
Squid	No	No	No	No	No	No	No	No
Tunas – Frozen, Chilled	No	No	No	No	No	No	No	No
Tunas – Canned	No	No	No	No	No	No	No	No**

** Annual quota on canned sardine and mackerel
Note: Above data based on latest information available.
Source: Major, 1989.

Bibliography

All of the following papers were prepared for the PECC Task Force on Fisheries Development and Cooperation Workshop held in Vancouver, Canada, May 29-30, 1989. Copies are available on request to Professor Gordon Munro, Department of Economics, University of British Columbia, Vancouver, B.C. Canada.

Campbell, H.F., "Problems in Pacific Fisheries Trade: An Australian Perspective", 1989.

Crowley, R.W., "Trade and Trade Barriers in Pacific Rim Fisheries: A Canadian Perspective", 1989.

Major, Philip, "Trade Barriers Affecting the Pacific Market for Fish", 1989.

Park, Seong Kwae, "Korea's Fisheries Production, Trade and Issues", 1989.

Shinohara, Takashi, "Fisheries Imports of Japan", 1989.

Pacific Rim Trade in Forest Products and Sustainable Economic Development

Luis Constantino and
Michael Percy
University of Alberta

Introduction

The notion that natural resources should be managed to ensure "sustainable development" has become a basic element of most informed discussions of resource exploitation, especially in regards to forestry in developing economies. However, the term has entered the global vocabulary so quickly that its meaning is often not clear. For our purposes we adopt the World Bank's definition that sustainable development is the effort of policymakers to:

> maximize the net benefits from existing resources (human, natural and produced capital) subject to maintaining the services and quality of these resources over time. More concretely, the concept of sustainable development means:
> (a) a transition away from economic growth based mainly on the depletion of exhaustible resource stocks, towards greater reliance on renewable resources;
> (b) a rate of utilization of renewable resources that does not consistently exceed their natural or managed rate of regeneration;
> (c) a pattern of resource use that does not foreclose too many options for the future through irreversible resource degradation; and

(d)   continued attention to allocative and technical efficiency, so that growth can proceed while aggregate natural resource consumption is stabilized." (World Bank, 1988, pp. 85-86)

The apparent high rates of tropical deforestation have led many observers to fear that the resource is not being managed on a sustainable basis. Two sorts of consequences from non-sustainable management are anticipated. The first is that the direct effects of deforestation on producing countries may be significant and result in large-scale economic and social disruptions in the future. The second concern is that the ecological and environmental costs to the global economy from the greenhouse effect and possible species loss may be large and irreversible.

This background paper briefly reviews the current literature on tropical deforestation and its links to both the trade in tropical timber products and salient features of the economic and institutional environment of developing countries. Part One is an overview of the world trade in tropical timber products mainly in the Asia-Pacific region and is undertaken at a high level of aggregation because of the space constraints. The evidence on tropical deforestation is reviewed in Part Two and the relative contributions of industrial and non-industrial timber production to the problem assessed. Part Three of the paper highlights the critical role of institutional reform and broad based economic development to reducing pressure on the tropical forest base.

1.   Trade in Tropical Forest Products

The public focus on tropical timber production and deforestation is overwhelmingly on commercial activities. This focus is somewhat misleading as we shall argue later, in light of the much larger volume of hardwood timber allocation to fuelwood demands and the loss of forest base to agricultural uses. Until the Second World War the trade in tropical forest products was a relatively small component of international trade flows of forest products and consisted mainly of timber used in the luxury trade. However, after the Second World War the demand for tropical timber increased significantly. Imports of tropical hardwoods increased 14 times between 1950 and 1980.

In 1970 all sources of hardwoods accounted for 29 per cent of total world roundwood production of 1.3 billion cubic meters, softwoods the remaining 71 per cent. By 1985, hardwoods accounted for 31 per cent of world roundwood production of 1.5 billion cubic meters and the timber from the developing regions of Southeast Asia, especially Indonesia and Malaysia, accounted for 32 per cent of the world's increase in new hardwood supply (Woodbridge, Reed and Associates, 1988, p. 85).[1]

Tropical timber exports come from three regions. In 1980, the Asia-Pacific region supplied 84 per cent of the world's tropical timber exports by volume; Africa supplied 14 per cent; and the remaining two per cent came from Latin America (Grainger, 1986, Table 7, p. 16). Table 1 highlights the pattern of trade in tropical timber products. The major role of Asia-Pacific in the tropical timber exports trade belies its small share of the world's tropical forests—24 per cent (Lanly, 1982). Less than 8 per cent of the total world production of wood for all purposes is exported from its country of origin (Gammie, 1981) but this is not so for tropical countries, especially in the Asia-Pacific region. Exports from tropical countries as a proportion of regional roundwood removals rose to more than one-half for the Asia-Pacific region by the 1970s. This stands in sharp contrast to the levels observed for Latin American and African tropical hardwood exporters (Harvard Institute for International Development (HIID), 1988, pp. 6-7).

Remarkable shifts have occurred in the composition of trade within this region both in products and origins of exports. Indonesia and Malaysia now account for the bulk of the region's exports supplanting the Philippines, the major exporter of tropical hardwoods from the region in the 1950s and 1960s. In 1984 Malaysia produced 45 per cent of the world's tropical industrial wood exports, including 60 per cent of all hardwood log exports. Spurred on by restrictions on the exports of logs and culminating with a complete ban in 1986, Indonesian exports of wood products have increased dramatically, from 13 thousand cubic meters in 1976 to over 3 million cubic meters in 1985 for plywood and from 600 thousand cubic meters to 2 million cubic meters for sawnwood. Indonesia's share of the world market for tropical wood products rose from zero per cent in 1976 to 70 per cent in 1985 for plywood, and from 12 per cent in 1976 to 33 per cent in 1985 for sawnwood (FAO Yearbook of Forest Statistics, 1985). Indonesia has now imposed restrictions on sawnwood exports and banned rattan exports in efforts to increase value-added production.

The efforts of major producers of tropical hardwoods within the Asia-Pacific region to promote further processing of tropical timber within the country have led to shifts in the locus of processing of tropical hardwoods through time. In the 1950s and 1960s producer countries such as the Philippines, Indonesia and Malaysia had limited manufacturing capabilities and exported their production mainly as logs and some sawnwood. Japan, for example, in the 1950s re-exported approximately one-third of its tropical log imports in processed form. Taiwan and Singapore adopted Japan's processing model in the 1960s and relied upon tropical timber products from Indonesia, the Philippines, and

Malaysia. Growth of domestic demand in Japan led to a decline in its role as the major exporter of manufactured tropical timber products but other countries within the region, such as Taiwan, Singapore, South Korea, and to a lesser extent Hong Kong, assumed the role (Reilly, 1989, p. 10). However, the decision of major exporting countries, such as Indonesia, to ban log exports and focus on value-added tropical timber products, such as plywood, has led their production to expand at the expense of other countries such as Taiwan and South Korea which had formerly processed tropical timber. Thus the structure of trade flows within the Asia-Pacific region reflects not only comparative production costs and resource availability but also barriers to the flow of natural resources among countries.[2]

Table 2 provides an overview of the value of tropical wood products by category by major importers for 1984. These data are for all tropical wood products, not just those from the Asia-Pacific region. In the global context of tropical wood products consumption, Japan, USA, and the EEC are roughly equal. However, Japan stands out in that 84 per cent of its imports are logs or sawnwood whereas the USA and EEC import a greater proportion of manufactured goods. Over 95 per cent of Japan's tropical industrial wood imports come from the Asia-Pacific region and in 1980 comprised almost half of the region's exports (Reilly, 1989, p. 13). This pattern in import composition reflects both the history of Japan as a processor and a pattern of tariffs common to most economies which escalates according to the extent of processing of the forest products in question. Tables 3, 4, and 5 depict the international trade in hardwood products (logs, lumber, and plywood) as of 1986.

Hardwoods are forecast to increase their contribution to world industrial roundwood supplies to 33 per cent of global supply by the year 2000 (Woodbridge, Reed and Associates, 1988, Vol II, Table 2.2). Hardwood supplies are estimated to increase by 156 million cubic meters with the Asia-Pacific region exclusive of Japan and Developed Oceania accounting for 22 million cubic meters. Most, if not all of the hardwood increment from tropical regions is forecast to come from plantations as the reserves of natural tropical hardwood forests continue to dwindle (ibid., p. 90). Brazil is predicted to be the most important producer of incremental hardwoods from plantations.

2.   Tropical Deforestation

Deforestation is taken to mean the conversion of natural forest areas to other uses including artificial plantations, agriculture and wasteland (Lanly, 1982). However, the shift of natural forest areas to artificial plantations or perennial tree crop production continues to provide some of the environmental services of natural forests including watershed regulations and soil protection. In any case, natural forest conversion to plantations constitutes only a small element of deforestation (HIID, 1988, pp. 9-10). A wide continuum of opinion exists concerning the extent of tropical deforestation and the threat it poses for producing countries (Sedjo and Clawson, 1984, pp. 155-66; HIID, 1988, pp. 18-22). This diversity of opinion reflects major gaps in our knowledge regarding timber inventory, harvesting rates, to cite just two of many variables and differences in definitions of deforestation.

It is worth emphasizing that the earth's forest area has declined from approximately 5 billion to 4 billion hectares from pre-agricultural times to the present. Repetto (1988, p. 3) notes that

Temperate closed forests have suffered the greatest losses (32 to 35 per cent), followed by subtropical woody savannah and deciduous forests (24 to 25 per cent), and tropical climax forests (15 to 20 per cent). Over the entire period, tropical evergreen rainforests have suffered the smallest attrition, 4 to 6 per cent, because until recently they were inaccessible and barely populated.

Thus the concern of the developed economies is somewhat belated and suspect since many based early economic growth on rapid deforestation.

Recent estimates of deforestation are reported in Table 6 for selected countries in the Asia-Pacific region. Other countries and group averages are included for the purposes of comparison. The evidence suggests considerable variation among counties in the Asia-Pacific region. Malaysia, the current major log exporter (Table 3) falls in the category of higher than average rates of deforestation and large areas affected, whereas Indonesia falls in the second category of low rates of deforestation but large areas affected. Projected rates of deforestation are extremely sensitive to assumptions regarding economic growth as shifting cultivation and agricultural expansion are major causes for conversion of the tropical forest to non-forestry uses. Grainger (1987) estimates that the forest area of the Asia-Pacific region could contract by as much as 23 per cent to at least 12 per cent depending on agricultural-forestry interactions.

The rates of deforestation reported in Table 6 arise from a variety of factors, of which commercial forestry is but one element. In 1984 wood removals for industrial forestry in the Asia-Pacific region amounted to 188.2 million cubic meters. In the same year, removals for fuelwood and charcoal amounted to 696.5 million cubic meters (Asian Development Bank, 1987, Table 15). Lanly

(1982) has attributed about 45 per cent of the deforestation of the closed forests to shifting cultivators. In tropical Asia deforestation is ascribed mainly to encroachment by lowland villages, shifting cultivators, and from planned transmigration and resettlement (HIID, 1988, p. 11). However, commercial forestry is often the catalyst for deforestation from non-commercial causes. Logging roads in particular increase access to heretofore unexploited forest areas for shifting cultivators.

Current harvest levels appear to be unsustainable. The rate of deforestation from all sources—commercial forestry and shifts to competing uses, especially agriculture—and the absence of adequate reforestation programs means that current harvest levels will lead to continued depletion of the forest base. A recent study has concluded that

> By the end of the century, the 33 developing countries that are now net exporters of forest products will be reduced to fewer than 10, and total developing-country exports of industrial forest products are predicted to drop from their current level of more than US$7 billion to less than US$2 billion (WRI, 1985).

The shift to plantation timber and a reliance on fast growing and high yielding species is viewed as the source of anticipated growth in new supplies of both soft and hardwoods. The Asian Development Bank has estimated that a comprehensive investment strategy for the forest sector of the Asia-Pacific region for the coming decade would cost on an annual average basis, US$5.5 billion (Asian Development Bank, 1987, Table 24). Approximately 17 per cent of these investments are directed to the environment including watershed management, arid land forestry, ecosystem conservation, and non-industrial plantings. Investments in fuelwood capacity account for another 10 per cent of proposed annual investment levels. A key element of the investment strategy includes investment in forest institutions, in education and training, research and extension to help strengthen forest management capabilities. Investment in institutions would account for an additional 17 per cent of proposed annual expenditures. The remaining 56 per cent of expenditures are in the forest industry including plantations and reforestation (ibid., Table 24).

Expenditures in the Peoples Republic of China account for a total of 40 per cent of the Asian Development Bank estimates of required investments in the coming decade. The required level of investments in the coming decade. The required level of investments in Indonesia are estimated at approximately at US$840 million per annum over the coming decade, and the corresponding estimates for Malaysia, the Philippines, and Thailand are US$250 million, US$172 million, and US$190 million, respectively (ibid.).

3. Deforestation and Institutional Reform

At the beginning of this background paper it was noted that public attention tends to focus on the link between commercial forestry and depletion of the tropical forest base. However, the evidence suggests that commercial harvest rates and the shift of tropical forest base to non-forest activities and waste is symptomatic of two fundamental problems—(1) the pattern of economic development, and (2) the failure of the existing institutional structure in many developing countries to value the forest resource adequately.[3]

Rapid population growth in many developing countries places enormous demands on the agricultural sector to meet domestic food requirements and leads shifts of the forest base to non-forest uses. A further consequence of population growth is an increasing demand for fuelwood, an additional pressure on the forest resource. The estimate for 1984 cited that in the Asia-Pacific region almost 700 million cubic meters of wood removals was for fuelwood and charcoal, and 188 million cubic meters for industrial wood should be recalled in this context.

The shift of forest base to agricultural uses is a key element in tropical deforestation. Improvements in agricultural productivity may be a key element in reducing the magnitude of deforestation as the ability for regions to produce more agricultural goods from a given land area will reduce demands on the forest land base. Grainger (1987) has concluded that:

> future trends in deforestation will probably be determined by the way in which processes in the agricultural sector move towards equilibrium. This has major implications for strategies intended to bring deforestation under control since it indicates that the focus of action should be in the agricultural sector, rather than in the forest sector as in previous strategies, e.g. those of FAO (1985) and the World Resources Institute (1985).

Deforestation associated with expansion of agriculture is often symptomatic of the more profound problem that the existing institutional structure both consistently undervalues the contribution of the forest base to economic development and manages the forest base in a manner that promotes deforestation. The typical forest provides a wide range of benefits that the market does not value directly and which are not reflected in commercial timber prices. The contribution of the forest to the regional environment through watershed protection and soil preservation is enormously important but rarely valued until lost. The tropical forest also provides a wide range of foodstuffs and other goods to forest dwellers which are quite significant in value but are highly underestimated as they do not show up as market transactions (Repetto, 1988, p. 10). Moreover, a wide-range of minor forest crops from resins to medicinal products are often overlooked when valuing the forest base. These sorts of benefits, with the appropriate institutional framework, can be included in efforts to value the forest base.

However, the tropical forest is unique in that a range of its benefits clearly extends beyond national boundaries. The role played by the tropical forest in the greenhouse phenomenon is just one example. The remarkable biological diversity of tropical forests and the potential for genetic materials found in them to contribute new medicines, new foods, and other products to benefit the global economy is another example. However, since these sorts of benefits are global in nature, international organizations, through grants and aid to developing countries with tropical forests, must help ensure the benefits are realized. The developing countries cannot be expected to bear the entire costs of ensuring that the transboundary benefits of the tropical forests are realized.

Failure to realize the value of the market and non-market benefits of the forest means that it is harvested more rapidly than is desirable and the forest base is allocated to other uses. Repetto (1988) has argued persuasively that government policies exacerbate tropical deforestation significantly. For example, land tenure policies tend to promote deforestation through granting title to land devoted to agricultural uses but not for forest uses. On the basis of detailed country studies, Repetto (1988, pp. 13-17) suggests six explanations for government policies that have contributed to deforestation:

1.   Continuing benefits from intact natural forests have been consistently undervalued.
2.   Net benefits from forest exploitation and conversion have been overestimated though exaggerating benefits and underestimating costs.
3.   Development planners have proceeded too boldly to exploit tropical forests for commodity production without adequate biological knowledge of their potential or limitations or awareness of the economic consequences of development policies.
4.   Policymakers have attempted without much success to draw on tropical forest resources to solve fiscal, economic, social and political conflicts elsewhere in society.

5.   National governments have been reluctant to invest enough in stewardship and management of the public forest resource despite its enormous value.

6.   National governments have overestimated their own capabilities for forest management while at the same time underestimating the value of traditional management practices and local governance over forest resources.

Tropical deforestation is a reality. The causes are far more complex than simply the extent of current commercial hardwood production entering international trade. Economic development especially through enhancing productivity growth in agriculture, and promoting non-wood energy usage where possible, will relieve pressure on the tropical forests. Institutional reform within producing countries, especially in ensuring that the full value—market and non-market components—of the tropical forest is considered when evaluating forest investments and potential forest base conversion, is another essential ingredient for tropical forest conservation. Finally, international organizations through aid must bear some of the costs for ensuring tropical forest conservation.

Table 1
Major Tropical Hardwood Trade Flows, 1980

A. Imports by Product and Source
(unit = billion cubic metres of log equivalent)

	Logs	Sawnwood	Plywd/vrs	Total
JAPAN	18.4	0.8	0.1	19.3
Africa	0.0	0.0	0.0	0.0
Asia-Pacific	18.4	0.8	0.1	19.3
Latin America	0.0	0.0	0.0	0.0
EUROPE	5.3	5.0	1.3	11.6
Africa	5.0	0.9	0.2	6.1
Asia-Pacific	0.3	3.8	1.1	5.2
Latin America	0.0	0.3	0.0	0.3
USA	0.0	0.6	2.1	2.7
Africa	0.0	0.0	0.0	0.0
Asia-Pacific	0.0	0.2	2.0	2.2
Latin America	0.0	0.4	0.1	0.5
OTHER ASIA	13.6	0.0	0.0	13.6
Africa	0.0	0.0	0.0	0.0
Asia-Pacific	13.6	0.0	0.0	13.6
Latin America	0.0	0.0	0.0	0.0

B. Trade Flows by Volume
(unit as above)

Exporter \ Importer	Japan	Europe	USA	Other Asia	Total
Africa	0.0	6.1	0.0	0.0	6.1
Asia-Pacific	19.3	5.2	2.2	13.6	40.3
Latin America	0.0	0.3	0.5	0.0	0.8
Total	19.3	11.6	2.7	13.6	47.2

Note: The Asia-Pacific exporting region includes other Asian processors.

Table 2
Value of Tropical Wood Products (excluding pulp and paper) Imported by Japan, the United States, Western Europe and the EEC in 1984

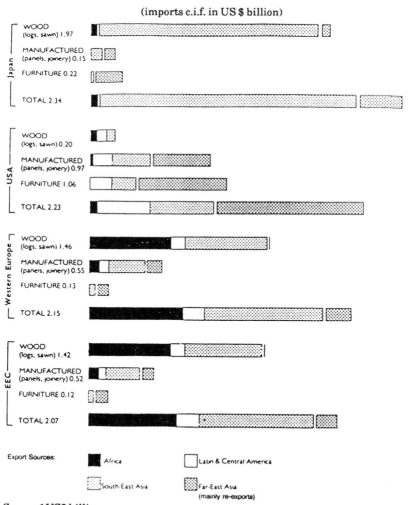

(imports c.i.f. in US $ billion)

Japan
- WOOD (logs, sawn) 1.97
- MANUFACTURED (panels, joinery) 0.15
- FURNITURE 0.22
- TOTAL 2.34

USA
- WOOD (logs, sawn) 0.20
- MANUFACTURED (panels, joinery) 0.97
- FURNITURE 1.06
- TOTAL 2.23

Western Europe
- WOOD (logs, sawn) 1.46
- MANUFACTURED (panels, joinery) 0.55
- FURNITURE 0.13
- TOTAL 2.15

EEC
- WOOD (logs, sawn) 1.42
- MANUFACTURED (panels, joinery) 0.52
- FURNITURE 0.12
- TOTAL 2.07

Export Sources:
- Africa
- Latin & Central America
- South-East Asia
- Far-East Asia (mainly re-exports)

Scm = 1US$ billion

Source: OECD (1986) as quoted in Smith, Yeo-Chang and Schrueder (1989).

Table 3
Trade Flows of Hardwood Log (1986)

(Unit: 1,000 M³)

Importing Country Exporting Country	Japan	Other Developed Countries	China (including Taiwan)	Sough Korea	Hong Kong	Developed Countries	Developing Countries	World Total
Malaysia	11,439	4	3,536	2,934	445	11,443	7,552	18,995
Ivory Coast	1	875	–	5	–	876	144	1,020
Papua New Guinea	797	0	36	464	3	797	503	1,300
Gabon	49	645	–	64	–	694	189	883
Cameroon	10	688	–	–	–	698	6	704
Philippines	255	38	40	6	–	293	59	352
Solomon Islands	271	0	–	–	–	271	78	349
Liberia	–	347	–	–	–	347	11	358
Developed Countries	45	3,245	–	27	–	3,290	316	3,606
Developing Countries	12,822	849	3,612	3,473	448	16,268	9,012	25,280
World Total	12,867	7,125	3,612	3,500	448	19,558	9,328	28,886

Source: FAO (1988) Yearbook of Forest Products—1986.

Table 4
Trade Flows of Hardwood Lumber (1986)

(Unit: 1,000 m^3)

Importing Countries Exporting Countries	Italy	Japan	USA	UK	West Germany	Nether-lands	Canada	China (& Taiwan)	Singapore	Developed Countries	Developing Countries	World Total
Malaysia	41	191	19	102	82	638	–	143	751	1613	1378	2991
Indonesia	207	365	51	64	45	77	1	274	455	919	1241	2160
USA	45	145	–	71	60	32	360	208	6	867	334	1201
Yugoslavia	520	1	–	3	6	7	–	–	–	649	132	781
Singapore	10	35	7	15	36	79	1	–	–	270	471	741
France	84	–	–	28	97	53	–	–	–	582	13	595
Philippines	1	133	41	164	6	9	1	10	1	436	59	495
Ivory Coast	95	–	5	43	13	17	–	–	–	419	56	475
West Germany	26	–	1	49	–	53	–	–	–	381	3	384
Canada	4	13	210	26	6	3	–	5	–	294	18	312
Developed Countries	689	159	212	215	289	148	360	213	6	3731	586	4317
Developing Countries	360	729	250	484	186	827	26	427	1207	4375	3802	8177
World Total	1049	888	462	699	475	975	386	640	1213	8106	4388	12494

Source: FAO (1988). Yearbook of Forest Products—1986.

Table 5
Trade Flows of Tropical Hardwood Plywood (1986)

(Unit: 1,000 m³)

Importing Countries / Exporting Countries	USA	Hong Kong	UK	Singapore	Japan	China (& Taiwan)	Saudi Arabia	Nether-lands	Developed Countries	Developing Countries	World Total
Indonesia	1094	853	264	419	601	297	186	90	2160	2458	4618
Singapore	7	56	65	–	13	23	49	48	273	302	575
Taiwan	323	–	–	12	5	–	59	–	344	168	512
Malaysia	–	44	126	184	4	–	2	6	161	291	452
Philippines	72	40	80	–	3	18	–	6	185	71	256
Brazil	23	–	63	–	–	–	7	3	128	90	218
South Korea	30	2	62	22	–	4	11	31	138	62	200
Others	–	–	–	–	–	–	–	–	89	91	180
World Total	1549	1042	660	637	626	342	314	184	3478	3533	7011

Source: FAO (1988). Yearbook of Forest Products—1986.

Table 6
Deforestation in Selected Tropical Countries

Country	Closed Forest Area 1980, (1000 hectares)	Annual Rate of Deforestation 1981-85, percent
Group 1		
Malaysia	20,996	1.2
Thailand	9,235	2.6
Philippines	9,510	1.0
Nepal	1,941	4.1
Nigeria	5,950	5.0
Ivory Coast	4,458	6.5
Av. (24 countries)	222,415	2.3
Group 2		
Brazil	357,480	0.4
Indonesia	113,895	0.5
India	51,841	0.3
Av. (13 countries)	908,005	0.3
Group 3		
Kenya	1,105	1.0
Mozambique	935	1.1
Av. (10 countries)	6,529	2.2
Group 4		
Pakistan	2,185	0.0
Ethiopia	4,350	0.1
Central Af. Rep.	3,590	0.1
Av. (15 countries)	23,458	0.4

Group 1 countries: higher than average rates of deforestation, large areas affected

Group 2 countries: relatively low rates but large areas affected

Group 3 countries: high rates and small areas of forests remaining

Group 4: low or moderate rates and small areas affected

Source: Repetto (1980, Table 1.2)

Notes

1. Total hardwood supply increased from 367 million cubic meters to 471 million cubic meters, with the Asia-Pacific region inclusive of Japan and Developed Oceania accounting for 28 million cubic meters of the increase. If we exclude Japan and Developed Oceania, the new increment of hardwood supply is 36 million cubic meters. (Woodbridge, Reed and Associates, 1988, Table 2.1).

2. Efforts to promote domestic employment and investment in processing industries through bans on the export of logs or rattan, for example, can be costly ways to promote greater manufacturing. If a country lacks infrastructure or the skills required to sustain a large processing industry the expansion of processing output may be more than offset by a decline in the value of the resource base being utilized. The fall in employment in the resource sector and decline in resource royalties accruing to the government may exceed the gains in value-added in the processing sector.

3. The failure of institutions to value the forest base is a problem to virtually all countries including the developed ones.

References

Asian Development Bank (1987), *A Review of Forestry and Forest Industries in the Asia-Pacific Region*, Manila.

Food and Agriculture Organization (FAO) (1987), *Yearbook of Forest Statistics, 1985*, Rome.

Food and Agriculture Organization (FAO) (1988), *Yearbook of Forest Products, 1986*, Rome.

Gammie, J.I. (1981), "World Timber to the Year 2000," Economist Intelligence Unit, Special Report No. 98, London.

Grainger, A. (1986), *The Future Role of the Tropical Rain Forests in the World Economy*, Ph.D. Dissertation, Oxford University.

Grainger, A. (1987), "A land use simulation model for the humid tropics" paper presented at the Land and Resource Evaluation for National Planning Conference and Workshop, Chetumal, Mexico.

Harvard Institute for International Development (1988), "The Case for Multiple-Use Management of Tropical Hardwood Forests," mimeo, a study prepared for the International Tropical Timber Organization.

Lanly, Jean-Paul (1982), *Tropical Forest Resources*, FAO Forestry Paper No. 3, Food and Agricultural Organization, Rome.

Repetto, Robert (1988), *The Forest For The Trees? Government Policies and the Misuse of Forest Resources*, World Resources Institute, Washington, D.C.

Reilly, Kathleen (1989), "The Tropical Timber Trade: With an Emphasis on the United States" Workshop on the U.S. Tropical Timber Trade, Rainforest Alliance, New York, April 14-15.

Sedjo, Roger A. and Marion Clawson (1984), "Global Forests," Chapter 4 of *The Resourceful Earth*, eds. Julian Simon and Herman Kahn, Oxford, Basil Blackwell.

Smith, Paul M., Yeo-Chang Youn and Gerard F. Schrueder (1989), "The Asian-U.S. Furniture Trade: a Background Perspective," paper presented at Workshop on the U.S. Tropical Timber Trade: Conservation Options and Impacts, New York, April 14-16.

Woodbridge, Reed and Associates (1988), *Canada's Forest Industry, The Next Twenty Years: Prospects and Priorities*, (6 volumes), Woodbridge, Reed and Associates, Vancouver.

World Bank (1988), *Indonesia, Adjustment, Growth and Sustainable Development.*

World Resources Institute (1985), *Tropical Forests: A Call for Action*, Report of a Task Force of WRI, World Bank, and the United Nations Development Program.

Appendix

This background paper focuses primarily on the trade in tropical hardwoods within the Asia-Pacific region. It does so for two reasons. The first is to do justice to the topic of reviewing the links among trade in forest products, deforestation, and sustainable development for the most important component of forest products trade within the Asia-Pacific region—tropical hardwoods. Size constraints for a background paper of this sort necessarily require a narrow focus if they are to provide substantive context to an issue. The alternative is simply a broad, descriptive review of trends in softwood and hardwood trade flows within the Asia-Pacific region. The second reason for the focus on the tropical timber trade is that it is increasingly an emotive issue in the public eye, yet in many cases the links between commercial forestry and tropical deforestation are exaggerated. The evidence discussed in this paper suggests that the causes of tropical deforestation are complex and linked as much, if not more, to the nature of economic development in some Asia-Pacific countries than they are to industrial forestry per se.

The focus on tropical hardwoods and sustainable development and lack of attention to forest management practices in temperate climates suggests, by inference, that no problem exists for the latter. Such is not the case. Certainly in North America a vast expertise in the theory of forest management practices in the context of sustainable development has emerged. Unfortunately, theory is not put into practice, especially in many regions of North America, primarily because of institutional rigidities. The evidence clearly suggests that the types of institutional failure so often highlighted for developing countries are also endemic in North America. Many regions in North America will be or are currently experiencing significant declines in harvest levels, especially as the transition from harvesting mature to second growth stands proceeds. Data indicates that reforestation efforts are not keeping pace with harvest levels and that the quantity of not satisfactorily restocked forest lands is increasing. Similarly, the contentious issue of the trade-off between environmental considerations and the economic activity promoted by industrial forestry permeates the management of North American forests. Finally, in some North American jurisdictions, government regulations regarding tenure (often too short a duration) and timber pricing often lead to harvest rates in excess of those most desirable from society's perspective.

In a larger paper, the focus would be more balanced, certainly in regards to common problems in the management of temperate and tropical forests. Such a paper would also clearly highlight those areas of technical expertise in management of temperate and tropical forests in which trade in knowledge and services would be mutually beneficial.

Subsidies and Countervailing Duties

J.M. Finger
World Bank, Washington, D.C.

By the normal meanings of the terms, a *countervailing duty* is an import charge imposed by one country to isolate itself from the effects of another country's *subsidy*. For example, if country A provides a five per cent subsidy on its exports to country B, and B, in turn, adds a five per cent countervailing duty to these goods as they are imported, there would be no effect on trade. B's countervailing duty prevents A's subsidy from having an effect on B's economy.

One might presume that General Agreement on Tariffs and Trade (GATT) rules about subsidies and countervailing duties would reflect this basic logic—when subsidies are allowed, countervailing duties are forbidden, when countervailing duties are allowed, subsidies are forbidden. Not true. When GATT allows subsidies is only loosely related to when it forbids countervailing duties, and vice versa.[1]

There are countervailing duty rules to control export subsidies and GATT rules to control both. Underneath all the rules, some countries see subsidies as the basic problem; some see countervailing duties as the problem that international agreement should control. Because the rules build on conflicting conceptions of what the problem is, the procedures they create tend toward obfuscation, not clarification of the underlying issues. The concern I want to bring forward in this note is that the international community has allowed the subsidy-countervailing duty questions to become too complex. My argument, in compressed form goes something as follows:

1. Among the major industrial countries subsidies are a major form of support only for agriculture. In manufacturing, import restrictions are the major form of support.
2. International discussion of the "principles" involved tends to have the effect more of justifying further import restrictions than of eliminating subsides.
3. Negotiations to reduce national programs that subsidize agricultural production are the important part of the Uruguay Round. Negotiations to reduce other subsidies might also be useful, but negotiations to reach an agreed statement of allowed or disallowed subsidies (or countervailing duties) are more likely part of the problem than of a solution.

Subsidies Matter Mostly in Agriculture

A society inclined to use its government to aid its own industries can do so in many ways. While agriculture and transportation tend to be heavily subsidized in industrial countries, industry, on the whole, is aided primarily by import restrictions. In the U.S., Canada, Australia and New Zealand (major net agricultural exporters) two-thirds or more of assistance to agriculture is provided through government payments and purchases while in Japan and Western Europe (net agricultural importers) two-thirds of assistance is provided through the transfer from consumers implicit in high domestic prices.[2] Similar country-by-country estimates for manufacturing are scarce, but a recent World Bank estimate for the industrial countries as a group suggests that $8 of every $10 of assistance to manufacturing is provided through the price effects of import restrictions.[3]

Subsidies to industry did expand widely after the first oil shock, and grew rapidly through the early 1980s. Even in countries in which such aid is traditionally low, such as the U.S. and Switzerland, there was a substantial rise. Much of the rise was assistance to help industry and transport adjust to increased petroleum prices; financial or tax incentives to save energy or switch to fuels produced at home, e.g., electricity from coal. That part of the increased assistance not aimed at energy tended to focus on a small number of sectors in difficulty: shipbuilding and steel, and, to a lesser extent, electronics, aircraft and autos. The balance of payments dimension of the oil shock created an interest in expanding exports, and this interest led to a considerable increase of indirect export subsidies provided through government export credits, insurance and guarantees. The subsidy element in such programs however, has been small—in the range of two to four per cent of total subsidies to domestic production.[4]

The expansion of direct aids to industry has stabilized since the mid-1980s. According to an Organization for Economic Cooperation and Development (OECD) report: "Almost all OECD member countries have begun to retreat on a number of interventionist fronts, especially on subsidies supporting specific industries or enterprises."[5] This stabilization has stemmed in part from contraction of the industries subsidized, in part from a shift to import restrictions as the form of support. The steel industry provides a good example. In Western Europe and the United States employment in the steel industry is now about half what it was in the 1970s. And, imports into the U.S. and the EC markets are now controlled by a system of 40 bilateral export restraint arrangements.[6]

In sum, subsidies are a big issue for agriculture, but not for other tradable goods. Import protection is by far the major means by which governments assist their manufacturing sectors.

Countervailing duties are used mostly by the United States

The relevant numbers are provided in Table 1. Seven out of eight countervailing duty cases are U.S. cases. In the seven years, 1980-86, there were 282 U.S. cases, 21 Australian, 16 Canadian, and 7 in the EC.

In a lengthier paper, Tracy Murray and I[7] have reviewed the pattern of U.S. unfair imports cases in the 1980s. (I have included as an annex several tables from that study.) The highlights of our findings are:

1. There were a lot of cases (on average, 86 per year, 1980-88) against a lot of countries—59 in all.
2. The patterns of antidumping and countervailing duty cases—in which industries, against which countries, to what outcome—were similar.
3. Nearly half (348 of 774) of the cases have been superseded by negotiated export restraints.

Our findings are consistent with the widespread feeling that unfair trade cases are where the action is. In the judgment of two of Washington's top trade lawyers, they "have become the usual first choice for industries seeking protection from imports into the United States.[8] The legal definitions of what is unfair provide so many possibilities that any U.S. producer who would be better off if imports were restricted can find a way to qualify; if not now, then after the next trade bill. The major limits on how much protection the unfair trade regulations will provide are the costs of pulling together and advancing a winning petition, and the tedium of negotiating a voluntary export restraint that will provide the exporters with enough extra profits to buy off their sovereign right to retaliate.

Table 1:
Number of Administered Protection Cases, 1980-86

	1980	1981	1982	1983	1984	1985	1986	1980-1986
Safeguards								
United States	2	6	4	2	6	3	5	28
Australia	1	0	1	2	0	0	0	4
Canada	0	1	2	0	0	1	0	4
EC	3	1	1	1	1	0	2	9
Countervailing actions								
United States	8	10	123	21	51	39	30	282
Australia	0	0	2	7	6	3	3	21
Canada	3	0	1	3	2	3	4	16
EC	0	1	3	2	1	0	0	7
Antidumping actions								
United States	22	14	61	47	71	65	71	351
Australia	62	50	78	87	56	60	63	456
Canada	25	19	72	36	31	36	74	293
EC	25	47	55	36	49	42	40	294
Other unfair trade practices - U.S.	28	19	73	39	33	39	28	259
All categories								
United States	60	49	261	109	161	146	134	920
Australia	63	50	81	96	62	63	66	481
Canada	28	20	75	39	33	40	78	313
EC	28	49	59	39	51	42	42	310
Total	179	168	476	283	307	291	320	2,024

Sources: United States data: U.S. International Trade Commission, ALLAD-CASIS Database; other countries, J. Michael Finger and Andrzej Olechowski, *The Uruguay Round, A Handbook on the Multilateral Trade Negotiations*, World Bank, Washington, D.C., 1987, Tables A8.1, A8.3, for numbers of antidumping and countervailing duty cases; GATT Secretariat: numbers of safeguards cases.

The Content of the Policy Debate

The Uruguay Round agricultural negotiations are important, and they are aimed at the right target—a mutual rollback of national programs that subsidize agricultural production, and their supporting web of import restrictions and export bounties. This is brutish, foxhole-to-foxhole warfare, but it is the right war, fought in the way it must be fought. Let us hope that the second half of the round produced an outcome of substance.

Negotiations to revise and to reform the subsidies/ countervailing duty code are another matter. They offer a more civilized debate, over rules that define what a subsidy is, over procedures by which a government may determine in an orderly manner when it will levy a countervailing action. These negotiations, I suggest, are more a part of the problem than of a solution. They mostly help national governments to avoid the underlying problems. They help to justify an increasing web of regulation of trade in manufactured goods which will require someday the nasty hand-to-hand combat that the international community now recognizes as the only way to deal with agricultural policies. I will present two examples: the content of the (mainly) U.S.-EC dispute over what is or is not a countervailable domestic subsidy, and the action-reaction of U.S. countervailing duties against Latin American export subsidies.

Actionable subsidy

The past decade's jousting between the U.S. and EC over what is an "actionable subsidy" is an attempt by each party to find a definition that provides sanctuary for its own policies and at the same time makes the other's countervailable. The 1988 U.S. trade law provides several examples. One relates to modification of wording that had been used for some time to preclude countervailing duties against the subsidy element in foreign assistance (the United States' own, or that of third countries) or international organizations' loans below the market rate of interest. The relevant limit was that the subsidy had been given by the government of the exporting country. Airbus, in the meaning of the matter in U.S. law, is an export of France, but is funded, not by the government of France, but by a consortium of governments. The 1988 trade bill makes it clear that enforcers of the countervailing duty law can add up subsidies provided by the members of such a consortium, yet at the same time the bill tries to avoid wording that would cover Japanese participation in production of the Boeing 767 airplane.

Another example concerns the general principle that a foreign government program is not a countervailable subsidy unless it is specific to an industry or group of industries within the country. Application of the principle brings forward some hard questions, however. The Mexican government, for example, sells natural gas inside Mexico for less than the world, or export price, and this price break is particularly valuable for producers of ammonia and other petrochemicals for which natural gas is the feedstock. When oil and gas prices were regulated in the U.S. the EC had insisted that internal U.S. prices below world prices provided an unfair advantage for U.S. producers of synthetic fibres. The U.S. government then, arguing that the EC claim was unjustified, was reluctant to interpret Mexico's natural gas pricing as a countervailable subsidy. Even after deregulation of oil and gas prices, in the U.S. wording the details of U.S. trade law, so as to justify countervailing duties against Mexican petrochemicals, could be dangerous. The same wording in foreign regulations could justify countervailing duties against U.S. agricultural exports that enjoyed cheap irrigation water, or other products that benefitted from a small business loans program. Wording enacted in the 1988 trade bill, its proponents hope, will define subsidies in a way that captures foreign practices yet does not provide the basis (if used in foreign regulations) to impede U.S. exports.

The tendency then is for each government to look for details that will justify its import restrictions, and, if possible, not justify those of other governments. What kind of accommodation might be struck when such conflicting details come together in an international negotiation? A common definition that allows the restrictions of neither—or of both?

"Fair trade" has proven to be good politics in the United States, and a popular "import" into other countries. Moreover, when trade issues are taken up within the context of "fairness," international politics tends to be an extension of national politics, not a counter to it. International negotiations provide another chance to impress the domestic electorate, by insisting that the limits implicit in the national sense of fairness be recognized in the international agreement.

This does not, however, mean that the resulting standards will reduce the amount of international trade. The interests that dominate the making of trade policy are often distributors as well as producers, all aware that international trade is quite profitable. What cuts into profits is not trade, but competition. These interests are quite happy with a system that tends to preserve trade, and at the same time, to gentrify competition—by providing a ready means to negotiate export quantity maximums or export price minimums.

Latin American export subsidies and U.S. countervailing duties

The ongoing conflict over U.S. countervailing duties against Latin American export subsidies is another situation in which emphasizing the international dimension risks intensification of the problem. The economics of the situation is that each party is taking actions that do not serve its economic interest.

On the U.S. or import side of this interpretation, the benefits of buying subsidized goods for what the seller asks are direct. The lower price is the better bargain. The reply, that such purchases provide, in the long run, a false economy, brings forward broader questions, brought out well by J. Bhagwati's rhetorical question: "Would one be wise to receive stolen property simply because it is cheaper, or would one rather vote to prohibit such transactions because of their systemic consequences?"[9] The rejoinder, in turn is that the use of antidumping and countervailing duties has been carried far beyond what systemic considerations can justify—the enforcement mechanisms have been captured by import-competing interests, and what they are producing is simply import protection. That is a major theme of Dr. Bhagwati's book.[10]

A colleague at the World Bank, Julio Nogués, has been studying the other side of the matter for several years—the economics of Latin American countries' export subsidies. Mr. Nogués begins with a familiar proposition from development economics—that export subsidies which are uniform across industries and equal in magnitude to the export disincentives from import restrictions and inappropriate exchange rates can be important parts of an effective development strategy. But Nogués finds that "The truth of the matter is that reality has been quite different from the world these models depicted."[11]

First, the pattern of actual subsidies is very different from the theoretical ideal. Each of the eight countries Nogués reviewed employed not a unified, single rate export subsidy, but a number of different programs that provided widely different subsidy rates to different industries—for example, from one to 25 per cent in the case of Argentina.[12] Furthermore, movements of the real exchange rate in the 1980s were found to be several times larger than average subsidy rates, hence the export subsidies cannot be justified as offsetting inappropriate exchange rates. To the extent that they were assumed to do so, or diffused political pressure to do so, the subsidies did a particular disservice to the national economic interest.

As to the effects of these export subsidy programs, Nogués summarizes his findings as follows:

> Twenty years ago, it was believed that export subsidies would produce more diversification and better export performance. This has not happened. Why?
> In most cases, export subsidies were not supported by more open import policies—so subsidies reduced only marginally the anti-export bias of Latin American

countries. Unstable real exchange rates have also hurt exports.

Export subsidies appear to have improved exports in Brazil, which also liberalized imports, significantly stabilized real exchange rates, and promoted other policies conducive to export growth. Yet Mexico, after reducing import barriers, also enjoyed improved exports—with minimum export subsidies, and with apparently lower social costs than Brazil experienced.

Export subsidies have failed in other Latin American countries—and particularly hurt development in Argentina, where fraud, corruption and rent-seeking have been rampant.

Finally, export subsidies compete with other government programs and—especially considering their failure rate—should be dismantled in this period when the welfare of Latin Americans has declined dramatically. The money would be better spent on infrastructure, health, and education projects.[13]

For the Latin American countries, export subsidies are a mistake; even so, for the United States, countervailing duties are a mistake. Yet each party takes action not in his own interests but in response to actions of the other party.

Policy Advice

Real-world export subsidies and countervailing duties are terrible. What each country does is worse for its own interests than doing nothing at all. The appropriate policy advice is obvious: Do not do it! Not creating the problem is better than finding the solution.

How can international negotiations move countries to act on that advice? GATT's history shows that rules put in place to implement and defend liberalization have been successful. GATT's history also shows that the other way—rules first—does not work. Rules intended to facilitate or motivate a subsequent liberalization have not been successful.[14] The intent of agricultural negotiations is to remove restrictions. This is the approach that has worked. Of course, agreement will not be easy. Reform of the subsidies/countervail code offers better possibilities for agreement, but lesser possibilities of the world economy working better. Put then, the best negotiators to work on agriculture.

Annex: Unfair Imports Cases in the United States, 1980-1988

Annex Table 1
Countries that are the Object of U.S. Antidumping and Countervailing Cases Compared with the Share they Provide of U.S. Merchandise Imports

(antidumping and countervailing duty cases completed, 1980-1988)

Country or Group of Countries	Total number of cases	Total cases against this country or group as a % of totals against all countries	Percentage of 1987 U.S. merchandise imports that originate in this country or group	Percentage with restrictive outcomes (including VERs)
All countries	774	100	100	70
Developed countries	450	58	63	65
Developing countries	286	37	36	75
Eastern European countries	38	5	0.5	87
European Community	304	40	20	64
Brazil	56	7	2	79
South Africa	20	2.6	0.3	100
Korea	36	4.7	4.2	86
Mexico	35	4.5	4.9	91
Taiwan, China	29	3.7	6.1	62
Hong Kong	1	0.1	2.4	100
Singapore	6	0.8	1.5	67
Canada	35	5	16	54
Japan	49	6	21	69

Annex Table 2
United States Countervailing Duty Cases, 1980-1988
By Country and Outcome (number of cases)

		Restrictive			Not	Total All
	VER*	Affirm- ative	Suspension Agreement	Total	Restrictive	Cases
Developed countries						
Australia	1	1	0	2	1	3
Austria	4	0	0	4	1	5
Canada	1	3	1	5	9	14
European community	95	5	10	110	67	177
Belgium	10	0	1	11	6	17
Denmark	0	0	1	1	6	7
France	14	2	1	17	11	28
Germany	11	0	1	12	6	18
Greece	0	0	1	1	0	1
Ireland	0	0	1	1	5	6
Italy	11	1	1	13	11	24
Luxembourg	7	0	1	8	5	13
Netherlands	5	1	1	7	6	13
Portugal	1	1	0	2	0	2
Spain	22	0	0	22	4	26
United Kingdom	12	0	1	13	5	18
EC Policies	2	0	0	2	2	4
Finland						
Japan	2	0	0	2	3	5
New Zealand	0	3	0	3	4	7
Norway	0	0	0	0	1	1
South Africa	13	1	0	14	0	14
Sweden	0	1	0	1	3	4
Switzerland						
Eastern European countries						
Czechoslovakia	1	0	0	1	0	1
East Germany	0	0	0	0	1	1
Hungary						
Poland	1	0	0	1	0	1
Rumania						
USSR	0	0	0	0	1	1
Yugoslavia	1	0	0	1	0	1

Annex Table 2 (cont'd)

	VER*	Restrictive Affirm-ative	Restrictive Suspension Agreement	Total	Not Restrictive	Total All Cases
Developing countries						
Argentina	0	3	1	4	2	6
Brazil	24	4	0	28	7	35
Chile	0	1	0	1	0	1
China	0	1	0	1	0	1
Costa Rica	0	2	0	2	0	2
Colombia	0	3	0	3	1	4
Ecuador	0	1	0	1	0	1
El Salvador	0	0	0	0	1	1
Hong Kong						
India	0	0	0	0	5	5
Indonesia	0	1	0	1	1	2
Iran	0	2	0	2	0	2
Israel	0	3	0	3	2	5
Kenya						
Korea	12	2	0	14	0	14
Malaysia	0	1	0	1	1	2
Mexico	6	17	4	27	2	29
Pakistan	0	1	0	1	2	3
Panama	1	0	0	1	0	1
Peru	0	3	0	3	2	5
Philippines	0	2	0	2	2	4
Singapore	0	1	1	2	0	2
Sri Lanka	0	0	0	0	1	1
Taiwan	2	2	0	4	3	7
Thailand	0	2	0	2	2	4
Trinidad & Tobago	1	0	0	1	0	1
Turkey	0	3	0	3	2	5
Uruguay	0	1	0	1	0	1
Venezuela	8	1	0	9	0	9
Zimbabwe	0	1	0	1	0	1
Totals						
All countries	173	72	17	262	127	389
Developed countries	116	14	11	141	89	230
Developing countries	54	58	6	118	36	154
Eastern European countries	3	0	0	3	2	5

* Voluntary Export Restraints

Notes

1. These matters are taken up in more detail in J.M. Finger, "Antidumping and Antisubsidy Measures" in J.M. Finger and A. Olechowski (eds.), *The Uruguay Round: A Handbook for the Multilateral Trade Negotiations*, (Washington, D.C.: World Bank, 1987).

2. Organization for Economic Cooperation and Development, *National Policies and Agricultural trade*, Paris: OECD, 1987, p. 132.

3. J.M. Finger and P.A. Messerlin, Part II of *the Impact of the Industrial Policies of Developed Countries on Developing Countries*, (Washington, D.C.: World Bank, Development Committee Pamphlet No. 20, 1989).

4. Donald Putnam Henry, *The Financial Cost of Export Credit Programs*, Rand Corporation, Publication No. 3491—United States—DP Santa Monica, California, 1987.

5. Organization for Economic Cooperation and Development, *Structural Adjustment and Economic Performance*, Paris: OECD, 1987, p. 232.

6. GATT, *Developments in the Trading System October 1987-March 1988* (GATT, Geneva, 12 August 1988) Appendix V.

7. J.M. Finger and Tracy Murray, "Policing Unfair Imports: The United States Example," Washington, D.C.: World Bank, April 1989).

8. Gary N. Horlick and Geoffrey D. Oliver, "Antidumping and Countervailing Duty Law Provisions in the Omnibus Trade and Competitiveness Act of 1988." (Washington, D.C.: unpublished, 1989), p. 1.

9. J. Bhagwati, *Protectionism*, (Cambridge, Mass.: MIT Press, 1988) p. 35.

10. This theme is emphasized in a review by N. David Palmeter, "The Capture of the Antidumping Law," *Yale Journal of International Law*, vol. 14, no. 1, 1989, pp. 182-198.

11. Julio Nogués, "The Experience of Latin America with Export Subsidies," (World Bank, PPR Working Paper No. WPS 182, April 1989), p. 4.

12. *Ibid.*, Table 6.

13. *Ibid.*, p. 11.

14. This matter is explained and documented in J.M. Finger, "Ideas Count, Words Inform," in Richard H. Snape (ed.), *Issues in World Trade Policy*, (London: Macmillan, 1986), pp. 257-280.

Subsidies: A Problem in International Trade? [1]

Michael Hart
Director, Centre for Trade Policy and Law
Carleton University

Introduction

In 1982 Gardner Patterson, formerly Deputy Director General of
the GATT, delivered a provocative paper to a group of trade policy
veterans gathered in Washington to consider the state of trade
policy in the 1980s. He entitled his paper "The European
Community as a Threat to the System."[2] Today it is tempting to
steal its theme and apply it to the United States in the context of
the international consideration of subsidies. The outraged tone
with which U.S. legislators and negotiators have approached
subsidies and their distortion of international trade has been out of
all proportion to the seriousness of the problem.

There is no question that subsidies distort market signals and
in the area of agricultural trade, are at the root of domestic and
border practices that have made a mockery of an ordered world
trading system. But it is not the United States that is the main
victim of world subsidy practices. Indeed, the United States is
itself a major subsidizer of agricultural production, high-tech
industries, military production and more. More importantly, the
zealous pursuit of unilateral antisubsidy measures by the United
States has created as much disorder in international trade as have
the practices they are meant to discipline. They are seen by others
as unwarranted attacks by the most powerful economy in the
system on their sovereign right to determine the relationship

101

between government and society. Additionally, U.S. pursuit of an international code aimed at ridding the world of all offensive subsidy practices has taken on the nature of a moral crusade and frustrates the negotiation of a pragmatic regime capable of curbing the excesses of both subsidy and antisubsidy practices. Perversely, U.S. insistence on too much is likely to lead to too little.

The problem of subsidies has persisted over the years because the issues are so intractable. Subsidy negotiations go to the core of modern trade and industrial policies and thus raise very sensitive concerns about national sovereignty. Nevertheless, efforts continue to find a way to resolve the issues involved. This paper seeks to place the international discussion of subsidies into some perspective and suggests some ideas that might profitably be pursued in the Uruguay Round of multilateral negotiations.

Is the Problem Real or Perceived?

Subsidies are considered to be a problem in international trade because they are "unfair." Unfairness, however, has no intellectual basis. What is fair to some is unfair to others. What for example, makes a 30 per cent tariff fair and a 10 per cent subsidy unfair? Why should a quota to protect market share be acceptable while a subsidy to help displaced workers or an import-impacted industry give rise to claims of unfairness and lead to countermeasures? Why should U.S. sugar quotas be any more acceptable than EC export restitutions on sugar? All involve political decisions to redirect resources and distort international trade flows for domestic political reasons. It is difficult to understand why firms harmed by subsidized imports have a higher claim to redress than those displaced by lower wages, technical innovation, quotas, tariffs or other factors. Yet the international rules make such a distinction and negotiations continue to develop more rules based on this distinction.

That governments subsidize is clear. Equally, there are more programs and policies that have a subsidizing effect today than a generation ago. Over the past 50 years, the governments of industrialized countries have entered into an increasing number of commitments. Some of these have led to increasing conflict between internal and external obligations because not all governments have assumed the same internal obligations or see their external obligations the same way. Thus the increasing role of government has sharpened philosophical differences about the proper role of government and the extent to which government programs and policies distort international trade and investment flows.

Domestic subsidies potentially involve a vast range and number of government policies and programs, many of which are perfectly justifiable as an exercise of sovereign activity within a country. They are an integral aspect of each country's basic social and economic fabric. The issue, therefore, is not whether governments do or should use subsidies or other economic intervention programs to further economic development and other objectives; rather, the issue centres on which forms of intervention are trade distorting and which are not. The question is whether it is possible to promote predictability and advance economic welfare by developing common definitions of what constitute trade distorting practices and agreeing on appropriate rules to control such practices. At the same time it should be recognized that reaching international agreement on which subsidy practices are to be acceptable and which are not will require a high degree of international consensus on a wide array of social and economic issues. It is unrealistic to expect such consensus to be reached quickly and easily.

Subsidies have long been recognized as a problem in international trade because they may cause three kinds of distortion:

- they displace potential imports from more efficient producers
- they enhance exports by less efficient producers
- they distort competition in third markets

Most economists agree that the greatest amount of harm caused by subsidies is in the economy providing the subsidy. Subsidies distort the allocation of resources and generally reduce net economic welfare. The decision to provide a subsidy is usually based on a political perception that the market allocation of resources in a particular circumstance is unsatisfactory and needs to be corrected with some form of government assistance—whether to compensate for the disadvantage of locating in a less than prime location, to encourage a particular economic activity, to maintain incomes at a desired level or some other goal. The economic effect is to reduce resources where they would have been allocated by the market and allocate them where it is perceived to be politically advantageous. Subsidies thus redistribute wealth and may reduce overall economic welfare. Goods and services that are able to be exported because they are cheaper increase the economic welfare of the importing country, although individual producers in the importing country may be adversely affected. Over time, both the subsidizing and other economies adjust to compensate for the effect of the subsidy. Richard Cooper concludes:

> ... in the case of government subsidies, and other actions that influence international trade, the interests of other countries reside in the proposition that they should not have to bear the costs, which are often

transitional or adjustment costs, arising from the
actions of other countries. . . . perhaps we should not
worry so much about government subsidies to economic
activity—or rather government intervention of all
types—as far as their effects on foreign trade are
concerned, provided that they do not impose acute
adjustment costs on economic activities outside the
country in question.[3]

The first proposition to keep in mind, therefore, in
considering approaches to the international negotiation of
subsidies is that, from a purely economic point of view, the degree
of harm that subsidies can cause can be easily exaggerated. A
related proposition is that the extent of subsidies that directly
distort trade flows is both much less than frequently alleged and
more concentrated than usually appreciated.

Various studies have sought to catalogue the extent of
subsidy practices in various countries. Fewer studies exist which
try to quantify the impact of such subsidies. The mere existence of
a government policy or program aimed at subsidizing economic
activity, for example, should not lead to the conclusion that
subsidies are actually being paid out. Many programs meet their
political objective merely by being announced. Others are so
poorly administered that they rarely meet their economic
objective.[4] The multiplicity of programs often results in one
program cancelling out another. Avinash Dixit, reviewing
analytical work in the United States, notes that any harm caused
by subsidies is largely of a political nature. Various producer
groups have found it useful to blame foreign subsidies as one
element responsible for some of their competitive woes and
politicians, particularly in the United States, have found these
claims credible and have helped to exaggerate the harm done by
foreign subsidies. He concludes that detailed research, both
theoretical and empirical, has found little evidence that the terms
of trade of the United States as a whole have been harmed by the
policies and practices of foreign governments, although individual
firms and sectors may be disadvantaged by some subsidy
practices.[5]

The economic literature also suggests that most antisubsidy
measures do not make much sense. In the importing country,
consumers typically gain more than producers lose. That gain may
be wiped out by the countervailing duty, but not sufficiently to
offset the disadvantage already suffered by the producer. As a
result, antisubsidy measures rarely have the desired effect. Notes
U.S. trade lawyer Gary Horlick:

Generally, once a government grant is allocated over total sales and amortized over the appropriate useful life, the resulting subsidy amount is very small. Thus the industry that brought the case often does not obtain any significant tariff benefit and the respondent industry may ultimately obtain a rate that is not a significant trade impediment, but at a heavy cost in terms of time, legal fees, and market uncertainty. In short, it is often a lose-lose situation for the parties.[6]

Thus, despite the conclusion of economists and other international trade experts that subsidies are neither a large nor a serious problem in international trade and that antisubsidy measures have little prophylactic effect, they have utterly failed to convince politicians. It is the political dimension of subsidies, therefore, that continues to be behind calls for a solution, based on the politically credible notion that one's own producers should not have to compete with foreign treasuries. Imported goods judged to have been assisted by the wealth of government are thus considered to be "unfair" and to require offsetting counter-measures. The pursuit of an international regime to discipline subsidies is, therefore, rooted in pre-economic mercantilist ideas and failure to grasp that fact has doomed many attempts to arrive at a balanced approach to the issue.

It is the pursuit of antisubsidy measures, particularly by the United States, that has made governments willing to seek consensus on which kinds of activities should or should not be allowed. Because antisubsidy measures bring government-policies or programs into question, they have assumed a high profile involving a heavy investment in government-to-government diplomacy. Negotiations, however, are not proceeding *de novo* but within the context of existing international and domestic law. Before examining what might be negotiated successfully in the Uruguay Round, therefore, we briefly consider the main features and flaws of existing international and domestic law.

The International Legal Regime

The international rules are ambivalent about subsidies and reflect the conflicting conclusions of economists and politicians. Tariffs, even though they are to be lowered progressively, are considered acceptable, while export subsidies, which have a similar economic effect, are proscribed. Domestic subsidies are considered acceptable unless they cause harm in which case countries can take countermeasures—either unilaterally or after multilateral authorization. There is also asymmetry in the ability of member countries to take countermeasures. Subsidies that may have an export enhancement effect can be unilaterally countervailed by an importing country while those that may have an import displacement effect or an export enhancement effect in third markets may only be countered following multilateral dispute settlement procedures. There are many examples of unilaterally imposed countervailing duties and very few examples of multilaterally authorized countermeasures. The practical effect of this distinction is that large economies with large domestic markets are given greater scope than small, export-dependent economies for engaging in their own subsidy practices and for countering the subsidy practices of others.[7]

GATT members originally thought that the major restraint on the use of domestic subsidies would be fiscal and thus saw no need for detailed disciplines. Experience during the 1960s and 1970s demonstrated that relying on fiscal restraint had been naïve. Attitudes toward subsidies, therefore, gradually shifted as governments became more heavily involved in economic activity; developing countries, many of whom used various kinds of subsidy programs, assumed a larger role in world trade; and the European Community made extensive use of export subsidies to dump its surplus agricultural production on world markets. In particular, the United States retreated from its tolerant attitude and began to make greater use of its countervailing duty statute, the only GATT member originally so equipped.

During the course of the Tokyo Round, there was a concerted effort to modernize the GATT regime. The results were disappointing. The 1979 GATT Subsidies Code is largely procedural in that it takes existing GATT rules regarding subsidies, countervailing duties and dispute settlement and spells out how these may be pursued by member countries. Its detailed provisions, however, clearly expose the original flaws built into the General Agreement. The Code classifies subsidies three ways:

- those that are unlawful, such as export subsidies on non-primary products
- those that are lawful unless they cause serious prejudice to the export interests of exporters to third markets—such as export subsidies on primary products—or nullify and impair benefits expected in the subsidizing market—such as production subsidies
- those that are lawful unless they cause material injury to competitors in an importing country, such as production subsidies

The Code thus clearly spells out that most subsidies are lawful and are pursued for a variety of important and useful reasons. But that lawfulness may be questioned if a subsidy causes harm. The harm that subsidies may cause is also classified in three different ways, based on their effect and the type of sanction that may be authorized:

- *material injury,* i.e., harm in the domestic market of an importing country which may lead to a unilaterally determined and imposed countervailing duty (based on GATT Article VI)
- *nullification and impairment* of expected benefits, i.e., harm in displacing imports in the subsidizing country which may justify multilaterally authorized countermeasures to restore the balance of benefits (based on GATT Article XXIII)
- *serious prejudice,* i.e., harm in displacing exports in third markets which may lead to multilaterally authorized countermeasures (based on GATT Article XVI)

These various distinctions are rooted in the GATT concept that the agreement involves a set of mutual and reciprocally balanced benefits. Very few practices are in fact a violation of the agreement. Rather, various national practices give rise to the right to seek a remedy if they cause harm in a system that GATT legal scholar Robert Hudec has called regulation without obligation.[8]

Only the first kind of harm has historically given rise to any serious jurisprudence and most of that is national. There is virtually no case history to provide any guidance as to what constitutes serious prejudice or nullification and impairment. There is no international agreement as to whether these standards are different from material injury. The principal flaw in the Code thus revolves around the ability of member states unilaterally to determine when a subsidy is lawful and when it is not, but only for one of the three types of harm for which GATT authorizes countermeasures. At the same time, there is no guarantee that any kind of subsidy is ever wholly lawful.

The disorder in the GATT system arises from the fact that it is a hybrid of two opposing attitudes. The first, based largely on political considerations, considers subsidies to be inherently bad and unlawful while the second, based somewhat more on economic considerations, believes that subsidies may not make much economic sense but should nevertheless be permitted except if they cause serious harm in which case they should be changed, removed or offset by a countervailing duty or similar measure. Confusion is further added by the distinction between export and domestic subsidies, and between export subsidies on industrial products and on primary products, for none of which is there much of an analytical basis, only one of political offensiveness. The GATT regime thus is a compromise that tries to maintain a balance between the right of governments to use subsidies and the right to take offsetting measures. It indicates that countries should seek to avoid programs and policies that seriously prejudice the interests of other signatories and at the same time enjoins countries not to introduce countervailing duties that would in themselves unjustifiably impede international trade. It is an uneasy compromise between conflicting points of view and in practice has made the GATT regime increasingly ineffective and perhaps even counterproductive.

Domestic Law

The GATT regime provides a relatively narrow base justifying reaction to foreign subsidy practices and there appears to be little disposition to broaden that base. U.S. law, on the other hand, provides a very broad base for imposing countervailing duties to offset the export enhancement effect of foreign subsidies and there is disposition to broaden that base. U.S. law is broadly conceived and has become steadily broader in its application. It is so structured as to encourage producer groups to identify as many foreign practices as they can find and enmesh them in a countervail suit. The reward is two-fold: foreign companies become embroiled in an expensive and disruptive quasi-judicial procedure where the burden of proof lies with them; should the U.S. government agree that these programs constitute subsidies and that the domestic industry is suffering some harm, a countervailing duty will be levied on imports. Other countries have followed the US lead and established their own analogous procedures, but in no other jurisdiction has domestic law and procedure developed to the same degree nor is it used as extensively by private parties.

There exists a substantial bias in domestic countervail procedures favouring domestic producers. U.S. law gives private parties in the United States the right to trigger an investigation whenever they believe that one of their competitors has benefitted from foreign government policies and programs they consider to be subsidies. It encourages complainants to cast their nets as widely as possible since the reward for a successful case is a penalty on foreign imports. It is up to the investigating authorities to determine whether the complainants' allegations are sustainable in a procedure biased against the foreign exporter. It should not be surprising, therefore, that the ambit of U.S. countervail has steadily widened over the years and subsidies appear to be a growing problem to U.S. officials.

U.S. countervail procedures also pay little heed to whether or not the offending practice has had any adverse effect on trade. The criteria are threefold—has there been any benefit to the recipient?

Has the recipient been favoured over other groups? Is the U.S. industry suffering any harm? If all three questions are positive, a countervailing duty is imposed without any regard to the question of trade distortion. In the case of Canadian assistance to East Coast groundfish producers, for example, a convincing case can be made that many of the federal and provincial programs found to be countervailable maintained an inefficient inshore fishery and that in their absence, Canada would have developed a much more competitive fishery based on factory trawlers. New England fish producers would have found such a Canadian fishery much more of a competitive threat. Were such an industry to be government financed, there would exist a much stronger case for trade distortion.[9]

Problems of U.S. law have become more acute since implementation of the GATT Subsidies Code in the Trade Agreements Act of 1979, for a number of fundamental reasons:

- The Act mandated that all subsidies that met the three-part test described above be countervailed, removing the discretion formerly exercised by Treasury officials
- It specifically rejected the export orientation test long favoured by Treasury officials in the administration of the law—programs were to be countervailed, whether or not there was any significant export enhancement effect
- Responsibility was moved from the Treasury Department to the Commerce Department, i.e., to the department charged with maintaining good relations with U.S. business
- It gave a false sense of security with the introduction of an injury test which in practice has proven to be a very low threshold of injury and, in the absence of any serious causal link between the complained of subsidy and that injury, almost derisory in its effect

The Tokyo Round thus had a perverse effect. Countries that believed they had placed some limits on the use of U.S. countervail in return for greater discipline on export subsidies and a clearer delineation of procedures and obligations instead found that the U.S. law became easier to use and was in fact being used more frequently.[10] The system is administratively costly and offends relations between states. In effect, because domestic countervailing duty procedures have taken on a task of disciplining trade distorting practices far larger than was ever envisaged in the General Agreement, they are becoming a substitute for multilateral agreement on rules covering subsidy practices and have become a protectionist device in themselves. In the absence of legislated limits (nationally or internationally) as to what constitutes a countervailable subsidy, there is likely to be continuous pressure to widen the ambit of countervailing duty procedures. There is an incentive for industry to make allegations and, in the absence of statutory limitations, it is hard for the administering authority to refuse. Writes British economist Brian Hindley: "The number of practices that might be regarded as conferring a subsidy is ... very large; if a tariff is offered as a reward for identifying such practices, there is likely to be a lengthy queue of applicants."[11] The U.S. countervailing duty statute, and its analogues in Canada, the EC and elsewhere, will thus continue to distort international trade, perhaps to a larger extent than the subsidies they are meant to discipline.

The Uruguay Round

Given the inadequacy of the international rules and the potential for conflict in the unilateral application of domestic procedures, it is not hard to understand why subsidies and countervailing duties are among the central issues in the Uruguay Round of multilateral trade negotiations. Not only is one of the 15 negotiating groups devoted exclusively to these two issues, but subsidies are the central challenge facing the Agriculture Group and are key elements in the discussions of the Resource Group, the Future of the GATT System (FOGS) Group and the Non-Tariff Measures Group.

Discussion to date has identified at least some common ground as a basis for negotiations. There appears to be consensus that:

- the 1979 Subsidies Code has worked poorly and fallen well short of expectations
- subsidies are on the increase (despite some evidence to the contrary)
- the use of remedies is on the rise leading to increased managed trade (evidence on this is also not convincing)
- the problem is most acute in the agricultural area where the lack of discipline has been exacerbated by the general lack of consensus on an appropriate international regime for trade in agriculture

There is less consensus on how to approach the issues. The key questions appear to be:

- whether stricter disciplines on subsidies can be achieved in the absence of agreement to place greater restraints on the application of countervailing duties. Many delegations seem to share the perception that a balance needs to be struck between discipline on the practice and the unilateral right to take countermeasures

- whether it will be possible to achieve greater balance in the application of countermeasures by adding teeth to those that counter harm resulting from import displacement and competition in third-country markets

- whether the list of agreed banned practices should be expanded and the exception for primary products eliminated

- whether there should be defined limits on how far countermeasures can reach, i.e., whether some government policies and practices ought to be inviolate just as some practices should be proscribed

- whether members are prepared to accept greater multilateral surveillance of compliance with the rules covering subsidies and the application of countermeasures

- whether it is possible to achieve greater consensus on what constitutes harm or injury and whether there needs to be one standard or three individual sets of criteria tailored to the three kinds of harm caused by subsidies

As can be expected, there are various approaches to these issues ranging from that of the U.S. to some of the major Less-Developed Countries such as India and Brazil. The United States believes it is both negotiable and desirable to enter into a code that would severely curtail the ability of governments to participate in their own economies while at the same time tightening what it perceives to be loopholes in the GATT rules covering countervailing duties.[12] Brazil and India, on the other hand, find the U.S. position on both subsidies and countervailing duties offensive. They believe there ought to be greater recognition of the right of GATT members, particularly developing country members, to determine their own domestic policy, free from the threat of unilaterally imposed countervailing duties. While not questioning the right of countries to take countermeasures, they believe these should be severely circumscribed to prevent abuse and limit actions to instances where there is clear evidence of harm. Most delegations find themselves between these two poles, interested in finding a solution to the subsidies/countervail conundrum that preserves a balance between the right to pursue domestic policies and the right to redress from those policies pursued by other members that cause harm. The key to success in the negotiations, however, lies in the United States, owing both to the impact of U.S. countervail procedures and U.S. zeal to deal with subsidies as a problem.

United States negotiators appear to remain unconvinced by economic analysis that demonstrates that it is the subsidizing country that is most harmed by subsidies and that, in aggregate, the United States economy benefits from foreign subsidies. They continue to be convinced that subsidies are a major problem in international trade and that it is the duty of the United States to rid the world of this problem. They are, therefore, continuing to use the considerable bargaining power of the U.S. government to effect discipline on the subsidy practices of others.

U.S. negotiators tend also to be generally unaware of the range of aids available to U.S. industries at the municipal, state and federal level, most of which have an import displacing rather than an export enhancing effect. This was the conclusion reached by Rodney Grey as a result of his experience during the Tokyo Round and one that remains valid today.[13]

Given the wide disparity in approach, particularly between the United States and the rest of the world, it would be unrealistic to expect a major breakthrough on subsidies. If there is to be any useful result at all beyond a cosmetic, procedural agreement, delegations will need to be realistic and not too ambitious. A key determinant of success will be whether it is possible to achieve some consensus on what constitutes a trade distorting government practice.

A Modest Proposal

Whatever conclusions are reached based on either a serious economic analysis of the issue of subsidies or an assessment of the international legal regime, political requirements will continue the drive to reach international consensus on both subsidies and antisubsidy measures. There is good reason, therefore, to try to effect a solution. Such a solution would need to satisfy, however, not only political requirements, but should also be reasonably grounded in principles of economics and law.

A sound international legal regime would include enforceable sanctions as well as multilateral surveillance and authorization. It would also provide more balanced recognition of the fact that subsidies distort trade in three ways. It would be a major shift from the current international regime which is a combination of unilaterally applied domestic legal sanctions dealing overly harshly and unsatisfactorily with one kind of harm and an international commercial diplomacy regime that deals inadequately—at least by comparison—with the two other kinds of harm. It could involve two complementary dimensions: unambiguous rules that can be enforced through clearly established procedures and lead to recognized sanctions as well as periodic negotiation leading to *ad hoc* solutions to the more complex and difficult problems. The latter could be made more predictable with agreement on a framework of general principles, but would continue to require a high degree of commercial diplomacy. Missing from this approach is the ability of governments unilaterally to determine what foreign practices they will tolerate. Any domestic procedures would have to be made subject to multilateral challenge and review.

A long-term solution to subsidies, therefore, does not lie in their prohibition—with the exception of some of the most politically offensive forms of subsidy—but in making the countervailing duty, serious prejudice and nullification and impairment tracks equivalent in procedure and remedy. This would require making the countervailing duty track less draconian and unilateral and the serious prejudice and nullification and impairment tracks more applicable. To achieve such a result would require scrapping the existing Code which most governments and observers now consider to have been a mistake. Making adjustments to the Code would not lead to the kind of serious changes that are required.

A new approach would recognize that it is neither necessary nor practical to condemn all subsidies *per se*. There is no reason, for example, for international trade rules to take a dim view of adjustment assistance to firms, which meets a socially desirable objective. Nor is a useful purpose served in outlawing subsidies aimed at promoting environmental responsibility or cultural autonomy. Negotiations would have to proceed, therefore, on both the practice and the remedy. The key to any long-term solution would require reaching agreement on which kinds of subsidies are actionable and which are not, accompanied by clear procedural and substantive limits on how countermeasures are to be applied in all three circumstances where they cause harm.

The Swiss negotiating paper[14] provides an attractive approach to the classification of subsidies. Based on its ideas, the following classification would make sense in a new subsidies code:

- *prohibited practices*, i.e., practices that are presumed to cause serious harm and thus give right to retaliation through unilateral countermeasures without any requirement to prove such harm. Multilateral litigation would only be required if there was dispute as to whether a particular practice was indeed prohibited. The ability to expand the list beyond the current prohibition of export subsidies on industrial products should be seen as directly related to the willingness of countries to develop a list of non-actionable practices. Among obvious candidates for inclusion on such a list are export subsidies on primary commodities.

- *non-actionable practices*, i.e., practices that are inviolate and are not subject to countermeasures, whether or not they cause harm. Such a list would need clearly to spell out the types and characteristics of government programs and policies that would not give rise to any right of redress. Obvious candidates for inclusion on such a list are government programs that are widely available, such as social programs. Other criteria may prove more controversial.

- *actionable practices*, i.e., practices that may give rise to litigation involving proof that they cause harm and the right to gain redress through countermeasures. No list would be required; government policies and programs that do not meet the prohibited or inviolate criteria would be subject to these procedures.

In order to make the system fair and more symmetrical, subsidies that fall into the last class would be actionable if they cause any of the three kinds of harm, i.e., harm through increased exports, harm through import displacement and harm in third markets. Standards for determining any such harm or injury would have to be similar or equivalent. Such harm would have to be clear and demonstrable and involve serious distortion of trade, i.e., the harm would have to be clearly linked to the programs or policies in question. Finally, the application of countermeasures would have to be subject to multilateral review.

Making such a system work would require efficient multilateral dispute settlement procedures involving, for example, a standing review body. No country would be prepared to subject its domestic countervail procedures to multilateral review unless it could be assured that the review would be swift, reliable and based on clearly established rules and procedures. Similarly, no country would be prepared to modify any programs shown to cause serious prejudice or nullification or impairment unless it was confident that the arbitrary application of countervail had been eliminated.

The challenge of this approach is two-fold. Governments must be prepared to break through the blockages that have prevented a sensible classification of subsidy practices. While initially experience could be gained through illustrative lists, governments must eventually be prepared to classify programs on the basis of precise criteria such as type of instrument involved (e.g., loans, grants, equity participation, regulatory requirement), purpose (e.g., social welfare, environmental protection, adjustment) and targets (e.g., generally available, small business, regional).

Second, governments must be prepared to cede some sovereignty in order to gain a more certain and predictable international business environment. They must be prepared to accept that some forms of government intervention cause unacceptable distortion of the economies of others and that unilateral solutions are no longer acceptable. A concomitant requirement is that governments must be prepared to accept a greater tolerance for the practices and policies of others that may raise complaints from domestic interests. Western governments have in the past 30 years come to grips domestically with the challenge of pluralistic societies. They must now show a willingness to make the same adjustment internationally.

Conclusions

In the words of Max Corden, "It seems to me that all this is desirable, little of it is probable, but some of it is at least possible."[15] The subsidies issue has bedevilled multilateral negotiations from the inception of the GATT to the present day. Many of the issues raised during the original negotiations are not substantively different from those being raised today. In addition, increasing government involvement in the economic life of countries as well as the unilateral application of countervailing duties, particularly by the United States, have made the issues even more complex and the need for solution even more acute. A long-term solution lies in a greater appreciation that subsidies are less of an evil than some believe and that unregulated antisubsidy measures may be a larger problem than the subsidies they seek to discipline. Such recognition is not likely to come within the time-frame envisaged for the conclusion of the Uruguay Round. A start, however, can be made during these negotiations and continued in the Canada-U.S. bilateral discussions over the next few years. A breakthrough in these talks may well prove critical to eventual multilateral success. Little would be gained, however, from a further cosmetic solution such as was devised during the Tokyo Round. The only useful purpose gained by such codes is to bring out in sharper relief the inadequacy of the existing rules and increase the penchant for unilateralism tolerated by those rules. Effort, therefore, should be directed toward the development of the three-fold subsidy classification scheme outlined above and toward the development of greater balance in the application of counter-measures.

Notes

1. This paper is an abbreviated version of a paper (available on request) which includes detailed references to the literature on subsidies and international trade. This paper has benefitted from work during the bilateral Canada-U.S. negotiations and in this regard I thank José Herran-Lima for his assistance.

2. William R. Cline, ed., *Trade Policy in the 1980s* (Washington, D.C.: Institute for International Economics, 1983), pp. 223-242.

3. Richard N. Cooper, "US Policies and Practices on Subsidies in International Trade," in Steven J. Warnecke, *International Trade and Industrial Policies* (New York: Holmes & Meier, 1978), pp. 119-120.

4. Jean-François Bence and Murray G. Smith, "Subsidies and Unfair Trade Laws: Implications for Canada-U.S. Trade", in *International Economic Issues*, Institute for Research on Public Policy, May-June, 1989. The authors have tried to quantify the extent of government assistance to non-agricultural firms in 1984 in Canada and the U.S. The study catalogues programs of assistance to business provided by the two federal governments and concludes that with very few exceptions, the level of assistance is not very high and has little impact on bilateral trade. Based on the type of programs analyzed, the study suggests that the overall rate of subsidy to non-agricultural business in Canada in 1984 was one per cent while the comparable rate in the U.S. was half of one per cent. The study concludes that the programs in both countries spread a relatively small amount of funds thinly over the whole economy and, with the exception of a few industry groupings, have almost no perceptible impact on trade.

5. Avinash Dixit, "How Should the United States Respond to Other Countries' Trade Policies," in Robert M. Stern, ed., *U.S. Trade Policies in a Changing World Economy* (Cambridge, Mass.: MIT Press, 1987), p. 254.

6. "The Free Trade Agreement Working Group: Developing a Harmonized and Improved Countervailing Duty Law," in American Bar Association, Section of International Law and Practice, *United States/Canada Free Trade Agreement: The Economic and Legal Implications* (Washington, D.C., 1988), footnote 5, p. 405. Examples of the relative insignificance of these subsidy programs can be gleaned from an analysis of the most important cases in the 1980s. In *Certain Fresh Atlantic Groundfish from Canada* (USITC Publication 1844, May, 1986), 55 of 85 complained of programs found to be countervailable, collectively amounting to 5.82% *ad valorem*; the most significant was the 1.876% assessment that federal equity infusions into National Sea Products and Fisheries Products International were not equity-worthy, subsequently proven to be a questionable conclusion since both companies

thrived following government-induced reorganization. In *Certain Live Swine and Pork from Canada* (USITC Publication 1733, July, 1985), 23 of 53 complained of programs found collectively to confer a subsidy of 4.39 cents per pound. In *Softwood Lumber from Canada* (48 Fed. Reg. 1983, p. 24168 and 51 Fed. Reg. 1986, p. 37453), 27 programs were found countervailable, but only the inclusion of stumpage practices in the second case, at an arbitrary level of 15%, lifted the collective assessment above the .5% *de minimis* level. See Annex I for a more detailed assessment of U.S. cases involving Canadian products.

7. Rodney Grey notes ". . . the anti-dumping and countervailing duty systems, as sanctioned by Article VI of the GATT, inherently protect producers in large economies more effectively than producers in smaller economies." "The Decay of the Trade Relations System," in R.H. Snape, ed., *Issues in World Trade Policy* (New York: St. Martin's Press, 1986), p. 27.

8. Robert E. Hudec, "Regulation of Domestic Subsidies Under the MTN Subsidies Code," in Don Wallace, Jr., Frank J. Loftus and Van C. Krikorian, *Interface Three: Legal Treatment of Domestic Subsidies*, (Washington, D.C.: The International Law Institute, 1984).

9. *Certain Fresh Atlantic Groundfish from Canada* (USITC Publication 1844, May, 1986). See also footnote 6 illustrating the need to cast the net widely in order to arrive at a sufficiently interesting level of subsidization to make the case worthwhile.

10. Between the enactment of the first general countervailing duty statute in 1897 and 1969 only some 65 countervailing duty orders were issued, roughly one a year. From 1970 on, the number of cases filed has steadily mounted. In 1982 alone, 146 investigations were launched, indicating the vast increase in the resort to countervailing duties as a standard weapon in the US trade policy arsenal. Since 1980, some fourteen cases have been filed against Canadian products, increasing concern in Canada about the security of access to the U.S. market. See Annex for an analysis of these cases and their impact on Canadian trade interests.

11. Brian Hindley, "Subsidies, Politics and Economics," in Don Wallace, Jr., Frank J. Loftus and Van C. Krikorian, *Interface Three: Legal Treatment of Domestic Subsidies* (Washington, D.C.: The International Law Institute, 1984), p. 31.

12. See, for example, Uruguay Round text MTN.GNG/NG10/ W/20 of 15 June, 1988.

13. See Rodney de C. Grey, "Some Notes on Subsidies and the International Rules," in Don Wallace, Jr., Frank J. Loftus and Van C. Krikorian, *Interface Three: Legal Treatment of Domestic Subsidies* (Washington, D.C.: The International Law Institute, 1984) and Michael Hart, *The Future on the Table*, a paper prepared for the conference *Living With Free Trade* in Ottawa on May 5, 1989 sponsored by the Centre for Trade Policy and Law.

14. Uruguay Round text MTN.GNG/NG10/W/17 of 1 February, 1988.

15. W. Max Corden, "On Making Rules for the International Trading System," in Robert M. Stern, ed., *U.S. Trade Policies in a Changing World Economy* (Cambridge, Mass.: MIT Press, 1987), p. 425.

Annex: U.S. Countervail and Canada

Since 1980, some 14 countervailing duty cases have been filed against Canada, increasing anxiety in Canada bout the security of its access to the U.S. market and raising concern about the ease with which the countervailing duty statute can be used to harass legitimate competition. The cases involved:

1. *Hard-Smoked Herring Fillets* (1981). No duty imposed due to a negative preliminary determination on injury by the International Trade Commission.

2. *Rail Passenger Cars and Parts* (1982). No duty imposed as U.S. complainant terminated the investigation by withdrawing its petition.

3. *Softwood Lumber* (1982). No duty imposed; countervailable subsidies were determined to be at *de minimis* levels. The complaint focused on Canadian stumpage practices which were not found to constitute a countervailable subsidy.

4. *Softwood Shakes and Shingles* (1982). Same as Softwood Lumber.

5. *Softwood Fences* (1982). Same as Softwood Lumber.

6. *Live Swine and Fresh, Chilled and Frozen Pork* (1984). Duties imposed on live swine at 4.39%, but not on pork, as imports of the latter were found not to have injured

U.S. producers. Since reduced to 2.2% as a result of a review in 1988. Breeding animals are not affected.

7. *Red Raspberries* (1985). No duties imposed as investigation was suspended by mutual agreement between U.S. and Canadian producers. Under the agreement, the B.C. government agreed not to provide the offending subsidies to Canadian exporters.

8. *Oil Country Tubular Goods* (1985). Duties of 0.72% imposed.

9. *Fresh Atlantic Groundfish* (1985). Duties imposed on fresh fish at 5.82% but not on fish fillets, as the latter were found not to have injured U.S. producers.

10. *Softwood Lumber* (1986). No duties imposed as the complainant terminated the investigation by withdrawing its petition after an agreement was signed between the Canadian and U.S. governments, whereby a 15% tax was imposed by Canada on exports to the U.S., following a preliminary determination that stumpage practices constituted a countervailable subsidy. In addition, the Canadian government undertook to negotiate an increase in stumpage fees with the appropriate provincial governments. The increase is to have the same effect on Canadian exports as the export tax it will eventually replace.

11. *Fresh Cut Flowers* (1986). Duties of 1.47% imposed.

12. *Probe Thermostats* (1988). Final negative on both subsidy and injury.

13. *Steel Rails* (1988). Duties of 103.55% imposed.

14. *Pork Products* (1989). Preliminary determination of 3.5 cents per pound.

Of these 14 cases, nine dealt with natural resources or agricultural products, namely, the three Softwood Lumber cases in 1983, the Swine and Pork case in 1984, the Fish and Raspberries cases in 1985, the second Softwood Lumber and the Flowers cases in 1986 and the Pork Products case in 1989.

A number of these cases have had the unenviable distinction of setting new landmarks in the expansionist ambit of the U.S. countervailing duty (CVD) statute. They have, therefore, continued the record set by earlier Canadian cases such as the 1973 Michelin decision which marked the first time U.S. authorities considered a purely domestic subsidy to be subject to countervailing duties; this determination was later codified in the *Trade Agreements Act* of 1979. In 1979, the Optic Liquid Level Sensor case further extended the ambit of the statute to domestic subsidies aimed at research and development, also a precedent-setting determination.

Before addressing the issues raised by the natural resource cases, there are two features of some of the remaining cases worth mentioning. The Rail Passenger Cars case was the first instance in which a CVD action was brought as a result of a single transaction, a contract between Bombardier and the New York City Transit Authority for the supply of subway cars. This was also the first U.S. case dealing with capital goods, a feature which was to become more common in Canadian and U.S. cases since, and which presents rather unique problems. The Oil Country Tubular Goods and Fresh Cut Flowers cases are good illustrations of the pernicious effect of the so-called "cumulation" rule. Under the rule, the International Trade Commission must assess the joint impact of imports from all countries under investigation on U.S. competitors, rather than the individual impact of imports from each country. The result has been to encourage actions against small-volume or marginal foreign suppliers resulting in unwarranted findings of injury, the very situation in which Canadian firms found themselves in these two cases. In the Oil Country Tubular Goods case, the Canadian market share was less than 6.5%. In the Flowers case, cumulation was carried to ridiculous extremes: Canadian exports represented some $200,000 out of total world imports of only $17 million.

The *Trade Agreements Act* of 1979 as interpreted by the Commerce Department prescribes a three-part test for making a finding of subsidization: first, the domestic subsidy must be targeted or, in the statutory words, "provided or required . . . to a specific enterprise or industry, or group of enterprises or indus-tries." Targeting has been deemed to include firms as well as geographic locations. This is the so-called "specificity test." Second, the subsidy must confer a benefit to, or compensate for a disadvantage of, the recipient. This is the so-called "preferen-tiality" test. Preferentiality has been interpreted to include special treatment to a recipient as well as the "non-commercial" nature of that treatment. Finally, all countervailable benefits from one source taken together must be higher than the *de minimis* level of 0.5 per cent.

The natural resource cases have developed both tests to the extent that the countervailing duty statute may now be used against any domestic subsidies or government policies which:

- target one particular group of recipients
- treat different recipients in different ways
- are limited, either by design or otherwise, to a "small" num-ber of recipients

- allow for any degree of administrative discretion in determining the eligibility of different groups of recipients
- treat different localities within a political jurisdiction in different ways
- provide special or differential treatment to the recipient from that of the private market, including situations in which the particular benefit cannot be obtained from the private market
- provide a benefit at no cost to the recipient, or at a cost lower than that payable by a recipient for an equal benefit on commercial terms. "Commercial terms" are based on an estimate of the reasonable expectation by the market concerning the future performance of the recipient, at the time the alleged subsidy was provided
- provide a publicly-owned resource at less than "market" value
- provide a publicly-owned resource to a "few" users, even if the quantity of users is not the result of government action, but is determined by the inherent characteristics of the resource, or the commercial feasibility of alternative uses.

The cases also have provided some guidance on characteristics that would not satisfy the two tests. In contrast to the characteristics that do satisfy the tests, these are conceptually so broad as to be almost undefined. Domestic subsidies and government policies are deemed not to be countervailable if they are either:

- neutral; or
- a "legitimate" government function in the "general public interest"; or
- provided at the equivalent of commercial terms.

"Neutrality" has been interpreted in the "natural resources" cases to mean a combination of the following features (i.e., existence of the corresponding opposite feature to any of these indicates "specificity"):

- universal availability or, conversely, targeting to a "sector" or to a "wide" group of industries. What constitutes a "sector" is unclear: the 1986 Softwood Lumber case took it to mean a large number of non-integrated industries
- applicability to every location within a political jurisdiction
- automaticity in considering eligibility
- equal terms for, or equal benefits directed at different industries, firms, products or individuals covered by the program

The cases under analysis have not elaborated significantly on the "public interest" criterion, since only one program, the Atlantic Fisheries Management Program, was specifically distinguished on these grounds. The only distinguishing feature (also appearing on programs dealing with certain government services to industry and with infrastructure) is the availability of benefits to the "general public."

The last general criterion, "commercial equivalency," has been generally straightforward in the Canadian cases. The test used is whether the "price" paid by the recipient to the government exceeds or is equal to the market price paid by the recipient to the government exceeds or is equal to the market price for an identical benefit. The only specific area of controversy has involved government equity infusions, where the determination of a "market" return on equity is extremely conjectural. Generally, though, the test attacks the legitimacy of governments supplementing the operation of private markets.

Until the 1986 Softwood Lumber case, expansion of the ambit of the countervail statute had been done exclusively through the "specificity" test. The Canadian natural resource cases appear to indicate expansion has been achieved by: (1) tightly defining the distinguishing features of offending practices, while (2) loosely defining the distinguishing features of permitted practices. Thus, the loose definition of what is permitted in one case may be eroded by the tighter definition of what is offending in a subsequent case. For example, prior to the Pork case, programs directed at agriculture were considered as not "specific" because agriculture was a sector, hence more than a "group of industries." When this argument was made on the Pork case, the Commerce Department added the tighter proviso of "differential treatment" to refute the claim. Again, in the 1983 Softwood Lumber cases, Commerce found that stumpage applied to a "group of industries"; in the 1986 case, Commerce found that "discretion" in providing stumpage licences meant this program did not, in fact, so apply. A "group of industries" was defined narrowly in the 1986 case as a large number of non-integrated industries. The net result of this approach is the inevitable encroachment on what is permitted by what is forbidden, until only the most neutral forms of government assistance (and from an economic policy perspective, the most ineffective in accomplishing micro objectives) will escape countervailing duties.

The argument used in the 1986 Softwood Lumber case further opened the "preferentiality" test to revisionism. The ambit of the test may include in the future the manner in which governments dispose of resources under public ownership. This represents a major departure from the existing test, limited, as it is, to determining whether the cost to the recipient of receiving a government benefit is less than the cost of a benefit of identical nature in the domestic market.

In sum, the interpretations given by the Commerce Department to the countervailing duty statute in the countervailing duty cases involving Canadian natural resource products may potentially preclude the use of any domestic subsidies or government policies which:

- are targeted in any fashion
- allow any administrative discretion in determining eligibility
- attempt to foster separate local or regional objectives
- supplement the operation of the private market in high-risk situations
- exploit government-owned resources in a "non-commercial" manner

These developments have serious implications for the ability of governments to carry out their traditional economic policies, as long as the current U.S. countervail regime prevails.

Up until 1985, there appeared to be some utility in carefully examining the precedents (Canadian or otherwise), in order to determine with some assurance what kind of program was most likely to be countervailed. Decisions since then, arrived at in the face of protectionist pressures and the threat of legislative change, have now suggested that precedent provides only meager predictability. If anything, precedent now suggests the statute is being used to reach practices hitherto thought unobjectionable.

On the Canadian side, there has been only one countervail case involving U.S. interests: corn. The case resulted in findings of subsidization and injury, and subsequent imposition of duties. The U.S. Senate passed a resolution mandating a Section 305-type investigation to ascertain whether the finding was in violation of Canada's GATT commitments. Canada underlined the fact that the investigation and subsequent determination were conducted under a very similar system to its U.S. counterpart, and in strict compliance with GATT rules on the matter. The margin of the duty was eventually reduced as a result of a public interest inquiry, a feature not available in the United States.

The Issue of Harassment

More fundamentally, there is evidence that the U.S. system has been used to harass Canadian imports:

- The percentage of final orders relative to the number of cases initiated against Canadian firms is low.

- Since 1980, 14 countervail investigations have been initiated against Canadian firms, all but one by private petition. Of the 13 investigations concluded, final duties were imposed on five cases. Of the five successful actions, three (Swine and Pork, Atlantic Groundfish, and Flowers) resulted only in partially favourable findings. Of the other cases, two were suspended or terminated due to undertakings. Hence, in six out of 13 cases the investigative authorities found insufficient evidence to justify the imposition of countervailing duties.

- In cases where final orders were issued, the amount of subsidization or the dumping margins were not large in a significant number of cases. Subsidy amounts of 4.4%, 5.8%, 0.72% and 1.47% were imposed in the Swine, Groundfish, Oil Country Tubular Goods and Flowers cases, respectively.

- The ease with which investigations can be initiated has led to dubious actions against Canadian suppliers.
  - Fresh Flowers: AD and CVD petitions were filed against eight countries. Canadian flower exports amounted to $250,000 in 1985 out of total U.S. flower imports of $17 million. Canada was included for two reasons: one, by cumulating all importers, the petitioner has a better chance of proving injury and discouraging new entrants; two, the petitioner was concerned that offshore flowers subject to future CVD or AD duties would circumvent them by transshipment or resale through Canada.
  - Oil Country Tubular Goods: Investigation against Canada was part of a series covering at least eight countries. Canadian imports accounted for less than 6% of the total market share.
  - Probe Thermostats: A small company in Vermont filed a petition alleging that a small company in Smiths Falls, Ontario was eligible for two federal programs—PMED and IDRP. Commerce accepted the petition and added nine programs of its own, ostensibly to gain further information for its own purposes. After a lengthy investigation, Commerce had to conclude the company had not benefitted from any of these programs. The case cost the company at least two years' profit.

- Countervail investigations have been initiated by U.S. industries that are also subsidized.
  - Fresh Atlantic Groundfish – U.S. East Coast fishermen benefit from a variety of government assistance programs.
  - Live Swine and Fresh Pork – U.S. agricultural support programs benefit U.S. livestock producers.

- Softwood Lumber – U.S. timber and related industries benefit from special tax treatment.
- Loose rules on the finality of findings have led to successive actions for different remedies:
  - Groundfish – One CVD investigation initiated in 1977 ended with a negative finding in late 1978. In the same year another CVD investigation was initiated which also ended in a negative finding in early 1979. A safeguard investigation was then initiated that also resulted in a negative determination in early 1980. A further investigation to review the previous two CVD investigations produced a negative injury finding in mid-1980. A study on conditions of competition for groundfish under s.332 was released in December of 1984. An additional CVD investigation was initiated in 1985, ending with duties being imposed on whole fish but not on fish fillets.
  - Softwood Lumber – One CVD investigation in 1983 ended with a *de minimis* determination of dumping and a finding that stumpage practices were not countervailable. U.S. lumber producers initiated another investigation in 1986, based on identical facts. Commerce reversed its previous ruling on the countervailability of stumpage practices at the preliminary determination stage.
- Erecting defences against contingency protection actions is very expensive. Expenses may become a strong deterrent of small companies.
  - Softwood I: C$4 million; Groundfish: over C$600,000 during the first six months; Softwood II: C$6 million.

Generally speaking, the record in Canadian countervail cases bears out the conclusion that the countervailing duty statute in the United States is more easily used to harass competition than to deal with serious problems of subsidization. Where there has been the perception of a serious problem, such as in lumber, the statute has proven unsatisfactory to both petitioner and respondent and the solution had to be found through diplomatic negotiations. With the exception of steel rails, the prophylactic effect of countervailing duties has also been minimal.

The Textile Trade Issue in the Uruguay Round Negotiations

Ippei Yamazawa*
Professor, Hitotsubashi University

Importance of the Textile Trade Issue

The textile industry is the first industry many developing countries introduce at the beginning of industrialization and for some countries, is the first major source of export earnings. It is also an area in which many developed countries have had difficulty adjusting their domestic production to rapidly increasing imports from developing countries. In the Pacific, among PECC members, there is both a big group of import markets and a group of the most competitive exporters. The textile trade occupies a significant percentage of the intra-Pacific trade.

For the past 15 years the textile trade has been under tight management, that is, the trade flow from an exporting country to an importing country has been kept under the maximum quantity set on individual products or product groups under the bilateral agreement between the two countries authorized by the Multi-fibre Arrangement (MFA). Contrary to its originally stated intention, this managed trade has recently been expanded to more textile types and implemented more strictly.

* The author has also been Jerwood Fellow at the University of Sheffield. He wishes to acknowledge benefits from discussions with the GATT Secretariat, especially Mr. Marcelo Raffaelli and Mr. Sanjoy Bagchi, in May 1989.

Nonetheless, the MFA has been admitted by the GATT as a temporary exception to its free trade rule. Being deprived of possible increase in export earnings, developing countries have long been complaining about this officially admitted managed trade and have requested termination of the MFA and a return to free trade, that is, to integrate the textile trade to the GATT rule. The termination was clearly stated in the GATT Work Program in 1982 and was incorporated in the 1986 Punta del Este Declaration that initiated the Uruguay Round negotiations.

Improvement of the textile trade system has given developing countries a major incentive to participate in the Uruguay Round and many regard it as a goal of that Round. The progress in the textile trade issue will encourage developing countries to accommodate more positively issues of developed countries' interest such as intellectual property rights and services trade, and will lead to overall success in the Uruguay Round.

However, as was anticipated, the textile trade negotiations seriously handicapped because of conflict between the extreme positions of exporting and importing countries. It could not be settled in Montreal in December 1988 as one of four difficult items and was postponed until the ministerial meeting in Geneva in April 1989. The Geneva meeting gave a "go" signal but further details are still to be discussed.

(a) "Substantive negotiation will begin ... in order to reach agreement *within the time-frame of the Uruguay Round** on modalities for the *integration of this sector into GATT ...*"

(b) "Such modalities for the process of integration into GATT on the basis of *strengthened GATT rules and disciplines* should cover the *phasing out of restrictions under the Multi-fibre Arrangement* and other restrictions on textiles and clothing not consistent with GATT rules and disciplines, the *time-span for such a process* of integration, and the *progressive character of this process* which should commence following the conclusion of the negotiations in 1990."

The current MFA 4 will be terminated in July 1991 and the textile committee will start discussion a year before as to whether there will be no new MFA or a modified MFA 5. Therefore, it is expected that a concrete modality for phasing out the MFA restrictions should be agreed upon by Spring of 1990 and

---

* All italics in the quotation is by the author.

implemented after July 1991. Both exporting and importing countries are invited to put forward proposals for alternative modalities by the end of June 1989 but no clear direction had been reported by November.

Problems with the MFA

The MFA was introduced into the GATT system in 1974 as a temporary measure for a four-year period in order to give importing countries breathing time for adjustment while ensuring exporting countries an orderly expansion of exports of at least six per cent per annum. There are two types of restrictions under the MFA. Article 3 provides a safeguard measure in the presence of market disruption regarding specific products by enabling importing countries to request an exporting country or countries for consultation to restrict exports at a fixed level for the twelve month period and to remove the disruption. Article 4 enables importing and exporting countries to conclude bilateral agreements in order to eliminate a real risk of market disruption in importing countries and disruption to the textile trade of exporting countries.

In reality, major importing countries (United States, the European Community and Canada) have resorted mostly to restrictions under Article 4 and concluded arrangements with individual exporting countries, mostly developing countries and Eastern European countries, making bilateral agreements on the base level and growth rates of imports of individual textile product, thereby establishing a managed trade network, instead of resorting to the Article 3 safeguard in the presence of actual market disruption.

Contrary to the assurance of generous implementation in Article 4, the MFA restrictions have tended to be strengthened in terms of coverage and implementation. The MFA was extended three times: MFA 2 for 1978-1982, MFA 3 for 1982-1987, and MFA 4 for 1987-1991. Quota has been expanded barely by one per cent, in keeping with the growth of domestic demand (justified as "rational departure" from the original rule). Neither carry forward nor transfer between product groups has been permitted. Recently the United States has included ramie products in addition to the original cotton, woollen, and synthetic products. Contrary to the temporary focus in its original intention, the MFA restrictions have provided domestic producers with vested interests in the form of restricted competition among imports, higher prices, but often greater sales values.

The MFA restrictions provide exporters with an awkward system of transaction as well. Individual exporting countries allocate their country's quota governing exports to a particular importing country among individual exporting firms who can increase exports only to the extent of growth of quotas. When some firms have not exported to the full extent of their quotas, unused quotas are redistributed among other exporting firms. This is a practice which, because of inevitable time lag in administration and redistribution, has tended to leave some quotas unused by the end of the year. This export quota system under Article 4 has tended to depress competition among exporters by restricting exports of competent firms below their potential while benefitting less competent firms with greater quota relative to their potential. The export price could thus be raised and the higher price constitutes a rent (additional income) to some exporters.

The MFA restrictions have had complicated impacts on both exporting and importing countries; providing rent to producers in importing countries and exporters with greater-than-capacity quota at the cost of declining shares of existing major exporters. As a matter of fact, in the Pacific major exporters of textile and clothing (Japan, Korea, Taiwan, and Hong Kong) decreased their shares in the U.S. market, while members of the Association of Southeast Asian Nations increased their shares under the MFA. The rent has created a vested interest for the past 15 years, which has tended to weaken the request by exporters to terminate the MFA in spite of objection in principle by exporting countries as a group.

Consumers in importing countries bear most of the burden in terms of higher prices and poorer quality, but their voice is seldom heard in the trade negotiations. In addition, there could be a dynamic loss to the industry as a whole incurred by the MFA restrictions, when they prevent the emergence of new producers and discourage innovative efforts by existing producers.

Japan has been in a unique position. She participated in the first MFA negotiations as an exporting country and her exports were restricted by the United States under a bilateral agreement. However, as her exports stagnated while her imports increased for the past decade, domestic producers have started to demand protection against increasing imports and Japan's policy stance has changed toward that of importing countries. Japan's imports of textile products increased by 27.4 per cent in 1986 and by 49.9 per cent in 1987. Imports of knitted outerwear increased 50 per cent in 1986, 51 per cent in 1987 and 54 per cent in 1988. Imports supplied 54 per cent of domestic consumption. The Japan Knitters Association sued its major exporter, Korea, for dumping exports last year, while the Japanese government requested that the Korean government place a voluntary export restraint on its exports of knitted wear. Japan has never resorted to the MFA restrictions to her imports, but she participates as an importing country in the current textile negotiations. Although the

Japanese government pledges to resort to the MFA restrictions in case of disruptive imports, it has managed to avoid it so far. But it had a hard time in Geneva last year when developing countries demanded the explicit statement of a freeze to further restrictions of textile and clothing imports.

How to Phase Out the MFA

The eventual goal is to return the textile trade to the GATT rules and disciplines in which both quota restrictions and discriminatory treatment are terminated and the trade is conducted on the basis of cost and prices. The MFA restrictions should be terminated in a progressive manner, say within a five to ten year period, thereby giving time for adjustment to both importing and exporting countries. However, there should be a definite time limit and no further extension; during the transitional period measures should be clearly stated and never reversed again. These two points are agreed upon by those in favour of terminating the MFA. But there are a variety of modalities proposed for its concrete implementation.[1]

One major group of modalities is the *tariffication* of the existing MFA restrictions. The idea is to convert all existing export quotas to their tariff equivalents, which is consistent with the GATT rules, and to leave more room for cost and prices to play, and then to reduce tariffs gradually. Although its logic is clear, there are various problems with its implementation. First, the estimation of tariff equivalents is not easy in reality on the basis of past performance of restricted imports. Second, the switch from export quotas to import tariffs deprives a rent from exporting countries and gives tariff revenue to importing countries. Some compensation is needed to persuade exporting countries. Third, the existing quota allocation, apparently with less severe restrictions to minor exporting countries and no restriction to developed countries, will give rise to differential tariffs for individual exporting countries, which contradicts the GATT's Most-Favoured Nation principle.

Modified proposals have been presented to incorporate these criticisms. An auction bid of import licences is proposed to determine the tariff equivalents at the market and a part of the revenue from the auction should be transferred to exporting countries in order to compensate for the loss of rent from export quotas. However, tariffication will result in even higher than the current high tariffs on textile products.[2] The explicit introduction of discriminatory tariffs (even during the transition period) and the transfer of tariff or auction revenue to exporting countries will introduce more complications.

Popular among economists is *tariff quota*, which admits imports at current MFN tariffs within existing quotas, while imposing on imports in excess of quotas differential tariffs which are prohibitively high at the outset but which will be lowered gradually to MFN tariffs when quotas lose any significance and the textile trade is governed by GATT rules. However sophisticated it may appear, the liberalization in excess of quota is subject to the same difficulty as immediate tariffication or auction bid.

The tariffication proposal seems to be overly concerned with the vested interest of producers in importing and exporting countries under the current system. However, the vested interest was not calculated at the start of the MFA and its maintenance need not be justified, apart from giving producers time to adjust to its loss.

The steady *expansion of existing export quotas* is straightforward and seems to be more practical. The expanded quotas will become non-binding and the quotas can be abolished. The new arrangement will be implemented in such a manner that MFA is extended for another five years after 1991 but under MFA 5 individual quotas will be expanded by 20 per cent every year and will be non-binding for many product groups by 1996. There will be no MFA 6.

The following measures may be added to increase the feasibility of this proposal.

1. Quota for minor suppliers (in terms of percentage of consumption) and under-used quota (say below 50 per cent) should be abolished immediately after 1991, leaving binding quota for major suppliers to be expanded as stated above.
2. Safeguard measures under Article 3 will be retained against disruptive imports during the MFA 5 but will be replaced later by the strengthened Article 19 of GATT.
3. Liberalization of tariffs and quota restrictions on textile imports from developing countries should be encouraged in order to match the liberalization efforts by developed countries.

Revival of the Textile Industry

The whole issue depends not so much on how to compensate the loss of vested interests as on how to encourage individual governments to terminate the MFA by a definite deadline. To this end we should warn our policy-makers against the current tendency to enjoy the status quo, which discourages their will to terminate the MFA. They should be warned against the detrimental consequences of the MFA in the long run, in spite of its temporary soothing effect on trade conflicts.

First, the MFA has already lasted for 15 years and there is no clear signal of termination by the United States or the EC after three successive extensions. Although the need for adjustment assistance has now been widely admitted, 15 years are too long to be justified as breathing time.

Second, the textile industry itself has changed over these years. Lobbyists have claimed that the protection to assert the revival of textile firms is no longer the same as it was 15 years ago. Many incompetent firms have left the industry either by switching over to other industries or simply by generational change. The protection under the MFA restrictions have tended to prolong the adjustment by some incompetent firms, but quite a few firms have achieved the necessary adjustment and have revived as competent producers.

The textile industry was regarded as typically labour intensive, with already matured technology, and production in developed countries being easily defeated by the catching-up of developing countries with cheap labour costs. This conventional perception no longer holds today. Many producers have adopted automatic, high-speed spinning and weaving machines, which increased their labour productivity so much that their disadvantage with high labour cost has lessened considerably. More important is the change in the consumer's taste in developed country markets. At the high income level, consumers have already been satisfied with a minimum need for clothing and will not increase their purchases only in response to cheaper prices. They will buy even more expensive clothing of better design and newer fashion. It will also encourage the invention of new synthetic yarns and fabrics. Fashion changes in much shorter cycles now.

Both closer market contact and the availability of new technology help producers in developed countries to compete with imports from developing countries. *Quick response* to changes in market demand through vertical integration has been a popular trend in the United States and other developed countries. Successful firms after these adjustments are not afraid of imports and no longer need protection. Furthermore, firms are now more active in international operations, less restrained from relocating their production overseas and changing supply sources from one to another. They easily circumvent conventional restrictions at national borders. Two leading Japanese spinning firms have started production in the United States mainly for reasons of cost that is, the depreciated U.S. dollar and cheaper electricity costs which have become more important than labour costs in fully automated production.[3]

Response to changing demand is also observed in some developing countries. Clothing producers of Asian Newly

Industrializing Economies (NIEs) have already been looking to their own domestic demand. Their own markets are smaller in size, but have an increased demand for better quality but more expensive clothing as the per capita income rises. A similar tendency has started in some ASEAN countries as well. Partly assisted by the recent exchange rate realignment and changes in cost competitiveness, the Asian textile producers are now shifting from big quantity to quality exports.

As a result of the shift to quality, textile exports from Japan, Korea, and Taiwan to the United States have recently been short of the quota set by the bilateral agreement (Table 1). Since utilization ratios are calculated by dividing the total export by the corresponding sum of the quota on individual product items (in terms of quantity), actual exports may have reached the full quota on some individual items. But the overall under-utilization suggests that in general imports have not been disruptive and quota restrictions have been redundant in recent years. On the other hand, current bilateral quota agreements of these countries with the United States will be terminated either by the end of 1989 (for Japan) or in the middle of 1990, and it is reported that bilateral negotiations will start soon for further extensions.[4]

Table 1
Export Quotas of Japan, Korea, and Taiwan to the United States and their Utilization in Recent Years

		Total quota (a) (100 million sm)	Utilization ratio (b) (%)
Japan	1987	6.4	73
	1988	6.5	59
Korea	1987	11.1	96
	1988	11.2	87
Taiwan	1987	13.9	96
	1988	14.1	83

Notes: (a) sum of all items, (b) estimates by industry experts

Source: *Japan Economic Journal*, August 5, 1989.

It is the best chance to terminate the MFA restrictions, at least for items with redundant quotas. However, the U.S. government wishes to continue the MFA with much reduced quota in order to compensate the increased quota for Caribbean countries, whereas the Japanese government wishes to extend the quota restriction unchanged. The cutback of quota contradicts the MFA rule. Both governments are concerned about the resurgence of exports, which suggests that bureaucrats and lobbyists tend to stick to quota restriction even after quota restrictions have become redundant.

Although the MFA in textile trade is an extreme case, less restrictive managed trade, Voluntary Export Restraints (VERs), proliferate in trade in major manufactured products, which weakens the GATT rules and disciplines. The GATT system cannot be strengthened without terminating the MFA.

Notes

1. See Sampson (1987), Silbertson (1988), Hamilton (1988), Bagchi (1989), and Sampson and Takacs (1989).

2. Ivanbrook (1986) reported that the Australian experience in quota auctioning in textile/clothing/footwear sector has been erratic.

3. The liberalization of the textile and clothing trade is often discussed differently on the ground that clothing production is more labour intensive and small-scaled so that it requires a longer time for adjustment. I am not well convinced by this argument for the following reasons. First, clothing production is closer to final consumers and their producers are equally active in revitalization through quick response to market changes by electronic devices. Second, textile and clothing production are inter-related so that different means of protection may misguide the resource allocations. The conventional argument should be re-examined in view of recent technical changes within the industry.

4. *Japan Economic Journal*, August 5, 1989.

Bibliography

Bagchi, Sanjoy, *Textiles in the Uruguay Round: Alternative Modalities for Integration into GATT*, presented at the workshop on "International Textile Trade, the Multi-Fibre Arrangement and the Uruguay Round," Stockholm, June 1989.

GATT, *Mid-Term Review Agreements*, TNC/11, 21, Geneva, April 1989.

Hamilton, C.B., "Sampson Proposal – A Reply to Aubrey Silbertson," *The World Economy*, vol. 10, December 1987.

Ivanbrook, C., *Determinants of the Price of Quota: The TCF Sectors of the Australian Economy 1982-1986*, Honours Thesis, University of Adelaide, 1986.

Raffaelli, Marcelo, *Some Considerations on the Multi-Fibre Arrangement: Past, Present and Future*, presented at the workshop on "International Textile Trade, the Multi-Fibre Arrangement and the Uruguay Round," Stockholm, June 1989.

Sampson, Gary P., "Pseudo-economics of the MFA – A Proposal for Reform," *The World Economy*, vol. 10, December 1987.

Sampson, G.P. and Wendy Takacs, *Returning Textile Trade to the Normal Workings of GATT: A Practical Proposal for Reform*, presented at the workshop on "International Textile Trade, the Multi-Fibre Arrangement and the Uruguay Round," Stockholm, June 1989.

Silbertson, Aubrey, "Impracticalities of the Sampson Proposal for Phasing out the MFA," *The World Economy*, vol. 10, December 1987.

Yamazawa, Ippei, "Renewal of the Textile Industry in Developed Countries and World Textile Trade," *Hitotsubashi Journal of Economics*, vol. 24, no. 1, June 1983.

The MFA and Trade in Textiles and Clothing

Chin-Kun Chang
Taiwan Institute of Economic Research

In the Ministerial Declaration that launched the Uruguay Round Multilateral Trade Negotiations, it was promulgated that negotiations in the area of textiles and clothing "shall aim to formulate modalities that would permit the eventual integration of this sector into GATT on the basis of strengthened GATT rules and disciplines, thereby also contributing to the objectives of further liberalization of trade." Because of the political sensitivity of the issues involved in textiles trade, it was clear from the very beginning of the new round of negotiations that a formidable task lay ahead.

When the Trade Negotiations Committee met in Montreal in December 1988 for the Mid-term Review Negotiations, ministers could not agree on the broad issues concerning trade in textiles and clothing. Nor did they reach agreements in three other sensitive subjects under negotiation—agriculture, intellectual property, and safeguards. The failure to make progress in all of the 15 groups under negotiation led many concerned observers to believe that the Montreal meeting was a major setback and that the hope for a more open and strengthened world trading system under the GATT was lost. However, agreements on these four deadlocked areas was reached at the Geneva meeting in April, thus concluding the work of the GATT Mid-term Review. Since then, there has been freshened momentum for the continuing of the Uruguay Round.

In the area of textiles and clothing, the broad issues of integrating textiles trade into the GATT system were finally agreed upon. Participating countries also agreed that future negotiations would focus on the specific means for achieving this aim, including eventually phasing out the Multifibre Arrangement (MFA) and other restrictions that are not consistent with the framework of GATT rules.

The MFA: Managed Trade in Textiles and Clothing

Currently trade in textiles accounts for 10 per cent of all world trade in manufactured goods and 25 per cent of manufactured exports from the developing countries. Rules governing trade in textiles and clothing however, are not subject to the GATT rules and disciplines, instead they are governed by a set of quantitative restrictions imposed by the importing developed countries beginning in the 1950s when Japan developed a strong textiles industry. Trade in textiles and clothing has become a classic example of managed trade and has drifted further and further away from the free trade regime of the GATT.

In the 1950-1960 period, large exports of low-cost cotton textiles from the developing countries led to the signing by the GATT contracting parties of the Short-Term Arrangement on Cotton Textiles (STA) in 1961. This agreement was extended twice to remain effective until September 30, 1973 and was subsequently known as the Long-Term Arrangement (LTA). On December 20, 1973 the Arrangement Regarding International Trade in Textiles (MFA) was concluded. In addition to cotton textiles it also covered man-made fibre and wool. The MFA has subsequently extended three times, in 1977 (MFA II), in 1981 (MFA III), and in 1986 (MFA IV). The current MFA will expire in 1991.

The MFA I allowed for a 6 per cent annual growth rate of textile exports from exporting countries. The MFA II subsequently lowered this rate and added the so-called "reasonable departure clause." The MFA III in turn dropped, the reasonable departure clause to protect developing exporting countries but added the anti-surge and outward processing clauses which effectively linked raw materials to processing and import quotas. The MFA IV further extended its coverage to include silk, linen and ramie.

Trade Regime Under the MFA

Although the MFA was negotiated under the auspices of the GATT, it greatly departs from the principle of non-discrimination that is central to the GATT system. The MFA also uses quantitative restrictions as a weapon, which is inconsistent with GATT rules.

From the perspective of a textiles exporting country, the MFA is protective and restrictive on several grounds:

(1) Article 3 justifies the introduction of new restrictions and/or intensification of existing restrictions on trade in textiles by importing countries to "the precise products and to countries whose exports of such products are causing market disruption as defined in Annex A . . . ." In practice, when the importing developed country makes the request with a view to removing such disruption by curbing exports, the exporting developing country concerned, being weak as always in international fora, usually has no other recourse but to agree.

(2) Paragraph 3 of Article 4 stipulates that bilateral agreements reached in order to eliminate real risk of market disruption in importing countries and disruption to the textile trade of exporting countries "shall, on overall terms, . . . be more liberal than measures provided for in Article 3 of [the] Arrangement." In practice, the importing countries seldom provide more liberal measures on sensitive textile products.

(3) From its origin, it is clear that the MFA is intended for the protection of the domestic textile industries in the developed countries. Exporting developing countries are no longer able to rely on exports of textiles to promote economic growth and development. Meanwhile, the protected textile industries in the importing developed countries have not taken advantage of the relief provided by the MFA by making the necessary adjustments to shift resources to other more economically efficient sectors. Instead they have adopted more and more technology-intensive and capital-intensive production methods in order to maintain their domestic market share of textiles and clothing. It is for this reason that the temporary safeguard measures have been extended for a period of time far beyond what is provided for by the GATT Article XIX, which permits suspension of obligations or concessions "for such time as may be necessary to prevent or remedy" serious injury caused by imports. In short, the MFA institutionalizes the emergency actions that are

supposed to be temporary, thus greatly undermining the credibility of the GATT system.

(4) The experience of the MFA makes it very tempting for countries to attempt to impose similar treatment to other sensitive areas such as trade in steel. The invention of Voluntary Export Restraints (VERs) and Orderly Marketing Arrangements (OMAs) are believed to have their origin in the MFA.

So, although the MFA was created and extended ostensibly for purpose of promoting "the development of production and expansion of trade in textiles" and progressively achieving "the reduction of trade barriers and the liberalization of world trade" in textiles, in practice these objectives have not been reached.   In each successive renewal, the MFA has instead become more and more restrictive on textiles exports from developing countries.

The above observation is confirmed by an OECD study, *Textile and Clothing Industries: Structural Problems and Policies in OECD Countries*, which plainly states that "[t]he new agreements always cover a wider range of products and/or fix lower annual growth rates than was the norm in the earlier period of the arrangement. The coverage of bilateral agreements has been more frequently modified. This is sometimes done at the request of exporting countries and the adjustments agreed may indeed facilitate their exports. But most of these requests come from importing countries and their objective is to restrain additional items."

Given its many flaws, the MFA must be ended if the GATT is to regain credibility as an institution that advocates the spirit of free trade.

Phasing-Out of the MFA

The eventual integration of the MFA into the GATT will, of course, depend on the overall outcome of the Uruguay Round Negotiations scheduled to be concluded by the end of 1990, especially the GATT rules in the area of safeguards. More specifically, safeguard rules must be strengthened to the extent that the availability of protection under them is sufficient to compensate importing countries for the loss of the MFA, and must be sufficiently transparent to be acceptable to both exporting and importing countries.

With regards to strengthening safeguards, the following improvements are suggested:

(1) The duration of import restrictions should be clearly spelled out;

(2) Restrictive measures should be gradually relaxed;

(3) Restrictive measures should be limited to tariff measures, with quantitative restrictions being justified under "highly unusual and critical circumstances";

(4) Bilateral prejudice should not be allowed when implementing restrictive measures. For instance, restrictive measures should be applied equally to all imports of a specific product in order to confirm the GATT principle of non-discrimination; and

(5) Exporting countries thus affected should not be allowed to take retaliatory action against justified safeguard measures by importing countries.

With regards to the eventual phase-out of the MFA, the following steps are suggested:

(1) The Uruguay Round must negotiate a mutually acceptable time-table for the gradual phase-out of the MFA, preferably no longer than five years after the completion of the Uruguay Round. In the meantime, all countries concerned must reaffirm their commitments on the rollback of restrictive or distorting measures in textiles trade inconsistent with GATT provisions;

(2) In the transition period leading to the end of the MFA, the number of textile products subject to restrictive measures under the MFA IV should be gradually reduced;

(3) The multilateral surveillance mechanisms of the GATT should also be strengthened in order to provide for effective monitoring of the liberalization process of textiles trade; and

(4) Importing countries should discontinue "grey area" measures such as VERs and OMAs.

In addition, all countries concerned should make efforts to promote international division of labour and technology transfer. Greater cooperation in these two areas would help ease the pain brought about by conflicts in the trade of textiles.

Recent International Trends in Intellectual Property Rights

Kensuke Norichika
Intellectual Property Division
Toshiba Corporation
Japan

Introduction

The World Intellectual Property Organization (WIPO) has in the past succeeded in keeping the Paris Union[1] under control and in adjusting the world intellectual property system. However, in the early 1980s severe conflict of interest between the developing countries (the 77 group), the developed countries (the B group), and the socialist countries (the D group) resulted in a deadlock in the negotiations to revise the Paris Convention with the exclusive compulsory license against non-working. More recently, the WIPO has been putting its effort into the worldwide harmonization of patent systems and has started to take action toward establishing a Harmonization Treaty.

In the GATT Uruguay Round started by the Punta del Este Declaration in October 1986, the TRIP (Negotiating Group on Trade-Related Aspects of Intellectual Property Rights, including Trade in Counterfeit Goods) attracted initial attention to three key issues concerning intellectual property—"Norm" (Protection Standards), "Enforcement Procedures", and "Dispute Settlement Mechanisms". Subsequent studies conducted by the TRIP group illustrated the wide difference in understanding of these issues between the developing and developed countries. Accordingly, at the Mid-term Review held in Geneva from April 5 to 8, 1989, it was agreed to start substantive negotiations on these issues, including the Norm. Their continuous examination is now being undertaken with a view to finding a final agreement by the end of the Uruguay Round in 1990.

The GATT and the WIPO can therefore be said to be at the centre of the international effort to reconcile the interests of the developed and developing countries concerning intellectual property. (See Annex 1 and Annex 2).

Multilateral Negotiation on Intellectual Property

GATT and the Private Trilateral Meeting

Japan, the U.S., the EC and other developed nations are aiming at establishing comprehensive rules regarding the protection of intellectual property through the GATT. On the other hand, the developing countries, led mainly by Brazil and India, insist that the GATT should not be used to establish such rules, because the preparation of such rules while strengthening intellectual property, accelerates the technical monopoly held by the developed countries and invades the authority of the WIPO.

In November 1987 and September 1988, Japan, together with Switzerland and the U.S., proposed a set of rules to the GATT concerning intellectual property which dealt with aspects of both "Enforcement" and "Norm". These proposals included the following items:

1. The principles extensively recognized GATT of most-favoured-nation treatment, national treatment and assurance of transparency shall also be applied to protect intellectual property;

2. Patents, trademarks, designs, copyrights, and semi-conductor integrated circuit layouts shall be protected;

3. Due process of law shall be guaranteed in procedures to enforce intellectual property rights, both in a domestic and international context;

4. An international mechanism to settle intellectual property rights disputes between nations shall be established;

5. A periodical review of rules shall be undertaken; and

6. An international information exchange and mechanisms for providing technical assistance to the developing nations shall be established.

In response to this GATT activity, the Japan Federations of Economic Organization (KEIDANREN-KDR), the Intellectual Property Committee (IPC) in the U.S., and the Union of Industrial and Employer's Confederation of Europe (UNICE) organized a private trilateral meeting to consider fundamental principles for protection of patent, proprietary information, trademark, design, copyright, semiconductor chip and enforcement mechanisms. This meeting resulted in the publication of the "Basic Framework of GATT Provisions on Intellectual Property—Statement of Views of the European, Japanese and United States Business Communities, June 1988". (See Annex 3 and Annex 4)

Since the release of that statement, the three organizations have continued to make known to their respective governments their views on the development of GATT provisions pertaining to intellectual property.

WIPO and the Trilateral Patent Office Meeting

In addition to the activity of the GATT, the commissioners of the Japanese, the U.S., and the EC patent offices have met to discuss each others patent systems and their harmonization. There are now 16 proposals under discussion between these patent offices. Among these, the biggest issue is the revision of the U.S.'s first-to-invent system which covers a period lasting for more than 150 years and is dramatically different from systems in place in Japan, Europe and almost all other nations. Given that Canada, whose patent system was close to that of the U.S., amended its patent law in January 1989 and that the Philippines is going to change its patent law to a first-to-file system, it is hoped that U.S. public opinion will gradually shift to support harmonization with other nations in terms of converting from the first-to-invent system to the first-to-file system, and from the 1-year patent duration from date of issuance to the 20-year patent duration from filing date. (See items 1 and 12, Annex 5) To accomplish this harmonization, the CLUB 15, which represents the 13 member nations of the European Patent Office, Japan and the U.S., has been very active.

Bilateral Negotiation on Intellectual Property

These discussions illustrate that bilateral negotiations between the two nations are progressing in parallel with multilateral negotiations. (See Annex 6)

In the meetings of the U.S.-Japan Trade Committee held in the late August last year and in March of this year it is reported that the U.S. proposed 12 items relating patent, copyright, design, and trade secret. Thus, bilateral negotiations between two nations are progressing in parallel with multilateral negotiations. (See Annex 6)

The Japan-U.S. Joint Task Force, which was left pending according to the joint statement of the 25th Japan-U.S. Business

Conference, repeatedly discussed the patent systems in Japan and the U.S. and their harmonization. Two sets of hearings held by Senator John D. Rockefeller IV criticized various aspects of the Japanese patent system, including non-acceptance of foreign language applications, narrow interpretation of patent claims, delay of patent examination, administrative interference or influence on the examination of patents, and other patent practices. However, many of these criticisms are based on misunderstanding about the Japanese patent system. At the multilateral negotiations, such problems had already been discussed where it was clearly realized that there was a large gap between Japanese and U.S.A. perceptions as to whether such issues should be negotiated bilaterally. Given this situation, the Japan-U.S. Joint Task Force is anxious to promote mutual understanding in order to reduce friction between the two countries. It is, therefore, expected that the both sides will compromise to some extent and announce a joint statement.

In the August 1988 meeting of the U.S-Japan Trade Committee it is reported that the U.S. proposed 12 items relating to patent, copyright, design and trade secret. These items were again discussed in the second meeting held in March 1989.

Important background to the bilateral negotiations is the U.S.'s use of Article 301 of the Omnibus Trade Act. For example, it concluded the U.S.-Korea agreement in July 1986, invoked Article 301 against Brazil in October 1988, and suspended GSP (general preferential duties) against Thailand in January 1989.

The USTR issued the 1989 NTE (National Trade Estimate) Report on April 28, 1989. In this report, trade problems, including 34 items relating to Japan, were pointed out including "delay of patent examination", "the absence of a discovery mechanism", the inadequacy of, "the type and level of protection for sound recording".

Furthermore, U.S. administration has recently singled out 25 countries whose practices deserve special attention under the so-called "special Article 301" which was of correspondence to super 301, and addressed the specification and sanction of a nation which infringed upon intellectual property rights. In the "Priority Watch List", eight countries, including India, Brazil and Korea, were listed as countries for which it was necessary to check, on November 1, 1989, their efforts to improve their record vis-à-vis intellectual property rights. Japan was included in a "watch list" and is expected to make significant improvements before the end of next year. In light of this type of pressure it seems apparent that U.S.-led bilateral negotiations will be very active in the immediate future.

Conclusion

As mentioned above, multilateral and bilateral negotiation concerning intellectual property are proceeding in parallel. However, the Paris Convention has long been responsible for adjusting the international patent system and the establishment of intellectual property system should be based on balance and harmony achieved among all nations, with problems resolved through multilateral rather than bilateral negotiations.

Notes

1. The Paris Union comprises the countries to which Paris Convention applies for the protection of industrial property. Paris Convention is the international convention for the protection of industrial property.

Annex I
Intellectual Property

```
Assets ── Technology
          Assets ──── Intellectual
                      Property ──┬── Industrial Property ──┬── Patent ──────── Invention
                                 │                         │
                                 │                         ├── Utility Model ── Small Invention
                                 │                         │
                                 │                         ├── Design ──────── Industrial Design
                                 │                         │
                                 │                         └── Trademark ───── Trademark
                                 │                                             (Good Will)
                                 │
                                 ├── Copyright ──────────────── Computer Program, Data Base
                                 │
                                 ├── Mask Work ──────────────── Semiconductor Chip Circuit Layout
                                 │
                                 ├── Service mark ───────────── Service Mark
                                 │
                                 ├── Unfair Competition ─────── Misappropriation
                                 │
                                 └── Proprietary Information ── Trade Secret, Know How


Patent
```

Annex 2
Multilateral Negotiation on Intellectual Property

GATT

(The General Agreement on Tariffs and Trade)
  * Uruguay Round (1986-1990)
    (the Punta del Este declaration)
  * TRIP
    (Trade-Related Aspects of Intellectual Property
    rights, including Trade in Counterfeit Goods)
  * Friends meeting

Private Trilateral Meeting

  - KEIDANREN (Japan Federations of Economic Organization)
  - IPC (Intellectual Property Committee)
  - UNICE (Union of Industrial and Employer's Confederation of
    Europe)

WIPO
(World Intellectual Property Organization)

  * Revision of Paris Convention
  * Treaty on Harmonization of Patent Laws
  * Treaty on the Protection of Integrated Circuit Lay-out

Trilateral Patent Office Meeting

  - JPO
  - USPTO
  - EPO

CLUB 15

  - JPO
  - USPTO
  - EPO-joined 13 nations
    (EPO is an observer)

Annex 3
Basic Framework of GATT Provisions on Intellectual Property

European, Japanese and
United States Business Communities

Introduction and Summary

Purpose of the Paper

This paper describes the trade-related problems that arise from the inadequate and ineffective protection of intellectual property, explains why the present international intellectual property regimes were never intended to address these trade distortions, and provides a thorough analysis of how the proposed GATT Provisions on Intellectual Property Protection (GATT IPP) can serve as a multilateral vehicle to reduce substantially these trade distortions.

Summary of Conclusions

- Despite efforts taken under the present international intellectual property regimes, the extensive losses to worldwide industry due to inadequate and ineffective national protection of intellectual property continue.

- The decision by the GATT Contracting Parties to include a strong negotiating mandate in the Ministerial Declaration on the Uruguay Round is a recognition of the serious distortions caused by inadequate and ineffective protection of intellectual property and demonstrates a commitment to solve the problem.

- The Ministerial Declaration does not restrict the negotiating approach, coverage, or structure of GATT Provisions on Intellectual Property.

- A code, similar in form to the Standards or Subsidies Codes already negotiated in the GATT, is the most appropriate approach among the various alternatives for dealing with trade distortions caused by inadequate and ineffective intellectual property protection.

- The objectives of the GATT IPP should be the elimination of distortions in the trade of goods, both tangible and intangible, caused by the lack of respect for intellectual property by taking two important steps that should not lead to barriers to legitimate trade: (a) the creation of an effective deterrent to international trade in goods where there is an infringement of intellectual property rights and (b) the adoption and implementation of adequate and effective rules for the protection of intellectual property.

- The objectives of the GATT IPP would be achieved by requiring signatories to the GATT IPP (a) to create adequate and effective trade and intellectual property laws for use by private rightsholders; and (b) to use multilateral consultation and dispute settlement procedures when other signatories fail to meet their obligations to provide adequate and effective trade and intellectual property laws.

- A set of fundamental principles for protection of intellectual property and of essential elements of enforcement procedures incorporated in the GATT IPP would serve as the necessary reference point for dispute settlement. These fundamental principles and essential elements can be drawn from those adequate minimum standards of intellectual property protection contained both in the laws of those countries which engage in most of the trade in products embodying intellectual property and in international intellectual property conventions that contain adequate standards of protection.

- Harmonization of the different national systems that already contain adequate and effective intellectual property protection is not a prerequisite to GATT Provisions on Intellectual Property.

- The GATT IPP must not permit a reduction in protection from levels already afforded. The maintenance of adequate and effective levels of protection will, therefore, limit the concessions that can be made and the incentives that can be offered to induce countries with inadequate levels of protection to adhere to the GATT IPP.

- However, a number of important incentives should be included in the GATT IPP (preferential treatment, transition rules and technical assistance), which could, when coupled with incentives outside the GATT framework (consultations, market access and assistance), expedite the process and encourage adherence by all GATT Contracting Parties.

- The primary focus of the negotiations should be on the nature and details of (a) effective, equitable and non-discriminatory enforcement mechanisms, including those at the border, to create a deterrent to international trade in goods which infringe intellectual property rights, (b) dispute settlement procedures to ensure that the domestic laws of the signatories effectively and adequately embody the GATT fundamental principles of intellectual property protection and essential elements of enforcement procedures and (c) preferential treatment to confer benefits on signatories and to encourage adherence to the GATT IPP.

Annex 4 Private Trilateral Committee (July 1988)
Fundamental Principles for Each Intellectual Property Protection

	Subject/Duration	Right and Licence	Enforcement
Patents (13 Articles)	• All kinds of devices, products, and processes meeting conditions such as novelty, utility, and non-obviousness. (Process patent directly applies to the product) • 20 years from filing date in general.	• Exclusive right of the manufacture, use or sale • Compulsory licence applies to only local manufacture and non-exclusive • Sufficient compensation to compulsory licensing • Non-working does not constitute revocation • Voluntary licensing conditions depend on parties negotiation	• Equitable civil procedures without discrimination • Sufficient remedies for damages, preliminary injunction, final injunction • To prove infringement, fair, reasonable and effective court procedure shall be available
Trademarks (17 Articles)	• Exclusive right derives from use or registration • Service mark is accorded the same protection. • No difference in subject and application • No less than 10-year registration • Renewal within no less than 10 years with no limitation.	• No special requirement applies to use • May lapse if not used for a reasonable time without any special circumstances • Free assignment between parties • Licensing accompanies adequate compensation but not discriminated by nationality or goods • Compulsory licensing not possible	• Counterfeiting is subject to criminal sanctions • Setting effective civil procedure without discrimination • Remedies shall give adequate compensation to owners, including compensation, preliminary and final injunction which are effective for infringement prevention • Provides special principles against counterfeit
Designs (8 Articles)	• Two- or three-dimensional external appearance of an article having a utility function • Novel but not having necessity of achieving a technical result, or not simply aiming at a utilitarian function • At least 10 years from the date of registration	• Not cancelled because of non-working • Registration grants exclusive right of prohibiting the manufacture, use or sale of a design which is identical or not substantially different	• Counterfeiting is subject to criminal sanctions • Effective and equitable civil procedure without discrimination • Remedies are identical with trademark (Marking registration is not an essential requirement for claiming damages)

Annex 4 (cont'd)

	Subject/Duration	Right and Licence	Enforcement
Copyrights (14 Articles)	• Automatic protection when created • All forms of original expression (literature, science, art) including computer program and data base • Sound recording is also protected by copyright or other specific rights providing comparable protection • Not extend to any idea, procedure, process, system, operation method, concept, principle or discovery • 50 years after the death of the author, at least 50 years from publication, 50 years from creation if not published, provided that photograph and applied art may be 25 years from creation	• Limitation, exemption and compulsory licence of the right shall be governed by the Berne Convention (Quite independent and same or similar creation may exist in parallel) • Involuntary licence shall secure consideration equivalent to strong safeguards and that of voluntary agreements • Exclusive right shall be freely and separately exploitable and transferable	• Includes right to copy, translate, arrange, or otherwise alter, distribute, import, and publicly communicate by performing, exhibiting, broadcasting and transmitting, or authorize doing so • Effective civil and criminal penalties and procedures and non-discriminatory are established within states • Criminal remedies and penalties include seizure of infringing materials and any apparatus and imprisonment, and fines having sufficient to deter infringement. Also civil remedies include adequate compensation and seizure, preliminary and final injunctions and orders for delivery materials
Semiconductor Chip Layout (18 Articles)	• Protection not extend to any idea or method of operation • Protection not deny other intellectual property right protection (e.g. patented process) • At least 10 years from the date of registration or the date of first commercial exploitation	• Layout design may be reproduced for the purpose of teaching, analyzing or evaluating without authorization • Copying and incorporating into product, and importing in selling or distributing are exclusively prohibited • Compulsory licensing not permitted	• Notice is not required for protection • Compensation for damage, injunctions and other relief consistent with national practices are prepared, so that a civil action can be taken against infringer
Proprietary Information (8 Articles)	• Information disclosed to Government as a prior condition for product registration or licensing • Technical know-how, tangible or intangible • Tangibly recorded secret business information • Valid as secret proprietary information as far as it is valuable to the proprietor and he is keeping the secret	• Confidential information not given exclusive protection such as is granted under a patent, and reverse engineering from published information, product, etc. is freely allowed as long as it is not against lawful contract or law • Information disclosed to Government is allowed to be exclusively used by the disclosing party for a reasonable period, and its disclosure is not allowed without consent • Technical transfer contract is not imposed unreasonably	• Wrongful acquisition is against law, and third party in good faith and negligence are dealt with by each national law • Protection mechanism is based on tradition of each nation's law system, and a combination of multiple protection systems is admitted

Annex 5
Trilateral Patent Office Meeting
Items on Total Harmonization

	USPO's proposal
1. First-to-invent system to First-to-file system	First applicant is given a patent. (First-to-file system).
2. Application by assignee	Makes it possible to file the patent application by assignee.
3. Grace period	Gives to an applicant one-year grace period prior to a filing date (or priority date).
4. Prior art effect	Whole contents of the published first application shall be prior art as of the time of its filing date (or priority date) to any application filed later in the same country.
5. Objective test for non-obviousness	Nonobviousness is judged by the following procedures: a. Decision of the scope and content of prior art b. Decision of difference between prior art and patent claim c. Comparison of the applicable difference with level of one skilled in the art.
6. Claim and its interpretation	(1) Claim shall clearly define the scope of an invention by its structural elements or means. (2) Each claim shall be able to be judged on its validity independently, and its validity and infringement shall be judged according to the following: a. Nature of invention b. Ordinary technical knowledge in the relevant technical field when the application was filed. c. Relevant prior art.
7. Scope of patentable subject matter	Patent protection shall be given to medicine, animal and plant, food and any useful method, product or composition, or its improvement.
8. Effect of process patent	(1) Effect of process patent extends to the import, use or sales of the product manufactured by that process. (2) In infringement litigation, the product manufactured by the process patent subject to the litigation is assumed produced by that process.

	USPO's proposal
9. Deferred examination	(1) Searching of every application shall be completed as soon as possible after its filing. (2) Examination of every application shall be completed soon after that. (3) Specific time limit shall be determined in future.
10. Post-grant re-examination	(1) Re-examination before patent granting is not permitted. (2) Re-examination can be filed anytime during the patent duration based on a publication or another patent.
11. New matter	No new matter shall be added to the specification, claim or drawing of a pending application.
12. Patent duration	Patent shall be valid for 20 years from the first domestic filing date, provided that the duration extension system may be introduced.
13. Laying open of application	(1) Application shall be laid open to public soon after 18 months from the filing date in general. (2) Compensation rights to demand is given based on the claim laid-open.
14. Description of invention	Specification shall describe its invention in sufficient, clear, concise and correct terms so that the invention can be carried out by those skilled in the art without unnecessary experiment.
15. Reissue of patent	Each patent office must give to patent owner an opportunity of patent reissue, when it is within 2 years from patent granting, claims may be expanded.
16. Compulsory license	Compulsory licensing is non-exclusive and may be given only when coping with emergency in the nation and so on.

Annex 6
Japan-U.S. Negotiation on Intellectual Property Main Subjects Proposed by U.S.A.

1. Patent
    *   Increase in the number of examiners to shorten the examination period.
    *   Allowing to file an application in English.
    *   Faster handling of litigation of patent infringement in court.

2. Copyright
    *   Hold the present 50-year protection of computer software.
    *   Prohibiting reverse engineering.
    *   Making the record reproducing right protection period to at least 50 years.
    *   Providing the same period copyright infringement as in the U.S.A.
    *   Even possession of copy infringing copyright being guilty.
    *   Rigid enforcement of regulations by police.

3. Trademark
    *   Increase of responsible personnel to shorten the period required for trademark registration.
    *   Establishing service mark registration system.

4. Trade Secret
    *   Introduction of effective protection measures of trade secret.

Intellectual Property and the GATT Negotiations: Some Areas for Discussion

D.G. McFetridge
H.E. English
Department of Economics
Carleton University

Background: The Role of Intellectual Property

The primary forms of intellectual property rights are patents, trademarks and copyrights. The general purpose of these rights is to encourage innovation and creative expression. They do this by bestowing upon the originators of qualifying innovative or creative works an exclusive but limited right to whatever returns their works may bring in the market.

Patent rights give the inventor the exclusive right to use or sell novel, non-obvious and useful inventions of a technological nature. Trademarks are words, names or symbols used by producers or merchants to identify their wares or services. The owner of a registered trademark has an exclusive right to use that mark. Copyrights grant the owner the exclusive right to reproduce, publish, display, perform or sell copies of literary, musical and artistic works and, in some countries, computer programs.

Intellectual property rights are generally limited both in time and in scope. The duration of a patent right is generally limited to between 15 and 20 years with a term of 20 years from date of filing being the most common.[1] Effective patent terms are further limited by provisions for compulsory licensing and by renewal fees which exist in most countries.[2]

The duration of a copyright is generally limited to the life of the artist plus a specified period generally between 25 and 50 years. A trademark, on the other hand, can be renewed indefinitely.

The scope of intellectual property rights is limited in a variety of ways. First there are a number of forms of technological innovation which are not covered by intellectual property rights. For example, patents cannot be obtained on basic research or in some countries on innovations involving some forms of life. The two major producers of computer chips, Japan and the United States, protect computer chip design under specific legislation rather than under copyright.[3]

Second, there are limitations on what constitutes infringement of intellectual property rights. For example, the copying of copyrighted audio or video material for personal use does not, at present, constitute an infringement of the copyright in the United States.[4] In addition, the "fair use" doctrine provides a number of defences, including copying for purposes of scholarly research of actions that would otherwise be infringing.

Third, patent, trademark, and copyright owners are limited as to the terms and conditions they can impose on their customers, agents or licensees. The doctrine of first sale, for example, effectively precludes a copyright holder from influencing the terms on which a copyrighted item is resold. To take a second example, competition or antitrust legislation in many developed countries including the United States and the member states of the European Economic Community limits, often severely, the ability of intellectual property holders to engage in trade practices such as tied selling, exclusive dealing, territorial restriction and resale price maintenance.[5]

These and numerous other limitations on scope and duration have led to the characterization of the intellectual property right as a limited monopoly. The extent of this monopoly varies among developed countries and has varied within individual developed countries over time. For example, the protection provided under the original United States copyright law was granted only to books, charts and maps, had a term of only 14 years and was not extended to works of foreign origin.[6]

The determination of the duration and scope of intellectual property rights, or what has been called "the intellectual property bargain", is part of a broader public policy decision regarding how best to stimulate and disseminate innovation and creative expression. There are other public policies by which this end might be achieved and there has been a continuing debate in developed countries regarding the relative efficacy of intellectual property and alternative policy mechanisms.

Each set of institutions has its costs. Intellectual property encourages innovation but at the cost of restricting its dissemination. Specifically, new technology or artistic expression has the characteristics of what is known as a public good. That is, its use by one individual does not reduce the amount available for others to use. Once information or ideas exist their use or dissemination is virtually costless. Efficient exploitation would dictate that they be freely available. But if new technologies and artistic works are freely available there will be no financial incentive (absent other forms of support) to produce them in the first place.[7]

Thus, in striking an intellectual property bargain society is trading-off dissemination against origination.[8] Specifically, the value of new innovative and creative endeavour encouraged by stronger intellectual property rights must be balanced against decreased access to innovations and creative works that would have occurred under a weaker regime.

The case for stronger rights turns on their effectiveness, both absolutely and relative to other incentive schemes, in inducing additional innovation. Those who have questioned the scope and duration of existing intellectual property rights within developed countries have frequently done so on the basis that these rights do not play a significant role in encouraging innovation.

There are two branches to this argument. The first is that a diminution of intellectual property rights would not reduce the value of resources devoted to innovation or artistic expression to any significant degree. The second branch is that while a diminution of these rights would lead to an exit from creative activity, this would serve largely to reduce duplication as well as both premature and hurried innovation. The flow of new usable knowledge would not be reduced.

There is evidence that patent rights are essential to the conduct of privately funded industrial research and development in several industries (pharmaceutical, fine chemicals and petroleum) and peripheral in others.[9] In these other sectors the costs of imitation provide a measure of "natural" protection to innovations and this is not enhanced materially by patent protection.[10]

Government funded industrial R&D is likely to be less sensitive yet to intellectual property considerations.

With respect to copyright, Palmer (1986) cites survey evidence to the effect that by 1977 some three-quarters of computer software developers had never rejected or abandoned a software development program because of the absence of copyright protection. Palmer also argues, however, that, given the spread of microcomputers, copyright protection is likely to have become more important since that time.

Students of the patent system have long been concerned that competition for patent monopolies might lead to wasteful duplication of research effort as well as hurried and premature research.[11] In this case a diminution of the patent right serves both to reduce the amount of wasteful research and to increase accessibility. As a consequence, the intellectual property bargain is tilted in favour of patent rights that are shorter in duration or narrower in scope. A recent theoretical study concludes, for example, that under conditions of R&D rivalry the socially optimal patent term is unlikely to exceed six years.[12] Similar considerations are likely to apply in the case of copyright.

It should be emphasized that what little empirical evidence exists indicates that research rivalry may not be as pervasive as is assumed in theoretical works on this subject.[13] Consequently, the socially optimal patent term may not be as short as the theoretical analyses suggest. This does not change the central point which is that the intellectual property bargain struck by society depends on the circumstances, specifically on the respective distributions of opportunities for and capabilities of innovation. There are no absolutes.

The existence of alternative means of encouraging innovation also influences the nature of intellectual property bargain. Tax incentives and subsidies play a prominent role in encouraging industrial innovation in most developed countries as do government R&D contracts. Universities and non-profit research institutes also play important roles.

Other policy measures can also be used to forestall imitation or limit access to the extent deemed desirable. For example, the taxation of audio and video tapes or recorders has been suggested as a means of reducing the extent of (unauthorized) copying of copyrighted audio or video material. To take another example, France taxes the sale of reprographic copying machines and rebates part of the proceeds to French copyright holders.

While intellectual property has the merit of providing a decentralized and market-driven incentive system, it is not necessarily superior to other incentive systems in all cases. This must be borne in mind when discussing the appropriate international intellectual property regime.

International Considerations

The process of striking an international intellectual property bargain is more complex yet. One reason for this is that some nations are predominately buyers of technology and artistic works while others are predominately originators. If they are able to copy or reverse engineer, individual using countries have little interest in maintaining a domestic intellectual property system which serves largely to reward foreign artists and inventors without noticeably influencing the global pace of innovative and creative activity. If copying is costly, it may be necessary to maintain a domestic intellectual property system in order to gain full access to foreign technologies. Although they may accept the necessity of paying for access to foreign technology, individual using countries will continue to attempt to minimize the amount they pay for this.

The income of originating countries depends on their ability to extract payment from users. Consequently, originating countries tend to favour a strong intellectual property regime. Attempts to fashion a set of intellectual property rights common to all countries have been burdened by this divergence of interests.

The originating countries, led by the United States, claim that using countries, specifically newly industrialized countries such as Korea, Taiwan, Singapore, Indonesia, Mexico and Brazil, are allowing their nationals to infringe upon the intellectual property rights of foreign, principally American, innovators and artists. This infringement is often called counterfeiting or piracy.

Counterfeiting is often defined as the unauthorized use of a trademark. Counterfeiters attempt to pass off goods of low or unknown quality as higher quality (trademarked) items. The ultimate effect of this type of practice is to destroy the value of a trademark as a quality signal and, possibly, to drive high quality goods from the market.

Piracy often refers to the unauthorized copying for resale of books, records, audio and video cassettes and computer software.

Counterfeiting and piracy are emotive terms implying a violation of the law.[14] This is not always the case as these activities do not necessarily constitute an infringement of intellectual property rights in the country in which they occur. The reason for this is that the countries involved may have weak or, in some cases, non-existent intellectual property regimes. In other cases, local infringement may be occurring but the enforcement of intellectual property rights may be so costly as to make control impossible. In still other cases foreigners may be handicapped, formally or otherwise, in the enforcement of their intellectual property rights.

Thus the concern of the originating countries is with non-existent intellectual property rights in some using countries and inadequate rights and/or excessively costly enforcement in others. This issue is difficult to adjudicate for several reasons. First, as the discussion in the background section indicates, the adequacy of intellectual property rights depends on the circumstances. There is no absolute standard of adequacy.

Second, intellectual property rights can be attenuated in a variety of ways by a country intent on so doing. For example, Japan maintains a strong intellectual property regime which does not formally discriminate against foreigners. Yet the operation of the Japanese system is such as to virtually require that foreigners license local producers which, in many cases, effectively cedes the market to those local suppliers.[15]

Notwithstanding the ambiguity regarding what constitutes a formally or effectively adequate set of intellectual property rights and thus what constitutes infringement, the United States has estimated its losses from both inadequate rights and infringement. The United States International Trade Commission estimates that in 1986 U.S. firms had their profits reduced by some $755 million and incurred additional losses in foreign royalty income in the amount of $3.1 billion (presumably also largely profit) as a result of either infringement or inadequate intellectual property rights. The bulk of these losses were borne by the computer and entertainment industries.[16] The major offenders are said to be Taiwan, Mexico, Korea and Brazil.

In its efforts to induce other countries to strengthen their intellectual property regimes the United States has made use of multilateral intellectual property for bilateral consultations and trade actions and, most recently, multilateral negotiations under the General Agreement on Tariffs and Trade (GATT).

From the standpoint of inducing other countries to strengthen intellectual property rights, the bilateral approach reinforced by threatened or actual trade actions appears to have been the most effective. The U.S. General Accounting Office cites the following accomplishments of this approach:[17]

1. Taiwan
    (a) Amendment of its copyright law in 1985 to increase penalties for piracy, to allow foreign firms judicial standing in copyright cases and to extend protection to computer software
    (b) Enactment of a new patent law in 1986 which extends protection to chemical and pharmaceutical products

2. Singapore
    (a) Passage of an improved copyright law in 1987 which is expected to protect audio and video tapes of U.S. origin from unauthorized copying

3. South Korea[18]
    After the institution of a Section 301 investigation by the United States in 1985, Korea agreed to:
    (a) extend product patent protection to chemicals and pharmaceutical
    (b) adopt a comprehensive copyright law
    (c) extend copyright protection to computer software
    (d) adhere to the Universal Copyright Convention thereby automatically extending copyright protection to U.S. works.[19]

The danger in the bilateral approach is that it tends to impose on other countries the intellectual property bargain which has been struck in the United States. As the discussion in the background section concludes, there are a variety of means by which innovation and creative expression can be fostered even for nations at the same stage of development. While it is difficult to conceive of an effective incentive system with no intellectual property rights, systems which assign intellectual property a less prominent role than the United States are entirely conceivable. This should also be kept in mind during the GATT negotiations on intellectual property and when choosing among institutions within which negotiations might proceed.

The GATT Negotiations

The stated purpose of the GATT negotiations on trade-related intellectual property issues (TRIPs) is to develop a common set of rules and disciplines which will provide adequate protection for intellectual property rights while ensuring that these rights do not disrupt legitimate trade. The key phrases are "adequate protection" and "legitimate trade." The task is to reach a consensus regarding the meaning of these terms. Given the minimal progress the World Intellectual Property Organization (WIPO) has made in its attempts to deal with this matter, a more realistic goal might be to define a minimum acceptable intellectual property protection which would, in turn, imply an upper boundary on what constitutes legitimate trade.

There are a number of reasons to believe that these issues can be addressed productively within the GATT framework. First, the GATT framework is essentially a bargaining one and, assertions to the effect that intellectual property rights are "moral rights" notwithstanding, the determination of what constitutes adequate protection of intellectual property has always been a matter of self-interested bargaining, motivated by the promise of mutual gain to be shared among users and originators.

Second, intellectual property rights are inextricably intertwined with international trade and have historically included the right to prohibit imports from infringing sources. International differences in intellectual property regimes can distort trade. The first challenge is to define what constitutes an infringing source. Secondly, to the extent that the definition of infringement varies from country to country how important are the trade distortions, and should they be removed by harmonization of regimes.

To take an extreme example, in the United Kingdom, copyright protection applies not only to blueprints and technical drawings but also to the objects depicted in them. Imports of products depicted in copyrighted blueprints (autoparts, for example) have been excluded from the British market on the grounds that they are infringing the British copyright[20]. It can reasonably be argued that this is an extension of copyright beyond the point necessary to provide an adequate return to the creator (of the blueprints) and, as such, constitutes an illegitimate restriction on trade. It is also trade-distorting in that the products in question could be exported elsewhere in the world.

The parallel importation of goods covered by trademark provides another example. Originators and users have a mutual interest in preventing confusion over the source of trademarked goods. This interest is protected by allowing the local owner or licensee of a trademark to prevent the importation of goods produced either by unauthorized or unrelated users of the mark. Prevention of importation from affiliated or contractually-related users of the mark (other licensees) is unjustifiable on the grounds of preventing confusion as to source, provided the origin of the goods is clearly indicated. It has been argued, however, that users also have an interest in inducing local licensees to make their own investments in the quality of the mark. In this case, grounds might exist for allowing the local owner of the mark to prevent importation of goods even by related and unauthorized users of the mark. The implication is that some restrictions on trade are collectively beneficial. It is a matter of determining the range of national circumstances in which this is the case.

A third reason that intellectual property issues can usefully be adjudicated under the GATT is that, as Stern (1987) rightly points out, a nation which refuses, as a matter of policy, to pay for the creative or innovative content of imported goods and services is imposing a tax on these imports which is, in principle, the same as a tariff. As such it is a legitimate subject for international bargaining in a GATT context and for adjudication under the GATT settlement mechanism.

The key issue, as Stern emphasizes, is that the originating countries recognize that intellectual property rights are not a moral absolute but a means to an end. They are and always have been the subject of bargaining. While there are benefits from harmonizing intellectual property regimes, this does not necessarily imply that prevailing U.S. standards should be imposed globally. In turn, the using countries must recognize that, to an increasing degree, innovation and artistic expression are what the originating countries have to sell. If the originating countries are unable to earn a return on their efforts in export markets their ability to import suffers and international trade will decline as a consequence.

With the recognition that both originating and using countries must be allowed to realize a return on their respective wares in the other's market, bargaining under GATT could seek a commitment for the using countries to enforce a minimum set of intellectual property standards in return for the originating countries' reducing tariff and non-tariff barriers on labour-intensive manufactured products as well as agricultural products.

Minimum intellectual property standards to which adherence might be sought include:

- the definition of the subject matter to be covered by the patents and copyrights
- a minimum patent term
- terms and circumstances of compulsory patent licences
- the definition of trademarks, trademark rights, and the means by which they are obtained.[21]

Failure to adhere to the minimum standards agreed upon would, of course, constitute infringement or, more colourfully, counterfeiting or piracy.

The term of a patent is effectively defined by the conditions under which compulsory licences can be awarded. A starting point might be a provision, already found in most national patent laws, for non-exclusive compulsory licences for failure to work a patent locally after a reasonable period. The rationale for this provision is that the intellectual property bargain involves an obligation to disseminate the patent technology as well as the products which embody it. It should be noted that non-exclusivity and/or provision for parallel importation gives a local compulsory licensee access to patented technology without restricting trade.

Compulsory licensing of some types of technology might also be contemplated regardless of local working. For example, Canadian patent law provides for limited compulsory licensing of pharmaceuticals. This implies a judgement that the gains from increased access made possible by compulsory licensing exceed any losses flowing from the reduced incentive to invent. There is little to indicate whether this judgement is correct, that is, whether the existing patent term provides the optimal balance between innovation and access in the case of pharmaceutical.[22]

Given the uncertainty regarding the optimality of the patent term prevailing in the developed countries, it would not seem unreasonable to provide for some flexibility in the conditions and circumstances under which compulsory licences can be awarded. This presupposes, of course, an acceptance of an undertaking to enforce the underlying patent right.

The establishment of simple common trademark registration standards is a priority. The terms on which trademarks are licensed is also an issue for both originators and users. In this regard, using countries might be willing to allow licensors more latitude in return for increased access by licensees to export markets. Provision for increased access to foreign markets could go as far as defining the trademark right to be exhausted after first sale of trademarked goods by authorized users. The ability of licensors to segment markets internationally would be reduced but this would hopefully be more than offset by a decrease in unauthorized use.

It is optimistic to expect even limited agreement on proposals such as this. Discussion of them does, however, have the useful by-product of clarifying the various national policies and practices on these matters and, perhaps, of increasing their clarity and consistency.

Notes

1. See Creel and Wintringham (1984), note 57.

2. Ibid., p. 264.

3. Wong (1985).

4. United States Congress, Office of Technology Assessment and Forecast (1986), pp. 192-3.

5. Blair and Kaserman (1985); McFetridge (1986).

6. United States Congress, Office of Technology Assessment and Forecast (1986), p. 190.

7. A discriminatory pricing system which charged the marginal user a zero price could bring about efficient dissemination, in principle, without reducing the incentive to create. Ironically, antitrust law in the United States and the European Economic Community forbids a variety of tying practices such as package licensing and block booking through which this end could be achieved.

8. The disclosure required of a patentee may also facilitate non-infringing uses of a technology which might not occur under a regime of trade secrecy.

9. Mansfield (1986, p. 175) finds that, of a sample of commercially introduced inventions, 60 per cent of the pharmaceutical inventions, 38 per cent of the chemicals, 25 per cent of the petroleum and 17 per cent of the machinery inventions would not have been developed in the absence of patent protection.

10. Mansfield et al. (1981) find that in other industries it is the cost of acquiring the requisite technical know-how which is the principal deterrent to imitation.

11. An early example is Plant (1934). Dasgupta and Stiglitz (1980) provide a contemporary analysis.

12. Kotowitz (1986), p. 59.

13. Mansfield et al. (1977) find little in the way of rivalry in the development of a sample of industrial innovations they examine.

14. Globerman (1986) notes that to define piracy is to define the boundaries of intellectual property rights. As noted in the background section, there is considerable disagreement within developed countries regarding where these boundaries ought to lie. In a Canadian context, for example, the right of intellectual property owners to prohibit importation from a non-infringing foreign source has often been questioned. Some would call this parallel importation piracy, others would not.

15. Wineberg (1988).

16. United States International Trade Commission (1988).

17. U.S. General Accounting Office (1987), pp. 50-4.

18. See Duvall (1988).

19. Section 301 of the U.S. Trade Act of 1974 as amended in 1984 empowers the President to take retaliatory trade action against foreign countries deemed to be denying adequate and effective protection to U.S. intellectual property.

20. Stern (1987), p. 200.

21. See Keon (1988) for further detail.

22. A lower elasticity of demand militates in favour of a shorter optimal patent term in both the Nordhaus (1969) and Dasgupta-Stiglitz (1980) models. It could be argued that since demand for pharmaceuticals is likely to be relatively inelastic the effective reduction of the patent term resulting from compulsory licensing is welfare-improving. Of course this argument could also apply to other technologies.

References

Blair, R. and D. Kaserman (1985). *Antitrust Economics*, (Homewood, Ill.: Irwin).

Creel, T. and D. Wintringham (1984). "Patent Systems and Their Role in the Technological Advance of Developing Nations," *Rutgers Computer and Technology Law Journal*, vol. 10, no. 2, pp. 255-302.

Dasgupta, P. and J. Stiglitz (1980). "Uncertainty, Industrial Structure and the Speed of R&D," *Bell Journal of Economics* (Spring), pp. 1-28.

Duvall, D. (1988). "Fair Trade and the Protection of Intellectual Property Rights in U.S.–Korean Economic Relations," *Law/Technology*, vol. 21, no. 1, pp. 18 ff.

Globerman, S. (1986). "Economic Issues Surrounding International Product Piracy," in R. Dunn (ed.), *Portfolio: International Economic Perspectives*, vol. 12, no. 1.

Grey, R. (1988). "Services and Intellectual Property Rights" (Victoria: Institute for Research on Public Policy), unpublished.

Keon, J. (1988). "TRIPs in current GATT Negotiations," *Les Nouvelles* (December), pp. 203-6.

Kotowitz, Y. (1986). "Issues in Patent Policy with Respect to the Pharmaceutical Industry," (Canada, Commission of Inquiry on the Pharmaceutical Industry).

Mansfield, E. (1986). "Patents and Innovation: An Empirical Study," *Management Science*, vol. 32 (February), pp. 173-81.

Mansfield, E., M. Schwartz and S. Wagner (1981). "Imitation Costs and Patents: An Empirical Study," *The Economic Journal*, vol. 91 (December), pp. 907-18.

McFetridge, D. (1986). "Government Intervention in Technology Transfer: More or Less?" *Canada-United States Law Journal*, vol. 11, pp. 331-44.

Nordhaus, W. (1969). *Invention, Growth and Welfare*. (Cambridge, Mass.: MIT).

Palmer, J. (1986). "Copyright and Computer Software" in R. Zerbe (ed.), *Research in Law and Economics*, vol. 8, pp. 205-26.

Plant, A. (1934). "The Economic Theory Concerning Patents for Inventions," *Economica*, vol. 1, pp. 30-51.

Stern, R. (1987). "Intellectual Property," in J.M. Finger and A. Olechowski (eds.), *The Uruguay Round Handbook* (Washington, D.C.: The World Bank).

U.S. Congress Office of Technology Assessment and Forecast (1986). *Intellectual Property Rights in an Age of Electronics and Information* (Washington, D.C.).

U.S. General Accounting Office (1987). "International Trade: Strengthening Worldwide Protection of Intellectual Property Rights," GAO/NSIAD-87-65 (Washington, D.C.).

U.S. International Trade Commission (1988). "Economic Effects of Intellectual Property Right Infringement," *Investigation No. 332-245* (Washington, D.C.).

Wineberg, A. (1988). "The Japanese Patent System: A Non-Tariff Barrier to Foreign Businesses?" *Journal of World Trade*, vol. 22, no. 1 (February), pp. 11-22.

Wong, R. (1985). "The Semiconductor Chip Protection Act: New Law for New Technology," *Journal of the Patent and Trademark Office Society*, vol. 67 (October), pp. 530-50.

The Uruguay Round and Trade in Services: the State of Play after April 1989

Geza Feketekuty
Office of the U.S.T.R., Washington

My role is to give you my perspective on where negotiations stand and how we should interpret the agreement that came out of the Mid-Term Review. In terms of an overall impression, it is certainly my view that the negotiations on services are going remarkably well, particularly in light of the stormy history leading up to the launching of the Uruguay Round. At the Mid-Term Review in Montreal in December 1988, agreement was achieved on services despite the fact that four other issues, textiles, safeguards, agriculture and intellectual property were not resolved until April. That has put a whole different cast on services. It is now seen as an issue that is being worked on in a very expeditious manner.

I am going to look particularly at the Mid-Term Review agreement on services and give you my interpretation, piecing together various elements of the text. My feeling is that this text was a major advance in the negotiating process. I know there have been many editorial writers who have tried to dismiss it, saying it was mere rhetoric. My own view, as you will see from my interpretation of it, is that some very major points were pinned down in that agreement. Of course, it is an agreement that was drafted at midnight by a committee and as a result would not win a Pulitzer Prize. But I think careful reading will reveal a great deal about the emerging consensus on the framework of a services agreement.

I have noted in reading the papers for today's session that there are some nuances in interpretation and I will undoubtedly inject an American perspective to my interpretation of the text. I will try to be as objective as possible by citing from the text of the agreement.

The first point I would like to make about the text that emerged from the Mid-Term Review is that it clearly establishes a very broad coverage for the scope of the negotiations. There is a very broad definition of trade in services in paragraph 4. It basically says "that trade in services should encompass not only cross-border movements of services, but cross-border movements of producers of services." This broad scope is also basically pinned down in paragraph 7(e) dealing with market access. It says that where market access is made available to signatories, it should be on the basis that . . . foreign services may be supplied according to the preferred mode of delivery. This gives the supplier a choice with respect to the preferred mode of delivery.

What do we mean by modes of delivery? What are these alternative modes of delivery? One means of delivering services across national borders, is by electronic transmission of information through a communications network. Another is by sending a person to a different country. A third means is to establish an enterprise in that country and deliver those services through a locally established facility. And, of course, there is a fourth means, by moving a product to which services will be applied in the other country. So between those two paragraphs, paragraph 4 on definitions and paragraph 7(e) on market access, the Montreal text pins down a very broad scope for the negotiations.

It has been pointed out by my colleagues here that the paper did not explicitly address right of establishment and labour mobility. That is true. But those two paragraphs clearly imply that the negotiations will cover right of establishment and mobility.

The Montreal text thus establishes important political, operational and "negotiating" links between various modes of delivery, including labour mobility, right of establishment and cross-border transfer of services by electronic means. Governments, when they negotiate market access commitments, are likely to link market access concessions to a preferred mode of delivery. Developing countries will put the emphasis on labour mobility, and developed countries will put the emphasis on right of establishment. The rational negotiating outcome is to provide for both.

By the way, electronic delivery may ultimately create the greatest problems because it bypasses the regulatory authority of the importing country. If you can deliver services electronically, the importing country, in effect, is prepared to accept services that were produced under the regulatory framework of the supplying country.

The second point I want to make on the text concerns sectoral coverage. The agreement makes it clear there are to be no *a priori* exclusions of particular sectors, and the goal is balanced coverage reflecting the balance of commercial interests among the various countries. This follows the traditional GATT approach. Of course, the text also points out that there should be special attention to sectors of interest to developing countries. I will come back to this point.

The next point is that the agreement clearly puts the focus of the negotiations on effective market access. An important debate has been whether the ultimate commitment by governments is to abide by agreed principles in the application of regulations or whether the ultimate commitment by governments is to effective market access. I think the agreement makes it clear that the ultimate objective of the negotiations is to achieve effective market access. Now where has this come through? The language in paragraph 7(c), which I cited earlier, says "where market access is made available, suppliers should be given the choice of methods of delivery." The text in this paragraph not only explicitly talks about market access, but also sets up an important principle that will help achieve market access. If our exporter's ability to gain market access through one delivery channel is blocked for one reason or another, the availability of alternative methods of delivery could nevertheless assure effective market access.

Paragraph 7(b) says that "the aim of these rules, modalities and procedures should be to achieve . . . a progressively higher level of liberalization." In other words, a distinction is made between the objective, which is progressive globalization, and the tool, which is the application of the principles. Paragraph 7(b) states that "to this end [i.e., progressive liberalization] the adverse effects of all laws, regulations and administrative guidelines should be reduced as part of the process to provide effective market access." In other words, it says we have to deal with all the various laws, regulations and administrative guidelines which adversely affect effective market access.

The text implicitly recognizes that achieving effective market access in services is going to be a very complicated matter. Regulations that limit effective market access in services are complex, so that going about the application of principles in a purely mechanical way could lead to little real market access. A number of papers prepared for this meeting point this out. The focus on effective market access is therefore crucial, and the agreement will need to provide an effective market access test that goes beyond adherence to the principles of the framework.

This brings me to the language on national treatment in paragraph 7(c), which establishes national treatment as a key principle, and ties its application to the negotiation of effective market access. The link between national treatment and market access is achieved by adding to the language on national treatment the words "when accorded with other provisions of the framework." While this language is a bit opaque, what it means is that when negotiations under other provisions of the framework result in market access commitments, foreign suppliers should be treated exactly the same way as domestic suppliers.

The text also clearly establishes that the Uruguay Round should aim not only at achieving agreement on a framework, but also on an initial level of liberalization. And it does this in paragraph 7(b) where it says "the aim of these rules, modalities and procedures should be to achieve, *in this Round and future negotiations*, a progressively higher level of liberalization." There are some who have argued that the aim of the Uruguay Round negotiations on services should be to reach agreement on a framework, an empty box which is to be filled in through the future negotiation of substantive commitments of market access. What this text seems to say is that, we want to do more than that. We also want to use the Uruguay Round to establish some initial set of commitments on market liberalization.

Next, the participation of developing countries. There is a very long section on this, and the subject is also treated in a number of other sections of the Montreal text. Let me make the following observations. Number one, the emphasis is on the positive side of creating export opportunities for developing countries, not on the negative side of relieving these countries of commitments and obligations (i.e., special and differential treatment). And that is clearly demonstrated by the fact that in paragraph 7(f), the first three paragraphs deal exclusively with export opportunities for developing countries.

A second point is that in establishing a balance of market access commitments, clearly there is a recognition that the level of development will need to be factored into the equation. Developing countries are not expected to make the same level of commitment to market access as developed countries. Therefore, in the evaluation of what constitutes a balance in sectoral coverage, the level of development is to be taken into account.

Number three, when the text talks about differential obligations for developing countries, it only mentions least-developed countries, it does not mention developing countries as a whole so there is a clear assumption that developing countries will be assuming obligations of the system and that only with respect to least-developed countries is there a sense that they might not be able to assume those obligations fully.

Fourth, there is an emphasis in the Montreal text on the objective of strengthening the capacity, competitiveness and efficiency of the services sector in developing countries, but it does not say how that is to be achieved. The lack of specifics is the result of a debate between developing and developed countries. Developing countries have argued that developed countries should guarantee technology transfer. Developed countries have said that in services, technology takes the form of human skills and knowledge. Technology in services is not transferable independently of the people involved. The most effective way to transfer those skills is through the establishment of services facilities by competitive foreign firms in developing countries, encouraging these firms to hire local people as employees, and training then to supply world class services. The validity of this approach comes out clearly in the paper by Mr. Tan, where the observation is made that in local Singapore banks, most of the senior and mid-level officials were trained in foreign banks established in Singapore. In any case, this was something that has now been resolved, so what was agreed was the objective but not the means of achieving it.

Finally there is a curious paragraph on the right to introduce new regulations consistent with commitments in the framework. I am not quite sure what that means because it says that developing countries that may not have certain regulations have a right to introduce them, provided they are consistent with the other obligations of the framework. The major obligation relevant in this case is that such regulations should not adversely affect trade.

The agreement also includes a basic transparency commitment. This has been the subject of extensive discussion in Geneva in recent months. In particular these discussions have focused on whether all the local regulations ought to be pooled in one place or whether the agreement should involve only an obligation to publish the regulations.

The Montreal text also pinned down the Most-Favoured Nation/nondiscrimination principle as an important principle, but not what it means. The meaning was not spelled out because there is still some disagreement on what the scope of it ought to be. The issue concerns the right of a group of countries who decide to harmonize their regulations in a particular service activity to open trade in that activity with each other on a more competitive basis. Should that be interpreted as being consistent with Most-Favoured Nation (MFN) or not? That I think is a very critical issue. The willingness of a government to permit international competition in some services may be tied to the establishment of a common regulatory structure. What happens when some governments are prepared to commit themselves to harmonized regulations as a basis for international competition, while others are not? Should they be required to allow countries that are not prepared to harmonize their regulations to compete on an equal basis?

Other elements of the text deal with safeguards and exceptions. Right of establishment and labour mobility are not explicitly addressed, but as I indicated earlier they are implicitly covered by the text.

Ministers at the Mid-Term Review also arrived at a Group of Negotiations on Services (GNS) work program for the final two years of the negotiations. They agreed that the next stage should address the testing of the general principles with respect to particular sectors. Since then, the GNS has consented to test a number of sectors. Telecom and construction were tested at the June 1989 meeting. The testing process led to a very comprehensive and exhaustive discussion of trade in telecom and construction services and of how the principles relate to trade in these sectors. The next discussion will focus on transportation and tourism in July and in September on financial services and professional services.

Ministers also agreed that by the end of the year the GNS should come up with a draft text of a framework agreement. It is the intention of the United States to circulate a U.S. proposal of the draft agreement by September or October 1989. I assume that in the September to December period, the negotiators will be very actively engaged in coming up with a draft agreement.

The Montreal text also called for an early determination on sectors to be covered. In fact it called for pinpointing sectors by May 1989 but quite wisely, non of the countries came forward with the list of sectors. I thought it was a foolish decision. This is going to be one of the politically more difficult things for governments to decide, and necessarily it is going to be done towards the end of the negotiations.

I expect that the negotiators will need to develop sectoral annotations or annexes for key sectors such as telecommunications, financial services, transportation. These annotations or annexes will elaborate on the application of the general principles contained in the framework with respect to these key sectors.

There is one major unresolved issue that was not addressed in the Montreal text, namely the nature of the framework commitments, that is, how the principles included in the framework agreement are to be applied. Are they legally binding, *ipso facto*, or do they come into force only after countries have negotiated market access commitment with respect to specific sectors and specific measures? This is something that will need to be resolved. The United States has argued that these principles ought to be legally binding unless a government takes an exception. Other governments have argued that these principles should become legally binding only after they have been positively bound through a negotiating process. I suspect that there may be some way of combining these two approaches. One idea perhaps would be to apply the principles in a legally binding way with respect to existing trade in services (to the extent existing laws and regulations permit such trade) and to negotiate the liberalization of existing barriers through the negotiation of new commitments.

On the basis of this reading of the text that I have given you, it is possible to foresee the nature of the outcome for the negotiations on services in the Uruguay Round. There is a lot of work to be done. It looks like a very intimidating agenda, but I suspect that success is possible if governments begin focusing on the very extensive amount of trade and services which already takes place, and if they are willing, as starting point, to apply the principles to that existing trade. They may even be able to go beyond the *status quo* in some areas, and roll back existing barriers. The most important result, however, will be that we will have a solid framework for restraining the introduction of new barriers and negotiating the reduction of existing barriers in future negotiations. It is hoped we will continue to maintain the track record of the Mid-Term Review, where services turned out to be one of the less controversial issues.

Asian NIEs and Liberalization of Trade in Services

Chungsoo Kim and Kihong Kim
Korea Institute for Economics and Technology
Seoul, Korea

Introduction

The Montreal Accord from the Mid-term Review of the GATT Uruguay Round on the basic structure of a multilateral framework on the rules and principles of service trade was a positive step in the direction of liberalization of trade in services. For the first time since services found its way into international fora (embraced as one of the 18 issues of the 1982 GATT Ministerial Declaration) the prospect of reaching a multilateral agreement that would govern this trade in the coming years was visible.

Although few developing countries have expressed interest in trade in services, it is not solely an issue of the industrial world. A time is rapidly approaching when developing countries must take part in the multilateral effort to establish the rules and principles of trade in services. Developing countries will need to pay attention to the issue of service trade not only because trade in services (with its own inherent dynamism) has come to constitute a considerable portion of international trade, but also because they have uneven sectoral interests in its liberalization.

For the Newly Industrializing Economies (NIEs) in Asia, which have registered remarkable economic dynamism and growth during the past three decades, the negotiation at the Uruguay Round on trade in services will have particularly far-reaching effects. For not only has the service sector come to play a major role in their domestic macro-economic scenes, but the NIEs have also begun to see areas of service trade where they may acquire international competitiveness in an era of liberalization.

NIEs, of course, share many common features including high economic growth, rapid expansion of exports and a high share of manufactured goods in total exports. However, there exists as many differences as similarities. Differences in types of government, degree of market opening and pressures from external debts make common positions concerning trade in services in general, and its liberalization in particular, difficult. This paper attempts to summarize the NIEs' interests in liberalization of trade in services. In order to do so, it will first provide an overview of the current status and underlying conditions of service industries in individual NIEs, and then account for how the positions of the NIEs on trade in services have evolved over the years, especially during the course of the Uruguay Round. This is followed by an analysis of the implications for the NIEs of the Montreal Mid-Term Review on trade in services and its liberalization. It concludes with suggestions on how and where the potentially diverse positions of the NIEs should be coordinated in order to help expedite the Uruguay Round negotiations on trade in services.

Services Industries of NIEs

Korea

Although the Korean economy is basically structured around a manufacturing sector which has provided the major impetus to the rapid growth of the economy, the growth of the service sector has also contributed to Korea's economic development over the last three decades. The service sector, which employed 35 per cent of the total employed workers as recently as 1975, has grown so that it provided jobs for approximately one-half of the total workforce in 1987 and produced 57 per cent of the nation's Gross Domestic Product (GDP).

Of course, the apparent successful expansion of the service sector does not tell the whole story. The Korean service sector is characterized by labour-intensive modes of production and fundamentally differs from the capital- and technology-intensive service sectors of industrialized countries. The changes in trade balance of services reflects the weak international competitiveness of Korea's service industries. (This paper adopts IMF statistics that exclude direct-investment incomes in calculating the trade balance of services. It relies instead on the aggregate data on the balances of merchandise trade and current account.)

Table 1 shows the surplus in trade balance of services is a new phenomenon. Korea has recorded chronic deficits in trade of services and only started to register a current-account surplus in 1987. The weak position of Korea's overall trade balance of services results from its unbalanced sectoral development. The surplus generated by trade in construction and travel services has not been enough to compensate for deficits in other sectors.

Korea's construction activities went international in the mid-1970s when it began to take part in the construction boom in the Middle-East. However, since its foreign activities peaked in 1981 (revenue from foreign construction activities in that year amounted to 13.7 billion dollars), Korea's construction industry has never regained its international competitiveness. As a result, although it still maintains some competitiveness in simple, labour-intensive construction projects, it is in urgent need of diversi-fication of foreign markets and technological enhancement. The pressure of structural adjustment built up by fast-rising wages, strongly suggests that serious efforts must be undertaken to upgrade the level of construction technologies simply to stay afloat in the international construction market.

Korea's maritime transportation industry showed rapid growth through the 1970s, spurred by the equally dramatic expansion of merchandise trade and fostered by, what turned out to be, excessive government supports. By the late 1970s, however, it entered into a phase of long-term recession. Business conditions had noticeably deteriorated by the second oil shock and the ensuing slump in international maritime transportation, which in turn brought down freight charges drastically. Although this sector has earnestly sought to rationalize its efforts, the effects of the recession still linger. Burdened with out-dated ships and mounting debts, the maritime industry of Korea is dubbed as a "problem" industry.

The strong showing in recent years by Korea's travel industry is deceiving and is not expected to be repeated in the future. With strict regulations on foreign travel still in place, there is not much room to allow trade debits from trade of travel services, although with the Asian Games and the Olympics recently held in Korea, many inducements were in place to generate the "apparent" surplus in trade of travel services.

At present, much attention is being paid to the deregulation and internationalization of Korea's financial-service industries. Accordingly, external liberalization of the financial sector, such as banking and insurance, is in progress. Whether Korea is internationally competitive after liberalization remains to be seen, but this trend is expected to accelerate regardless, as a result of Korea's fuller participation in the IMF and the plan for capital-market liberalization that is to be carried out until 1992.

Taiwan

Since 1980, Taiwan has continuously recorded a surplus in merchandise trade and current account balances and, as a result, it accumulated foreign reserves in the amount of 70 billion dollars (the third largest in the world) by the end of 1987. However by most measures (such as share in GDP or total employment), Taiwan's service sector is the smallest among the NIEs and in every major service trade it has registered a chronic deficit. Taiwan's deficits in service trades have in part resulted from the surge of foreign travel by residents (in 1986, one-third of the total payment for service imports were for foreign travel) and considerable freight payments for its merchandise exports (22 per cent of the total payment for service imports in 1986).

In short, Taiwan does not appear to have strong across the board international competitiveness in service trade. The service industries of Taiwan face similar problems to those of Korea. Externally, both are under persistent pressures from the U.S. to open their domestic banking and insurance markets. Internally, it is doing its best to promote liberalization and internationalization of financial industries in order to induce balance development between the backward financial sector and the fast-growing real estate sector.

Among the four NIEs examined by this paper, Taiwan appears to be pursuing liberalization of the financial sector most earnestly. It has recently dismantled regulations on the foreign-exchange market, including relaxation of restrictions of limits on foreign-currency remittance, and has begun to permit participation of foreign security firms in its market. Furthermore it has taken these measures with *a priori* understanding of how its individual service industries would fare in the face of new international competition. (Taiwan's liberalization of financial sector could also be interpreted as a move that has much to do with the future of Hong Kong as a financial centre after 1997.)

Singapore

As a percentage of its economy, Singapore's service sector is one of the largest of the four NIEs. It commands 70 per cent of Singapore's GDP, a level similar to that of Hong Kong, and provides employment for 70 per cent of the total work force. Of course, this service predominance is largely the result of Singapore being a port-city state.

The significance of Singapore's service sector is well reflected in its trade balances. The deficit it chronically experiences in merchandise trade is compensated by a surplus in service trade. Among the individual service trades, maritime transportation registers a deficit. This deficit is partly compensated by a surplus in trade of travel services which has emerged as a major industry, contributing 16 per cent of the total foreign-exchange earnings and six per cent of GDP over the last five years. The development of travel services in Singapore has much to do with the well-developed civil aviation services (i.e., Singapore Airlines) and the retail distribution network.

From the 1970s, Singapore has been supporting the development of its financial sector as an engine of economic growth. As a result, it is the third largest international financial center in Asia, next to Tokyo and Hong Kong. Its financial sector has experienced two-digit growth rates for the last ten years and commands 23 per cent of GDP and nine per cent of total employment. Within a grand plan to develop Singapore into a "Financial Supermarket" that can provide a wide spectrum of financial services including banking, insurance and securities-related services, the Singaporean government is ready to expand the functions of SIMEX.

Hong Kong

The service sector accounted for 77.5 per cent of Hong Kong's GDP in 1987. Among individual service industries, financial industries and trade-and-commerce industries are the largest. The former produced 17 per cent of GDP in 1987 and the latter 21.7 per cent. As is the case in Singapore, the heavy dependence on service industries in general, and financial and distribution industries in particular, reflects Hong Kong's characteristic as a port-city state.

It is difficult to glimpse at the industry-wide features of Hong Kong's service sector because relevant statistics are not made public. But it is generally understood that Hong Kong records a surplus in trade of services, reaching approximately 15 billion dollars in 1986. The main sources of surplus are the travel and maritime transportation industries. The number of foreign visitors was 4.6 million in 1987 alone, and in terms of tonnage, Hong Kong's fleets are the second largest in the world.

There is little doubt that financial industries such as banking and insurance are critically important to Hong Kong. The development of Hong Kong's insurance industry owes much to the fact that it is a free port and a centre for international trade, which should be reason enough for insurance business to flourish *pari passu* the development of maritime transportation. The development of Hong Kong as an international centre of finance also has much to do with early government deregulations. In spite of these favourable factors, the ability of Hong Kong's financial sector to continue to play a major role, not only for the economy of

Hong Kong but also for other economies in the region, crucially depends on its future after 1997.

The NIEs and the Uruguay Round

Traditionally the NIEs have shown little interest in the issue of liberalization of trade in services. This has been largely dictated by their pattern of economic development that has depended on the export-led industrialization of the manufacturing sector.

In the case of Korea and Taiwan, for example, it was the U.S.'s request for market opening that provided the opportunities for them to pay attention to the issue of service trade. With both countries recording considerable trade surplus with the U.S. in recent years (Korea from the early 1980s and Taiwan from the late 1970s), American requests for greater access to their domestic service markets have been complied with.

By contrast, Hong Kong and Singapore, whose economic development has depended on their roles as centres of international trade (as free ports) and as centres of international finance, have been more conscious of the related issues of service-trade liberalization. Thus, both have endeavoured to nurture service industries such as maritime transportation and travel and air-line services, while continuing efforts to strengthen the manufacturing sector and expand international trading activities. As a result, both countries offer relatively open service markets; a fact that is in their advantage when negotiating with the U.S.

This does not, however, necessarily mean that they are in comfortable positions to actively support the liberalization of trade in services. Except for few service industries, they do not have a clear edge or advantage, particularly *vis-à-vis* the service industries of the industrialized countries. In addition, both Singapore and Hong Kong have to be always conscious of the relative backwardness of service industries in their neighbouring countries.

The NIEs' apparent lukewarm positions concerning liberalization of trade in services therefore stem from their unique economic structures and one should not be surprised by their inactivity concerning these issues at multilateral fora such as the GATT.

Positions Prior to the Launching of the Uruguay Round

At the initial stage of discussions that launched the Uruguay Round, the NIEs started out siding with the position of the developing countries which opposed not only the launching of any new multilateral trade negotiations (besides the GATT work program), but also the inclusion of the issue of service trade in the

Round itself. However, the October 1985 GATT special session provided opportunity for the NIEs to amend their position, and they came out in support of including service trade in the Round. This switch divided the developing countries into those who were "mild" on this issue, including the ASEAN nations as well as most of the NIEs, and those who were "hard line" such as India and Brazil.

Ever since, it has been customary for the NIEs to passively side with the industrialized countries. This was exemplified by the participation of the NIEs in the G-32 Proposal for the GATT Ministerial Declaration at Punta de Este that was prepared mostly on the initiative of developed countries; a point that was amply revealed at various preparatory meetings preceding the Declaration. The G-32 Proposal was more comprehensive in coverage than the G-10 Proposal which had been presented by other developing-countries who were contracting parties of the GATT, particularly on new issues, such as trade in services, or trade-related investment measures.

Stances during the Uruguay Round

The GNS (Group of Negotiations on Services) of the Uruguay Round had discussed five major areas: definition and statistics, broad concepts and principles to govern trade in services, coverage of multilateral rules, existing international arrangements and principles, and measures that encourage or hamper service trade. The NIEs did not actively participate in these discussions as they tried to find a balance between the position of the developed and developing countries. Prior to the Mid-term Review, the developing countries' negotiating position on trade in services had four main elements. First, with respect to liberalization of trade in services, they maintained that economic development should be considered along with the expansion of service trade. Second, they advocated that special treatment of developing countries should be recognized as one of the basic principles of a future multilateral framework of trade in services. Third, they insisted that the multilateral framework should encompass cross-border movements of both labour-intensive services and workers. Finally, the developing countries put forward the proposition that prior to discussions on a multilateral framework, sufficient discussion should be carried out on the problems of multi-national firms and the national objectives of regulations on trade in services.

Throughout the Uruguay Round, the NIEs have maintained a so-called "mild-LDC" position based on a scenario that envisages establishment of a multilateral framework following sufficient discussion. This position yielded the passive postures of the NIEs at the GNS of the Uruguay Round and they made no serious attempt to strengthen their negotiation positions by establishing consultative channels among themselves.

The NIEs and the Montreal Mid-Term Review

In general, the NIEs view the Mid-Term Review accord on trade in services in a favourable light. They tend to think that it represents a balance of interests for both developed and developing countries. What particularly comforted the NIEs was the emphasis on encouraging greater participation of all contracting parties at different stages of economic development so as not to repeat the experience of the low participation of developing countries in Multilateral Trade Negotiations (MTN) codes of the Tokyo Round.

Examples of this middle ground abound. The accord permits that certain sectors, such as infant service industries, could be excluded from negotiations; accommodates varying levels of development in the process of progressive liberalization, by allowing developing countries greater flexibility in terms of opening fewer sectors or fewer types of transactions; and encourages greater participation of the developing countries in service trade liberalization by strengthening domestic services capacity and competitiveness by such methods as active industrial policies and the facilitation of effective markets for service exports of developing countries.

The above breakthrough was not the result of active mediations or negotiations by the NIEs, but rather by compromises struck between the developed and developing countries. The most significant compromise was struck between the exclusion of the principle of rights of establishment (which the industrialized countries, particularly the U.S., supported as one of the "pillar" principles of trade in services) and the inclusion of the principle of special treatment of developing countries (which the industrialized countries objected to on the basis that it would introduce another distortion in the multilateral framework of trade in services). The European Community joined in the compromise by relinquishing its long-standing position on the principle of reciprocity in market opening.

The compromise of the Mid-Term Review agreement on trade in services removed the major blockades to expediting the negotiation process. The agreement on the basic principles has in turn put pressure on the NIEs. It is high time that they formulated more concrete positions concerning the liberalization of trade in services and the necessity of restructuring their domestic service industries.

To be precise, the Mid-Term Review accord on trade in services amounts only to a indicative listing of basic principles for the purpose of negotiations. It is one thing for the NIEs to have a basic framework that they can agree to, but it is quite another to produce rules and principles in formal, contractual language on the basis of that agreement. Furthermore, it is uncertain whether during the course of negotiations that the interest of the NIEs in service trade could be properly represented. Specifically, NIEs may have concerns in two areas. First, it is taken for granted that special treatment of developing countries be included as one of the principles of a multilateral framework on trade in services. But whether or not the principle is applicable to all the service industries of NIEs, or only to certain backward service industries, or even to none of their service industries, remains to be seen. Accordingly, an understanding among the NIEs on how developing countries status is to be applied should be formulated. Second, the stronger part of the NIEs' service sector still consists of labour-intensive industries. The NIEs should therefore endeavour to bring these services to the fore at the negotiations on coverage of a future multilateral framework. For developed countries, the right of establishment is one of the most important issues at service-trade negotiations. It would be interesting to see whether a linkage might emerge at the GNS negotiation table between a guarantee on the free movement of labour and on the right of establishment, and whether the NIEs could play intermediary roles on these issues.

Interests of the NIEs at Future Negotiations on Trade in Services

This paper has reviewed the current status of service sectors in the NIEs and their positions on service trade liberalization as revealed at international fora such as the Uruguay Round. The study has found, first, that the NIEs share a common level of service sector development although there are some significant differences among them; and second, that the NIEs have played a passive role in formulating a multilateral framework for trade in services, thereby implicitly supporting a gradual approach to institution-alizing the liberalization of trade in services.

Such common features may not be seen in the future. This does not by itself mean that each NIE would go its own way at future negotiations on trade in services, but that the expedited negotiations, driven forward by the Mid-Term Review accord, will inevitably compel the NIEs, both as a group and individually, to formulate positions to present at multilateral trade negotiations. They can no longer postpone the day of decision or follow the "middle-of-the-road" non-position of the past.

In view of these new developments, one can classify the pending issues of the NIEs into two categories. First, for some years to come, there will remain the bilateral pressures from Korea's and Taiwan's industrialized trading partners to open their service markets, with or without a multilateral framework on rules of trade and liberalization. One should note that there is a common understanding that the liberalization of trade in services should be pursued within a multilateral framework, otherwise, trade in services will be hopelessly distorted by all kinds of bilateral or plurilateral arrangements. And that the NIEs lack of international competitiveness in trade in services was the major reason why they came to support the launching of the Uruguay Round that included service trade as a major issue. Therefore, the first issue for NIEs, as a group or individually, is how to reconcile bilateral and multilateral negotiations. Second, it is of utmost importance for the NIEs to come up with proposals to contribute to the GATT negotiations on service trade and they can do this by first formulating their own positions at the GNS negotiations.

Bilateral Pressures for Market Opening

From the mid-1980s, the U.S. has persistently requested the opening of service markets in Korea and Taiwan and to a lesser degree, Singapore. The result of this pressure has been that the liberalization of service markets in these countries has commenced although they may not yet be sufficient for the interests of the U.S.

If bilateral requests for market opening were made on specific trading partners under circumstances where there does not exist any generally practised rules or generally recognized multilateral framework for trade in services, it would directly conflict with the international trade principle of reciprocity. Furthermore, bilateral pressures put forward during a period when multilateral trade negotiations, such as the Uruguay Round, were launched or when such negotiations such as the GNS were in progress, weaken the foundations of such multilateral ventures.

It should be noted that some of NIEs reversed their initial, negative positions concerning the launching of the Uruguay Round that encompassed the issue of service trade because they were led to believe that doing so would ameliorate the pressure for bilateral arrangements and provide an environment conducive to multilateral negotiations on liberalization of trade in services. However, we have already seen that in the absence of a multilateral framework, pressures for market opening of services are mounting and it would not miss the mark too widely if one foresaw this trend to continue until the final accord is reached at the GNS negotiation.

Although one may support the idea of bilateral market opening as an alternative to multilateral liberalization, the international trading community would be better served if such trend were restrained. Furthermore, if bilateral arrangements were made, it should be done so with the understanding that if there were any conflicts between the bilateral arrangement and a future multilateral framework, the latter would take precedence.

Future Positions of the NIEs at the GNS Negotiations

It is very likely that in the future negotiations at the GNS, the NIEs will take a common stance on the basic framework (i.e. "umbrella" framework) of principles and rules on trade in services and their liberalization. But, it is equally probable that they will offer positions unique to each country when the negotiation moves to sector-specific issues.

Multilateral Framework of Principles and Rules

Concerning the multilateral framework of rules and principles for trade in services, the NIEs would have common interest in claiming the following four points: first, that the liberalization of trade in services should be progressive, yet, gradual; second, if the situation justifies it, the principles of special treatment should be applied to the NIEs as well as to the developing countries, particularly when liberalization of trade in specific services is on the agenda; third, labour-intensive services should also constitute an integral part of any international scheme for liberalization of trade in services; and fourth, before recognizing the rights of establishment, due considerations should be taken concerning the development of individual countries.

Note that the above set of positions on trade in services more or less encompasses positions advocated by both developed and developing countries. That is, NIEs might be ready to negotiate on a formula that would not only guarantee the right of establishment and the free movement of labour in principle, but also recognize its reality in full. The actual situation is that while developing countries strongly support the inclusion of free movement of labour (to ensure the liberalization of labour-intensive service trades) as a prerequisite to any serious negotiations on service trade, they still have doubts on the arguments for rights of establishments, particularly in connection with the establishments of multi-national firms. The exact opposite positions are taken by most of the industrialized countries.

Therefore, there might be room for a contribution by the NIEs in preserving the momentum generated by the Mid-Term Review accord. This could be done by the NIEs playing a more active role presenting their own positions at the GNS negotiations. In order to do so, it may be necessary for the NIEs to formulate a grand, middle-of-the-road framework, that encompasses toned down features of the negotiation positions of both developed and developing countries.

Sector-Specific Rules of Service Trade

When negotiations commence on questions of liberalization of individual service trade, it would be hard for the NIEs to develop common positions. A good example is the liberalization of trade in financial services. In financial services, Korea is clearly at a disadvantage, but Hong Kong and Singapore have undisputed international competitiveness. As a result, the former is bound to take a passive position at best, while the latter two will likely play active roles in promoting progress.

Special Treatment of Developing Countries

For the NIEs, the central question regarding the special treatment of developing countries, if included as one of the principles of multilateral framework of trade in services, would be whether or not the principle would be applicable to themselves. One cannot safely assume it, particularly under the present circumstances where NIEs are frequently subject to requests of "graduation" (i.e., they are asked to duly play their part in strengthening the multilateral trading system by opening their own markets).

An alternative that has often been suggested is to establish the concept of a "developing country in services". This concept would be applied to any country if the development of an individual service industry is judged to lag behind. That is, the right question to ask concerning liberalization of trade in services should not be whether a country's macro-feature appears to justify across-the-board liberalization but, whether or not particular service industries have developed enough to sustain the liberalization of its trade. This concept would provide a breakthrough to GNS negotiations, where there still lingers elements of doubt simply because development is not even among individual service industries in different countries. The past experience in the trade of manufactured goods where structural problems of a given individual manufacturing industry were enough to justify maintenance, or even introduction of trade barriers, should not be repeated. All parties involved would be better off if an under-standing on a multilateral framework on trade in services was arrived at.

Table 1
Trade Balance of Services of Korea and Taiwan
(Unit: million U.S. dollars)

		1981	1982	1983	1984	1985	1986	1987
Korea	Credits	6598.1	7476.3	7178.7	7316.3	6664.4	8051.7	10010.0
	Debits	8116.5	8030.5	7613.3	8193.9	8110.5	8679.2	9032.6
	Balance	-1518.4	-554.2	-434.6	-877.6	-1446.1	-627.5	977.4
Taiwan	Credits	2545	2524	2558	2775	2115	3869	
	Debits	-3468	-3745	-4436	-5513	-5679	-6194	
	Balance	923	-1221	-1878	-2738	-3564	-2325	

Notes: Direct-investment incomes are included in the Korean statistics.

Sources: Economic Planning Board, *Main Indicators of the Korean Economy 4th Quarter 1988.*
E.I.U., Taiwan, Country Profile, 1988-89.

Table 2
Asian NIEs and Liberalization of Trade in Services

	Korea	Singapore	Hong Kong	Taiwan
Service Sectors with International Competitiveness	Labor-related services (construction, nurse, medical services)	Travel services civil aviation, banking	Travel services insurance, banking, maritime transportation	Travel Services
Areas of Future Interests	Financial services: deregulations	Financial services: A Center of International finance	Financial services	Financial services: coordination with growth of real economy
Basic Stance on Liberalization of Trade in Services	Gradual, step-wise liberalization	the same	the same	the same
Positions at GNS Negotiation	Priority on multilateral rules & principles with sufficient discussions	the same	the same	Non-Contracting party of GATT
Degree of Liberalization of Service Trade	limited	Practically no restriction	the same	limited
Bilateral Pressure of Market Opening	High Pressures from the U.S.	little	little	Pressures from the U.S.

Table 3

Industrial Structure of the Asian NIEs

(Unit: %)

	Year	Agri-culture	Mining	Manufac-turing	Electricity & Gas	Construc-tion	Trade & Commerce	Transport-ation & Telecom-munication	Banking	Other Services	GATT-[1] Definition Services
Korea	1970	26.9	1.5	20.9	1.6	5.5	18.3	6.8	5.9	12.6	50.7
	1980	15.8	1.3	28.0	2.2	9.1	17.5	6.1	7.5	12.5	54.9
	1987	11.4	1.2	30.3	3.2	8.2	16.6	8.2	8.0	12.8	57.1
Taiwan	1970	15.5	1.4	33.5	2.5	3.9	14.8	6.0	2.6	19.8	49.6
	1980	7.8	1.0	41.5	2.6	6.3	13.4	6.0	3.9	17.5	49.7
	1987	5.3	0.5	43.5	3.8	4.2	14.2	6.0	2.9	19.6	50.7
Hong Kong	1970	2.0	0.2	30.9	2.0	4.2	19.6	7.6	14.9	18.6	66.9
	1980	0.8	0.2	23.8	1.3	6.7	20.4	7.5	22.8	16.5	75.2
	1987	0.5	0.1	21.9	3.0	4.5	21.9	8.4	17.0	22.7	77.5
Singapore	1970	2.3	0.4	19.7	2.8	7.3	30.2	11.2	14.2	11.7	77.6
	1980	1.4	0.4	29.0	2.3	7.0	24.3	15.0	16.9	3.7	69.2
	1987	0.5	0.2	28.6	2.3	6.7	17.6	13.8	28.8	3.2	70.7

Source: ADB, *Key Indicators of Developing Member Countries of ADB.*
Note: 1) Share excluding those of agriculture, mining and manufacturing.

Table 4
Industrial Structure of the Asian NIEs by Employment
(Unit: %)

	Agriculture Forestry & Fishery	Mining & Manufacturing	Utilities	Construction	Services Commerces	Services Transportation	Services Finance & Business	Services Other Services	Other
Korea									
1975	45.7	19.1	–	4.4	–	–	–	30.9	35.2
1985	24.9	24.4	–	6.1	–	–	–	44.5	50.6
1987	21.9	28.1	–	5.6	–	–	–	44.3	50.0
Taiwan									
1975	30.4	28.6	0.4	5.9	14.1	5.7	–	14.9	41.0
1985	17.5	34.0	0.5	7.0	18.0	5.2	–	17.9	48.5
1987	15.3	35.4	0.4	6.9	17.9	5.3	–	18.3	49.3
Singapore									
1970	3.5	22.3	1.2	6.6	23.4	12.1	4.0	26.8	74.2
1985	0.7	25.7	0.7	8.9	23.3	10.1	8.7	21.5	74.3
1987	0.9	26.8	0.6	7.7	23.4	10.1	8.9	21.5	72.3

	Manufacturing	Building & construction (1)	Financing, insurance, real estate, business (2)	Wholesale, retail & commerces (3)	Restaurants & hotels (4)	(1) + (2) / (3) + (4)	Other
Hong Kong							
1982	44.5	4.3	8.7	18.8	8.4	35.9	15.3
1983	41.0	13.4	9.8	21.8	8.5	53.5	13.4

Sources: Korea E.P.B., *Korean Economic Indicators*, 1988. 4/4; Republic of China, *Taiwan Statistical Data Book*, 1988; Singapore, *Yearbook of Statistics Singapore*, 1987; and E.I.U. *Hong Kong, Macau, Country Profile*, 1988, 1989.

Table 5
Balance of Payments of Asian NIEs
(Unit: million U.S. dollars)

		1974	1980	1985	1986	1987
Korea	Exports (f.o.b)	4515	17214	26442	33913	46244
	Imports (f.o.b)	-6452	-21598	-26461	-29707	-38585
	Trade Balance	-1937	-4384	-19	4206	7659
	Current Account Balance	-2023	-5321	-887	4618	9854
	Overall Balance	-1094	-1890	-1255	1700	5202
Singapore	Exports (f.o.b)	5547	18200	21533	21336	27277
	Imports (f.o.b)	-7764	-22401	-24361	-23402	-29817
	Trade Balance	-2217	-4201	-2828	-2066	-2540
	Current Account Balance	-1022	-1563	-3	542	539
	Overall Balance	295	662	1337	555	1106
Taiwan	Exports (f.o.b)	5592	19575	30466	39492	53224
	Imports (f.o.b)	-6422	-19498	-19296	-22635	-32442
	Trade Balance	-830	77	11170	16857	20782
	Current Account Balance	-1113	-913	9195	16217	18172
	Overall Balance	41	1092	7040	24104	31822
Hong Kong	Exports (f.o.b)	6027 [1]	19730	30184	35440	48476
	Imports (f.o.b)	-6766 [1]	-22409	29705	35366	48465
	Trade Balance	-739	-2679	479	74	11
	Current Account Balance	N.A.	N.A.	N.A.	N.A.	N.A.
	Overall Balance					

1. The amount for 1975 as 1974 figure not available. Current account balance also not available.
Source: Asian Development Bank, *Key indicators of Developing Member countries of ADB*, July 1988.

Table 6
Service Trade of the Asian NIEs
(Unit: million SDR)

		Maritime Transportation		Other Transportation		Travel		Construction		Management Services	
		credit	debit	credit	debit	credit	debit	credit	debit	credit	debit
Korea	1983	1,384	-401	885	-1,341	557	-520	1,769	-139	118	-229
	1985	1,304	-514	746	-1,324	767	-598	977	-212	196	-176
	1987	1,388	-621	700	-1,507	1,706	-478	783	-151	248	-136
Taiwan[1]	1983	293	-1,008	506	-860	990	-1,229	N.A.	N.A.	N.A.[2]	N.A.
	1985	606	-954	538	-1,089	963	-1,999	–	–	–	–
	1987	1,137	-1,594	692	-1,439	1,619	-2,641	–	–	–	–
Singapore	1981	652	-1,363	2,089	N.A.	1,866	-525	N.A.	N.A.	N.A.	N.A.
	1985	672	-1,485	1,929	N.A.	1,635	-604	–	–	–	–
	1987	680	-1,531	1,501	N.A.	1,714	-612	–	–	–	–

1. US$ million   2. N.A.: not available

Source: IMF, *Balance of Payments Statistics*, Yearbook, 1988.
For Taiwan, source is *Industry of Free China*, Oct. 1988.

Trade in Financial Services and the Uruguay Round

Dr. Edward P. Neufeld
Executive Vice President
The Royal Bank of Canada

I.   Introduction

At the Mid-term Review of the Uruguay Round in Montreal in December 1988, the Trade Negotiations Committee (TNC) agreed on a very broad conceptual framework of principles and rules for a multilateral agreement on trade in services. These principles and rules were developed and negotiated over a two-year period by the Group of Negotiations on Services (GNS). An attempt to determine the applicability and implications of this broad framework for specific service sectors has only recently begun. Exploratory meetings on the applicability of this framework for the construction and telecommunications sectors were scheduled by the GNS for June 1989 in Geneva, followed by similar meetings on the transportation and tourism sectors in July, and professional services and financial services (including insurance) in September.

In the hope of facilitating the future work of the GNS on financial services, this paper provides an overview of the more relevant issues in financial services trade, and then attempts to provide a preliminary assessment of the applicability and implications of the broad skeletal framework for services agreed upon in Montreal for a multilateral agreement on trade in financial services. In addition, this paper offers some suggestions on how the skeletal framework for trade in services might be refined, broadened and built upon in order to further increase its applicability to trade in financial services.

II. Some Key Dimensions of Foreign Trade in Financial Services

Entry and Establishment

Since the provisions of most types of financial services require some form of physical presence on the part of the supplier, the right of entry and establishment of a physical presence in a foreign country is usually a prerequisite to foreign trade in financial services. Depending upon the financial service being supplied, such physical presence could take any number of forms, including a branch, subsidiary, representative office or even an automatic teller machine.

The right of entry and establishment in most countries is usually subject to various types of approval criteria, regulations and impediments. For example, most countries require that a potential foreign entrant satisfy specific prudential criteria such as capital adequacy and other financial fitness tests. Many countries also apply a reciprocity criteria before determining whether or not to allow in a supplier from another country. In addition, the choice of presence established (e.g., subsidiary, branch, agency or joint venture) may be limited by regulation.

Other common obstacles facing foreign suppliers seeking entry and establishment include: general regulations/policies covering foreign direct investment in all sectors, specific regulations/policies restricting new investment by foreigners in all or parts of the financial sector, restrictions on the foreign acquisition of equity in existing indigenous financial services entities, regulations separating different types of financial services which thereby effectively bar foreign suppliers that do not satisfy a particular ownership-corporate structure, and geographical or numerical restrictions on branching.

Business Powers and Flexibility of Diversification

In addition to the right of entry and establishment, a second key set of prerequisites to foreign trade in financial services is business powers. Regulations affecting business powers and the flexibility of diversification have a major influence over the quantity and range of financial services traded, and the efficiency with which they are produced and delivered.

The regulation and range of business powers can vary substantially across countries. For example, at one extreme, national regulations may permit and encourage "universal" type financial services suppliers that can engage in all or most types of financial services. At the other extreme, national regulations can completely separate traditional commercial banking, securities related services, trusts and insurance activities and/or may separate activities within one of these categories (e.g., primary market activities versus trading in secondary markets).

Excessive regulations on business powers adversely affect the quantity of and efficiency with which financial services are supplied by both domestic and foreign suppliers of financial services. Moreover, differences across countries in regulations governing business powers can act as barriers to entry of foreign suppliers of financial services or can impede the operations of established foreign suppliers. For example, suppliers from countries that permit and encourage universal type financial services suppliers may face barriers or impediments to entry into countries that enforce a legal separation of various types of financial services suppliers.

Market Access

Once entry and establishment are achieved and business powers are defined, foreign suppliers of financial services may still face impediments to accessing certain markets within a country. Such impediments can take numerous forms including numerical or geographical limits on branching by foreign suppliers, restrictions on dealing with the general public at the retail level and ceilings on the share of business allocated to foreign suppliers in particular markets. Market access by foreign suppliers might also be restricted by non-regulatory factors such as government favouritism, local cartels, or tightly-knit corporate groupings.

Cross-border Transactions

Some types of financial services trade can take place when the supplier and customer reside on different sides of a national border, and hence, an established physical present is not necessary. For example, some portfolio-related transactions, such as securities purchases and sales, may be possible via telephone, wire services or mail. The quantity and range of such financial services trade will be affected by tax, regulatory and other impediments and barriers.

The creation of barriers/impediments to such cross-border transactions are frequently motivated by balance of payments concerns. Therefore, such barriers/impediments often take the form of various types of foreign exchange controls. For example, such controls can prohibit or limit domestic dealing in foreign securities in an attempt to restrict capital outflows and take downward pressure off the domestic currency exchange rate. Alternatively, such controls may restrict certain types of capital inflows, such as foreign purchases of domestic securities, so as to slow currency appreciation (and/or limit foreign ownership). In addition to outright exchange controls, discriminatory turnover taxes can be imposed on domestic transactions in foreign securities or central bank deposit requirements can be imposed on purchases of foreign securities.

In addition, barriers to cross-border financial services trans-actions can arise from differences in regulatory/prudential systems across countries. For example, legal compliance with differing national disclosure criteria and accounting practices can some-times prove too onerous and costly for selling securities in differing regulatory jurisdictions. Regulatory/prudential limits may also be put on the share of institutional investors' portfolios that can be invested in foreign securities. Additionally, regulatory restric-tions on the corporate structure and types of assets held in collective investments (such as mutual funds, unit trusts and investment trusts) may so differ across countries making multiple compliance difficult.

Domestic Ownership/Control

An issue related to entry and establishment concerns the optimal degree of foreign ownership and control of a country's financial services sector. In most countries, by far the largest share of local financial services institutions is still owned by nationals. While increased foreign participation can create healthy competition and improve the efficiency of national financial services sectors, governments and regulators will likely maintain some interest in ensuring that the majority share of local financial services institutions remains in the hands of nationals in order to better ensure the effectiveness of monetary, balance-of-payments and regulatory policies as well as for other national policy reasons. In addition, there might be concern that too much foreign ownership of the financial services sector could leave a country vulnerable to extraterritorial actions by foreign governments.

Supervisory/Prudential Regulations

Some degree of supervisory/prudential regulations exists in all countries in order to safeguard the solvency, stability and integrity of the financial system. Such regulations typically cover capital adequacy, deposit insurance, corporate governance, ownership policy, business powers, conflicts of interest, self-dealing, and disclosure, amongst others. While the purpose of such regulations is prudential, some can also have the unintended effect of restricting/impeding market access by foreign supplies/suppliers of financial services.

III. Core Principles on which Entry, Establishment, Business Powers and Market Access could be Based

As the previous section indicated, the key prerequisites to trade in financial services include entry and establishment, business powers, and market access. Therefore, among the most important and potentially far-reaching principles and rules that could make up a future multilateral agreement on trade in financial services are those that determine the availability of these prerequisites. This section briefly considers the strengths and weaknesses of three alternative principles on which the right of entry and establishment, business powers and market access could be based. These three principles are National Treatment, Equivalent Access and Home Country Rule.

National Treatment

The Principle of National Treatment implies that foreign supplies/suppliers of financial services in a given country are treated on the same basis as indigenous supplies/suppliers of financial services in that same country.

On the surface, National Treatment would appear to be equitable within a given country and supportive of foreign trade in financial services. However, situations can arise where the strict application of National Treatment can be used to deny entry and establishment rights to foreign suppliers. For example, when regulations or policies differ across countries, financial institutions from a particular regulatory/policy environment in their home country may find themselves ineligible for entry into a foreign country due to their corporate or ownership structure, even though financial institutions from the foreign country are able to enter the home country markets. This can happen even though both countries apply the principle of National Treatment.

The varying degrees of legal separation of different types of financial services activities across countries is only one of many examples where differences in regulatory systems can cause trade and competitive inequities, even if all regulatory authorities apply the principle of National Treatment. Another major present day example is the restriction on interstate branching in the U.S. which applies to both indigenous and foreign financial institutions in the U.S., while U.S. financial institutions do not usually face such geographical branching restrictions abroad.

In summary, when differences in national regulatory/policy environments exist across countries, the application of the principle of National Treatment to foreign suppliers, which on the surface would appear to be equitable, can in fact cause trade impediments and competitive inequities. Such impediments can take the form of barriers to entry and/or restrictions on operating freedom.

Equivalent Access/Reciprocity

Under the principle of Equivalent Access, supplies/suppliers of financial services in a foreign country are treated on an equivalent basis to which their respective countries of origin treat supplies/ suppliers from the foreign country.

Equivalent Access would appear to be equitable across countries (although not necessarily within countries). Moreover, this principle could be used as tool by a given government to encourage further liberalization of trade in financial services by offering more liberal treatment to foreign supplies/suppliers in the domestic market in return for more liberal treatment of indigenous supplies/suppliers operating abroad.

On the negative side, the principle of Equivalent Access could reduce negotiations for and agreements on trade in financial services to numerous different bilateral negotiations and agreements, which could be a step backward for multilateralism. Moreover, the principle of Equivalent Access could be used as a tool for protectionism whereby new foreign financial services are stripped of their existing rights of entry and business powers on the basis that their home countries have more restrictive regulatory environments.

Home Country Rule

The principle of Home Country Rule implies that a supplier of financial services is allowed to operate in a foreign country (the "host" country) under the rules of its country of origin (its "home" country).

The positive implications of this principle are that it would encourage the liberalization of financial services and trade in financial services as each country competes to become the most attractive regulatory environment for financial institutions to set up their head offices. There would be an evolution across countries towards a common denominator of least regulations. As long as this common denominator is still prudential, then financial services efficiency and trade in financial services will have improved.

On the negative side, such potential competition among countries to be the least regulated environment could introduce potentially destabilizing elements into some national financial systems and/or the international financial system. On more practical grounds, the vast differences that presently exist across national regulatory environments, among developed countries, but even much more so between developed and less developed countries, would seem to suggest that attempting to establish a multilateral agreement based on the principle of Home Country Rule would be extremely difficult. Therefore, prerequisites for the practical and prudential implementation of the principle of Home Country Rule, probably include a reasonable degree of homogeneity of prudential/regulatory systems across countries and/or a common agreement across countries on minimum acceptable prudential/regulatory standard.

Strengths and Weaknesses of the Three Core Principles

Each of the principles of National Treatment, Equivalent Access and Home Country Rule has its strengths and weaknesses. Each offers a different basis and approach towards the liberalization of trade in financial services as well as varying degrees of competitive equity and fairness. However, the principle of National Treatment can create barriers to entry and impediments to the operations of financial institutions that come from countries with more liberalized financial services sectors. Moreover, this principle can cause competitive inequities in that it allows foreigners full freedom to compete for market share in the more liberalized countries, while not ensuring that foreign countries reciprocate. The principle of Equivalent Access can be used as a tool for encouraging liberalization abroad, but also has the potential to degenerating into a tool for bilateralism and protectionism. Home Country Rule has the major weakness of being impractical to implement over the short- to medium-term in light of the vast differences in existing supervisory/prudential systems across countries.

As a consequence of the differing advantages and disadvantages offered by these principles, countries tend to align themselves with the principle that best suits their regulatory interests. In the case of financial services, the more liberalized countries tend to support Equivalent Access or possibly Home Country Rule, while the least liberalized tend towards National Treatment. For example, the U.S., which, among the major countries, has a relatively high degree of regulatory separation of financial services and restricts inter-state banking, advocates the principle of National Treatment which is embodied in their International Banking Act of 1978. For much the same reason, Japan in practice has also been an advocate of National Treatment. In contrast, the European Community and Canada, which take a more universal view of financial services, have a stronger interest in supporting the principle of Equivalent Access to ensure that their domestic financial institutions are not shut out of or are operationally-constrained in foreign markets.

However, it is worth noting that National Treatment, Equivalent Access and Home Country Rule need not be mutually exclusive principles. In particular, if all countries agreed to implement common regulations and supervisory standards, the application of any one of these three principles would also imply the *de facto* application of the other two principles (everything else being the same). Similarly, the gradual harmonization of regulatory/supervisory standards would imply a gradual convergence of all three principles in practice. While supervisory reporting relationships might initially differ, once common regulations are established, countries would have an interest in agreeing on a single reporting relationship for efficiency's sake.

It is also worth pointing out that in an environment of harmonized regulations across countries, many of the weaknesses of these principles would be eliminated. The principle of National Treatment would not by itself cause barriers to entry or operational impediments. The principle of Equivalent Access would not degenerate to bilateralism or protectionism since regulatory harmonization would tend to imply equivalent access without the need for protectionist threats to special bilateral agreements. Regulatory harmonization would also eliminate the major impracticalities of Home Country Rule.

Therefore, regulatory harmonization would appear to have the potential to contribute to a convergence in the self-interests in trade in financial services of differing countries. Consequently, such harmonization could greatly contribute to the achievement of more liberalized and equitable multilateral trade in financial services.

IV. Current Issues and Trends

This section briefly outlines some of the important current issues and trends in financial services trade that will likely play a major role in shaping and determining the success or failure of the negotiations for a multilateral agreement for trade in financial services. These current issues include: the differences across countries in the degree of regulatory separation of financial services, the global trend towards universal-type financial institutions, the concerns of the less developed countries (LDCs), and the problem of defining financial services in a practical way.

Varying Degrees of Regulatory Separation of Financial Services

One of the more controversial current issues that the GNS will need to tackle is the difference across countries in their degree of regulatory separation of different types of financial services. The issue is a critical one because of the wide-spread practice of the principle of National Treatment, which, as explained in the previous section, can cause barriers to entry and restrictions on the operations of foreign supplies/suppliers of financial services when such regulatory differences exist. At one extreme, national regulations may permit "universal" regulatory differences. At another extreme, national regulations may permit "universal" type financial services suppliers that can engage in all or most types of financial services including traditional commercial banking, trust business, securities and insurance activities. And yet at another extreme, national regulations can completely separate these types of activities and/or may separate activities within one of these categories (e.g., primary market activities versus trading in secondary markets).

The kinds of regulatory separations across countries and the justifications for these are not consistent. For example, in the U.S., banks are allowed to engage in the trust business, but not the insurance or securities business. In contrast, in Canada, for years banks have not been allowed to engage in either the trust or insurance business but, unlike those in the U.S. or Japan, can now engage in domestic securities activities. In Germany, for years banks have been allowed to engage in the trust, securities and insurance business.

The various justifications for regulatory separation of financial services are frequently based on "conflicts of interest" type arguments. However, the inconsistencies in regulatory separation across countries would tend to suggest that opinions on what constitutes potential conflicts of interest vary considerably across countries. More importantly, as has been demonstrated in different ways across countries, such concerns about conflicts of interest are either overblown or are "regulatable" without resorting to the extreme of legal separation. This measure can adversely affect the quantity and variety of an efficiency with which financial services are supplied by both domestic and foreign suppliers. What has been conjectured to be a conflict of interest situation in one country has been proven in practice not to be the case in other countries.

The Case of Banking versus Securities

Among the most publicized of these inconsistent regulatory practices has been the varying degrees of separation of traditional commercial banking and securities activities. In the U.S. and Japan, commercial banking and securities-related activities are largely separated by the Glass-Steagall Act and Article 65, respectively. In contrast, in much of Europe where regulations allow for universal-type financial institutions, financial services suppliers can engage in both commercial banking and securities activities (and in some countries, insurance and trust business). In Canada, commercial banks can own subsidiaries that engage in securities activities and will soon be granted some in-house securities powers.

Foreign commercial banks that are granted entry into European countries and Canada, including those from the U.S. and Japan, so far have been allowed to engage in securities activities either directly or through subsidiaries. For the most part, the European and Canadian authorities have voluntarily applied the principle of National Treatment to foreign banks (although the principle of Equivalent Access is embodied in Canadian banking legislation). In other words, once foreign financial institutions are admitted into the universal banking countries of Europe and Canada, they are treated largely on the same basis as indigenous financial institutions.

It is also true that, in the U.S. and Japan, most of the respective regulatory authorities have voluntarily applied the principle of National Treatment to foreign financial institutions entering their jurisdictions. However, while U.S. and Japanese banks (and securities companies) are allowed to engage in a broad range of securities activities in the numerous European countries with universal banking systems, and in Canada through securities company subsidiaries, securities companies from such European countries and Canada, because many of these are bank-related, are effectively barred from entering the securities market in the U.S. and Japan because of Glass-Steagall and Article 65. The Japanese authorities have shown some flexibility in recent years by allowing some foreign bank-owned subsidiaries to engage in securities activities if these subsidiaries are 50 per cent owned by non-bank interests. However, this compromise has proved inadequate and impractical for many foreign universal banks and securities companies, including the major Canadian securities companies, most of which are much more than 50 per cent owned by Canadian banks.

The arguments for separating commercial banking and securities business include the opinion that these two types of activities are fundamentally different, with securities activities subject to more volatility and risk than commercial banking.

Therefore, it is argued that allowing commercial banks to engage in securities activities would tend to increase the riskiness of the commercial banking system. Such increased riskiness might compromise monetary policy and/or increase the costs to taxpayers for losses incurred in securities activities, since most governments provide varying degrees of guarantees on bank deposits. Additionally, there is some concern that a bank involved in a significant depositor/creditor relationship with a corporate customer may develop conflicts of interest across business activities. For example, a bank marketing the securities of a corporate customer, with which it also has a significant depositor/ creditor relationship, may be tempted to conceal negative information about the corporation from investors, and thereby compromise investor interests.

In contrast to these arguments, in the universal banking countries underwriting and trading securities are seen as a natural extension of traditional commercial banking (i.e., deposit-taking and lending). According to this view, efficiency would dictate that a financial institution should be in a position to offer an array of financing alternatives to a corporate client in search of capital, and that same financial institution should be able to offer that same corporate client a variety of alternatives for managing and investing its cash-flow and surplus earnings. Moreover, the fact that universal banks can engage in many types of financial services is perceived as lowering these banks' overall risk and vulnerability because of business diversification and the likelihood that losses in any one activity will be more than offset by stronger performances in other activities.

Recent history would tend to support the advocates of the more universal approach to financial services. The securitization of loans (e.g., the development of new tradeable syndicated loans, the trading of outstanding traditional loans on secondary markets and the repackaging of entire loan portfolios into tradeable securities) tend to support the argument that investment banking is a natural extension of commercial banking, and has increasingly blurred the distinction between the two. Furthermore, recent history would suggest that universal-type financial institutions are no more risky (and, arguably, are more sound) than banks that have tended to specialize in traditional commercial banking. Moreover, there is no evidence that universal-type institutions have compromised investor interests by withholding information on securities issues of corporate customers with which such institutions also have significant commercial banking interests.

The continued separation of commercial banking and investment banking in the U.S., which, in turn, has heavily influenced regulatory policy in Japan, is an anomaly. U.S. banks are among the most active underwriters and traders in international securities markets outside the U.S. Hence, there would appear to be at least some inconsistency in arguing that regulatory separation of commercial and investment banking makes good sense at home, while not enforcing such regulatory separation on U.S. institutions operating abroad.

In any case, such domestic regulatory/policy practices which continue to enforce an artificial separation between financial services impede the liberalization of trade in financial services.

The Trend Towards Universal Financial Services Institutions

The financial services sector continues to undergo revolutionary changes due to technological break-throughs, financial innovations, internationalization, deregulation and re-regulation. As a consequence, an effective multilateral agreement on trade in financial services will need to be forward-looking, broad in scope and flexible.

Among the more salient global trends in financial services is the trend towards universal type financial institutions. Universal-type financial institutions have for many years been part of the financial landscape in a number of continental European countries. Off the Continent, beginning in the early 1980s, the distinction between commercial banking and investment banking became increasingly blurred with the securitization of loans. The "Big Bank" in the UK in 1986 and other changes have moved the UK to a universal financial system where banks can engage in commercial banking, investment banking, as well as trust and insurance activities. In Canada, commercial banks were allowed to own securities subsidiaries beginning in 1987, and further deregulation is expected to soon allow banks to participate in the trust and insurance sectors. In the European Community (EC), "Project 1992" and its "Second Banking Directive," which is based on the mutual acceptance of Home Country Rule, have set in motion forces that are expected to eventually result in a virtually fully-integrated EC financial market based largely on universal-type financial institutions.

Despite the separation of commercial banking and securities activities in the U.S. and Japan, "commercial banks" in these countries have for a long time had some degree of power to underwrite government securities. Furthermore, bank-related financial institutions from the U.S. are among the more active underwriters and traders in international securities markets. Moreover, regulatory authorities in the U.S. and Japan appear to be gradually realizing that the traditional arguments for separating commercial banking and securities activities may not have a sound basis. As a consequence, the effectiveness of the Glass-Steagall Act in the U.S. and Article 65 in Japan are being slowly eroded by both market forces and gradual deregulation. However, in this regard, the pace of deregulation in the U.S. and Japan lags well behind the rest of the developed world.

In the less developed world, particularly in Asia, local financial markets are becoming increasingly developed and sophisticated. A number of governments in South-East Asia are in the process of substantially deregulating local financial markets and granting local financial institutions greater business freedoms. Some LDCs like Taiwan appear to be in the early stages of a system of universal-type financial institutions.

In general, there appears to be considerable evidence of a natural evolution and global trend towards universal-type financial institutions, and this will need to be taken into account in the formulation of any lasting multilateral agreement in trade in services.

Less Developed Country (LDC) Concerns

In general, LDCs have been among the least enthusiastic about the prospects of a multilateral agreement covering trade in services. A number of LDC governments have expressed the view that liberalization of trade in services is from their perspective a situation of "all give and little take." These LDCs have argued that for the more tradeable high value-added services (including financial services), which tend to be technology and education intensive, LDCs are at a major comparative disadvantage because of their early stage of economic development. Moreover, these LDC governments argue that in the case of labour-intensive services like construction, where LDCs have a comparative advantage, existing immigration regulations/policies in the major developed countries are likely to impede genuine trade in services liberalization.

Therefore, many LDCs are expected to seek particularly special treatment in any multilateral agreement covering trade in technology, education intensive services, and financial services.

The governments of some LDCs argue that their indigenous financial services sectors are at the "infant industry" stage of development, and as such will need temporary protection from foreign competition if they are to be given a chance to fully develop to a competitive level. However, recent history has shown that the protection of so-called infant industries can have high hidden costs, including the indirect subsidization of the less-than-efficient infant industry by the rest of the economy, the loss of foreign investment and related employment and income, and the high risk that the infant industry never become a strong or competitive "adult" industry because of over-protection. Many LDCs, particularly the indebted ones, simply cannot afford these costs.

In a number of LDCs the financial services sector is not only used as a vehicle to implement monetary policy, but also as a tool with which to implement the government's economic development plans and strategies via government influence over credit allocation and hence the allocation of real resources. Despite the disastrous results that such credit allocation policies have had in many countries, some LDC governments may be unwilling to relinquish such control over their financial services sectors to market forces.

On more emotional ground, some within the LDCs feel that the opening of their fledgling financial services sectors to potential foreign domination would be tantamount to a reversion back to colonialism.

A number of LDCs, particularly those with foreign debt problems, are experiencing severe balance-of-payments problems and may find it difficult to liberalize the cross-border flow of capital until these balance-of-payments difficulties are overcome. This argument may have some validity over a short- to medium-term time horizon, until such LDCs are able to implement the policies needed to stabilize their balance-of-payments situations. However, the argument would apply only to cross-border financial services transactions.

In any case, regardless of the validity or lack of validity of these arguments, many of these LDC concerns will need to be seriously taken into account in the negotiations toward a potential multilateral agreement for trade in financial services, if only for political/practical reasons.

The Asian LDCs

A number of these LDC concerns may apply far less to many of the less developed countries of Asia, particularly South-East Asia. Many have witnessed rapid growth and increasing sophistication of their financial services sectors in recent years. The admittance of more foreign financial institutions together with the further liberalization of local markets would more likely accelerate the growth and development of indigenous financial institutions. Increased local participation by foreign financial institutions could accelerate the development of short-term and inter-bank money markets, offer new clearing technologies, introduce innovative financial techniques and, in general, contribute to increased efficiency of the local financial services sector and the economy. Moreover, fuelled by their substantial trade surpluses, banks from many of these South-East Asian LDCs are increasingly applying for entry and establishment rights in the major developed countries. Therefore, it may be in the interests of many of these Asian countries to take a more forward-looking and liberal view of multilateral trade in financial services than their LDC counterparts in other parts of the world.

The Problem of Definition of Financial Services

Defining the term "service," in a way that would be practical to a multilateral trade agreement in services poses a considerable challenge and will play a major role in shaping and determining the coverage of such an agreement. The same is true of the definitions and coverage eventually applied to individual services sectors such as financial services.

Conceptual type definitions could be useful in that they could provide a broad frame of reference and define the maximum scope of the negotiations and potential agreement. However, when it comes to defining the commitments of an agreement in legal terms, negotiators will need something more specific to "hang their hats on."

Therefore, for practical reasons, negotiators will likely eventually be driven to compile a list of such services and, then if need be, define these more specific services.

In the case of financial services, negotiators should avoid listing such financial services by products or sub-products if the eventual agreement is to be forward-looking and of lasting value. Additionally, detailed listings of current products or sub-products would potentially significantly complicate an agreement, particularly given the ongoing blurring of products and the introduction of new innovative financial products.

Similarly, negotiators should avoid listing services by institutional type given the significant differences in institutional arrangements, business powers across countries, and the global trend towards universal financial institutions.

Perhaps the most practical, flexible, forward-looking and least problematic approach to defining financial services might be to list all existing financial services by their broad functional type and then, if need be, reach an agreement on the definition of these broad functions and processes. Such broad functions could include: the borrowing of savings, the provision of credit, leasing, facilitation of payments, receipts and transfers, discounting assets and the provision of liquidity, portfolio management, portfolio advice, provision of financial information, underwriting, guarantees and commitments, enduring, trading of financial instruments and currencies, broking and safekeeping.

While such an approach is not problem-free, it would allow for the continued blurring of existing products, the introduction of new products and continued changes in institutional types and business powers (including the global trend towards universal financial services institutions). It is far less likely that a new financial services function will be invented compared to the high likelihood of new product innovations or changes in institutional arrangements and business powers across countries. In the rare event that a new financial services function is invented, this could be accommodated by occasional additions and adjustments to the agreement.

V. The Framework of Rules and Principles for Services Trade Agreed to at the Mid-term Review of the Uruguay Round

At the Mid-term Review of the Uruguay Round in Montreal in December 1988, the Trade Negotiations Committee (TNC) agreed on a skeletal conceptual framework of principles and rules for a multilateral agreement covering trade in services. This skeletal framework represents a minimum set of principles that would cover trade in all services, and could be built upon and broadened when applied to specific services sectors like financial services. The framework includes the following broad principles:

1. Transparency
2. Progressive Liberalization
3. National Treatment
4. Most-Favoured-Nation/Non-Discrimination
5. Market Access
6. Increasing Participation of Developing Countries
7. Safeguards and Exceptions
8. Regulatory Situation

(A fuller description of these agreed upon principles and rules is included in the appendix to this paper.)

The principles of Transparency, Non-discrimination, and Market Access are clearly essential to an equitable agreement aimed at liberalizing trade in financial services, and need little further comment.

As already discussed, the principle of National Treatment has both strengths and weaknesses. The strict application of National Treatment can lead to barriers to entry and establishment of foreign suppliers, and impede the operational freedom of foreign suppliers when differences in regulatory systems exist across countries. Moreover, this principle can cause competitive inequities in that it allows foreigners full freedom to compete for market share in the most liberalized countries while not ensuring that foreign countries reciprocate.

The principles of Progressive Liberalization, Increasing Participation of Developing Countries, Safeguards and Exceptions and Regulatory Situation would appear to be more than is necessary to accommodate the concerns of less developed countries. The danger lies in that too liberal an interpretation and coverage of such principles could weaken a potential agreement on trade in financial services.

VI. Concluding Comments and Suggestions

1. The skeletal framework of broad rules and principles for trade in services, agreed to at the Mid-term Review, has the potential to form the core of a substantive multilateral agreement for trade in financial services. However, many of these principles will need to be further refined and qualified with great care if they are not to result in an agreement for financial services that inadvertently supports existing barriers/impediments to trade in financial services and/or is too weak to contribute to the further liberalization of financial services trade.

2. The strict application of the principle of National Treatment to trade in financial services could support and give further rise to barriers/impediments to entry, establishment and operational restrictions. Therefore, there should probably be at least some consideration for allowing some degree of equivalent access in a multilateral agreement for trade in financial services. The definition of National Treatment agreed to at the Mid-term Review, implying that foreign supplies/suppliers would receive treatment "no less favourable" than indigenous supplies/suppliers, would seem to allow for this possibility. For example, foreign suppliers could be accorded greater freedoms than indigenous suppliers in cases where indigenous suppliers enjoy such additional freedoms in the foreign market. However, realistically, this possibility may need to be spelled out in an agreement to ensure that it is given due consideration.

3. Regulatory harmonization implies a convergence of National Treatment, Equivalent Access and Home Country Rule, and hence a convergence of self-interests across countries in trade in financial services. Therefore, regulatory harmonization would appear to offer the basis for maximum liberalization of trade in financial services under common prudential standards. Thus, a long-term goal that perhaps should be embodied in a multilateral agreement, along with related "hard" commitments to achieving this goal, is the harmoniza-

tion of supervisory/prudential regulations. Progress already achieved through the new Bank for International Settlements capital adequacy guidelines should be built upon.

4. In light of the benefits of regulatory harmonization, Pacific countries should consider jointly supporting a commitment to regulatory harmonization both within and outside the multilateral GATT negotiations.

5. Given the strong economic arguments in favour of universal-type financial institutions and given the strong global trend towards such institutions, a multilateral agreement, including a commitment to regulatory harmonization, should be based on the principle of Universal Financial Institutions. This would best ensure that such an agreement is forward-looking and of lasting value.

6. Until a much greater degree of regulatory harmonization is achieved, and given the complexities of the issues, it will probably still be necessary for some bilateral/regional discussions and agreements to accelerate the liberalization of trade in financial services within sub-groups of countries, and to accommodate concerns about Equivalent Access. As long as these sub-agreements adhere to the broad principles in multilateral agreement, they should make a contribution to the further liberalization of multilateral trade in financial services.

7. Probably the most practical, flexible, forward-looking and least problematic approach to defining the term "financial services" for purposes of a workable multilateral agreement would be to list all existing financial services by broad function. The alternatives of listing financial services by existing specific product-types or institutional-types, which are subject to continued frequent change, would not be flexible and forward-looking and would unnecessarily complicate an agreement.

8. In order to ensure that the concerns of the LDCs are taken into account, while at the same time ensuring that rapid progress is achieved towards the further liberalization of trade in financial services, a multilateral agreement aimed at the liberalization of trade in financial services should perhaps have two or possibly three (at most) levels or tracks. For example, as the level of an LDC's economic and financial services sector development progresses, it could graduate to a higher degree of financial services. Many of the Asian LDCs, particularly in South-East Asia, have more to gain over the

short- to medium-term by supporting rapid multilateral liberalization of trade in financial services. A number already have fairly well-developed and strong local financial services institutions capable of competing well with financial services institutions from the developed countries. Increased local participation by foreign financial institutions would likely increase the development of short-term and inter-bank money markets, offer new clearing technologies, introduce innovative financial techniques and, in general, contribute to increased efficiency of the local financial services sector and the economy. Moreover, fuelled by their substantial trade surpluses, banks from many of these South-East Asian LDCs are increasingly applying for entry and establishment rights in the major developed countries. Such rights would be more easily obtainable under a more liberal multilateral agreement for trade in financial services.

10. Care will need to be taken to ensure that the definition and coverage of the principles of Progressive Liberalization, and Regulatory Situation are not interpreted and applied too liberally if a multilateral agreement for trade in financial services is to have substance.

11. The principle of Standstill should be included in a multilateral agreement for trade in financial services, at least among the more developed countries, in order to better ensure that progress already achieved is not jeopardized.

12. In light of the complexities of financial services trade, some form of Dispute Settlement principle and mechanism will likely be needed, particularly to deal with non-regulatory barriers and impediments to trade in financial services.

Appendix

At the Mid-term Review of the Uruguay Round in Montreal in December 1988, the Trade Negotiations Committee (TNC) agreed on a very broad conceptual framework of principles and rules for multilateral agreement trade in services. These principles and rules were developed over a two-year period by the Group of Negotiations on Services (GNS). This framework includes the following broad principles:

(a) *Transparency*
"Provisions should ensure information with respect to all laws, regulations and administrative guidelines as well as international agreements relating to services trade to which the signatories are parties through adequate provisions regarding their availability. Agreement should be reached with respect to any outstanding issues in this regard."

(b) *Progressive Liberalization*
"The negotiations should establish rules, modalities and procedures in the multilateral framework agreement that provide for progressive liberalization of trade in services with due respect for national policy objectives including provisions that allow for the application of principles to sectors and measures. Provisions should also be established for further negotiations after the Uruguay Round. Specific procedures may be required for the liberalization of particular sectors."

"The aim of these rules, modalities and procedures should be to achieve, in this round and future negotiations, a progressively higher level of liberalization taking due account of the level of development of individual signatories. To this end the adverse effects of all laws, regulations and administrative guidelines should be reduced as part of the process to provide effective market access, including national treatment."

"The rules, modalities and procedures for progressive liberalization should provide appropriate flexibility for individual developing countries for opening fewer sectors or liberalizing fewer types of transactions or in progressively extending market access in line with their development situation."

(c) *National Treatment*
"When accorded in conformity with other provisions of the multilateral framework, it is understood that national treatment means that the services exports and/or exporters of any signatory are accorded in the market of any other signatory, in respect of all laws, regulations and administrative practices, treatment no less favourable than that

accorded domestic services or services providers in the same market."

(d) *Most-Favoured-Nation/Non-Discrimination*
"The multilateral framework shall contain a provision on m.f.n./non-discrimination."

(e) *Market Access*
"When market access is made available to signatories it should be on the basis that consistent with the other provisions of the multilateral framework and in accordance with the definition of trade in services, foreign services may be supplied according to the preferred mode of delivery."

(f) *Increasing Participation of Developing Countries*
"The framework should provide for the increasing participation of developing countries in world trade and for the expansion of their services exports, including *inter alia* through the strengthening of their domestic services capacity and its efficiency and competitiveness."

"Provisions should facilitate effective market access for services exports of developing countries through, *inter alia*, improved access to distribution channels and information networks. These provisions should facilitate liberalization of market access in sectors of export interest to developing countries."

"Autonomous liberalization of market access in favour of services exports of developing countries should be allowed."

"Particular account shall be taken of the serious difficulty of the least-developed countries in accepting negotiated commitments in view of their special economic situation and their development, trade and financial needs."

(g) *Safeguards and Exceptions*
"Further negotiations will be necessary on provisions for safeguards, e.g., for balance of payments reasons, and exceptions, e.g., based on security and cultural policy objectives."

(h) *Regulatory Situation*
"It is recognized that governments regulate services sectors, e.g. by granting exclusive rights in certain sectors, by attaching conditions to the operations of enterprises within their markets for consumer protection purposes and in pursuance of macro-economic policies. Asymmetries exist with respect to the degree of development of services regulations in different countries. Consequently, the right of countries, in particular of developing countries, to introduce new regulations is recognized. This should be consistent with commitments under the framework."

Bibliography

Baker, Anthony. "Liberalization of Trade in Services—The World Insurance Industry." In *The Emerging Service Economy,* ed. by Orio Giarini. Oxford: Pergamon Press for the Services World Forum, Geneva, 1987.

Feketekuty, Geza. *International Trade in Services: An Overview and Blueprint for Negotiations.* Washington, D.C.: American Enterprise Institute for Public Policy Research, 1988.

GATT. "Negotiations on Trade in Services." *Focus Newsletter,* (September/October 1988).

GATT. "Montreal Mid-term Ministerial Meeting." *Focus Newsletter,* (January 1989).

Gavin, Brigid. "A GATT for International Banking?" *Journal of World Trade Law,* vol. 19, no. 2, (March/April 1985).

Gibbs, Murray and Mina Mashayekhi. "Services: Cooperation for Development." *Journal of World Trade,* vol. 22, no. 2, (April 1988), pp. 81-107.

Kirmani, Naheed. "The Uruguay Round: Revitalizing the Global Trading System." *Finance & Development,* Washington, D.C.: IMF and World Bank, March 1989.

Koekkoek, Ad. "Developing Countries and Services in the Uruguay Round." *INTERECONOMICS,* (September/ October 1987), pp. 234-242.

Nayyar, Deepak. "Some Reflections on the Uruguay Round and Trade in Services," *Journal of World Trade,* Vol. 22, no. 5, (October 1988), pp. 35-47.

Nicolaides, Phedon, "Economic Aspects of Services: Implications for a GATT Agreement." *Journal of World Trade,* vol. 23, no. 1, (February 1989), pp. 125-136.

Organization for Economic Cooperation and Development. "Obstacles to International Trade in Banking Services." *Financial Market Trends,* vol. 27, (March 1984), pp. 15-44.

Organization for Economic Cooperation and Development. "International Trade in Services: Securities." *Financial Market Trends,* vol. 37, (May 1987), pp. 1-16.

Organization for Economic Cooperation and Development. "International Trade in Services: Para-Banking Services." *Financial Market Trends*, vol. 40, (May 1988), pp. 18-44.

Schultz, Siegfried. "Services and the GATT." *INTER-ECONOMICS*, (September/October 1987), pp. 227-234.

Financial Reform, Flows and The Pacific Basin

Tadao Hata
The Bank of Tokyo, Ltd.
New York, New York

Introduction

As the Pacific Basin is among the world's most economically dynamic regions, its nations need tremendous amounts of financial capital to sustain their dynamism. In addition, steps must also be taken in the areas of financial reforms and deregulation to assure a continued smooth flow of funds through the region. Freer and more open markets in trade and financial capital are absolutely essential to the vitality of the Pacific Basin.

Deregulation and Globalization of Financial Markets

Throughout the last ten years, the major industrialized nations in the Pacific Basin have, for the most part, made great strides in reforming and deregulating the increasingly globalized financial markets. To some extent, this progress has also taken place in the Basin's developing nations. Deregulation and globalization has contributed significantly to an increase in the flow of funds into the region.

Japan began to deregulate its financial markets in earnest with the Foreign Exchange Act of 1980 and the Banking Act of 1982. The spirit of reform was also catching on in the United

States at approximately the same time when Congress passed the Monetary Control and Deregulation Act in early 1980. It is clear that industrialized countries had little choice but to loosen their restrictive regulations as companies transcended national borders in their operations, thus requiring imaginative and innovative financing outlets to allow them to compete and survive in global markets.

In Japan, the push toward deregulation has taken several forms:

1. Deregulating interest rate ceilings on deposits;
2. Expanding the scope of financial markets; and
3. Deregulating the financial institutions which compete in those markets.

Let us look closely at these points. It is commonly acknowledged that placing a cap or ceiling on some interest rates while other rates are allowed to flex with changing market forces can disrupt—sometimes paralyse—financial flows. This is called disintermediation, and results in financial intermediaries such as banks losing deposits as market interest rates rise above deposit accounts ceilings. To stem the financial disruption of disintermediation, Japan has gradually phased out interest rate caps on large deposits by permitting banks to offer their customers new financial instruments that are sensitive to market interest rates. These instruments include negotiable certificates of deposits and money market certificates. Since the Spring of 1989, Japan has also begun to deregulate smaller denomination deposits of retail customers.

Japanese financial markets have changed quite notably in addition to interest rate deregulation. For example, in the interbank market, city banks have been authorized to buy bills and engage in so-called double option transactions in the dealer loan market. Also, in the government securities market, a public auction system—similar to that found in the U.S.—was introduced for the issue of treasury bills. Finally, in 1985, Japanese policy-makers initiated a yen-denominated bankers' acceptance market and in late 1987, a commercial paper market. While seemingly modest in scope, these examples of liberalization point to the need for the further deregulatory progress that is so essential to Japan's economic vitality, as well as to that of the Pacific Basin as a whole.

Along with interest rate deregulation and general expansion in the scope of financial markets, Japan has dared to thrust banks and securities firms into direct—although for now, limited—competition. For example, banks are now able to deal in and underwrite over-the-counter government bonds and to participate in the bond futures market. Securities companies, on the other hand, have been allowed to venture into activities that have heretofore been the preserve of banks, such as dealing in certificates of deposit and yen-denominated bankers' acceptances, and providing stand-by loans collateralized by government bonds.

The gradual regulatory and legislative blurring of the once clearly drawn line separating bank activities of from those of securities firms is inevitable if funds are to flow efficiently through an economic system. In fact, successful economic integration of all nations in the Pacific Basin requires further multilateral deregulation. To that point, one need only cite the tremendous strides taken by the federal reserve in recent years in expanding the securities powers of banking institutions in the U.S.

It would be incorrect—and a bit shortsighted—to concentrate regulatory and legislative on opening national financial markets to national players alone. With markets becoming increasingly globalized, it's important to include foreign institutions in these initiatives. For example, under the fair-play rules of cooperation and reciprocity, Japanese financial institutions have gained increased access to U.S. financial markets, as have U.S. firms in Japan. In fact, more than twenty foreign securities firms have recently gained membership on the Tokyo stock exchange and are participating in government bond underwriting syndicates.

Foreign banks have also been granted entry to Japan's financial markets. Since 1985, nine foreign banks have been permitted to conduct trust business in Japan even though ordinary Japanese city banks are prohibited from doing do. Also, some foreign banks—especially European banks—are permitted to engage in securities activities in Japan to the same extent they are able to do so in their home countries. These foreign banks certainly have a competitive—some would say unfair—edge over Japanese banks.

Changes in the Flow of Funds

Along with the economic evolution of the Pacific Basin countries through the 1970s and 1980s, there has been a noticeable change in the pattern of financial flows within the region. In the 1970s, the current account surpluses of the industrialized Pacific Basin nations were sufficient to finance the current account deficits of the region's developing economies.

In the 1980s, however, the patterns of financial flows changed. While Japan remained a supplier of funds, the U.S. became a net demander, as its current account turned negative. At the same time, among the developing economies, the newly industrialized countries, or NICs, became net funds suppliers, while the ASEAN countries became more heavily dependent on foreign lenders.

The Future of Financial Flows
within the Pacific Basin

It seems almost a certainty that the U.S. economy will remain a net demander of funds internationally—that is to say, its current account will remain in the red. Even though the dollar has fallen in the foreign exchange markets, since early 1985 the U.S. trade deficit (which accounts for the bulk of its current account deficit), while improving somewhat recently, is not likely to disappear. As long as the U.S. remains import-dependent, and as long as interest payments increase to finance its sizeable net external indebtedness, the U.S. current account deficit cannot be expected to drop below $100 billion annually, at least in the near term.

In contrast, the yen's overall appreciation since 1985 will tend to slow Japan's exports and, in turn, its trade surplus. However, Japan's current account surplus is not expected to diminish, especially in light of its expected income from its net holdings of foreign financial assets.

The future pattern of financial flows in the Pacific Basin is likely to be that the U.S. and the ASEAN countries will absorb increasing amounts of funds, while Japan and the NICs will be the region's suppliers. Since the capacity of the NICs to finance the external borrowing of other nations is relatively limited, Japan will probably remain the major supplier of funds in the Pacific Basin.

Smoothing the Financial Flows
in the Pacific Basin

Assuming that these changes in the composition of the demand and supply of funds in the Pacific Basin continue, what additional steps must be taken to guarantee continued financing of the region's economic expansion? Without doubt, the momentum of market deregulation must be sustained. Japan should move to eliminate all interest rate ceilings on deposits, expand the scope of the financial futures markets, further reduce regulations which restrict the operational flexibility of financial institution, and remove the legal and institutional barriers to entry by foreign financial firms.

Deregulation is a vote of confidence in the efficiency of the market mechanism. For markets to perform at their best, they must be free of burdensome and restrictive regulations. As a necessary condition of maintaining and sustaining the overall economic development of the Pacific Basin, financial deregulation must continue to be pursued; anything less would impair the rich future of the Pacific Basin.

Financial Services Trade Liberalization: A Perspective from Singapore*

Tan Kong Yam
National University of Singapore

Introduction

In September 1986 the ministerial meeting at Punta del Este, Uruguay agreed in principle to establish negotiating procedures within the GATT on services trade, parallel to a new round of negotiations on the reduction of barriers to merchandise trade. Long before that meeting, trade in financial services began to expand at a much faster rate than that of merchandise trade. While the value of world exports rose at an average annual rate of 14.3 per cent between 1966-1980, main indicators of international banking activity like gross international liabilities, net international bank lending, gross or net size of the Eurocurrency market have all expanded by an average annual rate of 25-30 per cent during the same period,[1] about twice the rate of expansion in merchandise trade.

During the first stage expansion in international financial activities from the mid-1950s to mid-1960s, development was largely driven by real sector activities like the expansion in trade-related financing, foreign exchange transactions and financial services servicing the internationalization of corporate activities.

* The views expressed herein are the personal views of the writer and they need not necessarily reflect the view of the institutions with which he is associated.

In the second stage from the mid-1960s to the early 1980s, the expansion of international financial services was greatly stimulated by the development of the Eurocurrency market, initially in Europe and later to other financial centres around the world, including the Asian Currency Unit (ACU) in Singapore. The impetus for this development was largely provided by the quest for cheaper and more efficient banking operations, to avoid the myriad regulations and controls in the domestic market like interest rate ceilings, reserve requirement on domestic deposits, capital and exchange controls and differences in taxation between domestic market and offshore financial centres. Growth during this period was further stimulated by the rising demand for international loan financing of industrial and infrastructural projects in the Less Developed Countries (LDCs) and for the financing of external imbalances associated with the two oil-price shocks. However, since the early 1980s, a period of rationalization and slower growth has set in, with increasingly greater emphasis being placed on profitability, capital adequacy, assessment of risks and exposures, tighter regulatory provisions and prudential restrictions as opposed to asset growth in bank strategy. With deregulation and technological innovation in telecommunication and information services, the past decade has also been characterized by the proliferation of new financial instruments, the integration of world financial markets, the internationalization of currencies and financial instruments and the multinationalization of financial intermediaries.

Financial Services in Singapore

The development of the financial services sector in Singapore, an offshore regional financial centre, roughly paralleled that of the global trends. Since the mid-1960s, Singapore embarked on her outward-oriented industrialization policy based on the promotion of foreign direct investment and the export of labour intensive manufactured products to the OECD markets. During the first 10 years of rapid industrialization, the manufacturing sector expanded at an average annual rate of 16 per cent. This period witnessed the setting up and expansion of financial services by foreign banks to service the Multinational Corporations (MNCs) and the expansion in international trade. Beginning in the latter part of the 1960s, the financial structure became progressively differentiated and began to experience very rapid rates of growth. One aspect of this remarkable growth is summarized in Table 1.

In line with the development of the Eurocurrency market, Singapore set up the Asian Currency Unit (ACU) in October 1968 by abolishing the withholding tax on interest payable to non-

Table 1
Financial Institutions in Singapore

Number (end of period)	1970	1975	1980	1985	1988	1989 (Mar)
Banks	36	69	96	134	134	136
Local banks	11	13	13	13	13	13
Foreign banks	25	56	83	121	121	123
Full	25	23	23	23	22	22
Restricted	-	12	13	14	14	14
Offshore	-	21	47	84	85	87
Finance companies	35	36	34	34	31	30
Merchant banks	2	21	37	55	64	65
Asian Currency Units (ACU)	16	66	115	179	188	191
Stockbroking companies	NA	19	21	44	84	91
Local companies	NA	19	21	25	25	25
Foreign companies	NA	NA	NA	12	21	23
Investment advisers	NA	NA	NA	7	38	43
Insurance Companies	80	69	71	84	105	110
Life	8	7	6	6	6	6
General	65	53	56	71	90	94
Life and general	7	9	9	7	9	10
SIMEX (Futures)						
Corporate clearing members	-	-	-	31	36	36
Corporate non-clearing members	-	-	-	36	42	42
Individual members	-	-	-	137	238	240
Commercial associate members	-	-	-	-	-	9
Individual trading permit holders	-	-	-	-	-	22
International money brokers	-	5	7	8	8	8
Representative offices	8	38	49	51	47	47
Banks	8	37	45	47	43	43
Merchant banks	-	1	4	4	4	4

Source: The Monetary Authority of Singapore

residents. This reflected the government's determination to develop the financial sector as an autonomous engine of growth, rather than merely as a sector which derived its growth from the expansion in real sector activities. In 1972, the 20 per cent liquidity ratio requirement was lifted from the ACU, bringing it in line with the Eurodollar market. The number of banks with ACU rose from 16 in 1970 to 115 in 1980 and further to 191 in March 1989. As a result, total assets increased by an annual rate of about 150 per cent in the initial years, moderated to 30-35 per cent in the 1970s and stabilized to around 20-25 per cent in the 1980s. By the end of 1988, total assets amounted to US$280.5 billion, of which 70 per cent consisted of interbank funds.

While less dramatic in the rate of expansion and liberalization than the offshore financial services of the ACU, since the early 1970s, the domestic financial services sector also underwent a process of gradual liberalization. In 1971, a new category of "restricted" licences was created to accommodate foreign banks. Restricted banks were allowed to deal in ACU and engage in wholesale corporate banking, but were not permitted to accept small time and savings deposits and could not do business in more than one location in Singapore. In 1973, another class of licences called offshore licences was approved for foreign financial institutions to engage in the ACU market and provide financial services to the regional economies. Two years later, domestic interest rates where liberalized. Exchange controls, which had been progressively liberalized, were completely lifted by June 1978. Since 1978, activities of offshore banks were further liberalized to include the provision of domestic loans as long as they did not exceed $90 million in total, generating even further competition to local banks in the domestic market.

As a result of this progressive step of liberalization, the pressure of competition from foreign financial institutions intensified throughout the 1970s. Competition arose not only in foreign exchange transactions, loans and bills financing, but also in personnel. As a result, each local bank which was content to service its share of the market, providing the same types of services and at the same charges, was forced to engage in intensive marketing, the upgrading of management expertise and training.

The competition from foreign financial institutions has spurred local banks to upgrade and innovate. It is interesting to note that while the foreign banks were most innovative and aggressive in the Asiandollar market in the 1970s and were also the first to introduce the automated teller machines (ATM) in 1979, it was the local banks which were first to introduce the telephone banking system in 1982 and the cashless payment system called NETS in 1985. It is also noteworthy that increasingly middle and upper management in the major local banks consisted of personnel who worked for varying lengths of time with foreign banks located in Singapore or at their overseas offices. Thus, competition from foreign banks has not only resulted in product innovation and service improvement but, more importantly, in personnel training and development for the local financial institutions.

Despite the government's attempt to promote the development of the financial sector and the willingness to liberalize, restrictions on the activities of foreign banks still exist. Present restrictions on foreign banks are confined largely to retail banking and include controls on the number of branches they can open and automated teller machines they can install. These restrictions have been raised several times by the U.S. Trade Representative in bilateral talks with Singapore. The Singapore stand is that foreign banks have already had one of the largest market shares in the provision of financial services in Singapore. For example, based on the data for 1987, foreign bank controlled 95 per cent of ACU assets, 85 per cent of domestic residents' foreign exchange deposits in ACU, 56 per cent of Singapore dollar domestic loans, 46 per cent of Singapore dollar domestic deposits and 80 per cent of trade financing. The rationale was that these were among the highest foreign penetration ratios in the world, indicating that the domestic financial sector has been open enough.

While the advantages of liberalization resulting in wider scope for competition, facilitating the introduction of new services, techniques, instruments, management strategies and fostering efficiency of the domestic financial system are well recognized, restrictions on the encroachment of foreign banks on domestic financial activities are likely to remain, even for a regional financial centre like Singapore. The argument against complete liberalization fundamentally rests on the perception that the financial sector is regarded as a strategic industry providing the community with money balances and payments' arrangements. These are vital to the proper functioning of the national economy and the attainment of national policy goals. This concern is further compounded by the fact that rapid integration of the domestic and foreign capital market, the increased international mobility and enhanced substitutability of financial assets have made it more difficult to conduct domestically oriented monetary policy. For a small open economy with no exchange controls like Singapore, there is hardly any room for an independent interest rate or monetary policy. The only price the central bank has some room to control through foreign exchange intervention is the exchange rate, which has significant effect on export competitiveness, imported inflation and the general level of confidence in the financial sector. Consequently, concern about destabilizing capital flight by uncontrollable foreign banks impinging on national sovereignty is another motivating factor in restraining further liberalization, particularly on internationalizing the Singapore dollar. From the regulatory perspective, there is also the concern that foreign banks, with their sophistication and links with parent banks abroad, could more easily circumvent domestic banking regulations of a monetary or prudential nature.

In sum, Singapore's policy on the financial sector has to balance three often conflicting objectives. First, there is the developmental objective of promoting the country as a financial centre by encouraging the location of foreign financial institutions in Singapore. This is achieved through a combination of tax incentives, regulatory measures, the maintenance of cost competitiveness, continuous upgrading of banking expertise and professionalism, and staying at the forefront of technology. Thus, the Asiandollar market, offshore fund management industry and the futures market (SIMEX) received generous tax concessions in their development. Second, there is the policy autonomy objective, particularly with respect to domestic banking activities and the management of exchange rate and monetary policies. Consequently, some protection has been accorded to the local financial institutions. Liberalization of financial activities in the domestic market has been more restrained and a "separation fence" has been erected to maintain differential incentives and constraints between domestic (onshore) and international (offshore) financial activities. Third, there is the usual prudential concern of preserving the resilience and soundness of the financial sector through banking regulation and supervision. Each policy and step in liberalization can be viewed as an attempt to maintain the final balance among the above three conflicting objectives.

Prospects in Regional Liberalization

Due to the limited size of the domestic market, financial institutions in Singapore, either foreign or local, have always performed a regional function. The offshore licence for foreign banks was created largely to serve the regional market. Initially, the ACU performed a largely regional role. For example, between 1968-1970, the bulk of deposits in the ACU were collected in the Asian region and remitted largely to New York and London for investment. However, since the early 1970s, the reverse has happened and funds from other regions and the developed countries have been intermediated and loaned to the regional economies for investment and development. For example, based on the net asset position of the ACU *vis-à-vis* other regions, Europe, the Middle East and Singapore have been net lenders since the mid-1970s. The major net borrower has been Asia (excluding Singapore). The net borrowing position of the Asian region has risen from about US$7 billion in the mid-1970s to US$14 billion in the mid-1980s. Thus, the ACU performed an important intermediating role, facilitating the flows of savings and investment in the region and internationally. This is particularly important for some of the regional economies where the financial sector has been relatively repressed or under-developed.

A development that could lead to the gradual liberalization of the financial services sector in the Association of Southeast Asian Nations' (ASEAN) is the recent surge in foreign direct investment into the region. Since 1985, as a result of the substantial appreciation of the yen, Japanese direct investment in the ASEAN region has risen at an annual rate of about 70 per cent. More significantly, driven by appreciating exchange rates, rising labour costs, protectionism in the OECD countries and environmental concern at home, newly industrializing economies (NIEs) like Taiwan, Hong Kong, Singapore and South Korea have been investing heavily in the ASEAN region since 1987. All the ASEAN countries have liberalized their foreign investment regime and adopted an increasingly open and outward-oriented development policy. As the flows of direct investment and merchandise trade are liberalized, international competition would be likely to generate pressure on lowering the domestic input costs, particularly intermediate inputs that are heavily regulated, or monopolized. Pressure could arise from industrialists and traders to clamour for the liberalization of the financial sector so as to reduce the high cost of the heavily protected financial services sector.

Despite the general trend for liberalization, the financial sectors of the developing countries in general and the ASEAN countries in particular are not likely to witness substantial liberalization in the foreseeable future. There will be a strong strive for self-sufficiency in financial services. The obstacles to liberalization are substantial. First, the major commercial banks and development banks in most ASEAN countries are directly or indirectly government-owned and the central banks often use the financial system for credit allocation purposes to achieve social objectives. Second, the financial services industry is largely technology and skilled-labour intensive and one where less developed countries have no comparative advantage. Liberalization of the sector can only lead to dominance by foreigners of the strategic industry. Moreover, from the successful industrial development experience of Japan, Taiwan and Korea, it is not clear that a liberalized and non-repressed financial services sector is necessary for the successful launching of industrialization, at least in the early stage of development.

Conclusion

As a small city state aspiring to be a regional financial centre and host to 13 locals banks and 123 foreign commercial banks with at least half of them ranking among the world's top 100 banks, Singapore has a very strong interest in seeing global trade in financial services liberalized. The general trend in ASEAN countries and the region is for liberalization, in direct investment flows, in merchandise trade and gradually in financial and other services. However, the process of financial liberalization has to be an extremely gradual one for developing countries. For those countries in the process of trade liberalization, too rapid a pace in financial liberalization may bring about an increase in domestic interest rates, leading to an appreciation of the domestic currency, to the detriment of the promotion of direct foreign investment and the expansion in merchandise trade. For the ASEAN countries that are liberalizing in investment flows and merchandise trade, it would be more prudent to follow in the footsteps of Taiwan and Korea by establishing a stronger industrial base before liberalizing in the financial services sector.

Services Sector Liberalization: Problems and Prospects for Aviation Arrangements

Christopher Findlay
University of Adelaide

Introduction

This paper reviews recent developments in the tourism and air transport sectors in the Pacific. The aim is to identify the pressures from those developments on policies on trade in air transport services, and to comment on how such policies might change. The demand for those changes is likely to come from within the industry. In that context it is argued that traditional principles for guiding trade negotiations, such as those of the GATT, have considerable relevance to air transport issues and are especially relevant to the smaller countries in the Pacific region.

Regulatory System

Air transport services between any pair of cities are controlled by an air services agreement (ASA) between the governments involved. The bilateral strategy was adopted in 1944 following the failure to agree on a multilateral exchange of market access. There are now about 1800 bilateral air services agreements in the world. The agreements specify:

- which airlines will fly on the route
- the capacity each airline will offer

> – the scope for airlines from third countries

to offer capacity on the route.

Airlines operating on a route will usually include one or more designated carriers from the countries at each end of the route, plus airlines from third countries. The bulk of capacity on the route will be provided by the end point carriers. As a result any country's imports of air transport services are determined by quantitative controls. In addition these "import quotas" are allocated to specific foreign firms.

Fares on each route are ultimately subject to government control as well. Traditionally target fares were negotiated by the airlines themselves then referred to governments for approval. Increasingly fares are set in the market place and governments are less involved in fare setting. Control of capacity is the more important policy instrument.

Various formulas are used to fix capacity. Some rely on rules based on traffic loads on a route, others fix capacity more rigidly in advance and then renegotiate at regular intervals and others review capacity after an increment when requested by the country whose capacity share has fallen.

The designated airlines are required to have a substantial local ownership and control. In many cases, the majority owner is also the national government. In those cases, the typical policy was to designate only that one airline as the international carrier.

One interpretation of the original motivation for the systems of agreements was that they avoided exploitation of market power by any one country. This power existed because of each country's controls over landing rights. On any route, one side was exposed to the fear that the other would unilaterally regulate either for profit or for other strategic purposes.

The system also overcame the perception that the market may not be competitive and that if allowed to operate freely, particular airlines even without explicit government action would come to dominate the market. At the time, this concern was focused on the U.S. airlines and that concern continues today.

A major problem in the current system has been the slow pace at which newcomer suppliers are admitted. Newcomer suppliers do not have much bargaining power unless their domestic market is also large, or they become a significant destination for traffic. Without bargaining power they must resort to diverting traffic from other routes in order to build up market share. This strategy has been applied successfully, by the ASEAN carriers for example. In general, however, the market share of the newcomer competitive suppliers is less than in the absence of regulation.

Developments in the Market

A number of developments in the market will have important implications for the regulatory system. These include:

1. the increasing density of traffic in the Pacific due to the increase in travel and tourism

2. the increasing number of competitive airlines in the region

3. the use of vertical integration in the tourist industry as a strategy for controlling and monitoring service quality; the same strategy is relevant in the freight market as well

4. the increasing role of computerized reservation systems (CRS) as strategic tools for airlines

5. the development of new aircraft (both twin- and four-engined) capable of long distance flights

6. the increased demand for, and options to supply (see 5. above) point-to-point services in the region, thereby increasing the number of international gateways and the presence of a large number of substitute routes

7. the trend toward privatization

8. confirmation of the importance of economies of networking, and the importance of access to mass markets, leading to integration of domestic and international services and the multiple designation of international airlines.

What will be the effects of these developments?

The combination of rapid growth in the travel market, the economies created by extending networks and the value of vertical linkages involving tourism industry firms and airlines are likely to lead to the creation of systems of firms in the air transport industry. Instead of services being packaged together by consumers, the consortia will provide the packages. Their activities could be coordinated through the use of the CRS.

The development of the consortia may extend further to the emergence of "global airlines" or "multinational corporations" in the airline industry although at present this step is restricted by rules on national ownership in the ASAs. On the other hand, the scope for ownership links will be extended by the diminishing role of government ownership in the industry. Ownership links may also be valuable because of their role in facilitating the monitoring of performance of other group members.

This sort of development could diminish the importance of the issue of accommodating newcomer suppliers.

The reason is that a typical strategy of a multinational corporation will be to situate production in the most competitive locations. This would naturally involve the newcomer suppliers as their competitiveness increased. The alternative strategy where ownership ties are restricted is to use a series of sub-contracting arrangements.

Such a course of action has implications for the pace of reform of the ASAs which will be determined by the attitudes of various groups with interests in aviation issues. Those of most interest are established suppliers, newcomer suppliers, national policy-makers and the tourism sector. The developments outlines may result in an alignment of interests between newcomer and established suppliers, especially in the Pacific where traffic volume is growing so rapidly. The established suppliers will have the incentive to encourage the entry of the newcomer suppliers, rather than to discourage it as has been the case.

Established suppliers may not need to decrease their absolute size, and could even grow. On the other hand their share of flying operations may fall. Their role would be to become the managers of the system, earning far higher proportions of their profit from commission sales rather than production. This new role for the established suppliers eases the structural adjustment pressures from the emerging new suppliers.

What will be the attitude of the consortia to the old regulatory system? They will find the regulations increasingly burdensome. As noted, they make the creation of ownership links more difficult; forming new networks or subcontracting services to low-cost members of the group will be more difficult. The divisions between market segments, such as domestic and international, will become more frustrating. As a result there could be a radical change in the operation of the system.

For a number of reasons, national policy-makers may be willing to sanction a more open system. Many of the original motivations for regulation are no longer relevant. There are now more airlines in the market, reflecting the great density of traffic; there are now more gateways increasing the number of routes which are close substitutes, at least in the view of consumers; as a result the market is regarded as more competitive than previously. In addition the moves to privatization diminish the concerns about unfair competition from subsidized airlines.

Finally, the interests of the tourist (export) industry in many countries are being given more weight. A regulatory system which inhibits capacity growth (in this import-competing industry) is criticized by the tourist (or export) sector, a consumer of the airline industry's. There may be a perception, at a national policy level, that at least one locally-owned and protected airline is a critical instrument for obtaining some share of the benefits of a tourism boom. Generally however, there are more efficient fiscal instruments available for this purpose. Furthermore, arguing this role for the airline industry is arguing for a position of the type which the original regulators of air transport were trying to avoid, that is, the exploitation of the market power provided by control over landing rights for national benefit.

However, there will be at least one major policy issue to consider—the effect of the emergence of the "mega-carriers" on the competitiveness of the market.

Operating within the ASAs, countries can influence the competitiveness of their local markets. Options include:

- promoting fare discounting, if necessary, with the use of more flexible rules on fare setting

- reviewing rules on fixing capacity, for example, moving to reviews of capacity after the event

- leaving open the option of multiple designation of local airlines

- permitting foreign entry into domestic markets

- easing the rules on the extent of foreign ownership of designated international carriers

Particular countries are already using some of these variations on the standard ASAs. In other words, the bilateral system need not establish a uniform market structure and conduct.

The bigger problem will be ensuring that local carriers have equal opportunity for access to markets in ASA partners and other countries to pick up passengers. Also the issues involved in market access have been expanded. Previously the main issues concerned capacity; in the current setting, there is increasing concern about access to complementary services for both airlines and their passengers as well as capacity.

The market access dilemma occurs because efforts to increase the degree of competition for local passengers reduces the national bargaining power in relation to access for its airlines into foreign markets. It "surrenders" conditions relating to market access which might be used to bargain for similar conditions at the other end of every route. In other words, the local air transport industry might argue that concessions have been made without obtaining sufficient aviation benefit in return.

The use of GATT principles may be very advantageous in managing this dilemma, giving a country an external standard against which to evaluate its access to foreign markets.

The extent to which the GATT principles are already embodied in the ASAs is reviewed in the first part of the following section, which later considers some options for extending the role of those principles in aviation negotiations.

GATT Principles
Non-discrimination

It is argued that non-discrimination is a feature of ASAs. However non-discrimination can be evaluated with respect to various conditions. One of these is access to complementary services, such as airport facilities. On these points, ASAs will often contain explicit statements of non-discrimination. (While there may be no discrimination between foreign suppliers, there is another question of whether they are treated like nationals; this issue is discussed below).

A second set of conditions concerns the rules by which capacity is negotiated. If any one country used the same set of rules for fixing capacity in all its ASAs, it could be argued that the ASAs were not discriminatory. In practice however, the rules vary, for example, according to the acceptance of multiple designation or the use of different systems for setting capacity. In terms of these conditions the ASAs are discriminatory.

Most-favoured nation treatment

Even if the rules for negotiating market access were not discriminatory, the ASAs still would not satisfy the Most-Favoured Nation (MFN) condition, since the allocation of rights to supply capacity are specific to particular countries (even firms) on any one route. Some airlines from other countries can fly a route while some cannot. The exchange of traffic rights is not governed by MFN principles but by a "balance of benefits" on the route.

National treatment

The national treatment principle is endorsed in the ASA system, once access to the market has been obtained. For example, it applies to items such as landing charges and air navigation fees. This principle is important therefore for exporters gaining access to the national air transport system infrastructure in an importing country.

Despite a statement of the rule, national treatment remains an issue, reflecting the difficulty of avoiding the problem within the ASAs. For example, one issue concerns rules requiring government officials to fly with a national airline. As explained above, complementary services have also become a major issue, such as;

- access to computerized reservations systems,
- access to ground handling services

– various landing fees, etc., as noted above but also access landing slots.

The national treatment principle presently does not extend to rights of establishment, because there are generally limits on the extent of foreign investment in local airlines. An extension in this direction would also facilitate market access.

Nor does the national treatment principle extend to access to points in the domestic market, where local carriers, while still often restricted in the points that can be served, are in an advantageous position compared to foreign airlines.

Transparency

Currently, all ASAs are registered with the industry organization, International Civil Aviation Organization (ICAO). The published agreements contain the general rules on setting of capacity, etc. However they are often accompanied by side agreements, which are not published, on particular decisions on capacity or other forms of cooperation. The system would be truly transparent if all aspects of the agreements were published.

Safeguards and dispute settlement

Dumping issues, which have arisen recently across the Pacific, and subsidy issues can be handled bilaterally within the ASAs, for example, in the case of dumping, by renegotiating capacity or the rules for capacity fixing. The ASAs specify consultation processes and also include the right to terminate, leading to negotiation of new agreement.

This bilateral system of disputes settlement does have some disadvantages. Disputes will be settled according to the bargaining power of the two parties. On the other hand a "rules orientated" system of settling disputes, such as the GATT tradition on dispute settlement of using panels and third parties, has the advantage of ensuring that the general principles are adhered to in the resolution of any dispute.

Summary

In summary, the ASAs

1. embody only to a limited extent the principle of non-discrimination in terms of the procedures and rules applied

2. embody the national treatment provision, although not as far as investment and access points, and even when

applied, the national treatment rules are difficult to enforce

3. include some safeguards provisions and a dispute settlement procedure, but one which is subject to distortions through the effects of relative bargaining powers and

4. are visible although not completely transparent while

5. the MFN condition is not met.

There are a number of options for trying to extend the influence of the traditional GATT principles into the air transport system in order to help resolve the current market access issues. These options include:

1. negotiating a binding agreement on air transport, embodying all the GATT principles perhaps as an addition to a more general agreement on services trade,

2. permitting countries to pursue their own conditional MFN agreements with other like-minded countries, and

3. negotiating a modified but binding agreement embodying some GATT principles and requiring "best efforts" on others.

Option 1 (a new and binding agreement) has the disadvantage that while it may be possible to negotiate a written agreement on air transport it is highly likely that every country would claim exception, for reasons given above.

Option 2 has the advantage of achieving some liberalization. A conditional agreement of this type will facilitate the development of the consortia of airlines. The fear is that the countries signing the agreement would then engage in new forms of discrimination against non-members, for example, concerning non-members' market access, which would strengthen the competitive position of the groups of airlines covered by the agreement.

This concern could be offset by pursuing simultaneously options 2 and 3. The multilateral agreement in option 3 would be a relatively simple statement of the relevance of the principles of GATT to air transport. It would bind the signatory countries to apply particular principles. This agreement would exist alongside the current set of ASAs and:

– should contain commitments to at least transparency, national treatment and dispute settlement,

– should reflect efforts to extend it to non-discrimination,

– is less likely to endorse MFN treatment on capacity.

The agreement would also sanction the pursuit of conditional MFN agreements by signatories. It would accept such initiatives only if any country which is willing to adhere to the obligations of that agreement is able to join. New signatories would then have market access rights equal to those of established members.

This strategy is likely to contribute to the emergence of a series of regional ASAs. Two countries may be like-minded but if there is not much traffic between them there is little benefit in negotiating a conditional agreement. Initially conditional MFN agreements are therefore likely to be negotiated by countries in the same network.

A group based on the Atlantic routes appears highly likely, even before European integration in 1992. Developments in the air transport industry suggest that any group of countries which can organize a multilateral agreement will be able to assist the competitive position of the airlines in the group. In anticipation, groups of "like-minded" countries in the Pacific ought to be exploring the opportunities to negotiate similar agreements involving others in their networks.

Selected Bibliography

Castle, L. and C. Findlay (eds.). *Pacific Trade in Services.* Sydney: Allen and Unwin, 1988.

Findlay, C. *The Flying Kangaroo – An Endangered Species: An Economic Perspective of Australian International Civil Aviation Policy.* Sydney: Allen and Unwin, 1985.

Industries Assistance Commission. *International Initiatives to Liberalise Trade in Services.* Inquiry into International Trade in Services, Discussion Paper no. 3. Canberra: Australian Government Publishing Service, January, 1989.

Kasper, D.M., "Liberalising Airline Services: How to Get from Here to There," *The World Economy*, March 1988.

PART III

MEMBERSHIP IN GATT AND OTHER ISSUES

China's Entry into the GATT

J.E.D. McDonnell
International Trade Advisor, Canberra

Introduction

At present China is part way through the process of joining the GATT. However, a number of key issues remain unresolved. The most important of these are the questions of whether China will be able to resume the original seat vacated by the Kuo-Min Tang government; whether China's statements as to the efficacy of this trade regime will be accepted by the contracting parties and more particularly whether China will be subject to special safeguards in its protocol of accession and finally whether China will be able to grandfather the wide range of measures which are currently inconsistent with the GATT.

It is fair to say that there is a large credibility gap which China has yet to overcome. Most contracting parties are sceptical about China's ability to conform with GATT rules. Many believe that the Chinese economy is not as open as it has been portrayed in the documentation presented by China's representatives. While it is acknowledged that the People's Republic of China (PRC) has moved a considerable distance towards opening up its economy, the contracting parties can point to instances where businesses have been severely disadvantaged by China's trade and investment regime. There is a sense that all is not as it seems.

The move for admission to the GATT comes at a difficult time. Economic reform policy in China, which since 1978 has

247

oscillated between periods of decentralization and economic expansion on the one hand, and recentralization and economic slowdown on the other, has once again swung back towards tighter central government control and retrenchment. Confronted with uncontrolled local investment and industrial growth, galloping inflation, supply shortages and concern about profiteering and corruption, China's leaders have announced measures aimed at cooling down the country's overheated economy, including a delay of planned price reforms.

Beijing's most pressing objectives are to reduce the double-digit inflation—conservatively estimated by official sources to be running at nearly 20 per cent, the highest level since the establishment of the People's Republic of China in 1949—and to slow the 20 per cent industrial growth rate. At the same time the retrenchment policy is more generally intended to make certain structural adjustments to the economy and to re-establish order in the country's business activities. Reassertion of centralized direction over the economy is viewed as crucial to these goals.

Reform of the Economic Structure in the People's Republic of China

Since 1979 the rural economy has been subject to limited introductions of market forces and the concept that remuneration is linked to output. As a result the rural economy has become more specialized, commercialized and modernized. More recently as a result of the decision on the reform of the economic structure approved in 1984, the restructuring of the national economy as a whole, with the focus on the urban economy, has been accelerated. The key to restructuring the national economy is the extension of the decision-making power of enterprises owned by the people (the so-called collective sector) and turning them into economic entities having full authority for management and full responsibility for their own profits and losses (as private sector business is in the West). As yet, this transformation has only been partial, however, a number of such enterprises have demonstrated considerable autonomy in both trade and investment decisions.

These reforms have been accompanied by a reform of the planning system which is based on the reduction in mandatory planning and the systematic extension of guidance planning, making possible further efforts to develop and improve the market orientation of the system. At the same time, measures are being taken to open up capital markets, to import technology and promote a rational flow of labour.

Further reforms await the promulgation of prospective new economic laws. A key element will be the reform of the systems of pricing and price control, which are seminal to the establishment and improvement of the market-oriented nature of the system. Through these reforms a system will be gradually established in which the state sets the prices of a few vital commodities and labour services, while leaving the rest of the price formation to occur as a result of market forces. For the time being however, the operation of market forces is within certain parameters laid down through the State Planning Commission. In addition the PRC is establishing a new macro-economic management system by gradually changing from mainly direct to mainly indirect controls in the areas of monetary, fiscal and credit policy. Further reforms have been contained in the new economic law. Important aspects of this law relating to foreign investment were promulgated on October 11, 1986. Additional key elements of the new economic law have yet to appear. From the point of view of the GATT contracting parties, the most important of these will be the new trade laws and the laws relating to the reform of the pricing system.

An essential part of the 1984 decision was the reform of the planning system as it relates to foreign trade. The emphasis of this reform is the realization of the role of foreign trade in the increased production and the introduction of new technology. The objective of the reform is to separate the function of government planning and intervention from that of business management. The PRC government has moved away from direct intervention and control, towards relying principally on the use of macro-economic measures. In this context the PRC will be relying more and more on the normal protective mechanisms to protect domestic industries from the impact of international trade. For the greater range of PRC imports the tariff only will serve as the protective mechanism. However, in some critical cases because of the shortage of foreign exchange quantitative restrictions will have to be relied on. Many PRC enterprises will be subject to international competition and their future will depend on the vicissitudes of the market.

An important ingredient in the open door policy has been the seventh five-year plan. This plan which is to operate from 1986 to 1990 was approved on April 12, 1986 by the Fourth Session of the Sixth National People's Congress.

The objective of the plan is that over the five years the gross value of the country's industrial and agricultural output should increase by 38 per cent and the gross national product by 44 per cent. Calculated in terms of constant 1980 prices, the total value of industrial and agricultural output in 1990 will reach US$595 billion and the GNP will reach US$372 billion. It is predicted that the total volume of imports and exports will grow at an average annual rate of 7 per cent, reaching US$83 billion by 1990.

The Trade Regime of the People's Republic of China

The PRC employs all the standard trade measures. The primary focus of its trade regime is the customs tariff which is employed to protect all those industries within the PRC that require protection. Where further restrictions are required because of scarcity of foreign exchange or for other reasons, quantitative restrictions are used. A number of complaints have been levelled at the present trade regime which would be overcome if the PRC becomes a GATT member. It has been asserted that customs valuations for tariff purposes are arbitrary and vary between ports of entry. This should be resolved if the PRC joins the GATT Customs Valuation Code. It has also been argued that the import restrictions which the PRC has implemented are not consistent with the GATT principles. The import restrictions have recently been reduced in number and where they have been introduced for balance of payments purposes they can certainly be justified under GATT rules. The PRC government argues that other fundamental laws which amount to import restrictions could be made the subject of a "grandfather clause" when the PRC signs its protocol of resumption.

The Customs Tariff

The present customs tariff legislation comprises the regulation on import and export duties and the customs tariff and the customs import and export tariff which became effective on March 10, 1985. The objective of the PRC tariff policy is to encourage the export of goods, increase the import of necessities like improved species of plants, fine breeds of animals, fertilizers, certain pharmaceuticals, scientific precision instruments, key machinery or equipment, so as to protect and promote the development of the national economy.

The basic principles for fixing duty rates are as follows:

- duty free treatment for imported necessities which cannot be domestically produced or which are insufficiently supplied
- low rates of duty on raw materials and higher rates of duty on semi-manufactured products
- higher rates of duty on products where the domestic production should be protected.

The tariff combines an element of protection with an element of revenue raising. This is consistent with the approach of many developing countries which have a low tax base and therefore rely on import duties to operate as a poll tax for revenue raising purposes. Where there is no domestic production use of import duties for revenue purposes is consistent with the GATT. There are very few duties imposed on the export of goods.

The levels of protection are set after an enquiry and report process has been completed. A Tariff Board, composed of representatives of the Customs General Administration, the Ministry of Foreign Economic Relations and Trade, the Ministry of Finance, the National Planning Commission and the National Economic Commission is responsible for amendments to the Customs Import and Export Regulations and establishing temporary duty rates pursuant to the principles laid down in the Regulations on Import and Export Duties. The Regulations on Import and Export Duties provide that all goods permitted to be imported into, or exported from, the People's Republic of China are subject to import or export duties to be collected by customs in accordance with the tariff. There are two columns of import duty rates, the minimum rates and the general rates. The minimum rates apply to imports originating in countries with which the PRC has a trade agreement containing a most-favoured nation clause, whereas the general rates apply to imports originating in countries with which the PRC has not concluded such agreements. Most import and export duties are *ad valorem* and customs valuation is broadly consistent with the precepts of the Customs Valuation Code. The Customs Import and Export Tariff is arranged on the basis of the Customs Cooperation Council nomenclature (BTN). Duties on imported or exported goods are levied by the customs authorities according to the relevant tariff headings. In addition, some sub-headings are added to give more precision to the description of particular import or export goods. The items and sub-items in the tariff amount to some 2,100 lines. Apart from those goods which come in duty free, minimum import duty rates vary from 3 to 150 per cent whereas general rates vary from 8 to 180 per cent. There are generally 17 different rates of duty which can be applied to any particular tariff line.

Subsidies

There are a number of types of subsidy utilized in the PRC which directly or indirectly affect imports or exports and therefore have possible implications for GATT obligations. These are:

1. Subsidies paid on certain foodstuffs, e.g., grain and edible oil due to the fact that the fixed retail price is lower than the purchase price paid to the domestic producer or to the importing agency. This is a subsidy which would encourage greater consumption and, if anything, encourage greater imports than otherwise would be the case.

2. Subsidies to the producer due to the fact that energy and certain industrial raw material prices are lower than the cost of production or import prices.

3. Subsidies which occur where a foreign trade enterprise purchases goods at determined domestic prices and exports them for lower prices thus operating at a loss for which the government compensates.

This type of operation is diminishing as the economic reform progresses and more foreign trade enterprises are becoming responsible for their profits and losses. The International Monetary Fund (IMF) staff has noted that under the agency system the domestic prices are normally equivalent to the international price adjusted for the trade corporation's commission. (P. 13 SM85/266)

> Final prices received by most export producers still do not reflect the [internationally traded price], because a major, though declining, share of foreign trade is conducted through foreign trade corporations whose transactions with domestic enterprises are settled at officially determined domestic prices; the difference between international and domestic prices is reflected in the financial position of the foreign trade corporation. (P. 15 SM/85/266)

The IMF staff and executive directors have stressed that an early rationalization of the price system, including strengthened links between international and domestic prices, would greatly improve economic efficiency (P. 18, 22 and 23 SM/266). It could be expected that this argument will be pursued in GATT also.

The Import Licensing System

The PRC's licensing system is designed to ensure that import and export trade is conducted in accordance with the laws and regulations of the state. The Ministry of Foreign Economic Relations and Trade (MFERT) is the administering agency for issuing licences.

Currently the PRC applies import licensing to 43 import commodities mainly raw materials, high grade consumer goods and motor vehicles. In the case of 16 items the licences are approved by MFERT in Beijing, in other cases they are approved by local authorities, under a delegation from MFERT. The authorized agencies issue the import licences according to the foreign exchange paying capability and the requirements of national economic development. The PRC's import licensing system is applied without discrimination as to source.

Reform of the Price System and Price Determination and Imports and Exports

Reform of the price system is the key to the reform of the PRC economic structure. The centralized system of price control is being reformed progressively, reducing the range of uniform prices set by the state and correspondingly enlarging the range of prices allowed to float within certain limits. There has also been an increase in the number of goods which are subject to totally unrestricted pricing. It is hoped that prices will then be more responsive to changes in labour productivity and that the relation between market supply and demand will better meet the needs of national economic developments.

The first year of general reform of the price system was 1985. The basic principle of the reform was to relax price controls while readjusting prices in stages. The reform was primarily carried out in the following three ways:

1. Controls on the purchasing prices and the selling prices of pork were relaxed, and price fluctuations within certain limits were allowed according to supply and demand.

2. The unified state purchasing price of grains was abolished and replaced by a contract purchasing price. Grains not purchased by the state were allowed to be sold freely on the market.

3. The charges for short distance railway passenger and freight transport were raised to encourage more short distance use of highway and water transportation.

In addition, enterprises were allowed to fix prices of from 10 to 20 per cent above the price previously set for industrial products. They were entitled to market these products freely to allow for adjustments to inventories. Prices in these goods and other minor commodities were set by market forces.

In summary, there are at present three main types of prices, state fixed prices, prices allowed to float within certain limits, and market prices. These prices apply to essentially domestic production. A separate set of criteria has been established for the price determination of imports and exports. These are:

1. *Method of Domestic Pricing for Imports.* Currently, the domestic prices for imports are basically set on the basis of import costs plus commission. The components of the prices for imports are as follows: prices on CIF basis (converted at the ruling rate of exchange) plus import duties plus internal taxes plus banking charges plus commission. The profits and losses that arise when import commodities are sold on the domestic market are borne by the importing enterprise. In the case of a few commodities whose prices are fixed by the

state, the profits and losses are borne by the Ministry of Finance.

2. *Method of Pricing for Exports.* Exports are generally priced according to world market conditions. At present, prices of exports are, in principle, set on the basis of export costs plus commission. The components of the prices for exports are as follows: purchasing price of foreign trade enterprises, or production costs plus internal transport changes, plus processing and packing costs plus cost of wear and tear plus storehouse charges plus banking charges plus commission. This price is then converted to the foreign currency concerned at the ruling rate of exchange.

Joining the GATT

The process for joining the GATT for most new members is relatively simple. Article XXXIII provides that a government not a party to the Agreement may accede to the Agreement on terms and conditions to be agreed between such government and the contracting parties. Decisions of the contracting parties in such cases are to be taken by a two-thirds majority.

There are usually two documents which comprise the instrument of accession: "the Protocol" which sets out the terms and conditions for compliance with the Agreement and the "Tariff Schedule" which comprises the bound items of the acceding governments' tariff (either unilaterally offered or resulting from negotiation).

The Protocol is usually straightforward in the case of acceding market economy countries. (See for example the Protocol for Thailand, BISD 29S/3.) However, in the case of non-market economy countries and selected market economy countries (notably Japan) special provisions were included in or linked to the Protocol which limited the rights of the acceding country.

In the respective Protocols of Accession of Poland (15S/47), Romania (18S/6) and Hungary (20S/4) there are provisions which, notwithstanding Article XII, allow other contracting parties to maintain quantitative restrictions on imports during a "transitional period," (it is difficult to know what constitutes a "transitional period"). If it is to be determined by the progression of these contracting parties to complete market economy status then it is likely that the transitional period will last indefinitely. The restrictions applied in the Protocols of Accession of these countries amount to selective safeguards, and there is no doubt that those countries which agreed to the insertion of such provisions within their protocol now feel that they have been badly disadvantaged.

The case of Japan reflects an entirely different situation. The restrictions which were placed on the Japanese economy at a stage when it was truly transitional, moving from war-time regulation to a full market economy status, reflect the fear which many contracting parties maintained and still maintain towards new members that are likely to be economically competitive. The contracting parties were prepared to admit Japan as a new member in the early 1950s, but when Japan finally acceded to the GATT in 1955, 14 of these contracting parties representing about 40 per cent of the foreign trade of the GATT elected to invoke Article XXXV against Japan. The effect of this was that they refused to apply the Agreement in whole or in part (notably Article II) to Japan. As Dam points out, "This massive decision to discriminate was motivated largely by a fear of low wage competition in manufactured goods," (Dam, 1970). Interestingly in the case of Japan it was the western European countries which were most concerned about the threat of Japanese exports. The U.S. saw it as being somewhat to its advantage to have Japan as a member of the GATT since it believed that increased Japanese exports would reduce the economic burden on the United States, (Patterson, 1966). In the present day case of the People's Republic of China, the Europeans appear to be relatively relaxed, however, there is greater concern in the United States about the effect of the PRC's entry into the GATT particularly because the PRC is the source of competitive low cost manufacturers. Ironically much of this concern stems from what Americans perceive to be "unfair trading" by East Asian countries, notably the Japanese.

As indicated earlier the contracting parties, after a great deal of obfuscation (Patterson, p. 285) agreed to Japan's becoming a member of the GATT, but then many invoked Article XXXV against it. There was no precedent for this action. Indeed the implications of applying Article XXXV had not been thought through. Did it, for example, preclude Japan from voting on matters affecting countries which had invoked Article XXXV? If it did then it would probably preclude Japan from participating in votes on most of the matters before the GATT? Did it mean that Japan had no resort to dispute settlement procedures of any sort where its trading partner had invoked Article XXXV? If so, what were the benefits that Japan could realize from GATT membership? Without resolution of these matters, Japan's GATT status was what is called in Australia a "Clayton's membership— the membership you have when you don't have a membership" (*derived from a commercial for a well known non-alcoholic beverage—the drink you have when you're not having a drink*).

The position of the PRC places it in double jeopardy. It is both a non-market economy, albeit one which is making a transition towards some aspects of a market economy, and a low-cost East

Asian country likely to have a dislocating impact upon western manufacturers. Therefore, it has to confront both the issues of selective safeguards as they are applied to non-market economies in their Protocol of Accession and the possibility that some GATT contracting parties may apply Article XXXV against it. Both these issues have been raised by U.S. negotiators in preliminary discussions, however, it should be said that the U.S. has not taken a firm public view on either of them. In addition, the present mood of the United States Congress makes it likely that, notwithstanding President Bush's affinity to China, the U.S. will take a defensive rather than a positive approach to negotiations with the PRC. The U.S. is the predominant negotiator on the PRC's accession to the GATT. In many ways this is unfortunate because U.S./China trade relations have peculiar systemic problems of their own.

At present trade relations between the U.S. and the PRC are governed by a Trade Relations Agreement, which was signed on July 7, 1979. The signature of this agreement in 1979 and its coming into effect in 1980 was an important step forward in the normalization of relations between the PRC and the United States in so far as it provided for the establishment of a diplomatic relationship and a policy of favourable treatment for the PRC which marked it out from the previous treatment which continued to be applied to the Soviet Union, that of less than Most Favoured Nation (MFN) status.

There is, however, a catch. Section 402 of the U.S. Trade Act of 1974 provides that before MFN status is extended to any non-market economy country the President must report to Congress that the country in question does not "deny its citizens the right or opportunity to emigrate; impose more than a nominal tax on immigration or on the visas or other documents required for immigration or any purpose or cause whatsoever; or impose more than a nominal tax, levy, fine, fee, or other charge on any citizen as a consequence of the desire of such citizen to emigrate to the country of his or her choice." The President may, however, temporarily waive this restriction if "it is determined that such waiver will substantially promote the objectives of the purpose of the statue; and assurances are received that the emigration practices of that country will henceforth lead substantially to the achievement of the objectives of the statue." In the normal course of events the President has granted this waiver after assurances by the Chinese government that they are committed to the freedom of emigration. This matter of itself has not become an important question in the review of the PRC's MFN status, however, there are indications that the provision might be used to lobby the President to take protective action against low cost imports from the PRC.

The more important question in relation to the PRC's accession to the GATT is what will happen to the 1974 Trade Act provision once the PRC becomes a full GATT member. In the event that the U.S. wishes to retain this provision it should invoke Article XXXV or to give an undertaking that the waiver will be virtually automatic. Once the PRC and the U.S. are both full members of the GATT it would be contrary to GATT rules for the U.S. to decline MFN status in the event that the waiver were not continued, however, no formal dispute would arise unless the PRC sought to have the matter brought before the GATT. There may be no reason for the PRC to complain about such a situation (indeed it may choose to acquiesce in the breach) but in the event that it did, the U.S. would have no response if it had not invoked Article XXXV. Were Section 402 of the U.S. Trade Act of 1974 to be revoked, the Congressional trade hawks might seek an alternative provision to restrain "unfair" and "excessive" exports from the PRC. In order to avoid this dilemma the U.S. might insist on selective safeguard provisions in the PRC Protocol of Resumption following the precedent of Hungary, Romania and Poland, but as in the case of Romania and Hungary this would also require the U.S. to invoke Article XXXV.

Resumption Versus Accession

Before discussing the possible mechanisms for PRC re-entry it is necessary to dispose of the question of whether the PRC is resuming its old seat or acceding as a new member. The answer is of course that it is doing neither. What the PRC seeks is to be acknowledged as an original member, but to negotiate the basis of its membership "*de novo.*" It will therefore declare its original tariff schedule a nullity and seek to negotiate a new "Protocol of Resumption." In this context the PRC does not use the term resumption to imply continuous membership or continuing rights and obligations, but rather in the Oxford Dictionary sense of "begin again." The only difference between resumption in this latter sense and new accession is in the import of original membership.

However, it appears that most of the contracting parties now agree with the GATT Secretariat that the withdrawal of the Kuo-Min Tang government in 1950 was valid; they therefore will not agree to China resuming its seat. Rather they will press China to negotiate a Protocol of Accession which can be supported by a large majority—if not a consensus—of contracting parties.

Possible Solutions to the PRC Membership Problem

Four broad solutions are indicated as possible bases for the PRC's resumption of its seat in the GATT:

1. Limited membership subject to the restrictions normally associated with non-market economy countries and restrictions pursuant to Article XXXV:
2. Provisional membership leading to eventual full membership;
3. The creation of a new set of obligations under the GATT to apply to countries such as the PRC (the so called Part V solution);
4. Unlimited membership similar to Thailand or Mexico.

Limited Membership

The particular problems associated with the use of restrictions in the Protocol of Accession and Article XXXV are discussed above. On a more general level the employment of such provisions does further harm to the GATT as a general instrument designed to encourage freer trade. This point was made by the working party that was appointed to review Japanese accession in 1960 (BISD 10S/69). The working party suggested that the principal use of the invocation of Article XXXV would tend to disappear if "satisfactory multilateral solutions" could be found for the problem of "market disruption."

The membership of the PRC raises the same general issue. Employment of "selective safeguards" against the PRC in the context of a renewal of its membership would undoubtedly be seen by some countries as a chance to renew one of the more fractious and counterproductive GATT debates. As no generally acceptable solution to the safeguards problem has yet emerged, this is a debate which is best avoided in a particular context. Moreover, there are strong economic arguments against the use of selective safeguards in any context (Robertson, 1977).

Provisional Membership

This has been suggested by a number of American commentators, particularly Robert Herzstein (Herzstein, 1986). Herzstein's contention is that the PRC lacks the necessary institutions to operate a market economy. In this view a mere affirmation by the PRC that it will reduce its external tariffs would be unlikely to satisfy the GATT contracting parties or achieve the objectives of the GATT. He therefore suggests that the resumption process take a number of steps from simple information gathering through a series of milestones to full GATT membership.

Herzstein admits that this staged procedure is more elaborate and time consuming than the steps followed with other centrally planned economies and herein lies the rub. One of the objectives of the PRC in joining the GATT is to use its membership to accelerate implementation of reforms within the country. The fact that the PRC is opening its markets is evidenced by the rapid increase in imports in recent years. It now has the legal and institutional framework necessary to support a trade regime which conforms with the GATT. However, as Herzstein has pointed out, "Even with steady progress in the direction set by its current policies, it may not for some years achieve the critical mass of policies, institutions, and behaviour which would make it a 'market economy' capable of interacting with other major GATT members without distortions and perceived unfairness." The pace of change in the PRC is necessarily slow. However, for this very reason the PRC is too big a country to have policy introduced on the basis of gradualism. The policy of conformity with the GATT will have to be introduced as a once and for all policy to avoid confusions. However, the inducement for the PRC to change will need to be the promise of reasonable reciprocity from contracting parties at the same time.

The Creation of New Obligations (The Part V Solution)

The first questions that arise in connection with the concept of new obligations or a new Part V solution are what are the new obligations and to which countries will they apply? Before attempting to answer, it is perhaps important to examine why suggestions for a Part V have arisen.

There is a strong argument that has been put forward by a number of GATT representatives, commentators and secretariat staff, that the entry into the GATT of centrally planned economies and developing countries has watered down the meaning of Article I. This is undoubtedly true. The reason why it occurred probably has as much to do with the fact that these countries constituted a relatively small proportion of world trade as anything else. While the centrally planned economies were given Part IV, a new set of obligations which amounted to an exemption from many of the GATT disciplines was applied to the industrialized countries. The rationale for this exemption from some of the disciplines was that such an exemption was necessary to promote economic development in developing countries. The fallacy of this is now apparent. If economic development is to be equated with economic growth then this is desirable for all contracting parties, not only developing countries. It would follow that all contracting Parties should be exempted from GATT discipline in order to promote economic growth. On the other hand, if economic growth is more readily promoted through adherence to GATT disciplines, then there is no case for developing countries being given such exemptions. There is therefore a strong case for the elimination of Part IV from the GATT rather than the proliferation of such parts to include a Part V.

Given that neither the existing centrally planned contracting parties nor the developing contracting parties are likely to change their present status the only member of Part V in the foreseeable future would be the PRC. (*Obviously a Part V restricted to large non-market economies and conferring only limited GATT rights would make it easier to bring the U.S.S.R. into the GATT.*) The PRC is ostensibly both a developing country and a centrally planned economy. To meet its requirements, Part V would therefore have to comprise all the exemptions presently allowed to developing countries and the restrictions required by the industrialized countries. In this case the PRC and other contracting parties would not offer and receive reciprocal concessions and most likely the industrialized countries would neither grant nor receive MFN treatment.

The arguments against such a proposal are obvious. The objective in having the PRC become a member of the GATT is to have it adhere to GATT disciplines. It is undesirable that it should be able to claim the exemptions which apply to developing countries and it is equally undesirable that it be permanently exempted from compliance with GATT disciplines by virtue of its centrally planned status when this is only a transitory situation. When the dimension of the PRC's prospective impact on world trade is taken into consideration (it is likely to be the fourth largest trader among the GATT countries after U.S., EEC and Japan before the end of the century) the need for the PRC to comply fully with the GATT disciplines becomes a matter of the utmost urgency if the GATT is to survive as a cornerstone of international trade.

Unlimited GATT Membership

The author concludes that the PRC should be treated in the same way as Mexico was in its accession. The reason for this is because the PRC is best characterized as a developing country moving rapidly towards the economic structure which characterizes many developing countries (a developing country mixed economy). The disciplines that were applied to Mexico were stringent and included reciprocal concessions (see L/6036, August 14, 1986). The

PRC which is a far more important country than Mexico economically should accept no lesser disciplines.

The question arises as to what safeguards the industrialized countries would have against a surge in Chinese exports. The answer is that they would have all the safeguards of the GATT together with the disciplines of the appropriate codes. There are strong arguments that some of these provisions are inadequate, but if this is the case they are not only inadequate against the PRC, but against all the contracting parties. It is for this reason that they are being reconsidered in the course of the new multilateral trade negotiations. In the meantime, countries have managed to co-exist with the PRC's burgeoning trade until now without special safeguards, and membership in the GATT will not in any marked respect change the "*status quo ante.*"

Two bilateral problems remain. The problem of the U.S. Trade Act adverted to earlier and the problem of the treatment of PRC exports for antidumping purposes. The first of these can be safely ignored. The fact that the PRC is not receiving "*de jure*" MFN treatment because of Section 402 of the 1974 U.S. Trade Law will not matter as long as the U.S. continues as a matter of fact to grant the PRC MFN treatment by extending the waiver. If this ceases, the matter will no doubt become a formal dispute within the GATT and will need to be resolved by the contracting parties in light of prevailing circumstances. In relation to PRC treatment under domestic antidumping legislation the onus rests with the PRC to show that its domestic pricing system will allow anti-dumping investigations of the sort carried out in similar market economy countries. This can only be shown once the transition in the PRC economy has matured.

In the author's view the only reasonable approach to PRC renewed membership is for the PRC to be treated in a way that is comparable to an acceding mixed economy developing country (e.g., Mexico). The PRC needs GATT membership sooner rather than later and on terms which will encourage economic reform, not stifle it. In taking an approach similar to that taken with Mexico, the industrialized countries would have little to lose other than the opportunity to introduce more protectionism.

Conclusions

The issues of economic reform within China and its admission to GATT are inextricably intertwined. In a sense the PRC administration may need admission to the GATT at a fixed point in order to move closer to deregulation, rather more than the rest of the world needs the PRC to be admitted to the GATT for its own trading purposes. This is yet again a snapshot view. The PRC economy is growing at a pace which could see it reaching the size of the American economy early in the twenty-first century. It will then be a motor economy of the sort which the rest of the world needs for sustained growth. It is far better that such an economy be absorbed into the world trading system within the GATT framework rather than remain outside it. Nevertheless, if the PRC is admitted to the GATT within the next one to two years there is no doubt that the combination of the PRC's restrictive import regulations and export subsidization policies will put its trading practices in danger of offending the spirit if not the letter of the General Agreement. There are therefore profound issues of constitutional reform which must be addressed within the PRC as well as the probably more superficial issues which will be involved in any negotiation of the PRC's Protocol of Resumption. Here the key issue is that the negotiation of the Protocol should be perceived by other countries, particularly those at the forefront of negotiations with the PRC, as being directed towards providing the impetus for the PRC to undertake real constitutional reform in the context of becoming a full GATT member. The contracting parties should avoid Sinophobia or some other derivative of the "Japanese problem." If the contracting parties were to dig in and use the Protocol as a means of preserving protectionist measures against PRC exports, the effect may well be to inhibit the movement of what is potentially one of the world's largest markets towards integration within the open multilateral trading system. However, momentum towards both economic reform and admission to the GATT must be seen in the context of the present economic and political realities within China.

The signs are ominous. If the trends generated by foreign-trade reform and domestic inflation are allowed to continue, China will once again enter the stage of serious trade deficits, just as it did in 1985 and 1986. To avoid this, the Ministry of Foreign Economic Relations and Trade (MFERT) adopted in October 1988 several measures to revise foreign trade reform.

The measures included recentralization of management of the export and import of commodities that have been in short supply in the country, or which have experienced great fluctuation in procurement prices or export or import prices. Administrative controls over foreign trade in the form of quotas, licences and permits were strengthened. In addition, economic measures, such as customs duties and taxes, are not being used more flexibly and frequently, as a means for the state to intervene in import and export activities.

In November and early December 1988, MFERT and the State Council reportedly attempted to revise the reform policy on imports by local authorities. It apparently wanted to re-establish a much more centralized foreign trade permit system. A more radical move has also been taken by the State Council to rectify unequal competition in exports and imports among localities. This takes the form of cutting the retention share of foreign exchange earnings from exports by the Special Economic Zones (SEZs) from 100 to 80 per cent.

At the same time three industrial sectors—light industry, arts and crafts, and garments—are now required to experiment with self-financing in foreign trade, and are to have their retention share raised from 70 to 80 per cent, thereby allowing equal competition between the SEZs and the rest of the country in the export of commodities from these sectors. The changes were effective from January 1989.

With the trade deficit rising to over U.S.$6 billion at the end of 1988, the central government has taken even more drastic steps to curb it in 1989. Under these circumstances, China's trade may not be as promising as it was in 1988. China's import growth is likely to level out and eventually decline. At the same time, exports are also likely to decline because of the need to restrict tradable goods for export in order to improve supply for the domestic market. The trade deficit may be stabilized, but most probably only at the expense of reform. China will once again enter into a stage of adjustment as it did in 1986 and 1987. But this time, it will no longer have the support of strong export growth.

All these realities are only serving to make the issue of China's admission to the GATT more complex and difficult for the rest of the world.

References

Dam, Kenneth W. *The GATT: Law – The International Organization*, Chicago, University of Chicago Press, 1970.

Herzstein, Robert. "China and the GATT: Legal and Policy Issues Raised by China's Participation in the General Agreement on Tariffs and Trade," *Law and Policy in International Business*, Vol. 18:2, 1986, pp. 371-415.

Patterson, Gardner. *Discrimination in International Trade – The Policy Issues, 1945-1965*, Princeton, Princeton University Press, 1966.

Robertson, David. *Fail Safe Systems for Trade Liberalization*, London, Trade Policy Research Centre, 1977.

China's Foreign Trade Policy Problems

Li Zhongzhou
Ministry of Foreign Economic Relations and Trade

Introduction

China's relations with the multilateral trading system known as GATT have been suspended for more than forty years following the imposition of a trade embargo by Western nations in response to its adoption in 1949 of a Soviet-style planned economy and a policy of autarky. However, as international political trends have changed, so too has China's international economic policies. Beginning in 1978, China has implemented national policies of opening to the outside world and invigorating the domestic economy. To improve economic efficiency, it has reformed its entire economy system, changed its economic development strategy and nurtured and perfected a socialist market. China has also adopted a completely new attitude toward international economic relations and has changed from a policy of absolute autarky to one of enthusiastic participation in the international division of labour. This is evident by the use of comparative advantage to enhance national economic development, the liberalization of foreign investment, and the energetic use of foreign capital to promote national economic activity through the combination of domestic and foreign production. In short, the status of foreign economic relations in the national economy has been greatly elevated.

On the basis of this policy transformation, China resumed its participation in the World Bank and the International Monetary Fund (IMF) in 1980 and in the process, integrated its monetary and fiscal system with the world's system. However, China remains outside of the General Agreement on Tariffs and Trade (GATT) which, along with the World Bank and the IMF is one of the three key international economic institutions established after the Second World War. If China does not participate in GATT, it cannot be a full participant in the world economic system and will suffer from a lack of coordination between its monetary-fiscal policy and trade policy.

The Preparatory Phase for Resumption of Status as a GATT Contracting Party

To adjust to the requirements of opening to the outside world and to invigorate the domestic economy, China has implemented significant economic reforms. Primarily among these has been the reform of the wage system, the development of different management models, and the expansion of enterprise autonomy. Private industry, both individually owned and collectives, have also developed and have become much more independent of state-owned enterprises. With the reform of the planning system and government management of enterprises, macroeconomic management is shifting from direct to indirect control, and the regulating functions of the market have increased significantly. Accompanying these charges is the opening to the outside, or the shift toward an open-door economy.

The reforms of the past decade have created an economic system that now basically conforms to the requirements of GATT and conditions are increasingly ripe for restoration of China's status as a contracting party, as in July 1986.

The Advantages of GATT Membership

China has given careful consideration to the pros and cons of resuming GATT status. In general terms, the GATT principles of non-discrimination and trade liberalization offer improved opportunities for Chinese products to enter international markets. More specifically, nine advantages seem apparent:

    (1)   Participating in GATT will strengthen the economic relations between China and other nations and improve China's role in the multilateral trade system. Accordingly, it will be able to work with other contracting parties to rescind protectionist measures and reform the structure of international production in order that

Chinese products will be able to enter international markets more readily, resulting in an improved export product mix and a more diversified economy.

(2)   Trade among GATT participants already accounts for 90 per cent of world trade and trade between China and GATT participants accounts for more that 85 per cent of China's trade. Resumption of GATT status will help China to rationalize the allocation of its resources and accelerate its economic development, thereby giving new impetus to a stagnant world economy. The expansion of world demand will in turn provide even larger export markets for Chinese products.

(3)   As a result of problems left over from the period of embargo and blockage, a number of the major developed nations have not provided China with preferential treatment in accordance with GATT rules. Some nations have granted China conditional "most-favoured-nation" treatment, but because of the reality of the increasing tendency toward regional groupings, China can be said to be receiving "least-favoured-nation" treatment. Furthermore, some industrialized nations impose discriminatory quantitative restrictions (QRs), anti-dumping procedures, and selective safeguard measures on China. China hopes that by resuming GATT status she will receive unqualified "most-favoured-nation" treatment and that all discriminatory trade practices against it will be abolished.

(4)   In addition, because China is a low income developing nation, it anticipates that she will receive the type of treatment offered other developing nations. For instance, import restrictions and flexible customs duties should be permitted for balance of payments reasons. For development reasons, protection of infant industries, governmental assistance, and export subsidies should also be permitted.

(5)   Participation in GATT will allow China to strengthen its position in trade negotiations by having access to more effective, just and fair rules for the settlement of disputes.

(6)   GATT status will help Chinese enterprises increase their international competitiveness, rationalize the economy's output mix, and overcome the blindness of industrial policy.

(7)   GATT requirements will increase the transparency of China's foreign trade system and uniformity of trade policies and laws throughout the country; thus gradually eliminating trade distortions, advancing the

reform of the economic system, and accelerating the transition to a socialist market economy.

(8) Participation in GATT will also strengthen the confidence of other GATT nations in the stability of Chinese economic and trade policies, facilitate the import of foreign technology and capital into China, and create an international environment conducive to China's outward-looking developing strategy.

(9) GATT is just now in the midst of negotiating new international regulations governing trade in services, investment and intellectual property rights. These negotiations will have a major influence on the world economic and industrial structure through to the beginning of the next century. Only through active participation in these negotiations can China's position in the world economy be assured.

The Price of Participation

Because China is a potentially vast market, many contracting parties welcome its return to GATT. However, some countries, either because they misunderstand the facts or because they are seeking a tactical advantage in negotiations, continue to characterize the Chinese economy as a centrally planned economy of the traditional type and request that China not only reduce tariffs but also accept adjustments in the non-tariff area, especially with regard to selective safeguards. Although this position contrasts sharply with that held by China, in order to achieve the benefits of GATT participation China, must accept the necessity of the following changes:

(1) China must continue to reform her economic and trading system in accordance with GATT requirements. Although this is generally consistent with the goals of the current reform effort, it will nevertheless impose some additional constraints on economic policy.

(2) China's resumption of GATT status will require a reduction of tariffs. Compared to the developed countries, China's tariffs, which have the dual purpose of protecting national industries and providing government revenue, are relatively high. Because Chinese industries are accustomed to a high level of tariff protection and the government faces fiscal deficits, a major reduction of tariffs will cause tremendous problems and must be considered a high admission to GATT.

(3) China's traditional system of considering trade in terms of bilateral balance on the basis of annual plans will

have to be replaced by a system in which balance is attained only in the aggregate accounts.

(4) An increase in the share of foreign trade in the national economy will magnify the impact of instability in foreign-linked facets of the Chinese economy such as finance, currency, and the exchange rate.

(5) China has a high demand for imports due to commodity shortages and the overvaluation of its currency. The resultant shortage of foreign exchange causes price inflation and pressure to restrict imports, both of which are likely to increase with China's greater integration into the world economy brought about by GATT membership.

(6) GATT contracting parties will request that China continue to reform its price system, reduce the degree of planning in the economy, decrease export subsidies, and ease restrictions on foreign exchange management.

Specific Concerns in the Uruguay Round

The Uruguay Round has not given adequate attention to the problems of the developing nations. Although there has been some progress on the question of tropical products, little advance has been made on textiles and other issues of concern to developing nations. The following points address more specifically some of these concerns.

Agricultural Trade

The major trading nations want to avoid discussing trade in agricultural products during the current round of negotiations even though it is an issue that has already severely damaged the credibility of the multilateral trading system. Resources have been allocated in a totally irrational way, with highly efficient producers going out of business, while producers enjoying massive government subsidies have flourished behind a wall of protectionism. Only after the U.S. and the E.E.C. have resolved the inconsistencies in their policies will it be possible to reach agreement on agricultural trade.

China is simultaneously an importing and an exporting nation, and in the interests of the fundamental principles of the multilateral trading system and the long-term global supply of grain, it supports the goal of liberalizing trade in agricultural products. This can begin with the short-term strategy of first freezing, and then reducing, export subsidies; and then moving to achieve the long-term goal of improving the orderliness of agricultural trade. Public health and quarantine measures also need immediate attention because of their significant adverse impact on all developing countries' exports of agricultural and value-added products.

Textile trade and the Multifibre Agreement (MFA)

Textiles and clothing are major exports for the developing nations, but under the MFA, the importing countries are permitted to impose limits on their export. This makes a complete mockery of the GATT principles of free trade and non-discrimination, and severely damages the credibility of the multilateral trading system. The Uruguay Round should address this issue in light of GATT rules and procedures, not that the elimination of the MFA is interlinked with the reform of the safeguard clauses. Textile importing countries have asked for increased protection in this sector even though their own industry is running at more than 95 per cent of capacity. They should instead immediately freeze the status quo and then gradually abandon the MFA limits. The possibility of adding even more import restrictions is certainly not acceptable. On the other hand, the application of Article 18 (concerning exceptions granted for balance of payments reasons and encouragement of infant industries) will accelerate economic growth in the developing nations and will be beneficial to the expansion of world trade.

Protection of Intellectual Property

The major developed countries have attempted to use the GATT retaliation provisions to increase the protection of intellectual property rights and block what are otherwise legal trade restrictions. Developing nations are obvious targets, since their legislation on intellectual property is incomplete. A GATT attempt to fashion a new global trade regime dealing with intellectual property is likely to be counter-productive because it will only protect the interests of the owners of intellectual property and not the interests of the users, thus creating an even greater imbalance between developed and the developing nations.

Trade in Services

As the structure of output in countries around the world changes, trade in services has emerged as an important facet of world trade. A framework of multilateral principles and regulations governing this trade is certainly necessary, but a new framework must promote economic expansion and the development of the developing countries. The new regulations must not simply mechanically apply the provisions of GATT. Services are an important factor of production and the competitiveness of exports from the developing world is affected by their availability. Accordingly, particular consideration must be given to the needs of the developing nations in this sector.

Multilateral Trade Arrangements: A View from Taiwan

Pin-Kung Chiang
Board of Foreign Trade
Taipei, Taiwan

The Weakening of the GATT and the Need for Multilateral Trade Negotiations

Because Taiwan is not a contracting party to the General Agreement on Tariffs and Trade (GATT) it is unable to participate in its activities and the current round of Multilateral Trade Negotiations (MTNs). But as one of the major players in international trade, Taiwan watches closely, and with great concern, developments in the world trading system and the MTNs. This paper outlines Taiwan's views about the ongoing Uruguay Round and suggests ways to improve the current process of negotiation and strengthen the existing world trading system. Views, I firmly believe that most Asian Newly Industrialized Economies (NIEs) share.

The postwar trading system, based on the open multilateral framework of the GATT, has contributed to rapid economic growth, rising employment, and higher real incomes and wages in all major trading countries. The substantial reduction in barriers to trade and capital flows carried out under the auspices of GATT and the International Monetary Fund (IMF) have facilitated a remarkable expansion in trade and investment. World trade grew nearly twice as fast as world production in the 1950s and 1960s, and international direct-investment grew at an average of approximately 12 per cent a year during the 1960-73 period. The postwar trading system as embodied in the GATT, provides a central, albeit loose, framework to guide trade relations amongst market economies. Consistent with the philosophy that economic benefits of international specialization in production and trade are maximized by maintaining open and competitive markets, many GATT rules attempted to reduce the degree of government interference in the transactions of private firms. Government interventions must be limited in accordance with the principles of non-discrimination (the MTN treatment) and national treatment.

However, since the 1970s, new protectionism has swept the world and threatened the growth of many developing countries, especially Asia-Pacific countries. In the process, central economic premises and key rules of the GATT have been weakened and undermined. Specifically, government actions to limit imports or expand exports in an effort to protect jobs or promote economic growth have increased trade tensions and eroded public support for the world trading system.

Although there is little evidence that the postwar trend toward a more open trading system has been reversed, great uncertainty does exist about whether current GATT rules and institutions are capable of dealing with trade pressures caused by increased government interventions in the marketplace. Unless something is done at the current MTNs to overhaul the existing world trading system, the threat of protectionism will cast a long shadow and affect the prosperity of the global economy.

Over the years, industries in the developed countries, particularly in the United States and Europe, have faced hard adjustment challenges. Developing countries, on the other hand, have been plagued with increasing balance of payments and debt problems. As a result of these challenges, coupled with increased economic interdependence and trade competition, protectionist pressures in both developed and developing countries have intensified recently. Through a variety of domestic policies, governments have increasingly intervened in their economies to attain various national objectives. Many of the actions taken to protect jobs or promote growth violate the letter and/or spirit of the GATT rules. Others which focus on international transactions in services, investment and intellectual property rights have increased tensions and weakened public support for the world trading system.

On the import side, government efforts have focused on providing protection to key sectors facing difficulty in meeting increased competitive pressures. Measures such as public subsidies, cartel arrangements, procurement policies, and customs procedures are utilized to limit import competition. Furthermore, many of the import-limiting measures are negotiated bilaterally, a process that is inconsistent with the multilateral approach to trade policy embodied in GATT. Many import restraints are also directed at individual countries, particularly towards the Asian NIEs, thereby undermining the central GATT principle of non-discrimination. At the end of February 1989, GATT identified 277 "grey area" measures—voluntary export restraints, market-sharing deals and other pacts—designed to circumvent GATT rules. In addition, activity under the discretionary import-relief provisions dealing with unfair trade practices has increased trade tensions.

Direct and indirect measures have been utilized to promote exports. Official export credit subsidies have grown dramatically, from approximately $500 million in 1977, to close to $7 billion in 1987. Ineffective international discipline over official export credits reflects different national attitudes towards subsidization. Various non-traditional measures to increase exports are also in evidence. Some countries have increasingly resorted to "counter trade" in order to improve their trade accounts. A recent survey indicates that 25 per cent of all international trade is now covered by arrangements linking export sales to repurchase agreements. Attempts to create jobs by tying foreign-investment permission to local labour or material-content purchase agreements or export requirements also are on the rise.

The arbitrary and unilateral definition of "unfair", "unjustifiable", "unreasonable" and "illicit" trade practices as required in the newly enacted U.S. Omnibus Trade and Competitiveness Act of 1988, as well as the EC's new commercial policy instrument (Council Regulation 2641/84) on the strengthening of the common commercial policy, with regard in particular to protection against illicit commercial practices, promise to cause increased trade tensions amongst the major trading countries. They paint an even gloomier picture for the integrity of the world trading system.

All of these developments cast a cloud of uncertainty over the GATT rules and institutions that are meant to deal with the current and future challenges of government intervention in the market place.

Actions to Strengthen and Improve the International Trading System

Given the seemingly inherent draw of the world trading system towards protectionism, the need for checks to combat the shift is readily apparent. International trade rules provide governments with the necessary discipline to pursue national economic policies broadly supportive of an international division of labour based on comparative advantage. These rules also create a certain and predictable environment conductive to long-term investment. It is, therefore, is of paramount importance that these rules be strengthened and improved in order to maintain the international trade order. I would like to suggest some ideas which I hope may contribute constructively to the functioning of the GATT and the current round of the MTN:

The first challenge is to halt the erosion of the international trading system and restore its credibility. This restoration is closely associated with the implementation of the "standstill" and "rollback" commitments which were accepted at the 1982 GATT Ministerial Session and at UNCTAD VI in 1983 and for which a surveillance mechanism was established by the Uruguay Declaration.

Second, the growing preoccupation with reciprocity in a narrow, bilateral sense under the banner of "fair trade", and resorting to bilateral negotiations and bilateral arrangements to achieve MTN goals, undermines the basic GATT concept of multilateral reciprocity. The tendency to judge openness of markets not by rules, but by quantity outcomes for one's exports must be corrected. Pressures to show "results" and to "balance" trade, regardless of the competitiveness of the country's industry, contradict the principle of comparative advantage on which the GATT is based. The international trading community should take concerted action in the perspective of overall trade and economic benefits and common goals, rather than in terms of concessions to be made in a particular bilateral negotiation. Such bilateral solutions and narrow sense of reciprocity must be kept in check and brought under control, especially during the MTN period, as they threaten to cripple the central canon of the GATT— multilateralism.

Third, the dispute settlement mechanism must be strengthened so that no country can block the adoption of GATT panel reports. Such hostile blockage undermines the discipline and the very credibility on which the GATT relies. (For example, in May 1989, the United States blocked, for the fourth time, the adoption by the GATT Council of a panel's conclusions that Section 337 of the U.S. Tariff Act of 1930 is inconsistent with GATT rules. This repeated refusal to accept the panel's findings has caused Japanese concern about American attitudes *vis-à-vis* the settling of disputes and the credibility of the GATT mechanism for doing so. Furthermore, the undue delay of the U.S. to implement in a timely manner the recommendations of the panel reports on the super-fund tax on oil imports and customs users' fee has come under severe criticism.)

Fourth, GATT trade rules—including those that may cover new areas, like services, agriculture and intellectual property rights—must take "due account of the different development levels of contracting parties". Although certain provisions were embodied during the Tokyo Round to allow derogations, and special exemptions from and special exceptions to GATT rules for developing countries, no adjustments have been made to these rules to reflect changes in the world trading system. For example, the emergence of the NIEs has introduced a new variable into the international trade scene and a consensus has emerged amongst industrialized countries that the NIEs should not enjoy the same exemptions from GATT obligations as developing countries. At the same time, the NIEs insist that their economies are not yet mature enough to accept the responsibilities required of developed countries, and that they have neither the capability to assume equal obligations, nor the capacity to compete with developed countries, particularly in the field of services. New policy solutions must be found that would help the NIEs accept increased international responsibilities during their transition into developed countries.

Fifth, the "trade-expanding" intentions of certain countries threaten to yield a world economy in which the politically powerful nations expand their exports, regardless of their competitiveness, to weaker nations at the expense of less powerful but more efficient rivals. These voluntary import expansions (VIEs), as described by Professor Bhagwati, create a new form of "export protectionism" which threatens the open trading system and disregards the underlying comparative advantage principle on which world trade should be based. The threat of retaliation waged by certain countries as a means to "liberalize" world trade and open world markets has shaken the foundation of multilateralism upon which the GATT was built. Such threats may not work at all times; those countries who retaliate may find themselves becoming the countries with the most closed markets and highest trade barriers. These measures should be abandoned as a precondition to overhauling the world trading system and the MTN.

Sixth, there is a need to harmonize the rules on origin within the GATT. Although the Kyoto Convention contains basic rules on origin, the complexity of issues involved have wrought confusion and tension on the international trade terrain. During the past years, a number of trade rows have broken out over the origin of garments and motor vehicles, and unless rules on origin are settled within the GATT, there will be more.

Seventh, regionalism in international trade is rising. Following the economic integration of Europe, the U.S.-Canada Free Trade Agreement (FTA) and Australia-New Zealand Common Market, there are now proposals for establishing an Asia-Pacific Economic Community. The fear of "Fortress Europe" is in fact not limited Europe and has already expanded to include other regional movements. Article XXIV of the GATT should be fine-tuned or adjusted to prevent further conflicts between current rules and the underlying GATT most-favoured-nation principle. The Uruguay Round and regional economic integration should and must be mutually reinforcing and add to the benefits the world gains from trade.

Lastly, distortive economic conditions which prevail amongst some major international traders should be corrected so as to make these countries more competitive in the international trade arena. Structural adjustments must be allowed to happen now, not postponed until it is politically convenient. Only the restoration of the health of the economies in the major trading countries will halt the continuing corrosion of the world trading system and the crippling of the MTNs.

In short, the key challenge is to make the GATT an important factor in the management of protectionist pressures that threaten to undermine the considerable benefits of the postwar, open trading system. The current Uruguay Round is perhaps a step forward in this direction. If ways can be found to resolve the above issues under the framework of the GATT, the MTN will be a constructive force for maintaining the law and order of international trade.

Joint Multilateral Actions with OECD, IMF, World Bank

The root tensions in the world trading system are caused in large part by imbalances in economic, fiscal and monetary fields within and between major trading partners. These imbalances lead to excessive fluctuation in exchange rates, inflation, unemployment and high levels of indebtedness. A major world economic disruption could induce a hasty resurrection of the protectionist walls of an earlier era. Thus, coordination of international economic policies is bound to expand and become ever more pervasive as cross-border trade in goods and services grows as a proportion of world output. Greater coordination of macro-economic policies amongst OECD countries could aim at stimulating economic growth and contribute to exchange rate stabilization. And, as NIEs are emerging as new economic powers, there is a need for policy coordination between the NIEs and industrial countries. However, the current suggestion that there is a need to establish an Asian OECD will cause more confrontation than cooperation amongst industrialized countries and the Asian NIEs. OECD membership must be open-ended, rather than a closed-door club for the "rich" countries. It will be beneficial to the stability and integrity of the world's economy if OECD membership is expanded to include the NIEs instead of them resorting to their own form of economic policy cooperation; a move which could contribute to the disintegration of world economic system. The conclusions reached at Mid-Term Review in Montreal should be endorsed. Solutions to imbalances whose origins lie in the monetary and financial areas require joint actions by major trading partners within the IMF, the World Bank, UNCTAD and the OECD.

The Importance of Integrating Taiwan into the International Economic System

Another important flaw in the international trading system is that some major trading nations are neither contracting parties of the GATT nor participants in the current round of the MTN and are thus not subject to GATT rules. Taiwan is included amongst these countries.

Taiwan now trades with more than 140 countries and its total trade reached U.S. $110 billion in 1988, making it the 13th largest trading nation in the world. In addition, Taiwan's growing foreign reserves, which have now reached U.S. $75 billion, are of concern to many countries. Clearly there can be no doubt that Taiwan occupies an important position in the world's economy. But to the regret of many, it is neither a contracting part of the GATT, nor a member of such important international economic and monetary organizations as the OECD, the IMF and the World Bank. International cooperation on economic and monetary policies and the application of GATT rules to all trading countries is absolutely necessary to combat protectionism and to preserve the integrity of the world trading system. Accordingly it would be mutually advantageous to Taiwan and its trading partners to integrate it into the international trading system as well as other international economic and monetary cooperation systems.

Taiwan's Accession to the GATT

As a strong supporter of international cooperation and maintenance of world trade order, Taiwan participated from the beginning in the drafting of the Havana Charter and is one of the 23 original signatories of the GATT. Although it withdrew from the GATT in 1950, Taiwan strives to develop its foreign trade under GATT principles. For example, as the Tokyo Round entered its final stage, Taiwan concluded a bilateral trade agreement with the U.S. in 1979. Under this Agreement, it agreed to reduce tariffs on a wide scale. Equally important, all these tariff concessions were applied reciprocally to all of Taiwan's trading partners under the most-favoured-nation principle. Since 1984, Taiwan has adopted "liberalization" and "internationalization" as two established policies. During the past years, the government had initiated a series of concrete measures to liberalize trade. Foreign exchange controls have been largely abolished and the currency is now determined by market forces rather than being pegged to any currency; import controls, except for a few agricultural products which are politically very sensitive, are imposed only for reasons of public health and national security; the government is reviewing its import licensing procedures by introducing a negative-listing, automatic-licensing system; and tariffs have been significantly reduced to a level comparable to that of developed countries. All these measures have been taken to bring Taiwan's trade policy in line with GATT principles.

As the world's 13th largest trading nation, Taiwan is ready to shoulder more responsibility and willing to participate in more global economic activities. Last year it established an "Overseas Economic Development and Cooperation Fund" of U.S. $1 billion to assist the economic development of the developing world. Taiwan is now anxious to rejoin the GATT to accept additional international responsibilities in the world trading community. These efforts demonstrate its earnest wish to contribute more to the world economy and the international trading system. Taiwan's trading partners should render full support for its accession to the GATT.

Bibliography

Ahearn, Thomas R. "An Overview of the International Trading Environment," in Seymour J. Rubin and Thomas R. Graham. eds., *1984 Managing Trade Relations in the 1980s*. (New Jersey: Rowman & Allanheld, 1983).

Baldwin, Robert. *The Inefficacy of Trade Policy*. Princeton University Essays in International Finance, No. 150, 1982.

Baldwin, Robert. "Inefficacy of Protection in Promoting Social Goals." *World Economy*, 8:109-118, 1985.

Baldwin Robert. *The Political Economy of U.S. Import Policy*. (Cambridge, Mass.: MIT Press, 1985).

Bardhan, Pranab K. *Economic Growth, Development, and Foreign Trade: A Study in Pure Theory*. (New York: Wiley-Interscience, 1970).

Bergsten, C. Fred, and William R. Cline. "Trade Policy in the 1980s: An Overview," in William R. Cline, ed., *Trade Policy in the 1980s*. (Institute for International Economics, 1983).

Bhagwati, Jagdish. *The Theory and Practice of Commercial Policy.* Princeton University Essays in International Finance, No. 8, 1968.

Bhagwati, Jagdish. "The Generalised Theory of Distortions and Welfare," in J. Bhagwati et al., eds., *Trade, Balance of Payments and Growth.* (Amsterdam: North-Holland, 1971).

Bhagwati, Jagdish. "Shifting Comparative Advantage, Protectionist Demands, and Policy Response," in J. Bhagwati, ed., *Import Competition and Response.* (University of Chicago Press, 1982).

Bhagwati, Jagdish. "Protectionism: Old Wine in New Bottles." *Journal of Policy Modeling,* 7:23-33, 1985.

Bhagwati, Jagdish. "VERs, Quid Pro Quo DFI and VIEs: Political-Economy-Theoretic Analyses." *International Economic Journal,* 1:1-12, 1987.

Bhagwati, Jagdish, and Douglas Irwin. "The Return of the Reciprocitarians: U.S. Trade Policy Today." *World Economy,* 10:109-130, 1987.

Bhagwati, Jagdish. *Protectionism.* (Cambridge, Mass.: The MIT Press, 1988).

Cline, William R., "Reciprocity: A New Approach to World Trade Policy?" in William R. Cline. ed. *Trade Policy in the 1980s.* (Institute for International Economics, 1983).

Economist. "The Myth of Managed Trade." 6-12 May 1989, pp.13-14.

Economist. "Double Standards on Trade: Mote and Beam." 6-12 May 1989, pp.38-39.

Economist. "Bashing American Trade Policy." 20-26 May 1989, pp.91-92.

Finger, J. Michael, and Andrzej Olechowski., eds., *The Uruguay Round: A Handbook on the Multilateral Trade Negotiations.* 1987.

Gadbaw, R. Michael. "The Outlook for GATT as an Institution," in Seymour J. Rubin and Thomas R. Graham. eds. *Managing Trade Relations in the 1980s* (New Jersey: Rowman & Allanheld 1984).

Golt, Sidney. *The GATT Negotiations 1986-90: Origins, Issues & Prospects.* British-North American Committee, 1988.

Grey, Rodney de C. "A Note on US Trade Practices," in William R. Cline, ed. *Trade Policy in the 1980s.*

Jackson, John H. *World Trade and the Law of GATT.* (Virginia: The Michie Co., 1969).

Long, Oliver. *Law and Its Limitations in the GATT Multilateral Trade System.* (The Hague: Martinus Nijhoff, 1978).

Long, Oliver et al. *Public Scrutiny of Protection: Domestic Policy Transparency and Trade Liberalization,* (Aldershot, England: Gower Publishing Co., 1989).

McGovern, Edmond. *International Trade Regulation.* (England: Globefield Press, 1989).

UNCTAD. *Trade and Development Report* 1988.

World Bank. *World Development Report* 1986.

World Bank. *World Development Report* 1987.

World Bank. *World Development Report* 1988.

The USSR, PECC and GATT

Namik G. Yakubov
Chief of General Department for Economic
Relations with countries of Asia
USSR Ministry of Foreign Economic Relations

Allow me to thank the PECC and our host Canadian National Committee for the invitation sent to the Soviet delegation to attend this session of the Pacific Trade Policy Forum.

As you probably already know, on March 25, 1988, representatives of the state, public, trade and economic organizations and also individual citizens of the USSR, attaching paramount importance to international cooperation in the interests of socio-economic development, peace and security in the Asian-Pacific region, reflecting the objective interest of development of the USSR and, in particular, the Far East and Siberia established the Soviet National Committee for Asian-Pacific Economic Cooperation (SOVNAPEC).

Some publications of SOVNAPEC have been handed over to Mr. English. The SOVNAPEC is concentrating its activities in the following directions:

1. to participate in formulating the guidelines of economic cooperation and coordination of foreign economic relations of the USSR with the countries in the Asian-Pacific region;

2. to establish and maintain working contacts with the Pacific Economic Cooperation Conference, its sectoral groups and forums, and to maintain contacts with national committees of the Conference member-countries;

3.   to prepare proposals on establishing and realizing business contacts with other regional organizations and groupings, individual firms, banks and organizations of the countries in the region;
4.   to assist in arranging, in the USSR and abroad, international conferences and seminars and other events devoted to the Asian-Pacific region problems.

Within the SOVNAPEC framework were set up the commissions and working groups on:

- coastal and border trade problems;
- new forms of economic cooperation;
- establishing ties with regional economic organizations;
- power engineering and mineral resources;
- transport, tourism and communications;
- fisheries

The SOVNAPEC working bodies are set up according to the pattern existing in the PECC.

At the last session of the SOVNAPEC in February 1989 the trade policy working group was set up. It included the representatives of a number of state, public, trade and economic organizations, and also R&D institutes.

The group understands its mission as follows:

- to study the trade and economic policy of the countries in the Asian-Pacific Region as well as the economic integration processes;
- to elaborate measures and proposals relating to the promotion of the trade and economic relations of the USSR, its Far East economic region with the countries in the Asian-Pacific region.

The Soviet Far East, this large economic region, is for the time being at the budding stage of development, its potential is expanding and its rich natural resources are being put into circulation. Dynamic and comprehensive development of the Pacific region of the USSR should secure for our entire country, of which two-thirds is situated in Asia, a natural interaction with the Asian-Pacific region.

The necessity is evident of transforming the Far East economic complex into a system with the "double integration" elements: it is important to integrate the region into the national economy and to fit it into the system of international division of labour.

It appears that the guidelines of the economic development of the Far East economic region of the USSR and, accordingly, its foreign economic cooperation with countries in the Asian-Pacific region might be:

- comprehensive processing of raw material resources, in particular, in the timber and fish processing industries;

- development of its own machine-building base;
- manufacture of consumer goods;
- construction of tourist complexes and hotels.

Under new more favourable conditions created by the ongoing economic reforms, the so-called perestroika in the USSR, and initiatives put forward in the speeches of Mikhail Gorbachev in Vladivostok and Krasnoyarsk, the trade and economic relations of the USSR with the countries of the region are stepping up. New forms of business partnerships, including border trade, establishment of joint ventures, in particular, in the Far East are being developed.

Recently in the USSR, a number of practical measures were taken to establish in the Far East a special foreign economic regime granting wider autonomy to the region in making foreign economic decisions and creating an economic mechanism which would enhance interest in the Far East enterprises and foreign partners in the Asian-Pacific region in foreign economic activities.

I consider it useful to inform you more about some aspects of the radical reforms in foreign economic relations being carried out in the USSR.

A long-term foreign economic strategy has been drawn up in the Soviet Union and was approved in October 1988. It sets out a new qualitative approach to the development of the foreign economic relations of the USSR, aimed at enhancing their role in accelerating the country's economic and social development and a more active and comprehensive involvement of the Soviet economy in the international division of labour. There is to be a speedy configuration of an advanced model of foreign economic relations. This model calls for the development of new forms of economic cooperation in addition to the traditional forms of trade. The objective is to improve the structure of Soviet exports and to increase the share in them of end-products, especially engineering products, as well as to rationalize imports.

New opportunities have been opened up by legislation for enterprises which are direct producers or consumers of goods and services to go into the foreign market, establish direct contacts with foreign partners and create joint ventures both in the USSR and abroad.

The decision of the Council of Ministers of the USSR, dated December 2, 1988, "On further development of foreign economic activities of State-owned cooperatives and other public enterprises, associations and organizations", provides that, from April 1, 1989, all the above-mentioned enterprises and organizations have the right to conduct direct export-import operations on the basis of their self-earned foreign-currency resources. They may freely establish various foreign economic organizations (associations, shareholding companies, trading houses, etc.)

Legislation is currently in preparation to cover shareholding companies, rules for competition, protection of consumer interests, procedures for foreign currency transactions and the economic activities of Soviet enterprises and organizations abroad. This is expected to lead to the adoption of an act on foreign trade and other types of foreign economic activity. Auctions are to be held for the sale and purchase of all foreign currencies for Soviet roubles. It is also planned to introduce on January 1, 1991 a new exchange rate for use in foreign accounts. Specific proposals are to be drawn up in 1989 for the gradual introduction of the partial convertibility of the Soviet rouble.

The decision of the Council of Ministers provides for other specific measures aimed at expanding the independent foreign economic activities of enterprises, production associations, producers' cooperatives and other organizations.

This decision simplifies considerably the creation of joint ventures with foreign capital participation. The respective proportions of Soviet and foreign capital are determined by agreement between the parties. The director of a joint venture may be either a Soviet or a foreign citizen. By now more than 300 joint ventures are established with the total capital investment of 1.5 billion U.S. dollars and another 200 are under discussion.

To further stimulate establishment of joint ventures in the Far East economic region such ventures are granted profit tax holidays for the first three years from the moment of the declared profit with abatement of the profit tax up to 10 per cent upon expiration of this period. Besides, a part of the profit payable to the foreign participant in the joint venture set up in the Far East economic region is not liable to a tax for a definite period of time in case of profit repatriation.

Proposals are being drawn up regarding the establishment of joint-enterprise zones where joint ventures involving foreign participation will be concentrated.

I would like to inform you very briefly of the principal position of the USSR towards GATT. The Soviet Union is considering joining GATT in the future. The USSR's intentions to participate in GATT are determined exclusively by trade and economic considerations, by the wish to partake on an equal basis in the multilateral trade system.

The USSR's interest is easy to understand. The world trade problems are being solved by the mutual efforts of all states. The problems are of global nature and the Soviet Union would like to partake jointly with other countries in the search of ways to their mutually beneficial solution.

The USSR involvement in the international trade system on the basis of GATT principles and rules corresponds not only to the USSR interests. Participating in GATT and USSR would be ready to take certain obligations and to make a contribution to the improvement of trade policy conditions.

The reforms being implemented in the USSR create economic preconditions for the USSR joining GATT.

This reform provides for creation of effective measures of international trade policy similar to those of the GATT member-countries.

The system of state regulation of foreign economic relations is being radically changed towards the development of economic methods of management. There will be transparent foreign economic legislation based on the rules and principles generally recognized in world practice, including the rules and principles of the General Agreement on Tariffs and Trade.

A new economically effective customs tariff is being prepared in the USSR which, in conjunction with the price reform and the establishment of a real exchange rate for the rouble, will serve as a major instrument in the formation of prices for imported goods.

Work is under way to shift the USSR from January 1, 1991 to the Harmonized Commodity Description and Coding System as the nomenclature for customs-tariff and foreign trade statistics. Customs statistics based on generally recognized principles are to be introduced by 1990.

A set of measures is to be developed and progressively introduced, from early 1989, for the operational regulation of the USSR's foreign economic relations, including the introduction of a system of licensing, as well as the establishment of export and import quotas for particular commodities, types of services and countries or groups of countries as may be required in view of the payments situation or other economic or political conditions. It is intended to publish detailed information about these and other regulatory instruments, as and when they are introduced. Implementation of these and other measures requires time but in our opinion will create preconditions for the USSR's obligation to GATT.

I would like to hope that these reforms as well as the Soviet National Committee for Asian-Pacific Economic Cooperation participation in the bodies of the Pacific Economic Cooperation Conference create favourable conditions for our full partnership in PECC. We believe it is not only in our interest, but in the interest of all member countries.

In conclusion I would like to congratulate the organizers of the present Forum.

Certainly there are many problems and difficulties. It is most important to solve them in the interests of business, and to unite in efforts for cooperation and progress. We are ready to do this. The radical changes taking place at the present time in the USSR confirm this.

We made a long trip to come to this beautiful city in order to meet you and to participate in this forum and today when we are leaving for home we consider this trip useful as well as pleasant. Thank you very much for your attention.

Mexico and Pacific Trade

Miguel Angel Toro
Director General for
International Trade Negotiations

It is an honour for Mexico to attend the Third Pacific Trade Policy Forum as an observer. This participation gives Mexico the opportunity to state our interest in the work of the Pacific Economic Cooperation Conference.

We have created the Pacific Basin Mexican Commission in order to adequately follow up the activities of the PECC. The Commission, in turn, has also established five subcommittees to address the different issues covered by each of PECC's forums and working groups.

Among them, the Trade Policy Subcommittee has already started its activities. It has been agreed that its working program will be consistent with the agenda of the Pacific Trade Policy Forum.

Before I present our comments on the different issues of the agenda established by this forum, I would like to review the most relevant aspects of Mexico's trade policy.

During the period 1983-1988 the Mexican economy underwent deep structural changes. The year 1982 represents a landmark in Mexican economic history. The 1982 crisis showed the structural deficiencies arising from the import-substitution model. The maintenance of such a development regime for over three decades involved high costs in terms of lower output and non-oil exports growth. Therefore there was a strong need to change the economic strategy, pursue trade liberalization and promote non-oil exports growth.

The trade liberalization program can be chronologically divided into three separate stages: from early 1983 to June 1985; from July 1985 to November 1988; and a third one which is currently being implemented with the objective of consolidating and extending previous reforms. When the liberalization program was first adopted in 1983, the trade regime was characterized by high levels of protection. As a result of the balance of payments crisis in 1982, the government licensed all imports. Additionally, the tariff structure had 16 nominal rates, which ran from 0-100 per cent.

The trade liberalization program advanced at full speed beginning in mid-1985. By then, it had become clear that the economy needed a lot more non-oil exports to return to a stable and positive growth rate.

On July 25, an executive decree eliminated the import licensing for 3064 tariff positions (out of a total of 5219). By the end of 1985 the percentage of import categories subject to licensing dropped from 64.7 per cent to 10.4 per cent, and the percentage import value subject to licensing went down from 83 per cent to 37 per cent; that is, a decrease of nearly 50 percentage points.

The stabilization program instituted in December 1987 compacted the tariff range to 0-20 per cent, with five rates being applied (0, 5, 10, 15 and 20 per cent). As a result, tariff dispersion was halved from 14 per cent in 1986 to 7 per cent by year-end 1987.

Due to the above tariff modifications, by the end of 1987 the unweighed average tariff dropped to 10 per cent whereas the import-weighted average fell to roughly 6 per cent.

This tariff structure contrasted sharply with that prevailing in 1982, when the unweighed average tariff was 27 per cent, the import-weighted average tariff was 16 per cent, and tariff dispersion was 25 per cent, including 16 tariff levels with a 0-100 per cent range. Using production weights, the average import tariff fell from 23 per cent to 12 per cent in December 1987.

The tariff reforms continued in 1988 by eliminating the 5 per cent import surcharge (which had been introduced in stages since 1985), and by abolishing the remaining official import prices. Furthermore, the percentage import value subject to licensing dropped from 31 per cent in 1986 to 20 per cent in 1988.

President Salinas took office in December 1988 and launched an economic stabilization and economic growth plan. This program aims at reducing inflation and recovering economic growth.

The trade reform package of President Salinas' administration includes an important effort towards equalizing effective protection rates through a reduction in nominal tariff dispersion.

The purpose of this policy is to furnish tariff protection without discriminating among sectors. Thus, with this objective in mind, two executive decrees were issued in January and March 1989, raising tariff rates for most goods previously import-tax exempt, or subject to a 5 per cent rate. As a result of these increments, by March 1989 tariff dispersion dropped to 4.3 per cent.

Mexico is also actively promoting foreign investment. With few exceptions, our new regulation allows automatic authorization for projects that do not exceed 100 million dollars, do not locate in controlled growth areas, include at least 20 per cent of the investment in paid-in capital and maintain balance of payments equilibrium for the first three years of operation. Investment projects of more than 100 million dollars will be considered authorized if the National Commission of Foreign Investment does not decide in 30 days.

The Government of Mexico has informed all GATT member countries of its commitment to continue its trade liberalization policy in strict compliance with GATT rules and principles.

We see with great concern that the multilateral trading system faces the most severe problems of its 40 years of history. Under adverse international economic conditions, governments have found it politically difficult to carry out internal structural reforms in order to improve their economies' international performance. Instead, they have adopted restrictive trade policies. This is an important cause of the recent rise in protectionism.

The proliferation of protectionist measures and the growing trend towards bilateralism by the major industrial countries are contributing to the erosion of the multilateral trade regime based on GATT rules and principles.

Developing countries have not benefitted as much as developed countries from the substantial growth of trade flows experienced since 1983. This is partly due to the fact that developed countries are increasingly resorting to voluntary export restrictions, antidumping and countervailing duties, unilateral retaliatory measures and technical barriers to trade.

If the protectionist forces prevail they could negatively affect the dynamic growth of the Pacific Basin. This would be a serious strike against the international trading system, since the region's growth has to a large degree been made possible by export growth.

Mexico considers that the region could make important contributions to the GATT's Uruguay Round of multilateral trade negotiations by promoting the strengthening and improvement of the multilateral trading system.

Mexico's Considerations on the Issues of the Agenda

Agricultural Protection, Livestock and Grains

Mexico considers that the Uruguay Round offers a unique and historical opportunity to put an end to the distortions affecting trade in agriculture. The outcome of the GATT's April Trade Negotiations Committee (TNC) meeting in Geneva illustrated the political will of the main exporters of agricultural products to overcome the problems of this sector. Although the results of the meeting in this particular area were not spectacular, the different interests were taken into account. The purpose was to obtain a balance among the different points of view.

One positive outcome was the understanding on long and short term measures. However, it is important to recognize that an additional effort will be needed to reach an agreement which clearly identifies the specific measures by 1990 for the elimination of subsidies and more complete trade liberalization in this sector.

Additionally, it is important that negotiations advance towards more extensive tariff bindings and harmonization of tariff rates, since there is a large disparity among countries. Equally important are negotiations on substantial tariff reductions; and the elimination of non-tariff barriers which impede agricultural trade, including unjustified or excessive sanitary and phyto-sanitary regulations.

In this respect, another important result of the GATT's April INC meeting was the standstill commitment. In order to avoid the proliferation of restrictive measures, this commitment froze restrictions for a 20 month period. This means that market access in 1989 and 1990 cannot be less than the average registered in 1987 and 1988.

Some of the member countries of the Pacific Economic Cooperation Conference are the main protagonists of Geneva's negotiations on agriculture. For this reason, it is important to Mexico that these countries are familiar with Mexico's problems in this sector and facilitate an outcome which does not affect our interests but which can be in accordance with the Punta del Este mandate.

Agricultural Products, particularly grains and livestock, are essential imports for many developing countries. Increasing pressures on their foreign exchange earnings because of higher prices, would represent an even heavier burden. Whereas industrial imports may be reduced when foreign exchange is less available such is not the case with food products.

All of the above characteristics imply that special and differential treatment must be awarded to developing countries which are net agricultural importers, at least for a short period, so that they can adjust their economies to produce food according to the availability of physical resources.

Therefore, while elaborating the rules that will govern future trade in agriculture, countries must take into account some measures that net food importers must be allowed to use to promote efficient production of agricultural products. In addition, better market access must be guaranteed to our agricultural exports, in order to compensate for the increase in prices resulting from the agriculture return to GATT rules.

We are confident that the PECC member countries will understand and support our position at the right moment.

Processed Natural Products

Mexico recognizes the interest of some PECC countries to identify as soon as possible the trade barriers affecting processed natural products, in order to initiate a rollback process and propitiate greater trade flows of these goods.

Tariff escalation affecting processed and semi-manufactured products is a source of concern for Mexico. This is because higher tariffs on more highly manufactured products provokes a market distortion which inhibits or discourages the development of this industry in countries with sufficient comparative advantages to engage in this activity. Therefore, an effort to eliminate tariff escalation in this area will be needed. On the other hand, Mexico considers that substantial negotiations aimed to remove non-tariff barriers should be initiated as soon as possible for the following products: non-ferrous metals and minerals, forestry products, and fish and fishery products.

At present, we do not favour a widening of product coverage in the group. Finally, Mexico is against the linkage of market access to supplies access.

Regional Initiatives on Tariffs and Non-Tariff Measures Affecting Trade in Manufactures

Textile Sector

The eventual integration of this sector into GATT rules and disciplines is of particular interest to Mexico.

The outcome of the April TNC meeting, was not as positive as desired, since some countries did not accept the commitment to avoid further import restrictions under the multifibre agreement (MFA). However, a positive result was the commitment to start negotiations in April 1989 regarding the modalities that would permit the reintegration of the sector to the GATT system. This process shall be initiated after the conclusion of negotiations in 1990.

Trade in textiles is a priority issue for developing countries. Mexico considers that PECC countries could make a good contribution to the Geneva Negotiations, by tabling a proposal to negotiate the phase-out of the MFA, with the process starting on the expiry of MFA IV.

The length of operation of the MFA permits belief that a structural adjustment process has already taken place in developed countries in this sector. For that reason Mexico would like to have the starting point of the phase-out of the MFA in a period not greater than five years.

Subsidies and Countervailing Measures

The problem of subsidies and countervailing measures is one of the most acute trade policy issues confronting the multilateral trading system. Mexico approves of the progress of the negotiation in the Uruguay Round, and favours the agreement reached regarding the elaboration of a common basis for negotiations on subsidies, countervailing duties, special and differential treatment, notification, surveillance and dispute settlement.

PECC countries could contribute to the negotiations process by elaborating a list of the three different types of subsidies mentioned in the Swiss proposal: (1) prohibited subsidies; (2) subsidies subject to requirement of material injury; (3) allowed subsidies.

Measures to Advance on Tariff Negotiations

According to the Montreal meeting results, substantive tariff negotiations in the Uruguay Round were to begin no later than July 1, 1989. This marks important progress in the negotiations. Countries agreed to have a tariff reduction of about 30 per cent. A relevant factor is that countries also agreed to grant "appropriate recognition" to unilateral tariff reduction measures adopted by certain participants since June 1, 1986.

Mexico has made an enormous liberalization effort as I explained at the beginning. All our commercial partners have benefitted from this process. We are actively participating in the fight against protectionism. The multilateral trading system becomes stronger with actions like this. Therefore, Mexico invokes all PECC countries to effectively give appropriate recognition to these kinds of efforts.

After the Uruguay Round the average level of tariff duties is expected to be driven to a minimum, therefore it is important that the maintenance of this level is guaranteed through additional bindings.

Mexico thus favours a harmonization formula approach, complemented with a request-offer approach to negotiate tariff reductions in the Uruguay Round.

New Issues

Umbrella Agreement on Guidelines for Liberalizing Trade in Services

Mexico considers that the work of the negotiating group in services in the Uruguay Round had developed in a dynamic way and important progress has been achieved. The Montreal meeting results which allowed the establishment of a set of guidelines and principles which will be incorporated into the agreement on services is an important achievement of the Mid-Term Review.

Mexico considers that the multilateral framework must allow a balance of interest among participants. Some countries have already defined a list of sectors of interest on this subject. At present, negotiations in Geneva have come to a point in which the guidelines and principles are now being tested in specific services sectors, in order to see how they can be implemented.

The specific actions that PECC countries could undertake from the Mexican point of view, would be the elaboration of studies to examine the extent to which these principles and guidelines can be applied to their sectors of interest.

The umbrella agreement on services must consider that progressive liberalization will have to take into account the degree of development of the participating countries. Additionally, the specific sectors of interest to developing countries will have to be included in the negotiations, in particular, those with intensive use of labour.

Intellectual Property Issues

If we consider the differences existing between developing and developed countries on this issue, we can certainly be satisfied with the progress of the April TNC meeting.

The text of the agreement reached a consensus because it managed to establish an ambiguous position in relation to the forum in which the negotiation results will be applied.

The negotiation results are not prejudged, leaving open the possibility that rules and disciplines regarding intellectual property rights can finally be implemented by GATT or by some other international organization related to intellectual property.

Mexico's interest is that GATT countries try to achieve an international balance which favours not only developed nations but also the developing countries.

Mexico has a law that protects intellectual property and supports the improvement of the protection of intellectual property rights As long as this protection does not become itself an unjustified barrier for developing countries' access to technologies produced in industrialized countries.

Mexico wants to make clear once more its deep interest in activities of the Pacific Trade Policy Forum and the Pacific Economic Cooperation Conference. This interest includes the private and academic sectors.

The Mexican private sector is present in this forum and working to re-establish closer trade and economic relationships with the countries of the Conference. Business councils with several countries in the region already exist in Mexico for this purpose. With them it will be possible to take advantage of trade, investment, and cooperation opportunities which could yield mutual benefits, within a framework of long-term economic relationships.

We are sure that the efforts of the Third Pacific Trade Policy Forum will be successful just as those in San Francisco and Singapore were.

Declining Industries, Mechanisms of Structural Adjustment, and Trade Policy in Pacific Basin Economies

Hugh Patrick*
Columbia University

The process of industrialization, and its spread to the developing economies, generates in its wake severe problems of structural adjustment for "declining" or "troubled" industries. These problems are of major policy significance for the Pacific Basin economies, though in somewhat different ways depending on the level of development (the advanced industrial countries, the newly industrialized economies, and currently industrializing nations). How inefficiencies are dealt with and the resources reallocated is an important domestic economic and political problem. Moreover, it has even more important implications for the relationships of these economies with each other and with the world, not simply in terms of trade flows but for the rules and nature of the international trading system itself.

Countries can simply leave the adjustment process to the marketplace and to market forces. However, in many instances governments intervene to slow down or smooth out adjustment, and often unilaterally impose or maintain import restrictions as the policy instrument. There is a direct linkage between structural adjustment problems, market versus government mechan-

---

* These are my views and interpretations for which I do not hold my colleagues in the project responsible.

isms of adjustment, the multilateral trading system, and the ongoing Uruguay Round of GATT negotiations.

One practical as well as conceptual difficulty lies in distinguishing between declining industries and those in trouble. It is of course politically more attractive for representatives to portray their industry as troubled rather than declining in order to justify government assistance as only a "temporary" measure. Declining industries are those facing the loss of long-term competitiveness (comparative advantage), due to rising relative costs of labor, natural resources, land, or capital. The prototypical example is the decline in competitiveness in many textile and apparel subsectors based on unskilled labor and relatively simple and standardized technologies, in all the advanced industrial nations and more recently in the Asian-Pacific newly industrialized economies as well.

Troubled industries have excess capacity or produce inefficiently for some sustained period but seemingly have not lost potential long-term competitiveness. Their difficulties may come about from sudden declines in world demand (shipbuilding in Japan and Korea), overvalued exchange rates (automobiles in the United States), or foreign import restrictions or export subsidies (the effect of European Community agricultural policies and United States reactions on New Zealand and Australia). Moreover follower country governments which aggressively pursue industrial policies to create more skill, technology, and capital intensive industries sometimes make policy mistakes (automobile assembly in all the smaller Pacific Basin economies). It is unlikely that these "troubled" industries will become competitively efficient within a reasonable time frame.

The Pacific Basin Studies Program at Columbia University in 1987 initiated a project to investigate these issues in a comparative Pacific Basin context under the direction of Professor Hugh Patrick. The purpose has been to describe and evaluate the mechanisms of adjustment in each country, to determine the effectiveness of and constraints on various policy choices, and to examine the implications for the country's trade policy. The five Pacific Basin advanced industrial nations—Japan, the United States, Canada, Australia and New Zealand—were obvious choices; each has well defined industries in decline or in trouble. Moreover, the four Asian-Pacific newly industrialized economies—Korea, Taiwan, Hong Kong and Singapore—are losing competitiveness in simple labor-intensive industries; and Korea faces severe problems of structural adjustments in certain troubled industries previously promoted by the government. Two countries earlier in the industrialization process—Malaysia and Thailand—were selected both because they have troubled industries (particularly automobiles) and because they represent problems of some possible decrease in competitive strength in certain agri-culture processing industries. One economist from each country has prepared the basic country studies that form the core of this project; the group held two workshop meetings, in July 1988 and January 1989, to review issues and manuscripts.

The focus of the project has been on manufacturing industries; agriculture enters only peripherally. At the same time, it was well recognized that certain highly efficient land-resource producers in the Pacific Basin, notably of grains and other agricultural crops, are unable to exploit their cost and market advantages fully because of import barriers in Japan, Korea, and increasingly Taiwan, and even more importantly the European Community. Agriculture trade policy issues, while conceptually very similar by economic criteria, have a different political and institutional agenda, and are being handled separately, though not unrelatedly, in the current Uruguay Round of GATT negotiations.

Analytical Conclusions

I derive a number of analytical conclusions from the project.

1. In every Pacific Basin economy analyzed, a great deal of adjustment has resulted through the marketplace despite substantial difference in the degree to which government policies attempted to inhibit or slow change. Market forces have simply been too strong at whatever level of protection. As firms lose sales and competitiveness, they reduce output, shift to new, higher value-added products, lay off workers, and adjust their physical capital. In every country there have been substantial declines in employment in specific manufacturing sectors; indeed this is one important measure of a declining industry.

2. Employment decreases in declining industries have been sub-stantially greater in the five advanced industrial countries, reflecting greater loss of competitiveness. Most workers laid off found jobs elsewhere or retired; few ended up unemployed and apparently few benefited substantially from government retraining, relocation or similar government-based pro-grams. In general, the higher the level of economic develop-ment (GNP/capita) the greater are the difficulties in adjustment. Human capital embodied in workers is both greater and more industry and/or firm specific (e.g., steel). Firms are larger, more capital-intensive, and their capital more specific in use. The political power of workers and firms in a declining industry is likely to be greater, and they are

more likely to seek government help. However, national differences in institutions, policies, and behaviour substantially determine an economy's flexibility, and hence its ability to rely on the market as the mechanism of adjustment (e.g., Singapore versus New Zealand).

3. It is incorrect to consider broadly-defined industries such as textiles or apparel as "dying," as likely to lose competitiveness altogether. Some segments are relatively capital and technology intensive (e.g., synthetic fibers); others maintain competitiveness through design, quick responses to changes in fashion, and nearness to market. Moreover, the process of sectoral decline is likely to be long-run; there is heterogeneity not only of product but of quality of producers. In textiles particularly many firms are small-scale, family-owned, and owners, workers, and machinery are aging. The opportunity cost of owner-workers and their physical capital is low; it may well make economic sense for them to produce until retirement and exit, even with lower incomes. The policy issue is whether society should enhance their incomes. If so, the political reality is that support is likely to be by protection from import (or domestic) competition rather than by direct subsidy. One policy objective should be to keep such support low enough not to attract inefficient new entrants into the industry, if more direct programs of support are not politically feasible.

4. The macroeconomic environment and macro policies strongly affect both the adjustment process and the degree to which sectoral policies are utilized.

   a) Rapid economic growth is the single most important factor easing the process of adjustment for declining industries. It creates new jobs and investment opportunities, and makes possible market-based adjustment. The best examples in the 1980s are Hong Kong, Korea, Singapore, and Taiwan, particularly in textiles, wigs, and other very labor-intensive declining sectors.

   b) A substantially overvalued exchange rate for a sustained period creates troubled industries and exacerbates the difficulties of declining industries. The United States (automobiles), Australia, and New Zealand are important examples. In addition to reducing price competitiveness, the overvalued exchange rate increases trade and current account deficits, which create trade fictions and an environment making protectionist actions politically more palatable. The United States experience in the 1980s has become a major problem not only for it but for all nations. In contrast an undervalued currency retards the process of structural adjustment and results in excessive current account surpluses. Japan is by far the most important example, but the surpluses of Taiwan and Korea have also resulted in serious problems.

c) New Zealand currently represents a special and extreme case of comprehensive sectoral deregulation and reforms in an adverse macroeconomic environment. The comprehensiveness and boldness of this policy package is impressive. Its successful implementation requires strong political will and a relatively long-term time horizon.

5. In virtually all economies—Hong Kong being the exception—governments have intervened selectively to help declining or troubled industries. The issues are those of degree, targeted group for assistance (workers, owners, financiers), and type of policy instruments used.

6. While most governments employ the rhetoric of market failure and/or infant industries as justification for intervention, and policies usually are driven by some sense of efficiency in resource allocation, in practice the policy objectives are more redistributive in nature, primarily in favour of interest groups with political power in affected sectors. The economic reality is that where government interference slows (or stops) the market forces of adjustment, resources continue to be inefficiently allocated, in some instances at great costs to consumers and with considerable net (deadweight) losses to the economy as a whole. However, these costs frequently are hidden in the form of high prices or low-interest-rate loans. The political reality is that powerful interest groups—which differ from country to country—are able to shape government policy to their advantage for sustained periods of time; in a second-best world they are able to stress social costs of adjustment (particularly unemployment). The policy battle in every country lies in tilting policies toward efficiency.

7. The advanced industrial countries—the U.S., Canada, Australia, New Zealand, and Japan—historically have provided assistance to both troubled and declining industries in one form or another. The major policy instrument was the *de facto* imposition of new import barriers, in new and increasingly pernicious forms of voluntary export restraints (VERs) and orderly marketing agreements (OMAs), as well as import quotas (textiles). While tariffs have in general been reduced, they remain higher than average in declining industries; and in many Pacific Basin countries (Australia,

New Zealand, Korea, Taiwan, Malaysia, Thailand) tariff or quota barriers remain high.

8. Japan is an exception among the industrial countries in that it now relies far less than earlier on trade protection to assist troubled or declining industries. Given its strong economic and trade position since 1980, it is very difficult for Japan to impose new import barriers (though not impossible, as selected "voluntary" restraints on imports of silk and knitwear attest). Rather, Japan has engaged in a constructive series of government-industry joint programs in selected declining ("structurally depressed") industries, which have been especially effective in concentrated industries. There is some evidence of collusive market-sharing arrangements in a few highly-concentrated industrial products, which have not been challenged by the government. The government has also provided support for small manufacturers and their workers in depressed industries and regions. The modest amount of government resources actually being provided suggests these programs have been ameliorative and smoothing, to mitigate political problems and pressures emanating from basic reliance on market forces.

9. The governments of the newly industrialized economies—Hong Kong, Korea, Singapore, and Taiwan—have not provided significant new assistance for declining labor-intensive manufacturing sectors. However, Korea and Singapore have assisted troubled industries. Korea, in particular, suffers from earlier policy mistakes which created today's troubled industries (shipping, shipbuilding). High tariff and other import barriers continue to protect Korean and Taiwan manufacturing. The policy problem, as earlier with Japan, is not the imposition of new protectionist support for (newly) declining or troubled industries, but the persistence of previously-established barriers which become increasingly effective as industries mature and begin to enter the process of decline.

10. Malaysia and Thailand are still in the early phase of their industrialization process; in general, labor-intensive industries are expanding, not declining. Yet each has its troubled industries, due mainly to policy mistakes. Automobiles are a clear case of highly protected, inefficiently small, local assembly and local component production. There also have been mistakes in the excessive expansion of capacity in the processing of certain agricultural products—sugar mills in Thailand and palm oil mills in Malaysia.

11. As noted, government policies to intervene in the process of adjustment reflect both a mixture of efficiency in resource allocation and social objectives, and a political response to powerful interest groups. Organized labor in declining industries has been an important player in the United States, Canada, and Australia, much less so in other Pacific Basin economies. (The current New Zealand case is remarkable in that powerful labor interests have gone along with the Labor Government's market-oriented reform program.) In most instances of intervention it appears the government has particularly sought to help owners and managers; in some instances major creditors (Japan, Korea) apparently have been the objective, or at least the beneficiaries, of government assistance to the industry. Immigrant labor has been a beneficiary in some instances (Australia, Canada, the United States); in contrast in Singapore the further utilization of foreign visiting workers has been deliberately restricted to prevent the pace of adjustment (textiles, shipbuilding) from slowing down.

12. In Taiwan (plywood), Korea (textiles) and Japan (aluminum, perhaps textiles) the government has provided some incentives for firms in declining industries to invest abroad in lower-cost countries. While this has not been studied carefully, it appears that the purposes are mainly ameliorative and political. To the extent that firms in declining industries invest abroad *and* import back to their home, utilizing their existing domestic marketing and distribution systems, it undermines the ability of the firms in the industry to unite to seek government protection from imports.

13. The political and economic realities of declining and troubled industries have been and are vexing problems for the GATT-based international trading system. While positive economic policies of domestic rationalization without using protectionist instruments has been widely touted (by the OECD for instance), in practice almost all countries have relied primarily upon import restriction policy instruments. The main exceptions are Hong Kong and Singapore which have systematically maintained free trade policies; and Japan in the past decade, which has been virtually precluded from using import restrictions to provide new assistance to declining or troubled industries by reason of its high trade surplus and strong U.S. and other foreign pressure. The major example of the bypassing (and undermining) of the GATT international trading system is the Multi-Fiber Agreement (MFA) which enables industrial countries to

impose comprehensive bilateral quotas on textile imports from developing countries.

14. In practice, the GATT system has not been effective in preventing industrial countries from raising import barriers unilaterally (Australian quotas on automobiles or textiles) or bilaterally (U.S.-Japan "voluntary export restraints" on automobiles, U.S. steel import arrangements with Japan, Canada, Korea, Taiwan). Existing GATT institution, mechanisms and powers do not provide an adequate basis in practice for restraining the intervention of national governments in assisting their declining/troubled industries by import restriction measures.

15. The declining and troubled industries problems of structural adjustment, and the proclivity of most governments to intervene by raising or maintaining import barriers, may well represent the key issues of the global trading system today: how to prevent official low trade barrier countries (U.S., Japan, Canada) from raising new barriers; how to cause high official import barrier countries (Australia, Korea, Taiwan, Malaysia, Thailand, and to some extent still, New Zealand) to reduce those barriers; and how to de-limit and restructure existing barriers, such as the textile MFA, into more market-oriented systems amenable to gradual liberalization.

Policy Conclusions

Several policy conclusions are suggested by these studies.

1. Since reduction in employment and output in industries having lost comparative advantage is inevitable and inevitably carries with it social and political as well as economic costs, generally it is less costly to allow the process of adjustment to take place sooner rather than later to reduce the cumulative inefficiencies and costs to consumers not only of delay but also of ever-higher protectionist barriers.

2. It is important to get the macroeconomic policies right: generation of employment and investment opportunities, and an exchange rate that is neither overvalued nor undervalued, are central.

3. The decision that the government intervene, to what degree, and particularly in what form, is quintessentially political and ideological. Nonetheless, it can and should be guided by objectives of economic efficiency and consumer welfare. It is the task of economists and government policy makers to

make clear that economic choices and associated costs to political leaders.

4. While labor adjustment seems to occur mainly through the marketplace, in slower-growing, advanced industrial economies governments could and probably should do more to develop constructive programs of retraining and relocation to minimize individual and social costs of job loss. However, the danger is that such programs in practice may simply become nothing more than schemes for additional income compensation; even so, they may be a politically-attractive, second-best ameliorative technique preferable to continued or enhanced protection.

5. The GATT-based international trading system needs to be strengthened, and GATT itself provided with a more powerful set of institutional structures, powers, and procedures to monitor individual country trade policy performance, and to press for domestically-based positive policies of adjustment rather than imposition of import restrictions under whatever guise ("voluntary" systems, orderly marketing arrangements, new quotas or tariffs).

6. The textile MFA is a pernicious and inefficient model of import restriction and managed trade. It should not be applied to other sectors.

7. Rather, textile trade arrangements should be gradually liberalized. A pragmatic sequence is first to move from country-by-country import quotas to global quotas; and then from quotas to equivalent tariffs; and then to a process of multilaterally negotiated binding tariff reductions.

PART IV

CONCLUDING PANEL
AND SPECIAL ADDRESSES

Pacific Trade Policy Initiatives – A Concluding Panel

The statements by the panelists represent the views of policy research specialists from universities and research institutions, who have been involved in the study of Pacific economic relationships, and in most cases have been active participants in the work of the Pacific Economic Cooperation Conference for several years.

Sir Frank Holmes
Institute of Policy Studies, Victoria University
Wellington, New Zealand

More and more politicians in the Pacific are saying that the Pacific is an idea whose time has come. They are acknowledging the dynamism and growing interdependence of the region's members in trade, investment, travel and communication. These developments, along with the pioneering work done by business people in PBEC and researchers in PAFTAD, and the growing scope and effectiveness of work of PECC, have encouraged politicians to see real possibilities of collective action by Pacific governments to advance their mutual interests in a difficult world. Our task at this Forum is to help to lay the foundations for fruitful meetings, of the PECC Conference in November and of Pacific ministers. We can help by using the PECC processes to assist ministers to determine priorities for that part of their agenda which will deal with trade policy; and by providing a basis for recommendations which we believe they could and should adopt collectively.

At this Forum, no-one has advocated a restrictive Pacific trading bloc. Indeed, the spirit of our discussions has been in favour of collective action against restrictive blocs and against resort to restrictive unilateral trade policy measures. We want the Pacific to be an outward-looking association of diverse and independent nations, who work actively for the expansion of investment and trade in our region and in the world. In 1989-90 our highest priority is the achievement of a successful GATT round.

In GATT, we are looking for progress towards liberalization on a wide front. We want a substantial reduction of all types of barriers, in primary and service industries, as well as in manufacturing. We want to improve GATT's capacity to protect members against the misuse of safeguard measures and other departures from the letter and spirit of the agreement. We want GATT to be able to settle disputes effectively and speedily.

We recognize that our own governments must be prepared to reduce restrictions in their own politically sensitive areas if others are going to do likewise. Each of us will have a somewhat different order of priorities. As you would expect, New Zealanders see agriculture as one of the make-or-break issues of the round. I hope that this forum will emphasize how important it is for the members of GATT to honour their commitments and to work through, seriously and expeditiously, the programme laid down by the Trade Negotiations Committee in April. Let us not forget that, in the short-term, there is an obligation on them not to increase existing levels of domestic and export support and protection, and to reduce the levels in 1990. Let us not forget that, in the short-term, there is an obligation on them not to increase existing levels of domestic and export support and protection, and to reduce the levels in 1990. Let us also not lose sight of the longer-term objectives agreed at Geneva to establish a fair and market-oriented agricultural trading system; operationally effective GATT disciplines; and substantial and progressive reductions in agricultural support and protection sustained over an agreed period of time, resulting in both correcting and preventing restrictions and distortions in world agricultural markets.

Most of us here, from developed countries at least, seem prepared to urge our governments to give a lead from the Pacific region towards a substantial phased reduction of tariffs and increase in the scope of tariff bindings. Credit is to be given in the Geneva agreement for unilateral liberalization after June 1986. I prefer an across-the-board formula for the tariff cuts as the best way to proceed. New Zealand is well on the way to eliminating its own quantitative restrictions, in our own interests. I trust that this Forum will support strong action to reduce or eliminate non-tariff barriers as part of an integrated approach to a significant reduction of protection and subsidies of all kinds. The liberalization should include services where I hope a negative list approach will be accepted. That is, there would be an agreement to free all services not specifically excluded by a particular member.

I would also advocate a strong statement supporting the strengthening of GATT rules on safeguards. We should strongly oppose capricious and selective misuse of safeguard provisions. Let us insist that measures taken should be temporary, degressive and subject to review by a greatly strengthened GATT system. Let us make that system capable of effective surveillance and speedy settlement of disputes.

My most important priority would be to get Pacific ministers and GATT members, from both developed and developing countries, to acknowledge that they should review, regularly and systematically, their own restrictions, subsidies and other measures which limit and distort trade and publish the results. This review would be a useful element of future GATT surveillance of the damage which we do to one another in international trade. But it would also help politicians and people in each country to see whether the benefits of the measures which they take are outweighed by the costs which they usually involve for consumers, for taxpayers and for more efficient unsubsidized industries and services.

I am suggesting that Pacific ministers should aim to provide constructive leadership in the Round, and more particularly to form alliances for progress on priority issues of mutual interest. The membership of the alliances may vary according to the issues concerned. They will sometimes include non-Pacific members. It might be timely, for example, to get Japan, Korea and Taiwan to work with Pacific members of the Cairns group to help build a base for a break-through with the Europeans in GATT on difficult issues of agriculture and processed natural products. We could form an alliance to develop the proposals made by Professor Yamazawa and Dr. Chang yesterday to phase-out the multi-fibre agreement. We can provide a sympathetic forum, probably via PECC, to work through the issues involved in getting the PRC, Taiwan and Hong Kong into GATT and better integrated into the world trading system.

I am not suggesting that collective Pacific action should be confined to the GATT round. But we should strive to see that what we do collectively and unilaterally is consistent with GATT principles. For example, in service transactions, we may be able to draft proposals for regional codes which provide for more rapid liberalization than can be agreed globally. But we should make our arrangements open to all who will adopt the agreed Pacific approach.

Countries with close affinities may wish to free trade among themselves, as have Australia and New Zealand in their Closer Economic Relations Trade Agreement and Canada and the United States in their Free Trade Agreement. We should not object to this if the arrangements are consistent with GATT rules, especially if they simultaneously reduce restrictions on imports from others, as Australia and New Zealand have. I would be happy however, to make such arrangements subject to surveillance by GATT and by any Pacific organization.

The issue of regional free trade areas is an important one which time will not permit me to discuss today. It is however, dealt with in a forthcoming book which will be published by my Institute, with contributions by Ted English and Murray Smith and other Canadian, Australian and New Zealand researchers. I have available for members of this Forum copies of the introduction to this publication.

I think that Mr. Bob Hawke's initiative to organize an early meeting of Pacific ministers is timely. It comes at a time when we are seeking to strengthen PECC and to bring its work more effectively to bear on activities by Governments, business and research institutions in the region. We should urge our governments, in their responses to the Hawke initiative, to build on PECC's good work, to use its tripartite processes, and to strengthen its capacity to do more, not weaken it.

Gradually and diplomatically, through its tripartite structure, PECC has brought into its membership countries whose governments were previously sceptical or apprehensive about Pacific cooperation or had political difficulties in coming together. Its membership provides a useful basis for an initial ministerial meeting.

We should urge our ministers to avoid unnecessary duplication of effort and creation of another expensive international bureaucracy. (We already have ESCAP.) Ministers should come together only when they have an agenda which offers reasonable prospects of agreement that they can act constructively together. I trust that, in arranging the Secretariat for meetings, ministers will draw on those who might serve on expanded PECC Secretariat and select staff from other continuing Pacific organizations such as ASEAN. In their decisions they should recognize that they can fruitfully work through the membership of PBEC, PAFTAD and PECC as well as through their own officials.

As I said at the beginning, the work of this Forum and those who will pull our positive suggestions together, along with that of the other task forces of PECC and the Auckland Conference in

November, can and should be used in the process of determining priorities for the Ministerial agenda and suggesting recommendations for action at their first meetings. The wide consensus which we have achieved here suggest that, at least on issues on trade policy, the outcome of the Ministers' meeting could well be most constructive.

Jeff Schott
Institute for International Economics
Washington, D.C.

I should start with the observation that Secretary Baker must have got an advance copy of Frank Holmes' speech, because he took Frank's advice this week. In a major policy address (on June 26, 1989)* that I think was timed to coincide with these meetings, he announced the first major U.S. support in the new administration for regional cooperative actions in the Pacific. He voiced support for a new mechanism for multilateral cooperation in the Pacific, one that went beyond trade issues to encompass a wide array of issues from trade and economic affairs to cultural exchange. He stressed that it must help, not hinder, existing efforts towards regional and multilateral cooperation in general. He voiced very strong support for Prime Minister Hawke's call for a ministerial meeting this fall as a first step toward developing such a new Pacific institution.

One should take that statement by Secretary Baker as a very significant step towards U.S. cooperation in the Pacific. While I think that institution building may be a bit premature, I would agree with a lot of the comments that we have heard today and in the last few days, that countries in the Pacific can do a lot to push multilateral efforts forward, particularly in the Uruguay Round, especially in the area of safeguards, particularly with regard to textiles and perhaps with regard to other issues such as antidumping or subsidies and countervail. There is a lot of work that can be done on a regional basis that could promote our common multilateral objectives.

I have been asked to summarize 280 pages of a book, including proceedings of another conference, entitled *More Free Trade Areas?*† I would like to perform the seemingly contradictory task of providing light on, while at the same time putting a cloud over a much-heralded option for Pacific cooperation, that is the negotiation of more free trade areas.

---

* See Appendix II of this book.

† A 1989 publication of the Institute for International Economics, edited by Jeff Schott.

It's difficult for me to come to Canada and be against free trade areas; in fact, how can anyone be against the concept of free trade areas? It's for trade liberalization. It's for cooperation. And one only has to look at the Canada-U.S. Free Trade Agreement to see what benefits can derive from two countries getting together, pursuing a course of trade liberalization, improving their bilateral relationship and at the same time providing building blocks for broader multilateral agreements and success in the GATT. The U.S.-Canada Agreement does all those things, and does them very well. In fact, the United States has pursued a two-track strategy, one that has been very effective in promoting both our bilateral relationship with Canada and with Israel and, at the same time, pursuing our common multilateral objectives.

But would more free trade areas result in the expected benefits of trade liberalization and help provide building blocks and help provide support for the GATT negotiations? Also would the negotiation of more free trade areas have negative side effects? I think the answer to those questions illustrates why there are problems with the concept of negotiating more free trade areas.

First, there are some common misperceptions about free trade areas. Most of the interest in free trade areas that focused on arrangements between countries in the Pacific and the United States results from criticism of the GATT process, concern that the GATT is not doing enough and that therefore one can achieve greater results by negotiating free trade agreements bilaterally. The interest in these bilaterals is based on criticism of the GATT, not on a persuasive analysis of the benefits to be derived from the free trade agreements themselves. It's much like a beauty contest where the judge looks at the first contestant, says "that's not very good and, having seen (a), I choose (b)". That's the way interest in free trade areas has developed in the U.S. and elsewhere in the Pacific. It has some dangers. It is likely to distract attention away from the GATT process because of the implicit criticism or lack of confidence that the GATT negotiations are going to achieve the results that we all hope they would. Therefore I think it would be quite distracting if such negotiations were to proceed while the GATT Round was underway.

Second, as we have seen in the U.S.-Canada negotiations, many important non-tariff barriers are not amenable to bilateral solutions. You need a bigger group in a trade negotiation to try to wrestle with the major problems in agriculture and to deal with the problem of subsidies and countervail. There just is not enough leverage in a bilateral negotiation to get the United States in particular to change long standing entrenched policies in return for concessions made on a bilateral basis. Many more countries have to participate.

Third, most bilateral negotiations don't achieve trade liberalization. If one looks at the results of many bilateral negotiations, what they achieve rather than liberalizing trade is voluntary export restraint that limits trade. We have seen that time and time again in the case of where the United States has got together with countries in the Pacific and the result has not been a broad opening up of the market but a limited restriction of the market, which has had very adverse implications for other countries in the region.

Another misperception is that we can replicate the Canada-U.S. Agreement in other contexts. I think the Canada-U.S. situation was quite unique. Without going into a long litany of reasons why, it is clear that we have already had substantial integration of our two economies prior to the negotiations. We have similar though not identical legal and trade regulatory backgrounds and we even have affiliated labour unions. Those type of conducive circumstances will not arise in other suggested free trade agreements.

Finally, and most importantly, the reason most countries are interested in negotiating free trade agreements with the United States is not because they are interested in achieving trade liberalization, but rather they are trying to safeguard the existing position they already have in the U.S. market. The primary objective that one sees in these countries in supporting free trade agreements with the U.S. is not broad trade liberalization but maintaining market access, really having a standstill. And it results from their concern, a valid concern, that the United States may be moving away from the GATT. If one listens to statements in the Congress, one can understand those countries' concern that the U.S. is moving towards protectionism; witness the passage of the 1988 Trade Act. But bilateral options really argue for securing market share, not general trade liberalization. In fact some of the countries involved, whose representatives are here today, have argued that the real objective of such a negotiation would be trade diversion, what one normally considers a cost of a free trade agreement. Trade diversion is buying more from one country at the expense of imports from another country. Another reason for pursuing bilateral deals is to avoid discrimination if another country suddenly negotiates preferences with the United States, and therefore puts your own country at a competitive disadvantage in the highly competitive Pacific market.

All of this led me to be quite negative on the concept of bilateral free trade areas as being a concept for broader cooperation within the Pacific Basin. And indeed I see that as rather a source of new conflict in the Pacific. If one looks at the bottom line of the prospects for more free trade areas, one sees that they would result in little trade liberalization because of the lack of progress that would be achievable on the major non-tariff barriers that inhibit trade. They would detract from the Uruguay Round and spur perverse reactions, they would perhaps promote better bilateral relations among the partner countries, but they would exacerbate regional frictions. Also they would have really no significant impact on bilateral trade balances with the United States, which would mean that there would continue to be strong protectionist pressure in the United States.

So in conclusion, I think one should follow the lead that Frank Holmes has put out, follow the lead of Secretary Baker to an extent, and particularly follow the lead of the PECC in seeking ways that countries in the region can work closer together to promote multilateral objectives in the current GATT Round. Therefore, make haste slowly until the results of the Uruguay Round are in. Don't pursue alternative trade initiatives, which are likely to distract from, rather than promote, the multilateral negotiations in the GATT and use the cooperative efforts in the region to strengthen prospects for a successful Uruguay Round.

Soogil Young
Korea Development Institute
Seoul, Korea

For the four years between the Second PECC which was held in Bangkok and the Fifth PECC which was held in Vancouver, I was one of the active participants in the PECC process as a member of Coordinating Group. In fact I had the very distinct pleasure of coordinating the first meeting of this Forum at San Francisco in 1986 and also of coordinating the Trade Task Force that preceded this forum, with very active and gracious support from such colleagues as Ted English and Sir Frank Holmes. So I know a bit about the history of this exercise.

Having returned from three years of what I might call retirement, I could not help comparing the work of this Forum this time with the work of the Task Force and the Forum three years ago. I am amazed at the remarkable gain that has been made in relevance, specificity and the depth of the works presented as well as the discussions on them. And in any case, I came to conclude that the Pacific Trade Policy Forum has developed or come to the stage where it may and should be utilized as an effective component in the policy making process in the Pacific countries and economies. The discussions at this Forum meeting show that the Uruguay Round has come to a very critical stage phase and also that the Pacific trade policy cooperation can be very crucial in bringing the Uruguay Round to a meaningful conclusion. We have only one and a half years left before the conclusion of that Uruguay

Round, and the nature or the quality of the deals to be made in the remainder of this time will determine the efficacy of the multilateral trading system on which prosperity of the Pacific economies in the 1990s will depend.

Now what can the Pacific economies do together in this regard at the Uruguay Round? I think they can make efforts to insure progress in the right direction. I think there are at least two specific issues on which they should make such efforts. I believe they will have to deal with these two as one package. One is agriculture. The other is an issue which cuts across such issues as safeguards, antidumping duties and countervailing duties. All of these so-called contingency protection measures, as papers by Mike Finger and others have shown, more often than not are employed to target protectionism at specific exporting countries. They do present a fundamental challenge to the most-favoured-nation principle of the GATT. The general issue here is of course discrimination. And I think it will be of critical importance to the long term health of the global trading system, as well as that of the global economy itself, to establish a lasting liberal order in agricultural trade on the one hand, and also to confirm the principle of non-discrimination both in spirit and in practice.

But our discussions also have shown that both politically and intellectually it may not be easy to make progress in the right direction during the Uruguay Round on these issues. But with a coalition among Pacific governments, and I think the coalition is possible if the two issues are approached as a package, the Pacific economies can push for a breakthrough at the Uruguay Round. Specifically they should collectively push for agricultural trade liberalization in a fundamental sense, on the one hand, and also push for the tightening up of safeguards, provisions to rule out selectivity; and press for reforming of codes on subsidies and other less-than-fair-value actions in order to eliminate confusion and to minimize protectionist abuse. They should also seek to support each other in other ways at the Uruguay Round.

Now in order to make this coalition possible or more effective, perhaps the developing countries of the Pacific might choose to make a special contribution. It can be argued that one major factor contributing to the abuse of contingency protections, as well as to the deadlock on the selectivity of safeguards, is the failure of the developing countries themselves to assume greater responsibility in the management of the trading system. More specifically developing countries have been asked to assume increasing obligations as they develop and they have so far not been responding very positively. The failure to accept this international call has also encouraged the policy makers of the developed countries to make it difficult for the policy makers of the developing countries to liberalize their trade regime for the purpose of promoting domestic efficiency as the level of development rises. There is self-interest for the developing countries in the regard, to accept this international call to assume greater responsibility in the management of the international trading system. The developing countries of this region may work out together a graduation formula. By formula, I mean some kind of approach, not necessarily an arithmetic formula. This might involve some revision or amendment of the GATT Article 18, would also affect the GSP, and might also refer to the role of developing countries in existing codes of the GATT, as well as new codes which might come out of the Uruguay Round. They will do so in exchange for the acceptance on the part of the developed world of non-selectivity of safeguards. So there will be an exchange, a trade-off, between Article 18 and 19. This would certainly require joint work among the newly industrializing economies and other developing economies of the Pacific.

What I have given you so far is a short term agenda for Pacific trade policy cooperation covering the period up to the conclusion of the Uruguay Round. Now let me say something also about the long term agenda for Pacific trade policy cooperation. The Uruguay Round will be over by the end of next year but will not have solved all the trade policy problems of the 1990s. The Forum should look beyond the 1990s. The Pacific countries should look beyond 1990 and will have to anticipate that there will be new trade policy problems arising over time, and many of them will be of common interest to the countries of the Pacific. Let me just name two. One is the need to continue the efforts to liberalize trade and investment in services. Mr. Feketekuty stated that the Uruguay Round will initiate the liberalization effort in this area, but will not complete this. So in the 1990s there will be further efforts to promote services liberalization, at sectoral levels. Of course this will have to be done on a global scale, but again the Pacific countries may want to work together to join and to lead this global effort.

We have heard of various indications that Europe 1992 is unlikely to create a fortress area. Nevertheless, Pacific countries will face many common problems in the course of living with Europe after 1992. So Pacific countries may find it useful to get together occasionally and share experiences and analyses of these issues.

I have covered briefly a possible short term agenda as well as a long term agenda for Pacific cooperation. Let me very briefly mention the role of Pacific Trade Policy Forum in particular. One role has been mentioned by Sir Frank, to present an agenda to the regional governments and also to offer assistance for the work that they would need to implement this agenda. So the Forum can work on agriculture, safeguards, less than fair value actions, services, Europe 1992, etc.

Finally, I would like to add this. This Forum might adopt and carry out work programs to help create a political momentum for trade liberalization in national capitals. The work of this Forum has so far mainly addressed government officials. But recent developments in some parts of this region show that it is one thing to talk to trade officials but, as implied by Ambassador Carlisle, it is another thing to talk to politicians. If anybody has to be told that unilateralism is a poor substitute for multilateralism, that there may not be much economic wisdom in the unfair trade laws, at least given the way they are implemented nowadays, or that the trade imbalances are largely a macroeconomic problem which has nothing to do with the so-called unfair trade practices, it is politicians I think rather than trade officials. The Pacific Trade Policy Forum may then want to develop work programs of a different nature, to more directly interact with the members of Congress and other political groups, as well as with the mass media to which they very carefully listen. For example, the Forum may organize a discussion session with members of Congress in Washington or it may devise ways of taking positions and announcing them in the public on current policy issues as they arise. There can be various kinds of "meet the politician" program or "tell the politician" program if you will.

Wilhelm Ortaliz
Philippines Council for Foreign Relations
Manila

The other speakers this afternoon are covering a lot of the issues that should be raised and what may be done by PECC as a contribution to the Uruguay Round GATT negotiations. Let me just focus on what we are doing in our country in the Philippines, that has been referred to as the "sick man" in Asia until now, even though we have managed a modest growth during the last two years.

When I was researching for a speech before an ASEAN meeting around two months ago, I stumbled upon a statement I think that is quite significant. It said that the lack of complementarity among the economies of ASEAN nations was less due to the fact that they had common natural resources and more because of the government intervention in business in each of the countries. With the exception of Singapore we have undertaken an import substitution policy that has continued until now. We have developed basically the same sort of industries and that explains why ASEAN cooperation until now seemed to suffering great difficulties with each country maintaining some sort of a very protective posture whenever we tried to negotiate concessions with each other.

Now yesterday morning at the end of the session dealing with countervailing action and textile trade policies, Michael Finger emphatically stressed the importance of every country making an effort to examining its trade and industrialization policies and consequently adopting programs and measures consistent with its development needs. In the Philippines it is a small group of government officials, and it usually is just a small group of government officials, whether in a developing country or a developed country, that does a lot of studies and exerts a lot of effort to push for trade liberalization. In the Philippines during the 1970s we had been met with quite modest success in terms of shifting industrialization policy from import substitution featured by very high tariffs, as high as 100 per cent, and a lot of import controls. In 1981 we launched an all encompassing tariff reform program and the lifting of quantitative restrictions on imports. The small group was very happy that it had the top government support to push for this. The reform programs consisted of a complete overhaul of the tariff structure. For a period of five years, we decided to set the maximum tariff from 100 to reduce it from 100 to 50 and to narrow the range between 10 per cent and 50 per cent. It also involved the lifting of quantitative import restrictions on some 1,600 items. It also covered the rationalization of the policy of fiscal incentives, based on the principle that fiscal incentives shall henceforth be extended to specific areas and activities in the economy to compensate for market distortions where such distortions cannot be phased out immediately. This is quite significant in that it focused government attention less on incentives given but more on identifying the distortions that existed in the economy and finding ways and means to phase them out.

In addition, the rationalization of the government's incentives program involved the adoption of a package of incentives that were more or less performance based. The package of reforms I wish to stress were formulated and put in place unilaterally, in other words, the country did not benefit from any concessions given by its trading partners. We were very much in a hurry to do this. Even though we had a five year phasing of the whole program, we decided that with or without concessions from our trading partners we needed to do this because this was good medicine for the economy.

Unfortunately the program for the face-lifting of import controls suffered a setback, a very major setback, when the country was struck by a foreign exchange crisis in late 1983. The foreign exchange crisis was so severe that we had to allocate foreign exchange for importations, basically confined initially to eight major industries which are quite basic. At that particular point in time, it did not make so much sense for us to be lifting import controls because we did not have enough exchange to import the basic necessities for the country. The new government that took over in 1986, notwithstanding the economic collapse that the country suffered after two years of negative growth, set the import liberalization program back on its track. It required a lot of courage for the Aquino government to do that.

During the last two days of the conference here, Dr. Medalla, who has been involved in the formulation of the reform programs, and I myself realized that perhaps we would have had less trouble implementing the program if we had not called it import liberalization and instead used the term we learned here, which was "tariffication". Perhaps the next time we do something again about lifting import controls we just simply call it tariffication, because it was precisely that. We were willing to accommodate certain adjustment, temporary upward adjustment of tariffs for certain industries for as long as they would reduce quantitative import restriction and just to make sure that the tool for protection became more transparent.

The reforms that have been put in place, and they are still in the process of being implemented, are actually just the first slice of what we intended for the country. Once this particular reform program is fully in place, the small group of people in academia and business as well as in government are looking forward to a second round tariff reform to further squeeze the tariff structure and limit the range from 10 to 30 per cent, and perhaps down the road by the end of the century really look at a uniform tariff of around 10 per cent for the country.

In addition we have our eyes set on the lifting of import controls, particularly for some very critical consumer products, home appliances, consumer durables and quite a number of items, including the progressive car manufacturing program, which are included in the progressive-manufacture program of the country. As you can imagine, it is no accident that the big business sector in the country are usually people who are producing products that are protected by very high tariffs of 40 or 50 per cent, 40 per cent even after the tariff reform, products where imports are also being controlled by the government.

Meanwhile something has happened in the country. From a autocratic government we now have a very democratic one and fortunately, or unfortunately, we now have a bicameral legislature and all of the reform program in order to be implemented has to go through a process of legislation. That should give you an idea of how much more difficult it may now be for the small group of people to push for reforms.

In addition news about Europe 1992 and protectionist legislation being passed by this or that country does not help the reform group. There is great doubt on the part of the public that the opening up of the country's domestic market to import competition will really be advantageous, considering that other countries seem to be closing up their own markets. The question that continues to be asked is, "Okay, we are opening up because you feel it is good for our export sector, but what markets are you looking at as being open for us when we finally get there?"

It needs to be emphasized therefore that while reforms are being designed by a group of technocrats and a group that are very passionately committed to this particular work, the final implementation is really dependent upon the mood of the country and the mood of government and the legislature particularly at this point of time. It therefore will help a lot if we can demonstrate that we are not alone in this particular effort, that all other countries in the region are in fact doing something similar, opening up their markets because it is good medicine for their particular economies. We need to demonstrate that the country's major trading partners are doing something complementary to what we are doing in the country and that our final exports that will come out of our effort will really have markets available.

When looking at the particular product groups that we are very concerned with, we are of course concerned with agricultural products but we are not in the big league, the agricultural products that are really in trouble are coming from developed countries. ASEAN and the Cairns Group are looking at the possibility of really making a special case for tropical products. As a basket this does not really represent much in terms of total trade but it is bread and butter for developing countries like us.

Another sector that we are looking at is the textile sector, covering from fibre production to garments. I hope that Yamazawa can be more more optimistic about his proposal. We would like to see his proposal considered as the basis for some sort of a scheduling for phasing out of the multi-fibre arrangement in the future. We are confident that, given the right phasing and given the right signals, even small countries like the Philippines could specialize in something that will contribute to exports.

Another sector that we are interested in looking at for partnership and complementarity would be the plastic products sector. Right now Philippine tariffs on the basic resin raw material (the import controls have just been lifted) are in the 30 to 40 per cent range so they are very heavily protected. In that particular sector, monopoly profits are directed against us and they buy a lot of newspaper space.

Another product, another industry that needs a lot of help would be the paper, paper product and packaging sector and still another is metal and metal fabrication. Reformers in PECC member countries really need to work together to influence the government towards adoption of more complementarity policies. With limited reciprocity, I think we can together work in a coordinated manner; we could find a package of concessions that would lead to more progress, a will to liberalize in our own governments and in our own industrial sectors.

Now in looking at these product groups I realize of course that some of these reforms are feasible for adoption during this Uruguay Round and others may require a little bit longer. What is important is that we start something now, we start the studies that need to be undertaken and we start defining exactly the scope and pacing and means of liberalization among the countries in the region.

Professor Ippei Yamazawa
Hitotsubashi University
Japan

Almost everybody has mentioned and welcomed Mr. Baker's proposal. I also welcome Mr. Baker's call for Pacific alliance and will elaborate how it can be related to our PECC activity in improving the trade and investment regime in the Pacific.

We Japanese welcomed Mr. Baker's proposal because it relieved us from a year-long nightmare. It started with a proposal for U.S.-Japan bilateral free trade made by Mr. Mansfield, the former Ambassador to Japan. Ambassador Mansfield was respected and liked by many Japanese and we never doubted his sincere intention to resolve the increasing conflict between the two countries. But why bilateral? Why a free trade agreement? In our relationship with the United States, a free trade arrangement cannot solve many of the problems raised between us. Why a bilateral agreement? We have already had a number of bilateral negotiations with the United States on individual items, each of which concluded with concessions to the U.S. interest. They irritated many Japanese. Nonetheless, it is never clever to turn down a U.S. request and we took it seriously, but we had a hard time to digest this proposal. A number of study groups started, by the Ministry of International Trade and Industry (MITI), by the Ministry of Foreign Affairs, and by the Ministry of Finance. They never worked together, they established separate working groups and the Economic Planning Agency and private research institutions such as the Japan Economic Research Center, the Foundation for Advanced Information and Research (FAIR) and others. I discussed it with U.S. International Trade Commission study mission sent by the Congress. Recently, many of them came up with a similar conclusion. The MITI proposal which was introduced by Mr. Kuroda during the Forum (on June 26) happened to be one of them. They came to a similar conclusion, supporting multilateral rather than bilateral approaches and no free trade arrangement. It covered a wide range of cooperation activities. The issues for cooperative actions they mentioned in their report have already been covered by PECC task force activity. Usually our government reports do not give credit to the original source of the ideas or proposal that appear in them, so the report of those study groups do not mention explicitly their indebtedness to the PECC reports. But the Japan Committee for the PECC has been distributing all materials the PECC report to them, so their indebtedness is quite clear.

However the PECC has had a weak political commitment to processes for connecting our discussions and recommendations to policy implementation. So I am very glad to see the new initiative taken by Mr. Baker, Mr. Hawke and others. Those new initiatives will lead to the holding of ministerial meetings and can lead to political commitments to the PECC recommendations.

But our next challenge is, how PECC, strengthened by stronger political commitment, can further improve trade and investment conditions of the Pacific. We have already started two PECC activities directly aimed at it. One is the Pacific economic outlook which discusses the decrease of macroeconomic imbalances in the Pacific through closer and more efficient coordination in macroeconomic policy. And another is to continue to improve the Trade Policy Forum and the trade and investment regime through studies by this Forum in close cooperation with other task forces like those dealing with agriculture, forestry and the environment, the minerals and energy forum and others. In this Forum we have already discussed such issues as agriculture, processed resource trade, the services trade and others.

I would like to attract your attention to another issue, the VER, the Voluntary Export Restraint which governs a large proportion of manufactures trade in the Pacific. VER covers steel, automobile, household electronics, semi-conductors and other products. According to a GATT report, nearly 40 per cent of Japan's exports is under these VERs. And each of these VERs has been a source of trade conflict between Japan and the United States. The VERs on these products are not as tight as MFA restrictions on textiles, which I discussed in a paper presented yesterday, but they are still managed, preventing new entry and discouraging technical innovation. These have been extended repeatedly so that there have emerged vested interest both for exporting and importing countries. These VERs also tend to prevent industrialization of the Asian NIEs and ASEAN countries, and delay the dynamic development of the Pacific.

Furthermore VERs contradict GATT rules and disciplines, and their proliferation undermines the GATT regime. I have to say that Japan is responsible for the proliferation of VERs. She has been responding to the United States request too easily and now she is starting to make similar requests to our neighbour countries. It does not make any sense to call for a standstill for VER, unless we find other better means of solving conflict. They will include the improvement of the safeguards and the strengthening of dispute settlement procedures and others. The problem here is there is no strong initiative to eliminate VER. In Geneva I found the GATT official in charge of the safeguards negotiation very pessimistic. Neither of the two governments involved in VERs complained. A third country government seldom complained except in the case of the U.S.-Japan semiconductor agreement. Neither exporting nor importing groups complained. Only academics criticized it. So it seems to me necessary to raise this issue in such multilateral groups as PECC and work out suggested solutions.

Yesterday I endorsed the importance of phasing out MFA in textile trade. This was taken up because it is on the agenda of the GATT negotiation as the exception to GATT rules. Another initiative should be take to remove VER which does not appear on GATT agenda. As regards to this issue I certainly welcome the suggestion made by Mr. Smith and also the reference to this important issue made by Mr. Carlisle during his luncheon speech today, and respond to this suggestion. I would like to include this issue in our trade policy statement.

Djisman S. Simandjuntak
Centre for Strategic and International Studies
Jakarta

At least 66 of the present 96 contracting parties to the GATT and another eight non-member participants in the Uruguay Round, can be identified as developing countries. No doubt, these countries differ widely in terms of stages of economic development and openness of their respective economies, making it very difficult to treat them in a uniform way in international trade talks and negotiations. Some of them have graduated or have been graduated in terms of compliance to the principles and rules of the GATT. Nevertheless, solidarity exists, however vague it may be, among developing countries in facing the developed countries which on their side, are increasingly heterogeneous, in terms of real commitment to the GATT. At least in one thing, the developing countries in the GATT take a common position, namely on the demand for a differential treatment based on Part IV or the development norm of GATT.

Addressing this demand for differential treatment is an imperative for the GATT. Apart from the fact that developing countries constitute a "majority" in the GATT—the term "majority" is basically of no relevance in an organization where decision making process is based on consensus—positive population growth, relatively high economic growth, and the existence of potential demand imply a growing importance of developing countries to future expansion of the global market, at least for some industries and services. The Seven Wiseman strongly recommended, therefore, that efforts be made to secure an active participation of developing countries in the GATT. It is in relation to this active participation, that is, participation which also includes the willingness to make concessions in exchange for concessions made by others, that the idea of limited reciprocity needs to be looked into with greater clarity.

Different Interpretations of Reciprocity

Both in theory and practice, trade liberalization does not have to be based on the principles of reciprocity. In fact, in the early days of GATT, the United States offered trade concessions virtually without expecting "compensations" from other countries, including the war-damaged Western European countries. Formally speaking, participation in the GATT which implies a commitment to liberalization, is bound to lead to reciprocity in due course of time. However, to rule out the possibility of free riding, reciprocity is explicitly mentioned as the second substantive principles of the GATT. The importance attached to it fluctuates over time. At present, demand for reciprocity is particularly strong in the United States. Countries with strong reliance on the American market cannot afford to ignore this demand as doing so is likely to be penalized. Therefore, developing countries participating in the GATT have both fundamental and practical reasons not to resist reciprocity. What needs to be sought is the kind of reciprocity commensurate with the economic conditions prevailing in the respective countries.

There are two kinds of reciprocity, though the boundary between them is difficult to draw. The first is referred to as general reciprocity in which the degree of reciprocity is measured in terms of a rough balance between concessions exchanged by two negotiating parties. In contrast, specific reciprocity known also as aggressive reciprocity or tit-for-tat reciprocity is measured in terms of result such as bilateral trade balance or even sectoral balance between two countries. A strict insistence on specific reciprocity is, therefore, likely to result in the collapse of world trade. If the United States and Indonesia for example, had to balance trade product by product, trade would cease to exist in a big number of products such as coffee and aircraft. The interest of all parties to the GATT is served, if developing countries refuse to enter into an agreement which is based on specific reciprocity. To refuse a general reciprocity, however, is likely to result in a situation where the agenda of GATT is shaped by the developed countries without due attention to the interest of developing countries. Moreover, developing countries need to abide to certain rules of trade-policy-making if they are to get rid of unproductive rent-seeking with all its damaging impacts on international competitiveness.

Arguments for Limited Reciprocity

Equality between concession and compensation is practically impossible to measure. A reduction of tariff by 10 per cent by the United States for example, is not necessarily the same thing as a 10 per cent tariff cut by Austria, given the different size of the two economies. Notwithstanding this problem of measurement, however, it still is possible to estimate the trade importance of certain concessions, and to say whether or not a country makes a more generous concession than another country. What is much more difficult, is to find strong arguments in favour of a deal where a developing country offers a compensation which is less generous than the concession it gets.

The infant industry argument is very well known. Its theoretical foundation is certainly contestable. In the real world, however, all countries adhere to it, if in different forms. Some countries impose restrictions on imports to compensate for the high costs of infrastructure, outdated machinery and equipment, transportation and telecommunication and government services. Others resort to it as a way of fostering the development and diffusion of new technologies. Industrial targeting, where the level of competition is consciously reduced through picking up the most prospective winners and a host of incentives such as R & D subsidy and government procurement are provided to the participants in the targeting, is a variant of infant industry argument. Such a targeting is now at work in many high-tech industries. Admittedly, there are many flaws in this infant industry argument. In a world with rapid technical change, the demand of an industry for a differential treatment tends to perpetuate. One day the demand may be asked because of infancy, another day because of a technically feasible reinvention. Therefore, eligibility for limited reciprocity should be judged on the overall level of economic development rather than on a sector by sector basis.

Another argument for limited reciprocity relates to the fact that some elements of protection are biased against developing countries. Whenever protection policy allows a sectoral selectivity, industries with declining competitiveness are likely to enjoy a level of protection above average. Yet, it is this category of industries where developing countries usually start to industrialize. In some cases such as the MFA, newcomers among the developing countries are even penalized because of the success of others, if by default rather than by design. The phasing-out of this bias should not be made conditional on the willingness of developing countries to reciprocate. Rather, it should be seen as a necessary part of sectorally neutral protection structure which requires the lowest possible level of dispersion of protection levels across industries.

Possible Forms of Limited Reciprocity

Most of the arguments normally put forward to defend limited reciprocity are certainly contestable. One can even hypothesize that developing countries would reap a greater benefit from participation in trade negotiations, if they fully comply to the principles of reciprocity rather than if they insist on getting concessions without the obligation to reciprocate as under such circumstances the concessions made will be binding. The continuous erosion of the Generalized System of Preferences (GSP) shows very clearly that unilateral concessions are highly unstable. However, the fact remains that resistance to full reciprocity is still found among many developing countries, in spite of the waves of deregulation which in reality lead to substantial trade liberalization. To secure an active participation of many developing countries in the GATT, flexibility is, therefore, needed in judging the equality of concessions.

Limited reciprocity can take different forms. A consequential compliance to the principles of transparency and a real commitment to standstill can be seen as an important concession. A limited reciprocity can also take the form of a longer time schedule to implement a certain agreement on trade liberalization. The experience of ASEAN with its Preferential Trading Arrangement is a good example in this connection. While a common target of intra-ASEAN liberalization was agreed during Manila Summit, Indonesia and the Philippines are allowed to proceed more slowly in implementing the agreement, namely within a seven-year period as compared to five years in the case of other ASEAN countries. The result is encouraging so far. It helps Indonesia to overcome its reluctance to engage in intra-ASEAN trade liberalization. Another possibility is to allow a developing country to limit concession to standstill in a few industries which it thinks are of crucial importance to its economic development, subject to the condition that rollback is offered in other industries.

Some developing countries are likely to continue to refuse to accept the limited reciprocity illustrated above. However, developing countries should not forget that they, too, have liberalized without getting a compensation from other countries for an obvious reason that the liberalization is not bound to the GATT. If a developing country has no choice but to liberalize, it should do so in such a way as enable it to seek compensation from other countries, the more so at a time when "reciprotarians" seem to have gained in importance in some major trading countries.

H. Edward English
Carleton University
Ottawa, Canada

How can the Pacific countries in 1989 and 1990 contribute to the maintenance of the world trading system, and its adaptation to the needs of the next decade and beyond? The answer is usually given under *headings* such as multilateral initiatives, regional initiatives and bilateral deals.

They can be complementary strategies, but conflict can also arise between approaches. Trade policy options include:

1. A reinforced and enlarged GATT, based on some of the changes being negotiated during the Uruguay Round.

2. Bilateralism or sub-regionalism as before—perhaps even new FTA's such as those reviewed critically in Jeff Schott's publication.* The nature of existing groups indicates that it is likely that such arrangements are more likely among countries at similar levels of development—e.g., that between Canada and the U.S. (a combined GNP of over 5 trillion U.S. dollars) that between Australia and New Zealand (with a combined GNP of about 180 billion). The ASEAN countries have a combined GNP of over 200 billion.

    Wider Pacific groups have been contemplated in the writings of Sir Frank Holmes e.g. Canada, Australia and New Zealand; or Canada, the U.S. and Japan; or these three plus Australia, New Zealand and perhaps Korea.

    This latter or anything approaching it in scope would clearly require attention to separate and distinct (not-fully-reciprocal) treatment of other PECC countries such as those of ASEAN and the Pacific Islands. Selective "ad hoc" arrangements with China, Taiwan and Hong Kong would also be important.

---

*   See the publication list of the Institute for International Economics.

Another kind of bilateralism, that based on pressure by larger countries or smaller economic units, is also likely to continue, but it is not clear that this will provide a balance of benefits from trade. It could instead induce the politically weak to resort to joint defense actions and inward-looking policies.

If larger free trade areas are unrealistic and bilateralism of unequals is unacceptable and risky for the system, what regional initiatives can be practical?

3.   The answer could be specific issue alliances that encompass the major trading interests of the PECC countries. These can include joint proposals for trade policy liberalization that are directly relevant to the Uruguay Round and the future of the GATT system. They can also include a package of proposals that go beyond what is likely to be accomplished in the Uruguay Round but will be open to adherence by other GATT members now or in the future.

Examples most of which have already emerged from the papers and discussion in this Forum, include:

(a)   Extension of the Cairns group proposals into commitments by PECC countries for the reduction of agricultural protection, such as reduction of domestic subsidies in the region and joint action on export subsidies, elimination of such subsidies by PECC members and joint response to such subsidies by non-PECC members. A timetable for liberalization should be considered. (Refer to the Brookins paper.)

(b)   Negotiation of agreements to reduce or eliminate tariff and non-tariff barriers on specific *processed* products of the resource industries:

(i)   tariffs on tropical fruits, coconut products, fish products, forest products (plywood, furniture and paper) and some mineral and chemical products;

(ii)   non-tariff barriers including out-of-date or unnecessary phyto-sanitary regulations, construction regulations, etc.; and

(iii)   harmonization of practices and recognition of economically acceptable differences in policies in resource taxation and sustained development. The importance of the forest and fisheries industries to PECC economies suggest that the PECC could take a lead in these matters. (Refer to the Munro, Findlay and Percy papers.)

(c) The variety of regional interests in trade distortions affecting manufacturers is evident. It was illustrated in the selective list of issues addressed in the Forum program.

Two of the issues were broadly sectoral in character— textile products and high-tech goods trade. The former category is governed by the multi-fibre arrangement. Here the failure of importing countries to live up to the minimum commitment to growth in trade is regrettable, as is the rigid commitment of established exporting countries to their specific quotas. The commitment by both exporting and importing countries to more flexible markets would benefit all parties. Collective action by importing countries of the developed world would make it easier for developing countries to move out of rigid export patterns. The developed countries of the Pacific might act together to liberalize imports. They are not acting alone these days, except perhaps for Japan. Specific Pacific developing countries have shown a capacity to move up-market in these products and might do more if quotas could be exchanged or even eliminated. (Refer to Yamazawa paper.)

Countries having comparative advantages in the high-tech sectors have shown considerable concern about counterfeit trade—the undermining of returns from intellectual property rights, but much less about the monopolistic abuse of such rights. Under bilateral pressure, developing countries have been persuaded to extend the application of basic patent, trademark & copyright legislation. What is now needed is a more collective effort to define and apply a more common standard of adequacy of rewards to such property and the development and application of means of reducing rigidities and encouraging competitive use of new technology while continuing to allow appropriate terms for compensation of the innovator. The instruments of compulsory licensing and the exhaustion principle are alternatives that deserve further consideration. The Pacific countries have a big stake in this, given their intellectual potential, and might give more unified leadership both in GATT and in the international intellectual property associations.

The third issue in the "manufactures trade" category discussed in the Forum related to subsidy and countervail. The link between distinctive national policies and trade pattern distortion has been getting more thought recently. The Canada-U.S. FTA negotiations addressed this issue and decided to allow five to seven more years for study and negotiation. Pacific countries clearly have a parallel interest notably over the application of "super 301" by the U.S. It is clear that there is much scope for better identification of those interventions that are subsidies, or equivalents that have significant trade distortion effects, and how the same ends of public policy might be served without inducing countervail. For example, income-support systems are clearly to be preferred to price supports or subsidies on particular commodities. (Refer to Finger and Hart papers.)

(d) Finally we have looked at the framework for services trade liberalization and the particular conditions of financial services and civil aviation and tourism services. Several conclusions emerge from the main papers.

  (i) There are several overlapping principles on which services trade could rely—national treatment, reciprocity and home-market treatment. But the differences among these are reduced by the harmonization of national practice. (Refer to the Feketekuty and Kim and Kim papers.)

  (ii) It must be recognized generally that infant industry or young economy arguments apply here. Response to this reality can be of several kinds. One is that serious consideration be given to service sectors of interest to developing countries, e.g. construction services and civil aviation and tourism are important to ASEAN NIEs.

  Secondly, principles governing services trade should allow for the needs of developing countries. The entry of imported services might be conditional on transfer of technology and training arrangements, even though in other respects national treatment would apply.

(e) Support for changes in the rules and procedures of GATT that make escape from GATT obligations more difficult and less appealing, including:

(i) a non-discriminatory system of safeguards that makes them relatively convenient to adopt but rapidly digressive, thus encouraging adjustment and the substitution of safeguard action under GATT for unilateral withdrawal of access to markets.

(ii) development of a system for analysis by the GATT secretariat of the impact of subsidies, and the conditions under which GATT signatories might resort to non-discriminatory countervail or other action; and accompanying this, the removal or severe restriction of unilateral determination of actionable subsidies and countervail action.

(iii) support for the other dispute settlement and surveillance mechanisms now proposed in Uruguay Round.

The agenda is large. The opportunities for specific issue alliances indicated by PECC members but open to others are substantial. The Hawke initiative will help to identify the most urgent priorities. The PECC Trade Forum with the advantage of its work to date, is well placed to address these priorities in a constructive way, reflecting private (business and academic) knowledge and perspective and thus enriching the basis for national policies and international negotiations.

GATT and the Uruguay Round: The Implications of the Round for the Pacific Region

Charles R. Carlisle
GATT Secretariat, Geneva

I have been asked to speak today about GATT and the Uruguay Round and about the implications of the Round for the Pacific region. My remarks concern four subjects:

1. the current status of the Uruguay Round and the challenges confronting us in the Round;
2. the importance of the Round to the world economy;
3. the importance of success in these negotiations for the nations of the Pacific; and
4. the health of GATT and the prospects for a successful Uruguay Round.

The Uruguay Round

We are now more than half-way through the most complex and ambitious trade negotiations the world has ever seen. Launched by ministers from more than 90 countries at Punta del Este, Uruguay, in September 1986, the Round is scheduled to be completed by the end of 1990.

Shortly after the ministers met we established 15 different negotiating groups, drew up negotiating plans, chose chairmen for the negotiating groups, and started to work. The negotiations cover not only traditional subjects such as tariffs and quotas. They also seek to bring agriculture effectively under GATT's rules and address new subjects such as services, trade-related investment measures, and the trade-related aspects of intellectual property rights. We also are trying to improve the way the GATT functions and, for the first time in a GATT negotiation, we are reviewing its rules to see how they can be made better.

In December 1988 in Montreal we had a mid-term review with, I might add, the very active participation of Canadian trade minister John Crosbie as well as other Canadian officials. The purposes of the meeting were to review our work to date and, more important, to agree on the scope and direction of the negotiations in the Round's final two years.

Many articles in the press characterized the Montreal meeting as a failure because we were not able to reach agreement on four key subjects—agriculture, textiles, intellectual property, and "safeguards" (GATT jargon for the measures governments take when import surges threaten domestic industries). And because we could not reach agreement in those four areas, a group of Latin American nations, desirous of a substantial result in agriculture, announced that they would not join any consensus on the other 11 subjects until agriculture was agreed. Thus, the entire Round was effectively put on hold.

This gave rise, perhaps understandably, to reports of "failure" and a "crisis" in the Round. Only after reading beyond the headlines was it clear that Ambassadors to GATT, meeting in Geneva, had reached agreement on six subjects before the Montreal meeting began and that Ministers meeting in Montreal had reached agreement on five others.

The Montreal meeting can be considered a success by any reasonable standard. For example, governments agreed to cut tariffs in this Round by more than 30 per cent; a number of governments agreed to reduce or eliminate duties on many tropical products and to do this, not at the end of the Round, but now; agreement was reached on speeding up and streamlining dispute settlement procedures; and agreement was reached on the establishment, on a provisional basis, of a trade policy review mechanism, which will systematically review the trade policies of all GATT members. This new review mechanism holds great promise in helping to curb protectionist practices.

The Montreal meeting scored perhaps its greatest breakthrough in services, one of the most vexing issues in the Uruguay Round and one that had produced sharp north-south divisions. At Montreal, however, Ministers were able to agree on how the negotiations are to proceed and that a draft framework agreement should be ready by the end of this year.

At the end of the Montreal meeting Ministers agreed that high officials should meet in Geneva during the first week in April to deal with the four remaining subjects. That Geneva meeting was a success.

The negotiating deadlock on agriculture was broken by agreeing that over the long term there should be "substantial progressive reductions in agricultural support and protection sustained over an agreed period of time...". Governments also agreed between now and the end of the Round "... to ensure that current domestic and export support and protection levels in the agricultural sector are not exceeded... within the scope of their existing legislation and their existing GATT rights and obligations...".

After two years of debate governments were also able to agree on the issues to be addressed in the intellectual property negotiations. In addition, agreements were reached on textiles and safeguards, thereby completing a package on all 15 negotiating subjects.

While we are pleased with the results of the Montreal and Geneva meetings, we are not complacent. Essentially, the first two years of the Round were spent discussing what we would be negotiating in the last two years. That first part was the easier part, but even that was not easy. Now, we must come to grips with, and resolve, some very difficult negotiating issues:

- How can we substantially liberalize trade in agriculture and bring this trade effectively under GATT's rules?

- Can we strengthen access to markets for manufactured goods and commodities? Do we have the vision—and the political courage—to begin freeing trade in such products as textiles and steel and to get rid of subsidies?

- What rules are needed for the new areas of trade in services, intellectual property rights, and trade-related investment measures?

The Uruguay Round and the World Economy

Just to ask those questions—and one could ask others—suggests the daunting challenges confronting us as we drive to finish the Round within the next 18 months. It is vitally important to the world economy that we overcome those challenges.

The massive indebtedness of a number of developing countries is still with us. That debt has *increased* from more than US$800 billion in 1982 to US$1,300 billion last year.

Trade liberalization by itself cannot solve the debt problem, but can we possibly get on top of that problem without trade liberalization? A successful Uruguay Round can help the indebted countries to expand their exports and to grow their way out of their great difficulties.

We also still confront huge current account imbalances. The Federal Republic of Germany had a US$54 billion surplus in the last 12 months, Japan had a US$77 billion surplus and the United States had a US$125 billion deficit.

These imbalances are simply unsustainable, if for no other reason that not even the United States can go on indefinitely adding to its foreign debt. Correcting the imbalances will mean a major shift in world trade, and the two most important questions are: *When* will the shift occur and *how* will it occur? Will it come about primarily through export expansion—and that seems to have been the case until now—or will it come about through import contraction? A successful Uruguay Round will increase the chances that the adjustment will be based on export expansion and economic growth, not on import contraction and recession.

Finally, we need trade growth to stimulate world economic growth. GATT's economists have calculated that the growth rates of both world merchandise trade and world merchandise production have been falling over the last two decades. World trade grew at an annual rate of 8.5 per cent in the 1960s, at a 4 per cent in the 1980s. Similarly, merchandise production expanded at a 6 per cent rate in the 1960s, and at a 2.5 per cent rate in this decade.

We did have a good year last year. Merchandise trade grew by an impressive 8.5 per cent, merchandise production by 5.5 per cent—just like the good old 1960s! We need more years like 1988.

Implications for the Pacific Area

The subject of economic growth takes me inevitably to the matter you asked me to address—the implications of the Uruguay Round for the Pacific. Canada, the United States and Mexico all have long coasts on the Pacific, as do several countries in South America, but by Pacific I mean, somewhat arbitrarily, Australia, the People's Republic of China, Hong Kong, Indonesia, Japan, South Korea, Malaysia, New Zealand, the Philippines, Singapore, Taiwan and Thailand.

These 12 countries and territories, which together have 1.6 billion—almost a third of the world's population—are diverse in many ways. But when one looks at the economic statistics certain things stand out.

First, their economic growth per capita, in real terms, has been increasing much faster than that in the rest of the world on average. From 1965 to 1986 annual per capita GNP growth, adjusted for inflation, was in the range of 2 to 3 per cent worldwide. In nine of the 12 countries and territories I have mentioned, however, the comparable figures were in the 4 to 7 per cent range, with Singapore at the remarkable level of 7.6 per cent. At that rate per capita GNP doubles in less than 10 years.

Second, their economies are heavily dependent on exports. According to World Bank figures, exports of goods and services as a percentage of total output averages 17 per cent for industrial countries and about the same for developing countries, 19 per cent. In seven of the 12 Pacific countries and territories the figure ranges from 21 to 57 per cent. In two, Hong Kong and Singapore, the figure is actually greater than one, 112 per cent and 187 per cent, respectively. In only three countries—Australia, China and Japan (with 12 per cent)—are the percentages below the general averages.

Third, as you might suspect, their exports have been growing faster than those of the rest of the world. Between 1980 and 1986, industrial country exports increased at an average annual rate of 3.3 per cent, those of developing countries by 4.8 per cent. Nine of the 12 countries topped those figures, with export growth of 5.5 per cent annually to 13.1 per cent (South Korea).

When we look at merchandise trade flows within and among regions a similar picture emerges. During the period 1980-1988 trade among the 12 grew at an average annual rate of 11.7 per cent, but trade between the 12 as a group and North America grew even faster—by 11.9 per cent. Moreover, trade between the 12 and Western Europe increased at a very respectable rate of 10.1 per cent a year. Trade within North America, within Western Europe and across the Atlantic grew at lower rates in the same period.

These few statistics confirm what we already know: that when one talks about the Pacific one is talking about a dynamic region characterized by strong, export-led growth.

Does such a region have a stake in the success of the Uruguay Round? The answer, it seems to me, is obvious. Yes!

I should add that the nations of the Pacific not only have an important stake in the overall success of the Round, they also have a direct interest in the success of many of the individual negotiations. Textiles is an obvious example. In the Uruguay Round we have the opportunity to begin phasing out the numerous restrictions that beset world trade in textiles and clothing.

Trade in other manufactured goods, which account for more than 50 per cent of all world trade, is another example. Just think of all of the manufactured exports from the Pacific nations.

Agriculture is a third example. A number of these nations are important and competitive producers of agricultural products. And why not services? Will all the services exports be from Japan, Europe and North America? Can developing nations produce software and undertake construction jobs in foreign countries? Of course they can.

But just a minute. Would not some sort of regional free trade arrangement serve just as well? To be blunt, the answer is no.

I hasten to add that at the GATT we are *not* opposed to customs unions or free trade areas such as the European Common Market and the Canada-U.S. Free Trade Agreement. Indeed, Article XXIV of the GATT specifically permits such arrangements. Paragraph 4 of that Article says:

> The contracting parties recognize the desirability of increasing freedom of trade by the development, through voluntary agreements, of closer integration between the economies of the countries parties to such agreements. They also recognize that the purpose of a customs union or of a free-trade area should be to facilitate trade between the constituent territories and not to raise barriers to the trade of other contracting parties with such territories.

The GATT looks with favour upon such arrangements, provided they facilitate trade and do not raise barriers to parties outside the arrangements. In our view, however, customs unions and free trade areas cannot be substitutes for a strong, liberalizing multilateral trading system. They can only be useful adjuncts.

This view is rooted not in a fear that GATT's 400 people will lose their jobs, but in economic truth: The larger the universe, the greater economic efficiency and income maximization. If the nations of the Pacific wish to have secure opportunities in the large, rich markets of North America and Western Europe, they will work hard for a successful Uruguay Round. Fortunately, they are doing just that.

GATT's Health and Prospects for a Successful Uruguay Round

In concluding my remarks I shall try to answer two separate but closely related questions: First, how healthy is the GATT? Second, will the Uruguay Round be successful?

I raise the first question because the answer to the second depends in part on the answer to the first, and also because one sees occasional articles by prominent economists and businessmen to the effect that the GATT is moribund or ineffective.

All of us will admit that the GATT can stand improvement, that, for example, it has not been able to prevent a number of "voluntary" and "grey-area" trade restrictive measures and that its mechanism for settling bilateral trade disputes is not as effective as we would like it to be.

But all of this is hardly an admission that GATT needs to be replaced or is about to go out of existence. Would a moribund institution tackle the kind of agenda GATT is now tackling? In fact, it would be hard to imagine a more ambitious agenda than the one we have set for ourselves.

Would Ministers of 100 nations have spent a week arguing and discussing night after night in Montreal—in December—if the institution were ineffective and needed to be replaced? We had more than 1,000 delegates at Montreal. Some of the delegations numbered over 70 persons and included several ministers and numerous representatives of the business community.

And would 10 more countries be applying to join the 96 nations already in GATT if the organization did not have a future?

Our dispute settlement process can stand improvement, but at Montreal Ministers agreed on measures to improve it; further changes may be agreed by the end of the Round. At the June meeting of the GATT Council, our regular governing body, 14 of the 28 agenda items concerned the settlement of disputes. Indeed, GATT's dispute settlement mechanism has never been put to greater use.

In short, we have in place a healthy institution, one that needs improvement but that will be improved, one that is squarely facing up to the challenges of the world trading system as we move toward the conclusion of the Uruguay Round. Will the Round be concluded successfully?

Certainly, the negotiating problems we confront are formidable. They are not only new, complex and extensive and involve hard commercial issues; they also raise fundamental differences, one might say cultural differences, in the way nations look at some of the issues.

Of course all of these things do not make the task any easier. Moreover, there are bilateral disputes and tensions, present and potential, which if not managed carefully, could seriously disrupt our negotiations.

Despite the obstacles—and we must not underestimate them—I believe that we shall achieve a substantial success by the end of the Round in 1990.

First, as I have tried to demonstrate, we have a fundamentally sound institutional structure to assist the negotiating process. Second, while the very sweep of the negotiations makes them more difficult in one sense, in another sense, it makes them easier. With 15 negotiating groups at work the scope for trade-offs between various issues increased dramatically.

Third, we have an extremely capable and experienced group of officials and negotiators at work, posted in Geneva and coming from capitals. While negotiating positions often are strongly held and exchanges are sometimes sharp, there is nonetheless a collegial and problem-solving spirit that pervades virtually all of our deliberations.

My fourth, last and, in my judgement, most compelling reason is that we shall be successful because governments everywhere strongly desire that the Round succeed. Whatever their political orientation, governments around the world are seeking to give market forces greater play—that is one of the most important developments in the last part of this century—and that is what the GATT and the Uruguay Round are all about.

In closing, I wish to pay tribute to the fine team of negotiators and officials which Canada has both in Ottawa and Geneva. Because Canadian proposals are well thought out and constructive, because Canada so clearly wants to strengthen GATT and is working so hard to ensure the Round's success, Canada's prestige and authority are high. Illustrating this point, Canada's ambassador to the GATT, John Weekes, is Chairman of the GATT Council of Representatives, a very important post in the GATT structure, and he also chairs one of the negotiating groups.

Pacific Trade and Economic Development

The Honourable John Crosbie, PC, QC, MP
Minister for International Trade
Ottawa

It gives me great pleasure to join you in this conference as we discuss the important issues of Pacific trade and economic development. Before I commence, I believe congratulations are in order for a variety of individuals and organizations. I would like to congratulate the Canadian National Committee on Pacific economic co-operation for their success in hosting the third Pacific Trade Policy Forum; the Chinese Taipei Committee for its financial support; The Institute for Research on Public Policy for its organizational role; and Professor Ted English, without whose hard work, none of this would have been possible.

Earlier today, Germain Denis, Assistant Deputy Minister, Office for Multilateral Trade Negotiations, offered a Canadian perspective on the Pacific in the Uruguay Round of multilateral negotiations. I do not wish to plough over furrowed ground. Rather, I felt it might be useful to place Canada's Pacific strategy in a broader context, so you can understand our national aims and aspirations.

Sitting here in central Vancouver, it is easy to forget that Canada is a relatively new entrant into the ranks of industrialized countries, with much of our development occurring only the past four decades. Indeed, we are a mere pup in the time frame of Asian history. And our national character is still evolving with

343

continuing immigration and urbanization. We are not the country we were even 20 years ago.

That national character has been shaped by geography, history and economic forces:

- Despite the percentage of Canadians who live in cities close to the U.S. border, our national mythology has been shaped in great part by our harsh northern climate and vast open space.
- Economics has caused ever-growing links with our southern neighbours.
- History has caused us to look back across the North Atlantic for our traditions and institutions.

In sum, north for mythology, south for commerce, east for our traditions. Rarely have we looked west beyond our shores.

While we have been a nation from sea to sea for more than a century, we have never truly turned our minds to the Pacific.

To most Canadians, Vancouver has represented the end of the line, far from the original Canada of Ontario and Quebec. And Asia was the far east, reflecting a European perspective that one had to round the Cape of Good Hope in search of silk and spices.

Our fundamental challenge, as we approach the twenty-first century, is to change the way Canadians see the world and ourselves.

In a very real way, it is to help Canadians see this city not as the end of the line, but as the beginning; not as a point of departure, but the port of entry into the Pacific domain; not as our far western edge over the Rockies, but our far eastern centre on the Pacific Rim.

Our plan to help Canadians adjust to the realities of the twenty-first century starts with a commitment to the multilateral trading system. As a middle power with a small domestic market, it is absolutely critical that we support the goal of an open world economy based on respect for the rule of law in multilateral trade.

We view the General Agreement on Tariffs and Trade as the door to development through trade—as the critical link between the three mega-economies of North America, Asia/Pacific and the European community.

I recognize that such a commitment to multilateralism might sound contradictory in light of our bilateral Free Trade Agreement with the United States. But there is no contradiction, for the FTA is an agreement linked tactically, strategically, substantively and psychologically to our objective of a more open world economy.

As a matter of tactics, the Agreement helped prevent a rise in damaging protectionism between Canada and the United States. And we believe it strengthened our negotiating position in the Uruguay Round of multilateral negotiations.

Strategically, the agreement secured better access to a world-scale market—a decisive response to Canada's age-old problem of market size. It lowers barriers to trade in value-added products and services—barriers that have long been obstacles to our development as a value-added economy. And in lowering these barriers, it increased our attractiveness as a location for world-scale manufacturing facilities—a gateway to the North American market for Asian and European manufacturers.

Substantively, the Agreement is based firmly on the concepts and principles of the GATT—in technical standards, procurement, export and import restrictions and elsewhere.

But perhaps most important, the Canada-U.S. Free Trade Agreement is a psychological watershed in our nation's history. It signals a new, outward-looking and more confident Canada.

Far from signifying a retrenchment of Canada into a Fortress North America mentality, this bilateral agreement is truly a stepping stone for our producers to offshore markets. It increases our ability to seize the opportunities in freer trade around the world—to participate in global developments from a position of strength.

Now, during our government's second mandate, we intend to build on that initiative by promoting a global orientation for our traders.

One action symbolizing that global thrust is our decision to change the working name of Canada's Department of External Affairs. Henceforth, the Department will be called External Affairs and International Trade Canada. We will be launching a corporate identity program during October 1989—our export month. The reasons for this change are twofold: first, to remind Canadians constantly the importance of international economic relations in the conduct of our foreign policy; and second, to ensure our exporters understand who and where to call in Ottawa for export assistance.

A second action will be our constant and continuing focus on the Uruguay Round of Multilateral Negotiations. Indeed, we believe it is no exaggeration to state that the continued health of the world economy depends on the progress we make in the current Uruguay Round.

Consider, for example, the link between agricultural trade reform and international finance reform, a link being pursued by the many Asia/Pacific nations in the Cairns Group. One of the benefits of agricultural reform would be higher returns to the LDCs for their exports, thereby easing their debt burden. But a second benefit would be lower budgetary deficits in North America through the lowering of wasteful subsidies. That, in turn, would surely have a beneficial impact on interest rates, which would ease the debt servicing costs of the LDCs even further. Combine meaningful progress on trade with a credible U.S. fiscal policy, and one has the foundation for growth into the '90s.

If agriculture is one critical issue, another is the need for disciplines on national trade laws governing alleged subsidies and dumping—laws that when abused, threaten to undo much of the benefit of past tariff reductions. For our part, we have done a great deal of work on this subject, and I am pleased to be able to release our multilateral position today. Our primary objectives in this areas are as follows:

- to seek improved disciplines on subsidy practices;

- to add greater precision to rules and procedures;

- to obtain clear multilateral understanding on acceptable government programs that are non-trade distorting; and

- to establish a better dispute settlement process.

It is my hope that other nations will find Canada's position compelling, in terms of both logic and practical effect.

Thus, one Canadian action will be the creation of External Affairs and International Trade Canada, while a second will be a continuing focus on the Uruguay Round. That leads me to a third action—our trade development strategy to seize the opportunities of freer global trade.

We call it our three-pillar strategy—geared to the mega-economies of the United States, the European Community and Asia/Pacific.

In other forums recently I have outlined our approach to the 1992 initiative of the European Community and our U.S. export development plan. Today, I would like to focus on our Pacific front.

As Prime Minister Mulroney declared during the 1988 election campaign, we intend to implement a Pacific 2000 initiative to ensure Canada is front and centre in the dynamic theatre of the Pacific Rim.

Today, the volume of trans-Pacific trade between Asia and North America exceeds $300 billion a year. By the turn of the century, that trade will likely exceed $500 billion. By that time, Pacific Asia will contain 60 per cent of humanity, 50 per cent of global production and 40 per cent of global consumption. Clearly, it is high time that Canada developed our own Pacific personality, and we intend to do just that.

- We will be strengthening our scientific and technological base through active partnerships.

- We will be promoting a greater awareness of Asian countries in Canada by encouraging cultural and language studies— awareness of Japan and the other nations that are part of the rich diversity of the Asia/Pacific region.

- We intend to promote a greater awareness of Canada in the Asia/Pacific region, by supporting exchanges and Canadian studies programs.
- We will be pursuing an aggressive regional trade strategy, identifying specific market opportunities in Japan, the four tigers (as they are called) India and elsewhere, and mounting promotional drives to translate those opportunities into exports.

But our Pacific personality goes beyond trade and investment. It is also about people. Fully 50 per cent of our immigration now comes from Asia/Pacific. By the year 2000, there will be one million more Canadians of Asian origin—a major force in our multicultural fabric and a solid link across the Pacific.

I have been focusing on Canada's continuing transformation into a global trader and a growing Pacific presence. But we also understand that the nations of Asia/Pacific are undergoing equally dramatic, if not even greater, change. In fact, I would suggest it is in the changes taking place on both sides of the Pacific that our full potential lies. It is through trade liberalization in sectors such as food products that we can develop a mutually beneficial trans-Pacific relationship based on comparative advantage.

Recent actions have shown that other trading partners, such as the United States, may exhibit impatience as they exert pressure to open Asian markets more fully and more quickly. We understand and support their objectives. We do not support their methods.

Rather, we believe the answer to current trans-Pacific problems lies in multilateral and regional co-operation—not bilateral confrontation; and that is why we are extremely interested in supporting the development of a Pacific Rim Forum and wholeheartedly support Australian Prime Minister Hawke's call for a ministerial meeting later this year.

We see this initial meeting as an opportunity to enhance the sense of community and common purpose among nations of the region. We see it as the beginning of a process of identifying, first, how we can work together to sustain growth, and second, where collaboration and co-operation might be most beneficial, for instance in resource management, transportation or telecommunications.

We hope that a Pacific ministerial forum might stimulate policy-oriented research in the region, and that organizations like the Pacific Economic Cooperation Conference could help channel data and analysis to where it is needed. We would look to the Forum to impart political energy to the fostering of business linkages, with a potentially key role for the Pacific Basin Economic Council.

Should the dialogue be restricted to economics and trade? We think that the agenda of co-operation, by its nature, is a broad one. And we see no reason why the topics covered by Pacific ministerial meetings could not eventually be extended to other areas, such as the environment.

In approaching the ideal of regional co-operation, I believe we should remember the unique qualities of past regional co-operation—our success in mobilizing private sector and academic involvement.

We should build on this success—and avoid building a big and expensive bureaucracy—by using what we have already. I am thinking, for example, of the Pacific Economic Cooperation Conference (PECC).

While matters of policy will obviously remain within the purview of governments, recent moves in PECC to acquire a small, permanent staff and to sharpen the focus of its work programs suggest that PECC might contribute analytical support to the process of regional co-operation. It is something that should be explored.

In summary, that is Canada's Pacific trade strategy for the 1990s, and beyond:

- a recognition that international economic relations are a key factor in our foreign policy;
- a firm commitment to multilateral trade and the rule of law as the door to opportunity for Canada and for all nations;
- using the bilateral Free Trade Agreement with the United States to strengthen our ability to compete in the Pacific arena;
- a Pacific 2000 strategy to develop our Pacific personality; and
- full-fledged support for Pacific regional co-operation.

We believe it is a coherent and realistic strategy that reflects Canada's needs and aspirations as an export-oriented middle power bordered by the Pacific and the Atlantic and situated north of the world's largest consumer market. It is our hope that, through this strategy, we can take our rightful place among the nations of the Pacific and ensure that all countries of the region can prosper in peace into the twenty-first century.

APPENDICES

Appendix I

Regional Cooperation: Challenges for Korea and Australia*

Right Honourable Robert Hawke
Prime Minister of Australia

Australia and Korea lie near the northern and southern extremities of the most dynamically growing region in the world: the Asia-Pacific region. This region generates more than one third of the world's trade, and is likely in the next decade to create more than half the world's economic output. This extraordinary growth gives nations such as ours tremendous opportunities and new responsibilities. Whether we can fulfil the predictions of those who see us entering a "Pacific Century," with all that would mean for rising living standards for our people, is in our own hands. But these opportunities cannot fully be exploited unless we are prepared, as individual nations and as a region, to do the hard work that will be involved.

Today I want to discuss one focus for that work: how we as a region can better cooperate so that our future, individually and regionally, is a secure and prosperous one.

First I want to pay tribute to your own spectacular achievements in Korea. When I came here last in 1984, I commented on the rapid economic progress you were making. Today, five years later, I find that not only have you managed to maintain the pace of economic progress, you have also undertaken

---

* Speech delivered in Seoul, Korea on 31 January 1989.

very welcome political reforms. This combination of economic dynamism and emergent democratic processes—so vividly and magnificently encapsulated in the Seoul Olympics last year—is justifiably pushing the Republic of Korea (ROK) into a more prominent place on the world stage.

Indeed it is no wonder that Korea will, before the turn of the century, join the ranks of the developed nations—a transition that will bring new responsibilities as part of your integration into the global political and economic system. As part of all this, Australia and Korea have built a very successful bilateral trade relationship. We are each among the eight most important trading partners of the other.

Two-way trade in 1987/88 was valued at almost $A3 billion. Over the last five years the trend rate of growth of Australia's exports to the ROK has been over 16 per cent per annum, while for imports it has been over 29 per cent per annum. This is spectacular growth.

There are excellent prospects for further expansion. Last year my government released a Korean Trade and Commercial Development Program as a means to develop further Australia's relationship with the Republic of Korea.

In addition I am pleased that we have an in-principle agreement to negotiate a protocol to the Australia-Korea Bilateral Trade Agreement which was originally signed in 1965. I look forward to its early finalization because it will help both our countries identify and promote areas which will expand our bilateral trade and commercial interests.

Australia enjoys excellent relations with Korea, the countries of North East Asia and the Asia-Pacific region as a whole. About two-thirds of Australia's exports and imports are directed to or sourced from our regional neighbours. About half of the total foreign investment in Australia has come from the Asia-Pacific region and almost three-fifths of Australia's total investment overseas is located within the region.

So we are keenly aware that the economic growth and structural change taking place in North East Asia, in particular, will have vital implications for us as well as our region and the wider international economy.

With this in mind we have asked Dr. Ross Garnaut, our former Ambassador to China, to review the Australian response to these changes. Dr. Garnaut is one of our most distinguished economists and a person closely associated with public policy.

His study will analyze and report on North East Asian changes over recent years and prospectively through to the end of this century and beyond. It will identify areas where our country can cooperate with you and other regional countries for mutual economic, political and wider benefits.

Dr. Garnaut will be coming to Seoul in April 1989 and proposes to discuss those issues with government and business leaders. I hope that these discussions, and the subsequent report, will be of value to Korean decision-makers as it obviously will be to those in Australia.

If one had to isolate the single key factor underpinning the growth of all the dynamically performing nations of the region, it would surely be their capacity to take advantage of a relatively open and non-discriminatory international trading system.

The multilateral system of global trade, under the auspices of the GATT, has provided more than four decades of growth for the world's economies.

North Asian economies, as major exporters, are enjoying growth rates much greater than the Organization of Economic Cooperation and Development (OECD) average. Given this centrality of trade to our region, we have cause for concern about our economic future. Serious cracks are appearing in the international trading system which have major implications for the future health of both our region and the world economy.

First, you will all be aware of the bilateral trade pressures associated with the significant trade imbalances between a number of regional countries and the United States.

Second, there is a trend towards the formation of bilateral or regional trading arrangements which run the risk of undermining a truly multilateral trading system.

Third, there are fundamental tensions within the GATT framework of multilateral trade, of which the Montreal deadlock of December 1988 is but the latest manifestation.

Each of these problems has prompted calls for some sort of regional action. But they are not the only driving forces behind calls for closer regional ties.

It has long been recognized—especially as the region's economic importance continues to grow—that the countries in the region are essentially interdependent; our economic futures are interlinked.

That realization led in 1980 to the creation of the Pacific Economic Cooperation Conference—PECC—of which Australia was a co-founder and of which we remain a consistent supporter.

PECC's work has illuminated large areas of common interests within the region. But its informality, which has helped to broaden its membership, has also made it difficult for it to address policy issues which are properly the responsibility of governments.

We have heard more recent proposals for new and closer regional consultations from both sides of the Pacific.

Former Japanese Prime Minister Nakasone has put forward a suggestion for a Pacific Forum for Economic and Cultural Cooperation.

Former U.S. Secretary of State, George Shultz, canvassed the need to a Pacific intergovernmental forum to encourage cooperation in specific sectors.

More recently, U.S. Senator Bill Bradley has proposed a Pacific coalition on trade and economic development designed to reinforce the Uruguay Round and remove barriers to economic growth in the region.

There have also been calls for various kinds of free trade areas in the Pacific, including one between the U.S. and Japan.

These different proposals have in common the perception that, as a region, we do have interests that can be advanced through greater consultation and cooperation.

I believe the time has come for us to increase our efforts substantially towards building regional cooperation and to investigate seriously what areas it might focus on and what forms it might take.

That is why Australia has recently launched a substantial and concerted diplomatic effort.

We have asked our missions in the region to gauge opinion within the region about how best to push forward our regional cooperation. Senior Australian ministers held constructive talks on this issue with the Japanese leadership earlier this week. We want to assess what the region's attitudes are towards the possibility of creating a more formal intergovernmental vehicle of regional cooperation. A meeting of ministers from throughout the region would be a useful forum to investigate the question.

What we are seeking to develop is a capacity for analysis and consultation on economic and social issues, not as an academic exercise but to help inform policy development by our respective governments.

I see merit in the model provided, in a different context, by the OECD.

I discussed these issues yesterday with President Roh, who is of course the leader of a major regional economy—one of the economies whose involvement would be vital to the success of any new regional institution.

I regard it as a significant step forward that President Roh gave his support to the proposals and expressed his enthusiasm for pursuing them through further regional consultation.

Let me spell out three areas in which I believe the Asia-Pacific region could profit from closer cooperation through such an institution.

First, effective regional cooperation can greatly improve the chances of success of the Uruguay Round and could thereby give a vital boost to the liberalization—and therefore the preservation—of the GATT-based trading system.

The GATT system now faces its most crucial test. The Montreal impasse, essentially due to lack of progress on trade liberalization in agriculture, must be overcome. If the Uruguay round fails, the underlying tensions which will have caused this failure will corrode the essence of the GATT system.

We must work together to save the GATT system. The region's role will be critical given its strong growth, reliance on trade and growing world importance and responsibility.

In 1983, in recognition of the importance of the liberalization of multilateral trade, I proposed a process of regional consultations on these issues.

The most recent meeting was held in Wellington in 1988, just prior to the Montreal Mid-Term Review. It was successful in providing a better understanding of the interests and concerns of regional countries in the multilateral negotiations.

I am pleased that Korea has been participating in that process and look forward to further regional consultations this year.

At the same time, regional cooperation could lead to a better understanding of, and a close monitoring of, the impact of international economic developments, including the 1992 integration of Europe and the recent U.S./Canada Free Trade Agreement.

Australia and Japan are currently undertaking a study of the potential regional impact of these new blocs. Because this study will, I believe, be of relevance and importance beyond our two countries, Prime Minister Takeshita and I will be discussing how best to familiarize other countries with its findings.

Second, we must be prepared openly to discuss obstacles to trade within our region.

From Australia's point of view, the success of the newly industrializing economies is an enormous opportunity, for us and for the whole region. Others see this very success as a threat, and it has led to frictions in trade relations within the region and beyond. There is undoubtedly room for dialogue and cooperation on this issue.

Australia's view is that the essence of a properly functioning trading system is, of course, that countries should seek multilateral trade balance, not bilateral balance, with all countries.

Equally, we believe the newly industrializing countries have a responsibility to liberalize further their own markets to reflect their phenomenal growth in trade and investment. And where such liberalization occurs, it must not be used to placate trade frictions being encountered with certain countries. This is anathema to the principles of free trade, and only invites counter-retaliation by those third countries whose interests are damaged.

As a region we must investigate the scope for further dismantling of barriers to trade within the region, consistent with the GATT framework.

It is a noteworthy source of opportunity that each of us has tended to impose the greatest barriers to trade in areas in which regional partners are most competitive. Some progress has been made in this area. In Korea, for example, we recognize and appreciate reforms which have lowered tariffs, liberalized imports and reduced restrictions on foreign traders.

We give the Korean government high credit for this and look forward to further dismantling of barriers to trade and investment, including agriculture in which the problems of trade barriers are greatest. The recommendations of your recent Presidential Commission on Economic Restructuring, if implemented, would be a worthwhile move towards a more open Korean market.

In Australia, we have implemented a range of reforms to liberalize our economy. We are intent on continuing this process and the reforms to date are already providing new opportunities for countries such as Korea.

We have floated the Australian dollar, deregulated our financial markets, liberalized our foreign investment policy, cut the rate of company taxation, reduced by a third the level of tariff protection afforded to Australian manufacturing industry, and made our primary industries more responsive to changes in the international market place.

The third area in which we could benefit from regional cooperation is through identifying the broad economic interests we have in common. We should try to investigate whether through co-ordinated policy-making we might better capitalize on the extraordinary complementarity of the economies in the region. Australia's Industry Minister, Senator Button, has, for example, just this week cited the enormous benefits we can reap from harnessing our diverse science and technology research efforts. Surely this is an area in which we should assess our capabilities to see where we can boost each other's efforts in this crucial field.

I have already referred to the regional trading consultations. I initiated in 1983, and to the valuable work of the PECC. Bilateral exchanges such as my visit to Korea and that of President Roh to Australia in 1988 form valuable avenues of cooperation. Studies such as Dr. Garnaut's inquiry into North East Asia, and the joint Japanese Australian inquiry into the impact of the trading blocs will provide valuable information with which to guide our future decisions.

But I believe we should be striving for a more effective means of analysis of and consultation on the central issue we face as a region.

Before I leave this topic, I must stress that my support for a more formal vehicle for regional cooperation must not be interpreted as suggesting by code words the creation of a Pacific trading bloc.

Australia's support for non-discriminatory multilateral trading solutions in the GATT framework is clear, long-standing and unambiguous.

I have made it clear that a major priority of any regional effort would be the strengthening of the GATT system.

Australia attaches particular significance to our relationship with Korea. We would like to work with you, not just in developing our bilateral ties, but also in developing our mutual interests and opportunities in third countries.

The Asia-Pacific region is at a pivotal point in history. And the region is located at a pivotal point in the global economy.

We have much to offer each other. We have substantial shared political and economic interests, and a powerful complementarity in our economic skills, resources, and business, cultural, and political links.

Cooperation offers the region the opportunity to influence the course of multilateral trade liberalization, avoid alternative approaches which would undermine this objective and enable us to enter the next century with confidence that our potential will be fulfilled.

Comment on the Progress of the Hawke Initiative*
by Anthony Hely
Department of Foreign Affairs and Trade
Australia

Most people familiar with Pacific economic relations know about the Australian proposal for enhanced regional economic cooperation, which our Prime Minister Bob Hawke put forward in a major address in Korea in January of this year. The proposal was made against the background of rapidly changing economic developments both within the region itself and in the international trading system.

---

* Statement at Trade Forum, June 28, 1989.

Very briefly, what the Prime Minister proposed was the convening of an initial exploratory ministerial meeting later this year which would be designed to discuss economic issues of common interest to the Asia-Pacific region, to seek to identify potential specific areas for cooperation and to address how they might be advanced. Given that the Prime Minister had in mind that the process would be an ongoing one, he also spoke in terms of the need to address the establishment of a modest new form of institution that would support an ongoing process. Consultations have now been held with a number of regional governments and the head of the Department of Foreign Affairs and Trade in Canberra, Dick Woolcott has recently finished consultations with New Zealand, the six ASEAN countries, Korea, Japan, Hong Kong, People's Republic of China, the U.S.A. and Canada. I shall now summarize where we think we stand with the proposal after those consultations.

I thought I might quickly just refer to some general points where there was quite clearly a convergence of view among countries that were visited. The first, and at the broadest level of generality, there was certainly an agreement in all countries, either at head of government level or senior ministerial level, of the concept of regional economic cooperation itself, which won't come as any particular surprise to this group.

Secondly, there was an agreement that the focus of the cooperation should be on economic and trade issues and not on political and security issues, and that the process of cooperation should be designed to reinforce and support the multilateral trading system generally and the Uruguay Round of negotiations currently. And that view was expressed, I think, in the context of a realization that the export-led growth strategies of regional countries require unfettered access to global markets and that the pursuit of an open and free multilateral trading system is the best way of enhancing that.

There was certainly unanimous agreement that the proposal should not be in any sense seen as a forerunner to a regional trading block. Apart from the various reasons that were identified by Jeff Schott, a number of countries expressed that view in the context of a desire to avoid sending the wrong sorts of signals to the Europeans, for example, a desire to avoid encouraging in any sense the Europeans to turn inwards and protectionist in the development of their own single market.

In terms of membership in a regional grouping, again there was agreement that this should be based on pragmatic and economic criteria, not ideological criteria and that to be manageable, the initial focus should be on those countries that have the strongest economic linkages within the region, which I think argues, as Sir Frank Holmes mentioned, for a membership that is pretty well in line with the PECC membership. It was certainly in agreement throughout the region that the proposal should not in any way detract from or compete with the effective role played by existing regional organizations such as ASEAN at the intergovernmental level and the PECC at the non-governmental level. That is a view that we certainly share.

In terms of the process of the cooperation again I think there is a general feeling that it should be one of dialogue that is designed to better inform policy development, and not negotiating forum reflecting the narrow interests of any one participant. I think a number of countries were concerned to ensure that they were not going to be subject to pressure from larger economies and that the process should be one of an equal partnership based on common economic interests.

So much for the generality of it. If I could just turn to a couple of specific issues that were discussed with all the regional countries. Our first question was the crux of the proposal, the initial ministerial meeting in the region and I think we have now reached a stage where as a result of the consultation and as a result of the recent comment in his speech by U.S. Secretary of State Baker that there is a consensus around holding a ministerial meeting in the region later this year, possibly in November.

I should say that the position of the Japanese government on that was that its willingness to attend a meeting was subject to the full support of ASEAN. But recently I think we have seen the Japanese government both in MITI and the Foreign Ministry, as pretty favourable. At the time the consultations were held with the United States, the process of inter-agency coordination of thinking had not been finalized and we were promised a coordinated response from the United States at the time that our Prime Minister Mr. Hawke was to visit Washington. This is taking place right now. I have not heard the results of those discussions, but as I have mentioned and others have mentioned, Secretary of State Baker has indicated and in principle, a willingness to attend a ministerial meeting.

On the question of an agenda for a ministerial meeting, with our consultations we had prepared and left with countries an indicative agenda which contained a very wide range of economic and trade issues. There was not a lot of detailed discussion on the agenda but I think an acceptance that at the outset we should start off with a very broad agenda of economic issues but then try and move fairly quickly into potential specific areas of cooperation. And in that latter context, some countries placed priority on trade issues such as market access and support for the Uruguay Round, other countries had a preference to focus more on broader macroeconomic issues and cooperation in specific industry sectors, such as transport and telecommunications, science and technology, and I think the environment was mentioned by one country. Both those views are compatible with the underlying principle that we start with a broad agenda and then try and refine specific areas of cooperation through a process of consultation.

We noted in the context of the agenda that the PECC at the Standing Committee Meeting in San Francisco has volunteered to put forward some ideas and we look forward to receiving those.

One question that I think did attract considerable sensitivity in the consultations was the sort of institutional arrangement we might need to create to support an ongoing process of regional dialogue. Our basic standpoint was that we did not want to have just one ministerial meeting, create a warm glow and then go home and forget about it. We were looking for an ongoing process that was going to set the scene for cooperation, certainly in the course of the Uruguay Round, but beyond maybe in the context of the next round of negotiations. And from that standpoint it seemed to us that it was only sensible to have some form of regional organizational capacity to support an ongoing process of dialogue. Mr. Hawke, when he announced the proposal, referred to the OECD as a possible model and I think that did create some impression in the minds of some countries that we were looking at establishing a costly and massive new regional institution that was going to sweep away all others, which certainly was not in our mind but if it was we have been disabused of that by our regional consultations. It is very clear that no one wants, nor do we, a massive new regional bureaucracy. I think countries were reassured that we had fairly modest objectives and were simply looking for an organizational capacity to bring together and draw on existing resources, such as the PECC, to supply policy-relevant advice for ministers and to provide the necessary administrative and logistical support for ministerial meetings. So I think there is becoming a degree of acceptance about that.

Another question I think did attract considerable discussion in our consultations was the relationship between the proposal and existing organizations such as ASEAN and the PECC. Certainly in the minds of a lot of those consulted, particularly in ASEAN, there was an implicit feeling that in some way or another the proposal was going to downgrade the effective role that ASEAN has played at the government level and we were at pain to reassure them that was not the case, we have always been a very long standing and strong supporter of ASEAN and our view was that the sort of process we had in mind could strengthen the capacity of ASEAN and other members to protect themselves in international fora and hopefully provide a better basis for structural adjustment and economic improvements within the region itself.

There was also considerable discussion about the question of the relationship with the PECC. I think we have always felt and certainly the Prime Minister acknowledged in his address that the PECC has played a very valuable role in building regional cooperation, not just through building the necessary human networks for cooperation but in terms of providing high quality policy research and analysis on common economic issues. It is certainly our intention that the attributes of the PECC would be drawn heavily upon in developing the Prime Minister's proposal and in that context we welcomed the strong support that the Standing Committee of PECC gave in San Francisco.

Again I think it was certainly clear in that all countries wanted to see a rational linkage and a convergence of position between the sorts of processes involved in the Hawke initiative and those that are involved in the PECC. That I guess relates not only to the question of the timing relationship between a ministerial meeting later this year and that of the PECC but also to the need to dovetail the sort of institutional or secretariat structure that the PECC has contemplated establishing in its own organization and the sort of institutional arrangements that might emerge from the Hawke initiative. The latter issue is a bit further down the track, Ministerial meeting and PECC VII in Auckland is a more immediate issue. I think there has been some concern by some members here at this particular meeting that the thought of holding a regional ministerial meeting prior to PECC VII, which looks like being the case at the moment, would in some way downgrade the importance of the PECC meeting. We did not really see it that way. Our feeling was that the PECC had an important role to play in setting the agenda for the ministerial meeting both through making agenda suggestions and also submitting policy papers for a ministerial meeting and that the PECC VII would be able to take the results of the ministerial meeting and work out timing and other means of carrying forward those processes. It probably is a little bit early to be talking about these questions.

That is basically where we are Mr. Chairman. In terms of the next step, I guess the issue is one of consolidating regional support and there will be a meeting of the ASEAN Post-Ministerial conference in Brunei in early July when ASEAN meets with its so-called dialogue partners, the U.S, Canada, New Zealand, Japan and Australia. We are anticipating a positive discussion on the proposal in that context, in a way that we hope will enable us at a fairly early stage to firm up a senior officials regional meeting to prepare for a ministerial meeting. Timing of an official's meeting at this stage we think will probably be late August or early September at a venue to be arranged, with the thought of then moving on to a ministerial meeting later in the year.

I conclude by noting the relevance of the proposal to this PECC Forum. As I mentioned on the opening day, we see a very close relationship between the two, we share common objectives I think of building stronger regional support for the Uruguay Round and look to the Forum to play an active role in setting the agenda for ministers to consider. I think that one of the things we have been talking about today is how that process might take place.

Appendix II

A New Pacific Partnership: Framework for the Future*

The Honourable James A. Baker, III
U.S. Secretary of State

Thank you for that introduction, and I am honoured to be here. I am especially happy to appear before the Asia Society in the company of Japan's Foreign Minister, Hiroshi Mitsuzuka. As the representative of a great democracy, the Foreign Minister understands, as we all do, that a free government depends upon well-informed citizens who are active in public affairs. The Asia Society can therefore reflect with pride upon its contribution to America's understanding of East Asia and the Pacific Rim. Each one of you, by participating in the Society, makes a unique contribution to our national interest.

Our understanding of events in Asia and the Pacific has become all the more important because the post-war era is over. In Asia, as in Europe, a new order is taking shape. While the rites of passage will be painful—China proves that—it is an order full of promise and hope. I believe strongly that the United States, with its regional friends, must play a crucial role in designing its architecture.

These are major challenges to be met as the new order emerges. In Asia and the Pacific, as elsewhere in the world, the demand for democracy is the most vital political fact of our time.

---

* Speech delivered to The Asia Society in New York, June 26, 1989.

The Philippines and South Korea have made the transition to free government. But, as we have seen to our sorrow in 1988 in Burma and more recently in China, there are no guarantees of progress.

Another challenge stems from the very fact of the Pacific Rim's economic success. Economic achievements carry new responsibilities. Explosive growth has been accompanied by imbalances that threaten the integrity of the open trading system.

Finally, we continue to face security challenges. Conflict continues in Indochina. And on the Korean Peninsula, there remains a heavily armed stand-off. Elsewhere in Asia, the postwar security arrangements are being strained by economic constraints, changing threats and rising nationalism. Yet without a regional consensus on defence, all other achievements will be put in doubt.

The Pacific region is clearly of great and growing importance to the United States. That is why President Bush and Vice-President Quayle visited Asia within the first hundred days of the new Administration. In a few days, I will be travelling to Tokyo to meet with other donors to the Philippines Multilateral Assistance Initiative. Then, I'll go on to Brunei to meet my colleagues in the Association of South East Asian Nations (ASEAN), one of the Pacific's most constructive regional organizations.

The purpose of my trip is to establish the framework for a New Pacific partnership. To build that new partnership, we need continued American engagement in the region's politics, commerce and security. We need a more creative sharing of global responsibilities with Japan. And we also need a new mechanism to increase economic cooperation throughout the Pacific Rim.

Elements of the New Partnership: American Engagement

The foundation of the new Pacific partnership must be the engagement of the United States. President Bush has declared rightfully that America is a European power and will remain one. America is also a Pacific power. And we will remain one.

The stakes are great. In 1988, for example, our transpacific trade totalled $271 billion, far exceeding our transatlantic commerce of $186 billion. U.S. trade with East Asia has more than doubled since 1982.

Eight of our top 20 export markets are now in the Pacific. U.S. investment there, exceeding $33 billion, accounts for 23 per cent of all overseas profits earned by U.S. corporations.

The prosperity of the Pacific, however, depends upon the peace of the Pacific. For four decades, the United States has provided a framework of security that has permitted the region to prosper. America's forward-deployed deterrent remains more essential than ever to the security of the Pacific. And, as we demonstrated through the treaty abolishing intermediate range nuclear forces, we will not seek to improve the security of another region at Asia's expense.

Today, our allies are stronger and more prosperous than ever. And, there may be new opportunities to reduce both political tensions and threatening military capabilities.

Surely we will be able to find creative, new ways to assure our mutual defence. Just as surely, we must avoid false complacency. We have fought three major wars in East Asia in the past 45 years. Neither we nor our allies want to fight another.

I think that the facts are clear and the conclusions inescapable. America's unique political, economic and military capabilities provide the foundation for a prosperous and secure Pacific. And that foundation can be strengthened further through improved regional partnerships that reflect the achievements of our friends and allies.

The U.S.-Japan Global Partnership

Among those relationships in the Pacific, none is more important to the region or the world than our alliance with Japan.

Over the past decade, that alliance has experienced a fundamental change. Japan has become a world power. We applaud this achievement which holds so much promise for the future. But to make the most of that promise, the United States and Japan must build a new and truly global partnership.

The foundations for that global partnership are now being laid:

- Japan is shouldering more of the mutual defence burden and provides 40 per cent of the cost of stationing U.S. forces in-country.

- The recently concluded FSX fighter co-development project is an important advance as we strengthen our cooperation in defence and technology.

- Japan will soon be the largest donor of overseas development assistance. Its role in the Philippines Assistance Initiative offers a prime example of the good Japan can do in bolstering emerging democracies and sharing responsibilities.

- Finally, Japan has offered to help in alleviating the international debt problem.

There are, of course, other issues that will find their way onto the agenda of a global partnership, including environmental protection and international peacekeeping. But the message is clear. The time has arrived for Japan to translate its domestic and regional successes more fully into a broader international role with increased responsibility. And I am glad to say here today to my Japanese colleague, Foreign Minister Mitsuzuka, that I look forward to a new closeness of coordination with Japan.

This expanding relationship will require a transformation of outlook and policy in both our countries. That is already evident in the area of trade, where our bilateral relationship continues to be troubled. Prime Minister Uno himself put it best when, in his first major speech to the Diet, he urged Japan to "embark upon rectifying those institutions and practices that are objectively viewed as unfair." Though we have seen some progress in the trade area, the full opening of Japanese markets must still be achieved. And at the same time, we look forward to the full implementation of the structural reforms advocated by the Maekawa Report.

We and Japan must recognize how interconnected we really are. That is why we are looking to begin a structural economic initiative. Its purpose is to identify, on both sides, impediments to the reduction of economic imbalances—and to develop action plans to remove them.

Change will be required of the United States, not just of the Japanese. That is why President Bush is determined to put our American house in better order—to improve our education, to sharpen our competitiveness, to reduce the trade and budget deficits that weigh so heavily on our economy. And we will continue to oppose the protectionist pressures that menace the world trading system. The challenge of structural change is not Japan's alone.

Pacific Economic Cooperation

Let me turn now to the next part of the framework—a new mechanism to increase economic cooperation throughout the Pacific. Last year intra-Asian trade approached $200 billion, reflecting the rapid pace of Pacific Rim economic integration. Yet unlike Europe, there are inadequate regional mechanisms to deal with the effects of interdependence. Many distinguished states-men and influential organizations have suggested ways to fill the gap—among them Australian Prime Minister Hawke and MITI during the time Hiroshi Mitsuzuka headed it. All their sugges-tions share the objective of improving economic cooperation and offering a regional forum to discuss a range of common problems.

Clearly, the need for a new mechanism for multilateral cooperation among the nations of the Pacific Rim is an idea whose time has come.

Our involvement in the creation of this new institution will signal our full and ongoing engagement in the region. And by furthering the development and integration of market economies within the international system, we strengthen the collective force of those that share our principles.

I want to explore the possibilities for such a mechanism in detail during my trip. The United States will not offer a definite blueprint. We will be looking instead for a consensus, drawing on the best elements from varying plans. This new mechanism should be based on the following key principles:

- First, any mechanism should encompass a wide array of issues, extending from trade and economic affairs to issues such as cultural exchange and the protection of the Pacific region's natural resources. As such, it would embody what the President has called "creative responsibility sharing," meaning that each government should act commensurate with its resources and capabilities. All our economies have benefitted from the world trading system and all should act commensurate with their resources and capabilities to help strengthen it.

- Second, any Pacific-wide institution must be an inclusive entity that expands trade and investment. It must help, not hinder, already existing efforts, such as the Uruguay Round of GATT, the Organization for Economic Cooperation and Development (OECD), or a regional group, such as ASEAN.

- It should be based on a commitment by market economies to facilitate the free flow of goods, services, capital, technology and ideas.

- Third, a pan-Pacific entity should recognize the diversity of social and economic systems and differing levels of development in the region. At the same time, we should recognize that private initiative and free market policies offer the best route for individual opportunity and higher living standards.

Today, Minister Mitsuzuka and I talked about the possibility of such a new entity. And I will be discussing how we can create this new mechanism when I see Prime Minister Hawke this week and our ASEAN friends next week. If a consensus can be reached, we would support the Prime Minister's call for a ministerial meeting this fall as a first step toward developing such a new Pacific institution.

Constructive Relations with China

Full American engagement, a global partnership with Japan and a new political mechanism for Pacific economic cooperation are critical pieces in the puzzle of Asia's future. But that future will be incomplete without China. And today, more than ever, China casts a long shadow over the Pacific.

China had made great economic strides. Per capita income doubled in a decade. An open window to Western trade, technology and investment was an essential part of reform. To sum it up, if I can, China had decided to join in regional progress rather than remain isolated from it.

History shows, however, that economic and political reform are but two sides of the same coin. Now it has become all too evident that the pace of political change in China did not match the aspirations of the Chinese people.

The President has condemned in the strongest terms the brutal events of June 1989. We and other nations have suspended business as usual. But we and the rest of the world must not let our revulsion at this repression blind us to the pressures for reform.

China has suffered a tragic setback, but the story is not over. As the President said, "the process of democratization in communist countries will not be a smooth one and we must react to setbacks in a way that stimulates rather than stifles progress."

That is why we have acted in a measured way. The hasty dismantling of a constructive U.S.-Chinese relationship built up so carefully over two decades would serve neither our interests nor those of the Chinese people. Above all, it would not help those aspirations for democracy that were so obvious in the millions who marched to support the students in Tiananmen Square.

Having said that, let me be clear: the United States government and its people will stand for the democratic values we hold dear. China's current leadership may have cleared the Square. They cannot clear the conscience. China's rendezvous with freedom, like its rendezvous with the advancing nations of the Pacific, cannot be long delayed. We will be there to help when the day follows the night.

Conflict in the Pacific

Finally, we and the entire region must deal with the remaining major conflicts that threaten peace: the Korean Peninsula and Indochina.

I must note with regret that the North Korean regime has yet to abandon its self-imposed isolation of its pressure tactics intended to destabilize the Republic of Korea. We will continue to probe for hints of progress in reducing tensions between North and South, looking for signs of a willingness to engage in greater *glasnost* and military transparency. Our policy is to facilitate reconciliation through dialogue with all concerned parties, above all through direct talks between South and North. We will maintain fully our security commitment to Korea to facilitate such progress and prevent armed conflict.

In Cambodia, the shooting continues and the danger of renewed civil war is real. Hanoi's announced intention to withdraw its troops by the end of September 1989 has accelerated efforts towards a negotiated settlement. Our principal objectives are to bring about a verified Vietnamese withdrawal, to prevent a return to power of the Khmer Rouge, and to provide the Cambodian people a genuine opportunity for self-determination.

We believe a comprehensive agreement, backed by a credible international presence under U.S. auspices, is the best way to achieve these goals.

We believe that Prince Sihanouk's leadership is essential to the process of creating an independent Cambodia at peace with itself. That is why we have asked Congress to authorize additional aid to the non-Communist Resistance. Such aid will strengthen the Prince's position in the political process now underway and increase the prospects for a settlement which can ensure that the Khmer Rouge never again take power.

As we examine the possibilities of resolving the remaining Pacific conflicts, I want to note here some new developments in Soviet policy. For much of the post-war era, Soviet actions in Asia could only be described as ominous. Moscow has deployed a formidable military presence able to project naval and air power well into the Pacific.

Three years ago, at Vladivostok, General Secretary Gorbachev announced a new approach to Soviet interests in Asia. After easing Sino-Soviet border tensions, withdrawing Soviet troops from Afghanistan and influencing Vietnamese restraint, Mr. Gorbachev was able recently to visit Beijing. President Bush welcomed this development. It confirms that a constructive Soviet approach is possible if Moscow changes its policy of military intimidation and support for aggressions.

Now, it is time for new Soviet deeds to match new Soviet thinking. Let Moscow end its occupation of Japan's northern territories. Let Vladivostok become an open port, as Mr. Gorbachev proposed three years ago. Let special economic zones bloom in the soviet Far East, as Mr. Gorbachev suggested a year ago. Let the Soviet Union cooperate in resolving the tensions and hostilities in Korea and Cambodia.

Conclusion

A political philosopher once wrote that "there is nothing more difficult to take in hand, more perilous to conduct, more uncertain in its success, than to take the lead in the introduction of a new order of things." Yet today in the Pacific and East Asia, as in Europe, we face the inescapable challenge of building a new order.

There are perils. There will be difficulties. Yet I believe that despite these uncertainties, the rewards of a free, prosperous and secure Pacific are within our reach.

That calls for a new Pacific partnership, based on a global sharing of responsibilities with Japan. We also need a new mechanism to enhance economic cooperation in the Pacific Rim. And we need to address the points of conflict that still threaten the peace of the Pacific.

Let me close on this note. I believe that ultimately what beckons us to our Pacific destiny goes beyond the reckoning of material interests. It is the ideal of a creative harmony, the product of many different nations, each with its own approach, but drawn together around certain principles. It is the faith that we can create a Pacific community reaching out to the rest of the world. It is, in short, the belief that free peoples, working together, can emancipate our region at least from historic burdens of poverty and conflict. That is our vision, to which we this day dedicate our new Pacific partnership.

Joint Statement
Ministerial-Level Meeting
November 5-7, 1989, Canberra

Ministers from Australia, Brunei Darussalam, Canada, Indonesia, Japan, Republic of Korea, Malaysia, New Zealand, The Philippines, Singapore, Thailand, and the United States gathered in Canberra, Australia on 6-7 November 1989 to discuss how to advance the process of Asia Pacific Economic Cooperation.

Discussions covered a variety of topics under four agenda items:

- World and Regional Economic Developments;
- Global Trade Liberalization—The Role of the Asia Pacific Region;
- Opportunity for Regional Cooperation in Specific Areas; and
- Future Steps for Asia Pacific Economic Cooperation.

At the conclusion of this first meeting, Ministers expressed satisfaction with the discussions, which demonstrated the value of closer regional consultation and economic cooperation on matters of mutual interest.

Ministers also expressed their recognition of the important contribution ASEAN and its dialogue relationships have played in the development to date of APEC, and noted the significant role ASEAN institutional mechanisms can continue to play in supporting the present effort to broaden and strengthen regional economic cooperation.

Multilateral Trade Negotiations

The discussions on world and regional development, and on global trade liberalization, focused particularly on the need to advance the present round of Multilateral Trade Negotiations. Every economy represented in Canberra relies heavily on a strong and open multilateral trading system, and none believes that Asia Pacific Economic Cooperation should be directed to the formation of a trading bloc.

Ministers agreed that continued close consultation within the region should be used wherever possible to promote a positive conclusion to the Round. In this respect, it was agreed that Ministers concerned with trade policy should meet in early September 1990 to discuss the emerging results and consider how to unblock any obstacles to a comprehensive and ambitious MTN result. Ministers would then meet again in Brussels in early December on the eve of the concluding session. In the meantime, senior officials should consult regularly in Geneva to exchange views on MTN progress.

Ministers expressed strong support for the timely and successful completion of the Uruguay Round. They noted that much remained to be done if the December 1990 conclusion was to be achieved. They called on all contracting parties to work with them more vigorously to that end.

Future Steps

Ministers agreed that it was premature at this stage to decide upon any particular structure either for a ministerial-level forum or its necessary support mechanism, but that, while ideas are evolving, it was appropriate for further consultative meetings to take place and for work to be undertaken on matters of common interest and concern.

Accordingly, Ministers welcomed the invitation of Singapore to host a second ministerial-level consultative meeting in mid-1990, and they also welcomed the Republic of Korea's offer to host a third such meeting in Seoul during 1991.

Ministers asked their respective senior officials, together with representation from the ASEAN Secretariat, to meet early in 1990 to begin preparations for the next ministerial-level consultative meeting.

They asked senior officials to undertake or set in train further work on a number of possible topics for regional economic cooperation, on the possible participation of other economies in future meetings, and on other issues related to the future of such cooperation, for consideration by Ministers at their next meeting.

Summary Statement

Attached to this joint statement is Chairman Evans' concluding summary statement which records the substance of discussions during this meeting.

Visiting participating Ministers and their delegations expressed their deep appreciation to the government and people of Australia for organizing the meeting and for the excellent arrangements made for it, as well as for the warm hospitality extended to them.

Ministerial-Level Meeting
Summary Statement by the Chairman
Senator the Honourable Gareth Evans, Q.C.
Minister for Foreign Affairs and Trade of Australia
Canberra, November 7, 1989

Introduction

1.   This meeting has brought together in an unprecedented way key decision-makers from 12 dynamic economies in the Asia Pacific Region: Brunei Darussalam, Canada, Indonesia, Japan, the Republic of Korea, Malaysia, New Zealand, Philippines, Singapore, Thailand, the United States and Australia.   The presence here of Ministers from across this vast region, addressing constructively and with great goodwill and commitment our common economic concerns, has shown that the time is indeed right to advance the process of Asia Pacific Economic Cooperation.

2.   The stimulus for this meeting was Australian Prime Minister Hawke's call, in January 1989, for more effective Asia Pacific Economic Cooperation.   That proposal stemmed from a recognition that the increasing interdependence of regional economies indicated a need for effective consultations among regional decision-makers to:

- help strengthen the multilateral trading system and enhance the prospects for success in the Uruguay Round;
- provide an opportunity to assess prospects for, and obstacles to, increased trade and investment flows within the Asia Pacific region; and
- identify the range of practical common economic interests.

3.   In making and following up this proposal Australia, working closely with ASEAN and other participants, sought to give a sense of direction to a range of earlier proposals for closer regional economic cooperation. The intense process of consultation which has taken place since January, and culminated in this meeting, has succeeded in those terms;   for the first time we have had the opportunity to assess collectively, and in some depth, the economic prospects of the region, the factors which can help us to maintain the impressive momentum of growth of recent years as well as the problems which, if not anticipated, could impede future development.

4.   A key theme which has run through all our deliberations in the last two days is that the continuing economic success of the region, with all its implications for improved living standards for our people, depends on preserving and improving the multilateral trading system through progressive enhancement of, and adherence to, the GATT framework. By contributing to that effort through the Uruguay Round and beyond, this region can not only help assure its own economic future but improve economic prospects globally. We are all agreed that an open multilateral trading system has been, and remains, critical to rapid regional growth. None of us support the creation of trading blocs.

World and Regional Economic Developments

5.   Our exchanges on world and regional economic develop-ments have underlined the extent to which the economic prospects of regional economies are interconnected. Our discussions have highlighted the pace of structural change which has occurred in the region in recent years, and to the opportunities provided by emerging new patterns of regional and international special-isation. They have also underlined the strong contribution which sound macro and micro-economic policies and market oriented reforms have played in the region's growth, and provided a useful opportunity for us to compare experiences on these matters.

6.   Participants noted the changing relative strengths and the growing interdependence of regional economies. Participants noted that the non-inflationary economic expansion of the United States, now nearly 7 years in duration, has played a key role in the economic performance of the region. They also welcomed the extent to which Japan and other Western Pacific economies are acting increasingly as engines of growth for the region as a whole. The increase in living standards in all parts of the region in recent decades was particularly welcome. It was agreed that an impor-tant aspect of Asia Pacific Economic Cooperation is to maintain conditions which will lead to accelerated development in the currently less developed parts of the region, including the Pacific Island countries, and that open access to developed country markets is essential for such development.

7.   Ministers also noted some potential threats to further growth and to the further productive interdependence of Asia Pacific economies. The positive trends of recent years could be disrupted if, instead of continued willingness to undertake struc-tural change, there were to be increased resort to protectionism and if instead of positive joint international action to further

liberalise trade, there were to be increased resort to retaliatory or defensive measures.

Trade Liberalisation—The Role of the Asia Pacific Region

8.   There was general recognition that the Uruguay Round represents the principal, and most immediate and practical, opportunity before us to strengthen and further liberalise the multilateral trading system. All Ministers emphasised the importance, both for the region and for the world economy, of a timely and successful outcome to the Uruguay Round. In this regard, Ministers agreed that continued close consultation, and where possible, support for each others' Uruguay Round objectives could contribute significantly to achieving such an outcome.

9.   In this respect, it was agreed that Ministers concerned with trade policy should meet in early September 1990 to discuss the emerging results and consider how to unblock any obstacles to a comprehensive and ambitious MTN result. Ministers would then meet again in Brussels in early December on the eve of the concluding session. In the meantime, senior officials should consult regularly in Geneva to exchange views on MTN progress.

10.   Ministers expressed strong support for the timely and successful completion of the GATT Round. Ministers noted that much remained to be done if the December 1990 conclusion was to be achieved. They called on all Contracting Parties to work with them more vigorously to that end.

11.   Ministers agreed that the Asia Pacific region has a long-term common interest in promoting world-wide trade liberalisation. By working together, the region can inject positive views into a range of important international economic forums, including not only the GATT but the OECD, and sectoral bodies (e.g., the International Telecommunications Union). It was acknowledged that our regional economies would be better placed to show such impediments to trade among ourselves, without discriminating against others. It was further agreed that the prospects for such further liberalisation of trade in the region would need to be based on better information about emerging regional trade patterns and developments, as well as the economic impact of such developments.

Regional Cooperation in Specific Areas

12.   Rapid growth and increasing interdependence in the Asia Pacific are giving rise to both challenges and opportunities at the sectoral level.

13.   It was agreed that it would be useful to focus further on the scope for cooperation in the area of investment, technology transfer and associated areas of human resources development. Areas which warrant consideration include:

- cooperative programs for human resource development;
- the scope to enhance exchange of information on scientific, technological and industrial indicators, policies and developments;
- the scope to enhance the comparability of foreign direct investment statistics; and
- the scope for collaborative research and development projects.

14.   In discussing the adequacy of regional infrastructure, Ministers concluded that there would be merit in seeking to develop techniques which might help countries in the region to better anticipate the kind of bottlenecks which might occur as a result of rapid growth.   There was general support for work to explore further cooperation in specific areas relating to infrastructure, including telecommunications, maritime transport and aviation.

15.   Ministers also noted the need to identify more clearly the scope to extend cooperation in other areas, including energy, resources, fisheries, the environment, trade promotion and tourism and it was agreed that officials should carry forward preliminary work in other areas for consideration at future meetings.

General Principles of Asia Pacific Economic Cooperation

16.   The discussion of all these areas has served to underline the broad areas of economic interest participants have in common.   In particular, a consensus emerged on the following principles of Asia Pacific Economic Cooperation:

- the objective of enhanced Asia Pacific Economic Cooperation is to sustain the growth and development of the region, and in this way, to contribute to the growth and development of the world economy;

- cooperation should recognise the diversity of the region, including differing social and economic systems and current levels of development;

- cooperation should involve a commitment to open dialogue and consensus, with equal respect for the views of all participants;

- cooperation should be based on non-formal consultative exchanges of views among Asia Pacific economies;

- cooperation should focus on those economic areas where there is scope to advance common interests and achieve mutual benefits;

- consistent with the interests of Asia Pacific economies, cooperation should be directed at strengthening the open multilateral trading system: it should not involve the formation of a trading bloc;

- cooperation should aim to strengthen the gains from interdependence, both for the region and the world economy, including by encouraging the flow of goods, services, capital and technology;

- cooperation should complement and draw upon, rather than detract from, existing organisations in the region, including formal intergovernmental bodies such as ASEAN and less formal consultative bodies like the Pacific Economic Cooperation Conference (PECC); and

- participation by Asia Pacific economies should be assessed in the light of the strength of economic linkages with the region, and may be extended in future on the basis of consensus on the part of all participants.

Carrying Forward Regional Economic Cooperation

17. Further Consultative Meetings. It is evident that there is a large range of significant issues confronting the region, and affecting each participant's fundamental economic interests. Ministers agreed that it was premature at this stage to decide upon any particular structure for a Ministerial-level forum (or its necessary support mechanism), but that—while ideas were evolving—it was both appropriate and valuable for further consultative meetings to take place and for work to be undertaken on matters of common interest and concern. Accordingly, Ministers welcomed the invitation of Singapore to host a second Ministerial-level Consultative meeting in mid-1990, and they also welcomed the Republic of Korea's offer to host a third such meeting during 1991. It was further agreed that it would be appropriate, in the case of

any future such meetings, for at least every other such meeting to be held in an ASEAN member country.

18.   Work Program.   Ministers agreed that if cooperation is to lead to increasingly tangible benefits, the process of cooperation needs to progress beyond agreements on general principles. This will involve the identification and implementation of specific projects as well as enhancing the capacity for objective professional analysis to allow a more systematic identification of our common interests. In this context, Ministers identified the following broad areas as the basis for the development of a work program:

- *Economic studies:* including the review and analysis of the economic outlook for the region and its implications for policy, and the improvement of regional economic and trade data;

- *Trade liberalisation:* with an initial focus on consultations among participants at Ministerial as well as official level to pursue a timely and comprehensive outcome for the Uruguay Round of multilateral trade negotiations;

- *Investment, technology transfer and human resource development:* including programs for information exchange and training; and

- *Sectoral cooperation:* in fields such as tourism, energy, trade promotion, environmental matters and infrastructure development.

19.   Within these categories, Ministers further identified a wide range of specific activities or projects which has significant potential for enhancing the process of regional economic cooperation: these are listed in the Attachment to this Summary Statement. It was agreed that these subjects should be closely considered by senior officials, together with any other proposals that may be made by participants, with a view to setting in train a viable short to medium-term work program. Progress in the implementation of that work program would be reviewed at the next Ministerial-level meeting.

20.   Ministers agreed that two particular projects should proceed as soon as possible, viz:

(a)   Review of data on regional trade flows and developments (covering trade in goods and services) and on capital flows (including direct investment) in order to:

- identify areas where there is a need to improve the comparability of regional data;

- identify gaps in data and improve country and industry sector coverage; and

- develop new data bases as necessary.

(b)   Examination of mechanisms to facilitate the identification of trade, investment and technology transfer opportunities in regional countries, which might include:

- the establishment of joint sectoral industry groups to identify specific projects; particularly the small and medium scale industry;

- a data base on commercial opportunities;

- the promotion of regional confederations of chambers of industry;

- specific joint project investment studies; and

- enterprise to enterprise linkages.

It was agreed that senior officials would settle the detailed arrangements for implementation of these projects at their next meeting.

21.   Support Mechanism.   While some Ministers expressed a preference for moving as soon as possible to servicing the future needs of the APEC process through specifically identified structural arrangements of one kind or another, it was agreed that consideration of the structure of a support mechanism would benefit from a further period of reflection and evolution of the cooperation process. Accordingly, Ministers agreed that arrangements for the next one or two Ministerial-level Meetings should be overseen by senior officials from participating economies, joined by representation from the ASEAN Secretariat.

22.   It was agreed that this group of Senior Officials should convene at an early date, preferably no later than January 1990, in the first instance to advance a work program in the way outlined above.

23.   It was agreed that follow-up work should draw on existing resources for analysis in the Asia Pacific region, including the work of PECC task forces. The Chairman of the Standing Committee of PECC indicated PECC's willingness to assist in this regard.

24.   Participation.   Ministers have noted the importance of the People's Republic of China and the economies of Hong Kong and Taiwan to future prosperity of the Asia Pacific region. Taking into account the general principles of cooperation identified above, and recognising that APEC is a non-formal forum for consultations among high-level representatives of significant economies in the Asia Pacific region, it has been agreed that it would be desirable to

consider further the involvement of these three economies in the process of Asia Pacific Economic Cooperation.

25. It has been agreed that it would be appropriate for senior officials to undertake further consultations and consider issues related to future participation in the APEC process by these and other economies, including those of the Pacific Islands, and to report back to the next APEC Ministerial-level Meeting.

Conclusion

26. I believe we have made very worthwhile progress during our two days of discussions. We have been able to build on the efforts of those who have sought to promote Asia Pacific Economic Cooperation in the past and are able to look forward to a further positive process of evolution. Such evolution will take place on the basis of further careful consensus building, drawing constructively on existing mechanisms, such as the valuable institutions and process of ASEAN as well as the analytical capacity of the PECC.

27. We have all been pleased with the way in which leaders from this diverse and dynamic region have been able to reach consensus on a range of important issues. There is good reason for confidence that, by sustaining the spirit of goodwill and flexibility which has been shown at this meeting, we can develop Asia Pacific Economic Cooperation to benefit not only the region, but to enhance world wide economic prospects.

* * * * * * *

Attachment

Specific Elements of a Work Program

A)   Economic Studies

- Convene regular consultations on the economic outlook for the region and factors influencing economic prospects, drawing on, for example, the work of the Pacific Economic Outlook work of the PECC.

- Review data on regional trade flows and developments (covering trade in goods and services) and on capital flows (including direct investment) in order to

  - identify areas where there is a need to improve the comparability of regional data

- identify gaps in data and improve country and industry sector coverage
- develop new data bases as necessary.

- Feasibility study as to what kind of analytical capacity might be desirable and affordable in order to project regional growth, investment patterns and trade flows, including for the purpose of anticipating potential infrastructure bottlenecks.

B) Trade

- Intensify regional consultations at appropriate levels (both Ministerial and official) to pursue a timely and comprehensive outcome to the Uruguay Round negotiations;

  - this would be usefully complemented by a working group of regional officials to support these consultations and other trade matters of regional interest.

- Review the differences in regional customs practices and procedures and the possibilities for harmonisation, including the liberalisation of business visa requirements.

- Form a regional association of trade promotion organisations to promote intra-regional trade.

- Explore the scope for developing greater intra-industry trade including the establishment of a regional program of sub-contracting and multi-sourcing for finished products and industrial intermediates.

C) Investment, Technology Transfer and Related Aspects of Human Resources Development

- Examine mechanisms to facilitate the identification of trade, investment and technology transfer opportunities in regional countries, which might include

  - the establishment of joint sectoral industry groups to identify specific projects; particularly the small and medium scale industry;
  - a data base on commercial opportunities;
  - the promotion of regional confederations of chambers of industry;

- specific joint project investment studies; and
- enterprise to enterprise linkages.

- Coordinate regional trade promotion events and regional business seminars including consideration of an Asia Pacific Fair to promote regional trade, investment flows, technology transfer and human resources development.

- Examine the feasibility of establishing a "clearing house" mechanism (e.g., an Asia Pacific Information Centre for Science and Technology) for the exchange of information on scientific, technological and industrial indicators, policies and developments, including the implications for new skills in the region;

- Establish a comprehensive program for Human Resources development including the identification of critical skills and gaps in know how; and the establishment of a data base on education and human resources planning and an informal information exchange network to share the expertise of regional countries

  - consider programs to establish networks among education and related institutions, the exchange of managers, scientific and technical personnel throughout the region and the establishment of regional training programs including fellowships and scholarships
  - particular attention might be given to the needs of small and medium scale enterprises.

- Consider the concept of industrial/technology parks (centres of technical excellence), their possible contribution to infrastructural development in the Asia Pacific region and associated training programs.

- Undertake a survey of research and development activities and policies of each country in the region and assess the potential for regional R&D cooperation

  - areas for cooperative R&D might include micro electronics, information technology, genetic engineering, biotechnology, resources, biosphere, ecology and the environment.

D) Sectoral Cooperation

- Formation of groups of experts in each of the major infrastructure sectors (electric power, telecommunications) to assess national needs in the region, including technical studies of existing facilities and their development needs, the nature and extent of current bilateral assistance programs, the adequacy of bilateral and multilateral financing facilities to support infrastructure development and the scope for harmonising telecommunications standards in the region;

- Consider cooperative efforts in regional transportation links, including consultations and improved data collection, designed to provide cost effective capacity to meet anticipated growth in demand;

- Examine how to manage fisheries resources in the region in a way which maintains their long term economic viability and ensures a proper economic return to the owners of the resource

  - recognising the scope for using existing organisations, such as the South Pacific Commission or the Forum Fisheries Agency, to build a framework for enhanced fisheries cooperation;

- Consider the scope for cooperative regional efforts to improve the long term economic viability of tropical forests, including research, and improved harvesting and management techniques;

- Examine the scope to improve regional exchanges in relation to the basic energy resource supply and demand outlook, and energy policies and priorities, including the environmental implications of growing energy use;

- Examine regional tourism trends and prospects, including the potential for cooperative measures to facilitate regional tourism;

- Improve remote sensing on a global scale, inter alia to provide early warnings of natural disasters and improved climatic change studies;

- Examine the interaction between environmental considerations and economic decision-making, initially in the area of ocean pollutants and other threats to the Pacific environment with a view to strengthening marine resource conservation.

List of Participants
Pacific Economic Cooperation Conference
June 26-28, 1989, Vancouver

Australia

Christopher Findlay
  Senior Lecturer
  Department of Economics
  University of Adelaide

Tony Hely
  Representative of the National Pacific Cooperation Committee
  of Australia

Peter Lavery
  Lavery International Pty. Ltd.

John McDonnell
  International Trade Consultant

China

Li Zhongzhou
  Representative of the Chinese National Committee for Pacific
  Economic Cooperation
  (contributed paper but unable to attend)

Indonesia

Djisman Simandjuntak
Center for Strategic and International Studies

Japan

Tadao Hata
Chief Economist
N.Y. Office, Bank of Tokyo

Masaki Ishikawa
Representative of the Japan National Committee for Pacific
Economic Cooperation

Nobuyori Kodaira
Staff member
JETRO

Makoto Kuroda
Special Advisor to MITI & Japan Economic Foundation
Advisor to the Long-Term Credit Bank and Japan Ltd. and
Salomon Brothers Asia Ltd.

Kensuki Norichika
Toshiba Corporation

Miyohei Shinohara
Chairman
Institute of Developing Economies

Ambassador Hideyuki Ukawa
Representative of the Japan National Committee for Pacific
Economic Cooperation

Ippei Yamazawa
Professor of Economics
Hitotsubashi University

Korea

Byong Kyun Kim
Representative of the Korean National Committee for Pacific
Economic Cooperation

Chungsoo Kim
Korea Institute for Economics and Technology

Yong Jun Kim
Representative of the Korean National Committee for Pacific
Economic Cooperation

Soogil Young
  Senior Fellow
  Korea Development Institute

Malaysia

Encik Haron Siraj
  Representative of the Malaysian National Committee for Pacific
  Economic Cooperation

New Zealand

Barry Brill
  Goodman, Fielder, Wattie

David Gamble
  Representative of the New Zealand National Committee for
  Pacific Economic Cooperation

Sir Frank Wakefield Holmes
  Emeritus Professor, Visiting Fellow
  Institute for Policy Studies, Victoria University

The Philippines

Wilhelm G. Ortaliz
  Vice-Chairman
  Philippine Economic Cooperation Committee
  Executive Director
  Philippine Council for Foreign Relations Inc.

Linda Medalla
  Research Fellow
  Philippine Institute of Development Studies

Singapore

Hank Lim
  Coordinator, Singapore National Committee for Pacific
  Economic Cooperation
  Senior Lecturer, National University of Singapore

Lee Yuan
  National University of Singapore

Chinese Taipei

Wang Chang-Ching (Chief Delegate)
  Representative of the Chinese Taipei Pacific Economic
  Cooperation Committee

Pin-Kung Chiang
Representative of the Chinese Taipei Pacific Economic
Cooperation Committee

Tsu-dan Wu
Chinese Taipei Pacific Economic Cooperation Committee

Paul S.P. Hsu
Professor of Law, National Taiwan University

Tai-Ying Liu
Director-General
Chinese Taipei Pacific Economic Cooperation Committee

Chin-Kun Chang
Associate Research Fellow
Taiwan Institute of Economic Research

Hsin Liu
Senior Assistant
Chinese Taipei Pacific Economic Cooperation Committee

Li-Ping Chou
Junior Assistant Research Fellow
Chinese Taipei Pacific Economic Cooperation Committee

Thailand

Karun Kittistaporn
Representative of the Thailand National Committee for Pacific
Economic Cooperation

United States of America

Carol Brookins
Consultant

Brewster Denny
United States National Committee for Pacific Economic
Cooperation

Geza Feketekuty
Representative of the United States National Committee for
Pacific Economic Cooperation

John Hatton
McClellan and Marsh

Jeffrey Schott
Senior Fellow
Institute for International Economics

Michael Smith
    Representative of the United States National Committee for
    Pacific Economic Cooperation

David Tappan
    Chairman and Chief Executive Officer
    Fluor Corporation

Other Participants and Guests

Miguel Angel Toro
    Director General of International Trade Negotiations
    Mexico

Jorge Berguño
    Ambassador of Chile

Charles Carlisle
    Deputy Director-General
    General Agreement on Tariffs and Trade (GATT)

Jaime Villalobos Torres
    Consejero de Mercado Para Paises de Oriente
    Banco Nacional de Comercio Exterior, S.N.C.
    Mexico

Fernanco Gutirrez-Saldivar
    Presidente Ejecutivo
    Grupo Idesa
    Mexico

Michael Finger
    Principal Economist for International Trade
    World Bank

Peter Lo
    Minister
    Hong Kong Economic and Trade Affairs
    Washington

Jaime Pomareda
    Consul of Peru
    Vancouver

Namik Jamidovich Yakubov
    Representative of the Union of Soviet Socialist Republics

A. Romanoff
    Representative of the Union of Soviet Socialist Republics

Canada

George Adorjany
Executive Director, Investment Promotion
Ministry of Economic Development and Trade, Alberta

John Baldwin
Vice-President
The Progressive Group

Philip Barter*
Senior Partner
Price Waterhouse

Mike Carter
Director
Trade Negotiations and International Economic Policy
Ministry of International Business and Immigration
British Columbia

K. Lorne Brownsey
Research Associate
The Institute for Research on Public Policy

The Honourable Pat Carney
Former Minister for International Trade
Government of Canada

Peter Cornell
University of Ottawa

The Honourable John Crosbie
Minister for International Trade
Government of Canada

Stuart Culbertson
Executive Director
Trade and International Economic Policy
Ministry of International Business and Immigration
British Columbia

John Curtis
Senior Advisor
Office of Multilateral Trade Negotiations

Germain Denis
Assistant Deputy Minister
Office of Multilateral Trade Negotiations

Martine Desbois
  Investment Branch
  Ministry of International Business and Immigration
  British Columbia

Rod Dobell
  President
  The Institute for Research on Public Policy

H.E. (Ted) English*
  Coordinator, Trade Policy Forum
  Professor of Economics, Carleton University

Oksana Exell
  Coordinator for International Competitiveness
  Ministry of International Business and Immigration
  British Columbia

Terry Ford
  Director, Bilateral Trade Policy
  Industry, Science and Technology Canada

Bob Fraser
  Senior Policy Analyst, Business Cooperation Branch
  Canadian International Development Agency

Francois Gauthier
  Assistant Coordinator for Multilateral Negotiations
  Department of External Affairs

Heather Gibb
  Secretary, Canadian National Committee on Pacific Economic
  Cooperation
  Director, Pacific, Canadian Chamber of Commerce

Michael Hart
  Director, Centre for Trade Policy and Law
  Carleton University

Ralph Huenemann
  Director
  Centre for Asia Pacific Initiatives
  Professor of Economic Relations with China
  University of Victoria

David Iwaasa
  Department of Finance
  Canada

John Klassen
  Canadian Embassy, Tokyo

Scott Lawrie
 Manager - Project Development - Asia
 Novacor Chemicals Ltd.

Harvey Lazar
 Economic Council of Canada

Janet Lucas
 International Policy Analyst
 Ministry of International Business and Immigration
 British Columbia

Helmut Mach
 Executive Director
 Federal/Provincial Relations
 Alberta

Ronald A. MacIntosh
 North East Asia Relations Division
 Department of External Affairs

Sunder Magun
 Economic Council of Canada

Donald McFetridge
 Professor
 Department of Economics, Carleton University

Barry Mehr
 Assistant Deputy Minister
 Ministry of Agriculture
 Alberta

Rabin Mendis
 Director, Investment Promotion
 Ministry of Economic Development and Trade
 Alberta

Dianne Morash
 MLA – Calgary Glenmore
 Alberta

Gordon R. Munro*
 Coordinator of the Task Force on Fisheries
 Professor, University of British Columbia

Edward Neufeld
 Executive Vice-President
 Economic and Corporate Affairs
 The Royal Bank of Canada

Arthur C. Perron
  Director General
  Asia Pacific North Bureau
  Department of External Affairs

Michael Percy
  Department of Economics
  University of Alberta

Shane T. Pospisil*
  Senior Policy Advisor
  Ministry of Economic Development and Trade
  Alberta

Harry Quinlan
  Coordinator of Trade Policy
  Department of Commerce and Technology
  New Brunswick

Balbir Sahni*
  Professor of Economics
  Concordia University

William Saywell*
  Chairman
  Canadian National Committee on Pacific Economic Cooperation
  President, Simon Fraser University

R. Lorne Seitz*
  Deputy Minister
  Ministry of International Business and Immigration
  British Columbia

Chris Watts
  Special Advisor
  International Relations
  British Columbia

* Members of the Canadian National Committee on Pacific
  Economic Cooperation.

Related Publications Available – March 1990

To order, please contact:

The Institute for Research on Public Policy
P.O. Box 3670 S
Halifax, N.S.
B3J 3K6

1-800-565-0659 (toll free)

Conference Papers	*Canada and International Trade. Volume Two: Canada and the Pacific Rim.* 1985 $15.00
Richard W. Wright with Susan Huggett	*A Yen For Profit: Canadian Financial Institutions in Japan.* 1987 $15.00
Zhang Peiji and Ralph W. Huenemann (eds.)	*China's Foreign Trade.* 1987 $12.95
William M. Miner and Dale E. Hathaway (eds.)	*World Agricultural Trade: Building a Consensus.* 1988 $19.95
Jeffrey J. Schott and Murray G. Smith (eds.)	*The Canada-United States Free Trade Agreement: The Global Impact.* 1988 $15.95

Donald M. McRae and
Debra P. Steger (eds.)

Understanding the Free Trade Agreement. 1988 $19.95

K. Lorne Brownsey (ed.)

Canada–Japan: Policy Issues for the Future. 1989 $19.95

Frank Stone

Canada, the GATT and the International Trade System. (2nd edition) forthcoming

International Economic Issues

"The Uruguay Round at Half-Time: Strengthening the Trading System" (December 1988). $10.00

International Economic Issues

"Subsidies and the Trade Laws: The Canada-U.S. Dimension" (April/May 1989). $20.00

Murray G. Smith

Canada, the Pacific and Global Trade. 1989 $20.00

65512

HF   Pacific Trade Policy
1642.55   Forum (3rd : 1989 :
.P32   Pacific initiatives i
1989   global trade

DATE DUE

FEB 2 8 1991			
OCT 2 9 1991			
DEC 1 0 1991			
MAR 0 6 1992			
MAR 2 8 1992			
DEC 1 4 1992			
OCT 2 2 1998			
OCT 2 1 1998			